Hawaii 2000

HAWAII 2000

CONTINUING EXPERIMENT IN ANTICIPATORY DEMOCRACY

Edited by George Chaplin and Glenn D. Paige

The University Press of Hawaii for the Governor's Conference on the Year 2000
Honolulu

CONTENTS

5. Neighbor Island Futures

6. Conference Observer Responses

7. Toward the Futures

Appendix

Bibliography

ACKNOWLEDGMENTS

T his book could have come about only through the efforts of hundreds of people — as, in fact, it did. All but ten were citizens of Hawaii; the exceptions were guest speakers for the Governor's Conference on the Year 2000 from Ceylon, Israel, Austria, Japan, and the American mainland; and consultant-observers from Japan, Korea, and the Mainland. Each of the seven hundred participating islanders left an imprint on what happened during and after the conference and each deserves public recognition and appreciation. Their names are proudly carried in Appendix B.

But, as in every endeavor, some were asked to, and did, carry more responsibility than others and these deserve special gratitude. These include particularly those who were members of the conference advisory committee and the chairmen of the task forces. And the interim programs which warmed up the islands for the conference could not have achieved success without the leadership of Floyd Matson and Mildred Kosaki and the speakers and panelists. To all we are indebted.

The advice and continuing assistance of James A. Dator and the counsel of Reuel Denney were essential in shaping the program of the conference. Anne King and Walter Dods, Jr., quietly and effectively directed conference arrangements.

The "Water of Kāne," the moving chant which opened the conference, was recorded by Ka'upena Wong, with facilities provided by the John J. Harding Co., Ltd. as a *public service. Volunteers from the Junior League handled physical arrangements for the workshops. Student leaders in the Pacific and Asian Affairs Council under Stephanie McCandless provided a variety of services, in the process adding enthusiasm and momentum to the project. The Junior Advertising Club, which undertook publicizing the conference in advance as a public service, spread the word through TV and radio spots and contributed space in print media. Special thanks go to club president Larry Post and to chairman Philip Kinnicutt and members of the project committee.*

Conference luncheon and dinner meetings began in an atmosphere of thoughtful stimulation because of the creative reflections voiced by Monsignor Daniel J. Dever, the Reverend Yoshiaki Fujitani, and the Reverend James Swenson. As "new breed" clergymen, they cut across traditional lines to encompass the needs and hopes of all humankind.

Of course, no project the size of the conference is possible without a team which handles the paperwork, the multitude of physical details, the receipt, disbursement, and accounting of funds, the almost unbelievable number of required chores. That the conference moved smoothly and without overt mishap is a testimonial to the staff director, Tyrone Kusao, then head of the Center for Governmental Development, College of Continuing Education and Community Services, University of Hawaii; the dean of the College, Ralph Miwa, and the always willing staff, including James Kawachika, Janice Teramoto, Eleanor Lau, Kunio Nagoshi, and Karolyn Hickman; assisted by student workers Brian Dion, June Kiyabu, Mae Yoshihara, and Leonard Hoshijo. Mr. Kusao's colleague and successor Kunio Nagoshi continues as a patient pillar of strength for the Commission on the Year 2000. Secretarial assistance for the conference chairman was also cheerfully provided by Nani Crowell, Betty Hooten and Jane Arita of the Honolulu Advertiser.

No conference — and certainly not one concerning itself with the future — should go without present-oriented needling and questioning. And so thanks are acknowledged to John Witeck, Marie Stires, Tom De Wael, Paul Sullivan and others who prodded and kept the pressure on throughout. They created discomfort and even annoyance to some, but since the goal was not to divorce the future from past and present, this was, in itself, a helpful contribution.

To Governor John A. Burns, State Senate President David C. McClung, former Senate President John J. Hulten, House Speaker Tadao A. Beppu, and many others in government, a special note of thanks is owed. They saw the need and provided funding and support.

For assistance in preparing the manuscript for publication we are deeply indebted to Glenn F. Baker, who copy edited it; to Susan Fukushima, who typed it; to Kathy Orr, who helped with research; to Glenda Naito, who made final manuscript corrections and assisted with proofreading; and to Richard J. Barber, assistant director of the Social Science Research Institute, University of Hawaii, and coordinator of the Hawaii Chapter of the World Future Society, who smoothly coordinated our efforts.

To all named and to others inadvertently overlooked who gave us their time and understanding, their aid and ideas, we express warmest aloha.

George Chaplin
Glenn D. Paige

1 INTRODUCTION

Hawaii 2000: Origin of an Idea
Editors

telephone call from a bank economist to a newspaperman was the initial circumstance in a chain that led to Hawaii's becoming the first American state — and possibly the first place in the world — to embark on a widespread, lay exercise in "anticipatory democracy."[1] In August 1967, Dr. James Shoemaker, then vice-president of the Bank of Hawaii, asked George Chaplin, editor of the Honolulu Advertiser, to give a talk. The audience was to be members of the Hawaii Economic Association and the Hawaii chapter, American Statistical Association. Chaplin responded that statistics and economics were hardly his forte, whereupon Shoemaker said, "Talk about anything you want."

That night on leaving his office, Chaplin took home with him — "mostly because it was handy" — a copy of the 1967 summer issue of Daedalus, the journal of the American Academy of Arts and Sciences. It was titled "Toward the Year 2000: Work in Progress" and was devoted entirely to papers under discussion by the Academy's Commission on the Year 2000. The group, initially funded by the Carnegie Corporation, was chaired by sociologist Daniel Bell, with a wide-ranging membership of scholars and other professionals.

1. For this concept we are indebted to Alvin Toffler who introduced it in Future Shock (New York: Random House, 1970), pp. 316–330. When Future Shock appeared we realized that Hawaii already was engaged in an anticipatory democratic experiment similar to that envisioned by Toffler.

The commission's work, as Bell put it, was "an effort to indicate now the future consequences of present public-policy decisions, to anticipate future problems, and to begin the design of alternative solutions so that our society has more options and can make a moral choice, rather than be constrained, as is so often the case when problems descend upon us unnoticed and demand an immediate response." [2]

The next Sunday editor Chaplin combined a sunbath with reading Daedalus. *The more he read the more stimulated he became with the notion that if any place was ready for long-range creative planning, and could benefit from it, it was Hawaii. On our island chain of 6,464 square miles, separated from the U.S. mainland by twenty-four hundred miles of ocean, live 800,000 people concentrated mainly on the third largest island (Oahu, 604 sq. miles). This physical isolation and small scale give it a unique sense of identity and provide an unusual opportunity for measuring, projecting, and evaluating the processes of a total society. The newness of statehood, the multiethnic population with its great emphasis on education, and its awareness of the opportunity and responsibility to play a meaningful role in East-West relations — all conduced to an interest in having the people try to shape the islands' destiny.*

On December 14, 1967, Chaplin gave his talk to the statisticians and economists. It was titled "Plan Now for 21st Century Hawaii"; and two days later it was printed in full in the Honolulu Advertiser. [3] *He began with this statement: "The press, it is often said, should be the cutting edge of change. But so should be the university, the legislature, the corporation — in fact, all substantial public and private institutions. The real question is not just*

2. Daniel Bell, "The Year 2000 — The Trajectory of an Idea," *Daedalus* (Summer 1967), p. 639.
3. December 16, 1967, p. B–2.

change, but change for what? And over what period?"
He spoke of "currents of change which never before ran
so swift or so wide and deep" and of "the need for a
great capacity to adapt, to be as versatile as required."
Chaplin observed that computers, automation and espe-
cially research on an unprecedented scale "are altering
our lives at a fantastic rate. . . . Knowledge, with all that
it implies, is our most important resource for development.
And it urgently needs to be applied creatively in trying
to fashion the kind of future we want — nationally and
locally."

He quoted extensively from Daedalus, *from articles*
by, among others, economist Martin Shubik, zoologist
Ernest Mayr, microbiologist René J. Dubos, social psychol-
ogist Lawrence Frank, and psychiatrist Leonard Duhl. A
question raised by Ronald Schon, president of the Organ-
ization for Social and Technical Innovations of Cambridge,
Massachusetts, especially intrigued him: "How does one
bring the uses of intelligence into the service of the
future?"

The challenge of that single statement, said Chaplin,
was a sufficiently valid rationale for the establishment of
a Hawaii commission looking toward the year 2000. Three
of four in Hawaii alive today, he pointed out, would be
alive when 2000 arrived: "the twenty-first century is much
closer than it seems — only thirty-two years and fifteen
days off." He further explained,

We need talent, motivation and positive, aggressive plans.
Most of our plans are too small — and even these we
frequently abort. Given big goals, we need public policies
devised to achieve them. We need the highest caliber
of people to carry forward the implementation, both in
government and in the private sector. A Commission on
the Year 2000 for Hawaii, involving not only academics
and professionals, but also the young for whom the
twenty-first century will exist, could help us focus on

**where we want to go and how to get there. The poet
Yeats said, "In dreams begin responsibilities." We should
fear neither, but welcome both.**

*About two weeks later, Alvin Shim, a Honolulu
attorney specializing in labor relations, said to Chaplin
that Hawaii has got to face up to long-range problems
or face dire results. Chaplin lightly replied that he'd printed
a speech giving all the answers, and that since Shim had
obviously missed this piece of wisdom, he'd mail him
a copy.*

*He did, and the next day Shim phoned to say that
he wanted Chaplin to accompany him to see the then
President of the State Senate, John Hulten, and the
Speaker of the House, Tadao Beppu. They went together,
and Chaplin outlined his thoughts for a commission. Afterward they talked to Governor John A. Burns. This led to
a session which included the mentioned legislative
leaders, plus Governor Burns, Judge Samuel P. King,
University of Hawaii President Thomas H. Hamilton, State
Planning Director Shelley Mark and several others.*

*From this emerged legislative funding [4] and an execu-
tive order by Governor Burns on June 30, 1969, creating
the Governor's Conference on the Year 2000. The governor
asked Chaplin to serve as chairman of a twenty-
one-member advisory committee with the functions of
planning and conducting the conference, evaluating it and
making recommendations for carry-over activities. [5]*

4. $50,000, subsequently supplemented by $15,000 to support the work
of three neighbor-island committees.

5. The committee, in addition to its chairman, consisted of Glenn
Paige, conference program chairman; Reuel Denney, vice-chairman;
James Dator, advisor; Mrs. Samuel P. King, conference arrangements
chairman; Walter Dods, Jr., vice-chairman; Floyd W. Matson, interim
program chairman; Mrs. Richard Kosaki, vice-chairman; Albert Akana,
Jr., Herbert Aronson, Mrs. Barry Chung, Thomas H. Creighton, Harry
Flagg, Keiji Kawakami, Miss Rebekah K. Luke, Ralph Miwa, Taylor Pryor,
Robert Strand, Claudio Suyat, Representative Charles Ushijima and
Senator Nadao Yoshinaga. Tyrone Kusao was named staff director;
assistance was provided by the Center for Governmental Development,
Division of Continuing Education and Community Service, University
of Hawaii.

In appointing the committee, Governor Burns said: "It is the thinking of many of us that a serious effort should be made now to assess Hawaii's future economic, political, cultural, and social systems and to identify the objectives that are desired and the action programs necessary to reach those objectives."

The advisory committee set the conference for August 5–8, 1970, so as to immediately precede an East-West Center conference planned for August 9–15 related to the future of Asia and the Pacific [6] — and to enable a sharing of speakers and other resources.

At the first meeting of the advisory committee on October 16, 1969, Chaplin said,

We are embarking on what I believe will be an exciting adventure — one which can be stimulating and helpful to the people of Hawaii. It is not the first such project. But, as far as I can determine, it is the first to be undertaken by an individual state. Nationally there is the commission on the year 2000 sponsored by the American Academy of Arts and Sciences. In England there is the committee on the next thirty years, operated by the English social science research council. France has its *futuribles* project, chaired by Bertrand de Jouvenel. Scandinavian, Italian and Czech groups are concerning themselves with Mankind 2000. Japan has its association on futuristics. There is a World Future Society. An international conference on futuristics was held at Oslo in 1967; another is scheduled for Kyoto in April, 1970.[7] A substantial body of literature

6. This was the second International Conference on Problems of Modernization in Asia and the Pacific. Conference cochairmen were Chancellor Everett Kleinjans, East-West Center, and philosophy Professor Sang Eun Lee, chairman of the first conference initiated by Korea University in Seoul on its sixtieth anniversary in 1965. The second conference program chairman was Fred W. Riggs. Conference proceedings, edited by Everett Kleinjans, are forthcoming.

7. Advisory committee members Dator, Kawakami, and Paige attended the Kyoto conference. Dator presented a paper, "A Framework for Futuristics in Hawaii." As a result of their participation, the distinctiveness of the Hawaii experiment became clearer. Also, we were able better to appreciate and assess world intellectual resources in futures thinking.

has already been developed on what man can do about his future — and it will grow larger.

He reported on a meeting which he and advisory committee members Miwa and Paige had held with Dr. Yehezkel Dror, who at the time was on leave from the Hebrew University of Jerusalem and had been visiting in Hawaii. Among Dror's suggestions, he said, was that we should plan not only goals, but alternatives. We should try to tie in the future with present policies. We should ask what current decisions have significance for the future. The main aim should be sensitizing to the future for present action. Again, what are the decisions today which have impact on the future? How can we organize present policy-making systems to take the future into account?

Chaplin reported also that the university was offering several new seminars under the general title of "Hawaii 2000." One was called "Hawaii 2000: Planning Hawaii Now," taught by planners Tom Dinell and Ruth Denney, a seminar "to determine what is likely to be and could be the shape of Hawaii." Another, "Hawaii 2000: the Hawaiian Environment" was taught by geoscientist Doak Cox, botanist Charles Lamoureux, and general scientist Jan Newhouse, dealing with population, pollution, and environmental quality. There was also "Hawaii 2000: Toward a Prescription for Survival," taught by Arnold Schwartz, M.D., a public health specialist; and "Hawaii 2000: Values and Utopias," taught by political scientist Dan Weaver; and with two other Hawaii 2000 courses planned, one on economic conditions, the other on legislation for the future. Thus there was already developing significant interest in the future at the higher education level.

From the first advisory committee meeting in October 1969 to the final conference day of August 8, 1970 — one week short of ten months — events unfolded at a rapid pace. During January and February 1970, ten statewide task forces on aspects of Hawaii's future were organized.

On February 23, a mini-conference to stimulate the task-force members was held. Consequently, in March, additional task forces for the islands of Hawaii, Maui, and Kauai were organized. Throughout the spring and into the summer a series of interim program activities were held. About two weeks prior to the August conference, draft task-force reports were published.[8] Then the governor's conference itself brought together some three hundred task-force members plus four hundred other persons, drawn widely from the community, who had not participated in the preparatory task-force activities. The reports were critically evaluated on this basis and subsequently revised in the fall of 1970. On March 23, 1971, a temporary Hawaii State Commission on the Year 2000 was appointed; in November of that year it was made permanent.

There were other related events, simultaneous occurrences, or unanticipated consequences, but this is the core chronology of what took place as a result of the chain of initiatives and responses that led from banker Shoemaker's call to editor Chaplin, to attorney Shim, to legislative, executive, and other community leaders, to the August 1970 convocation of seven hundred Hawaii citizens, and beyond, in continuing reverberations and extensions.

In this book we have gathered together the record of this pioneering community endeavor and have attempted to share what we think we have learned from it thus far. We have tried to present results and to explain underlying processes. We hope that this will be stimulating and useful for present and future citizens of Hawaii and for those persons everywhere who may seek creatively to adapt and advance Hawaii's anticipatory democratic experience.

Part Two describes how we began to educate ourselves

8. State of Hawaii, Governor's Conference on the Year 2000, August 5–8, 1970, *Preliminary Task Force Reports (July 1970)*, mimeographed, Honolulu, 1970.

and to involve larger groups of people in thinking about Hawaii's future. Part Three explains the process of the main conference and presents some outstanding contributions to it. Part Four contains the ten subsequently revised task-force reports; Five offers future views of the neighbor islands; Six presents evaluations of the conference effort by outside consultant-observers. Finally, in Part Seven, we reflect upon what we think we have learned and peer provocatively, we hope, toward some alternative futures for Hawaii.

To whatever it may be attributed — our island geography that reminds us of our shared fate, or the distinctive Hawaiian concept of aloha that recalls our shared humanity — the Hawaii 2000 experiment, from its origins down to the present, continues to provide glimpses into the creative potential that lies within a diverse, but basically tolerant, community.

2 ORIENTATION TOWARD FUTURES THINKING

Overview
Editors

ight from the outset different opinions as to correct approaches to the future were expressed in our advisory committee. In one form or another they have persisted right through the 1970 conference down to the present time. An early issue was whether we should seek primarily to generate specific proposals for present legislative action or whether we should play a more broadly educational role. That is, should we think of ourselves as a "futurist legislature" or as a creative catalyst of public thinking about the future. We chose the latter, but this did not satisfy everyone.

Another source of continuing tension emerged from different modes of thinking about the future. One view favors a from-here-to-there approach; that is, on the basis of a careful assessment of past experience, present problems and capabilities, with some view to future goals, a careful priority plan for concrete action should be prepared and provisions made for effective implementation. The other view emphasizes a from-there-to-here approach. It is much more tolerant of radical imagining about future states of affairs on the basis of which retroductive reasoning should produce guides for present action. This view often argues that radical imagining is not a luxury but a necessity if man is to break out of the self-defeating cycles that seem pushing him toward physical and psychological catastrophe. The distinction is not so simple as the familiar quarrel over means and ends because both

approaches contain complex clusters of means-ends elements. Undoubtedly both modes of thought will be important for the creation of alternative future human societies.
The most dramatic changes are likely to occur when the
creative spark of futures imagination gains the energetic
attention of the more present-oriented futures thinkers
and actors.

But whatever our preferences for intellectual style and
action, we were agreed that it would be useful to stimulate
ourselves and others to think more seriously and more
creatively about the future. We were committed to the
view that what we wanted to achieve was the complete
diffusion throughout Hawaii of a propensity to think very
creatively about our future goals, about the ways in which
we might reach them, and about emergent assets and
liabilities of the objective future over which we might have
little if any control. Rather than depending upon a few
professional academic, government, military, or business
forecasters we were fully committed to the view of mass
participation of laymen in futures thinking and futures-
oriented action.

This meant that we had to begin to educate ourselves.
Fortunately, in the fall of 1969, a year before the governor's
conference, a scholar, whose self-defined pioneering spe-
cialty was "political futuristics," had joined the political
science faculty at the University of Hawaii. He was a product in part of eight years of study and teaching in Japan
where he had become sensitive to growing Japanese concern with study of the future. When he arrived in Hawaii
in September 1969, he did not know that in less than
five months he would be addressing a joint session of
the Hawaii State legislature (twenty-five senators plus fifty-
one representatives) in a plea for innovative thinking about
Hawaii's future. From the start, the Hawaii 2000 adventure
benefited greatly from the broad grasp of futuristics, imagination, catalytic leadership, and unusual communication
skills of James A. Dator.

In "Why Futuristics" we present a transcript of the first talk he gave before our advisory committee, as a good example of where we began in our attempts to rethink Hawaii's futures. In a later address to a colorful, flower-laden, joint session of the legislature on January 26, 1970, Dator reviewed reasons for compelling concern for the future, urged Hawaii's political leaders to take a forward-looking systematic view of legislation rather than a "squeaky wheel" approach designed to silence the most noisy current protests, called for experimental legislation with built-in provisions for scientific evaluation, and urged rewards for "nonviolent social deviants and nonconformists".[1]

A survey of legislative thinking about Hawaii's past, present, and future conducted just prior to Dator's speech — although limited in number of respondents (only twenty-nine of seventy-six legislators) — nevertheless provides interesting indications of the views of some political leaders at that time.[2] First, the legislators were asked to describe their "best" and "worst" aspirations for Hawaii 2000. Then they were asked to give an overall rating of Hawaii's position on a ten-point scale (1 "worst", 10 "best") for several different points of time: 1959, the year Hawaii attained statehood; 1970; 1980; and 2000. Figure 1 presents a frequency distribution of their responses that reveal diverse views of the past, moderate positive consensus on the present, more optimistic expectations about the short-run future, and signs of a sharp divergence between extreme optimism and pessimism in evaluations of 2000.

The "best" Hawaii 2000 was described in terms of economic well-being, environmental quality, social har-

1. James A. Dator, "Address Before Joint Session of the Legislature of the State of Hawaii." Mimeographed. January 26, 1970.

2. Glenn D. Paige, "Hawaii's 1970 State Legislators View 'Hawaii 2000'; Report to the Legislature on Responses to a Questionnaire," Department of Political Science and Social Science Research Institute, University of Hawaii. Mimeographed. January 26, 1970.

At Statehood (1959)

```
                X           X
                X           X   X
    X   X   X   X   X   X   X   X
    X   X   X   X   X   X   X   X
    X   X   X   X   X   X   X   X
1   2   3   4   5   6   7   8   9   10
Worst                               Best
```

Today 1970

```
                X
                X
                X
                X
            X   X
            X   X
            X   X       X
            X   X       X
        X   X   X       X
        X   X   X   X   X
        X   X   X   X   X           X
1   2   3   4   5   6   7   8   9   10
Worst                               Best
```

Next Decade 1980

```
                            X
                        X   X
                        X   X
                    X   X   X
                    X   X   X   X
            X       X   X   X   X
    X   X   X   X   X   X   X   X   X
1   2   3   4   5   6   7   8   9   10
Worst                               Best
```

Hawaii 2000

```
                                    X
                            X       X
                            X   X   X
                            X   X   X
    X                       X   X   X
    X       X               X   X   X
X   X       X   X   X   X   X   X   X
1   2   3   4   5   6   7   8   9   10
Worst                               Best
```

Figure 1. Legislators' Evaluations of Hawaii's Past, Present, and Future
(X indicates the response of one legislator)

mony, quality of life, educational opportunity, peace, and a leadership role in the Pacific. The "worst" was seen as economic breakdown, environmental pollution, overpopulation-overcrowding, social disintegration, and war.

On February 28, 1970, one month after Dator's speech to the legislature, we invited about three hundred members of the ten emerging task forces to hear a provocative and persuasive talk by Robert Theobald, an outstanding future-oriented socioeconomist noted in part for his unusual skills in engaging others in dialogs. This talk is presented at the end of Part Two. Coincidentally, Theobald spoke in the large laboratory demonstration auditorium of the University of Hawaii's chemistry building, Bilger Hall, at the entrance of which are carved Louis Pasteur's words, "Laboratories are the temples of the future." After Theobald's talk, the ten groups caucused separately to decide how to proceed between then and the August 1970 conference, only five months away.

Another important part of our initial orientation toward the future was a series of interim program activities conducted throughout the spring of 1970, led by American studies professor Floyd Matson[3] and educational researcher Mildred Kosaki. Panel discussions open to the public were held mainly in high schools scattered throughout Oahu on the following subjects: Hawaii — its identity and place in the world; ecoproblems — the avoidance of catastrophe; human value — the quality of life; education — high and low; economics and technology; culture and the arts; government, law, and the body politic; and the future of the future.[4] These local discussions

3. Author of *The Broken Image: Man, Science, and Society* (New York: Doubleday, Anchor Book, 1969).

4. Chairmen were George Chaplin, Thomas Creighton, Floyd Matson, Claudio Suyat, Harry Flagg, Reuel Denney, Charles Ushijima, and James Dator. Speakers were Thomas H. Hamilton, Jan Newhouse, Francis Hsu, Richard Kosaki, Thomas K. Hitch, Murray Turnbull, Stuart Gerry Brown, and Herbert Cornuelle. Panelists were Robert Goodman, George

expressed our desire to decentralize the program and to make it easy for ordinary citizens to participate. Although participation was not high at this point, many of the discussions were lively and useful, convincing us of the potentials inherent in creating opportunities for neighborhood involvement.

Thus, through Dator's talks to our advisory committee and the legislature, Theobald's warming up of the task-force participants, and our interim program activities, the highlights of which were sometimes communicated more broadly through press, radio, and television, we began to educate ourselves and to engage wider participation in thinking about Hawaii's futures.

These initial activities evoked four principal responses. Two of them came from student groups, one came from a younger group of advertising executives, and the fourth came from community leaders in our neighbor-island counties — Hawaii, Maui, and Kauai.

The first student response in early 1970 came from the leadership of the Pacific and Asian Affairs Council (PAAC). Sparked by the creative enthusiasm of executive director Stephanie McCandless, PAAC conducted an extracurricular world-affairs program involving more than four thousand high- and intermediate-school students on a statewide basis. The purpose was to broaden the horizons of the island youngsters to encompass international and world problems. Much emphasis was placed upon the nurturance of student leadership and initiative. When the high-school-student leaders of PAAC learned of the

Kanahele, Pat Saiki, and Robert Midkiff; George S. Walters, Fujio Matsuda, Eddie Tangen, and Willie Newberry; Paul Hooper, Dianne Armstrong, Daniel Dever, and John McDermott; Linda Delaney, Ralph Kiyosaki, and Everett Kleinjans; Henry Epstein, Shelley Mark, Joseph Miccio, and Albert Nagy; Mrs. Russell Cades, John Murray, and Lee Stetson; Mrs. Sherman Grossman, Tim Leedom, Richard Schulze, and Shunichi Kimura; and Charles Lamoureux, Alexander Wylly, Marion Saunders, and Alan Moon. Meetings were held in Kalani, Farrington, and Castle high schools, in the University of Hawaii, and in the Honolulu International Center.

Hawaii 2000 activities they decided to adopt "Hawaii 2000 — Make It Your World!" as the theme of their 1970–71 school-year program. To prepare student leaders for the program, they decided to enroll ten of their members in a special 1970 spring-semester cluster of Hawaii 2000 courses at the University of Hawaii.[5] Furthermore, these students were invited to participate in the ten task forces on Hawaii 2000 being created by the advisory committee. These were: Hawaii's people and life-style; the quality of personal life; the natural environment; housing and transportation; political decision-making and the law; the economy; science and technology; education; the arts; and Hawaii and the Pacific community.

A second important youthful response came from a group catalyzed by Youth Action, an organization led by a former political science graduate student, John Witeck. The thrust of Youth Action was to mobilize young people to challenge the Establishment — "to comfort the afflicted and to afflict the comfortable" — on a wide variety of issues. Predicting that the advisory committee and PAAC activities would fail to come to grips with the "real" issues of Hawaii, which were viewed as the product of an industrial-military-academic-racist-capitalist structure, the Youth Action leaders organized a coalition of other youth-related groups to convene a conference on the future prior to the governor's conference planned for August 1970. "Hawaii Youth Congress 1970" was held from June 8 to 12, 1970, with financial support from the State legislature, the advisory committee for the governor's conference, and other private and governmental sources. About one hundred sixty young people from eighty youth and youth-oriented organizations registered for the conference held in the university's Frear Hall. Speakers included Arthur

5. The students and their schools were: Lee B. Gomes, Saint Louis; Gail Harada, Punahou; Derrick Ho, Farrington; Robert J. Kasher, Kalani; Melvyn K. Kono, Kaimuki; Tom Keogh, Saint Louis; Nengin Mahony, Roosevelt; Joe Tanega, Radford; Patricia Won, McKinley; and Gordon Wood, Kailua.

Waskow (of the Institute of Policy Studies, Washington, D.C., who urged the young people to live the future "now"), John Kelly, John Holt, and Elladene Lee.

The students, including neighbor-island representatives, lived together as "families" in dormitories, where explicit attempts were made by the activists to radicalize the uninitiated. Meetings were open to the public. The language was frequently obscene, in the style of the "revolutionary" confrontation tactics that swept American universities from Berkeley to Harvard in the 1960s, justified by the claimed bourgeois obscenity of the Establishment, the perceived spokesmen for which were often shouted down. The radical youth leaders were encouraged and supported by antibusiness, antimilitary, antiwhite, and antipoverty adult radical counterparts.

The youth conference produced a report of its own, copies of which were provided for all members of the governor's conference when it convened on August 6.[6] In general, the resolutions passed by the congress were much milder than the militant rhetoric that had preceded them. The record of the youth congress shows that a "radical caucus" made fourteen proposals. No votes are recorded for them, as was done for proposals presented by other groups, nor do they contain a notation "not voted upon" or "not considered on the floor," as was done in other cases. The radical caucus proposals concerned change of the educational system ("discontinuing culturally biased tests, racism, sex-typing . . . and imposition of middle-class values on people who do not share those values"); population control and "birth-control legislation"; the establishment of "strict air- and water-purity standards with strong powers of enforcement"; the establishment of a mass-transit system and State pressure on industries to immediately provide nonpolluting sources

6. Hawaii Youth Congress, *Peace: A Common Goal, Report on the Hawaii Youth Congress 1970: An Aquarian Perspective on the Year 2000* (Honolulu: Vanguard Press, n.p., n.d. [1970]).

of energy; the ending of "dependence on tourism as a major industry," with hotels converted to local housing and factories; unilateral withdrawal of U.S. military forces from Vietnam and other Pacific countries; the ending of the U.S. military presence in Hawaii; the cession of all military lands to the people of Hawaii; the elimination of the profit motive in the economic system, and ending the exploitation of women and minorities; State support of cultural and artistic expression of Hawaii's people, with free access to all; compelling the construction industry "to build free homes for local people"; control of industries by workers and by the people environmentally affected by them; local ownership and diversification of agriculture; and the redesigning of Hawaii's economy to achieve self-sufficiency and freedom from "outside economic or political manipulation."

Among proposals made by other individuals and groups that were voted upon favorably by the congress were those to establish a noncompulsory educational system (65 in favor to 34 opposed to 9 abstentions); to support a student bill of rights (69–4–13); to abolish grading (32–0–1); to seek voluntary restriction of families to two children (100–6–13); to "legalize spiritual discovery" through free choice of drugs (54–35–13); to recognize health care as a right, not a privilege (acclamation); to facilitate the secession of Hawaii from the United States of America (60–37–15); to immediately abolish the draft (66–8–10); to lower the voting age to 17 (69–4–11); to abolish the two-party system (67–36–13); to return estate lands to people of Hawaiian ancestry (54–17–20); to support a milk cooperative (by acclamation with 3 abstentions); to abolish money and "to establish a democratic-socialist system based on need rather than greed" (34–19–20); and to create nonmilitary-related jobs (55–0–2). Among measures adopted by acclamation was the following proposal by Leilani Lewis and her "family" group:

Youth Congress 1970 urges that the Governor's Con-

17

ference of [sic] the Year 2000 recognize that the design and planning of Hawaii's future include as many visions from as many individuals and groups who want to participate. We believe that there should be no elite groups who decide how Hawaii in the year 2000 will be designed. A pluralistic vision, including the ideas of every individual, not just a majority, should be included in the final master design. Therefore, we urge the Governor's conference to work toward the design of a society of alternative futures in which many different life-styles will not only be tolerated, but encouraged as well.[7]

Overall, the youth congress on the future accurately expressed the angry frustration and disillusionment with the American dream that characterized the mood of large numbers of young people throughout the nation in 1970.

A third response to the initial activities of the advisory committee was a decision by the Junior Advertising Club of Honolulu, led by Philip Kinnicutt, to take up publicizing the governor's conference as a public service activity.[8] *The club preceded its campaign by an opinion survey to discover citizen attitudes about the future. Hawaii's people were found to be alarmed and perplexed, with special concern for pollution, prices, and housing. The young advertisers then developed the theme "Hawaii 2000: Somebody Better Care About Tomorrow," through such media as bumper stickers, bus cards, posters, brochures, newspapers, magazines, radio, and television. One of the most effective creations was a television picture of a tiny baby's hand being held by an adult, with folk singer Bob Dylan's words ". . . You'd better start swimming or you'll sink like a stone, for the times they are a-changin' " in the background. The criterion used by the advertising club to measure success was the frequency of telephone or*

7. Hawaii Youth Congress, *Peace: A Common Goal*, pp. 26–27.
8. Other members included John Farmer, Mrs. Alex Wade, Mike Datisman, Frank Hajek, Ken Sanders, Lee Allison, Nora Jane Killalea, Louise Cavanaugh, Donna Stockwell, Linda Leppe, and Clara Shigemura.

letter requests to the advisory committee office for further information about the Hawaii 2000 project. Although the campaign was not regarded as highly effective by the club itself, it contributed to the enthusiasm of Hawaii 2000 participants, and won the club national recognition for its efforts by the American Advertising Federation. The campaign demonstrated again the great latent propensity for public service of Hawaii's people: that is, for less than five hundred dollars in advisory committee costs, approximately a quarter million dollars of advertising space and time was contributed.

Finally, the beginnings of the Hawaii 2000 project evoked a demand for separate identity and participation by neighbor-island groups. Neighbor-island participants in the February mini-conference asked help in organizing counterpart groups that would explore Hawaii 2000 in terms of their own local needs. The advisory committee secured supplemental funds for each of the three neighbor islands from the legislature. Community college leaders in Hilo, Wailuku, and Lihue were asked to serve as local coordinators. These groups were free to proceed in any way most appropriate for local circumstances. Opportunities were provided for them to present the results of their deliberations at the August conference.

But this overview has now taken us far from where we began in early 1970. For an understanding of how we got started, we must recall the talks by James Dator and Robert Theobald that provided initial stimulation.

Why Futuristics
James A. Dator

James A. Dator is professor of political science at the University of Hawaii where he specializes in the study of futuristics. Educated at Stetson University, the University of Pennsylvania, and The American University,he taught previously at Rikkyo University in Tokyo, the Training Institute of the Japanese Ministry of Foreign Affairs, and at Virginia Polytechnic Institute before joining the Hawaii faculty in 1969. A pioneer in undergraduate, graduate, and community education in futures thinking, his educational television program ''Tune to the Future'' has attracted wide attention. He has written on Japanese and American society and politics as well as alternative futures. His most recent book is *Human Futuristics* (1971), edited with Magoroh Maruyama. A member of the World Future Society, he served on the continuing committee of the International Future Research Conference (Kyoto, 1970) which prepared for the Third World Future Research Conference (Bucharest, 1972).

First, I want to give as complete, though brief, a picture as I can of my understanding of futuristics. To do that, I will start with a number of quotations from people who state the themes of futuristics in ways that make sense to me. Next, I'll give a brief definition of futuristics, and then several reasons why I think that to engage in futuristic activities is not just a luxury, something that we can either do or not do, but rather a necessity, something we must do. Finally, I'll present some examples of ways in which we as a committee can engage in futuristic activities, or support others in undertaking futuristics.

First, here are some key observations:

"We shape our tools and thereafter our tools shape us." (Marshall McLuhan)

"Our future may lie beyond our vision, but it is not beyond our control." (Robert F. Kennedy)

"Education means developing the ability to live humanly in the technological culture *by changing with it.*" (Anthony Schillaci)

"When faced with a totally new situation, we tend always to attach ourselves to the objects, to the flavor, of the most recent past. We look at the present through a rear-view mirror. We march backwards into the future." (Marshall McLuhan)

"Anything that is theoretically possible will be achieved in practice no matter what the technical difficulties, if it is desired greatly enough. It is no argument against a project to say: 'the idea's fantastic!' Most of the things that have happened in the last 50 years have been fantastic, and it is only by assuming that they will continue to be so that we have any hope of anticipating the future." (Arthur C. Clarke)

"Not using our planning capabilities is, of course, no solution as such: it's simply a decision to do something else. We are almost certain to face disaster if we don't plan; we are almost certain to increase the likelihood of having a better world if we plan well. But we are also almost certain to be in deep trouble even with planning because our best plans will be developed and fostered by limited human beings picking and choosing among limited knowledge, very often ignorant of the extent of their own ignorance." (Donald Michael)

What is futuristics ? It is the study, forecasting, and design of social values, environments, and organisms for the immediate, intermediate, and distant futures. *From one point of view that is an extremely sweeping statement. I will mention something about the techniques and about the objects of these processes, mainly relating to social values, environments, and organisms.*

But first, why is this field necessary? I'm going to try to develop eight major lines of argument, starting with what I believe to be the most forceful and obvious and of pressing demand, and ending with the ones which still to me, personally, are extremely persuasive, but which may be of considerable argument among you.

First, the reason that it is necessary to engage in broad future planning is environmental pollution; that is, because of the unintended consequences of our technological development: ecodisaster. You're completely familiar with this if you just read the newspapers, especially on Sunday, when it seems to be the intention to scare us to death with the very real truth of environmental pollution. But if you've read anything recently you should be completely aware that if we don't do something about the unintended consequences of our technologically based activities, then we have no future. Just to mention a number of genuinely impending disasters which you are familiar with: the level of DDT in plants and organisms at the present time is threatening to destroy life. The amount of DDT in mother's milk makes it unfit for human consumption, according to government standards. Indeed, the amount of DDT found in all organisms is already beyond tolerable limits, and if you are familiar with the article by Paul Ehrlich called the "Death of the Oceans" you know that he considers it possible for us to act in such a way that the oceans will be dead by the summer of 1979. So DDT and other pesticides and detergents that have been dumped into our waters may be polluting us out of existence.

Second, as you all know, the high level of carbon monoxide, particulates, and lead in our atmosphere means that we are going to have to do something very drastic about the unintended effects of the internal-combustion engine. I will mention just two alternatives. One is to outlaw the automobile. The other is to modify our lungs.

There certainly are other things you might think of, but to do nothing means to commit suicide.

Third, thermal pollution: that is, the rising temperature of water and air as a result of energy transfer and fuel consumption. The rise in temperature around hydroelectric plants, nuclear reactors, and so forth, is greatly altering the water ecology there, and radically changing the physical environment of man — changing it in ways that he does not intend, and in ways that he knows little about or, in any event, is not anticipating or controlling.

Another example of environmental pollution is the disposal of radioactive wastes, which take a very long time to disintegrate, and which we are now placing in holes in the earth around Denver, Colorado (possibly causing earthquakes), or else dumping them in the middle of an ocean in containers which we hope won't crack. If they do, well then, the result could be rather unfortunate.

Similarly, the disposal of wastes from biological warfare testing is also a major problem. And finally, the simply enormous increase in ordinary human waste — paper, plastics, bottles, cans, and so forth — would be important even if we were not likely to experience a very rapid increase in our total population. Indeed, aside from all the other types of environmental pollution, the simple increase of population and the subsequent difficulties in disposing of human wastes will present a terrifying problem in the very near future.

There are essentially three schools of thought about environmental pollution. One is represented by scientist Jan Newhouse and a number of other people at the University of Hawaii. They seem to feel essentially that nothing can be done; that it's already too late; that there is no future for the world. These people, as I understand them, are extremely serious when they say, "Woe, woe, all is over! Repent your sins, because there's nothing you can do but die in the awareness of what you have done."

A second school of thought believes that even though we know these terrible things are happening, and even though we know technologically and ideally that something should be done, nonetheless, our political and social institutions are such that nothing is going to be done. This seems to me to be an even more tragic opinion than the first. I feel that it is bad enough that the human race and the world generally may be doomed because of human foolishness. It's even more awful to think that knowing our doom, and furthermore knowing that there are ways to prevent it, still nothing will be done.

So, third, there is my point of view which is essentially that we can prevent disaster, and I hope we can get on the road toward preventing it. I also hope that this will be one of the major focuses of this committee: to stir up the public's awareness of our environmental pollution as well as its awareness that there are ways, perhaps painful ways, to solve it, and that we've got to make the effort to change our institutions and values and organisms, simply in order to make the continuation of any sort of life possible.

Now that's only one of the eight reasons why I think futuristics is necessary, but I think that's the only reason we need, unless we are really in favor of extinguishing life. But let me continue down the list.

The second reason for futuristics is the population explosion; again, something that you're completely familiar with. In fact I think you'll discover as I proceed that there's nothing new; that I'm presenting old stuff; that you're going to say, "Jim, I knew this all along. What's the big deal about it?" Fine. If we knew it all along, then let's do something about it, unless there's really nothing to do.

But consider the population explosion. The world population at the present time is around three billion; by 1980 it probably will be four billion; by the year 2000 (our target date) perhaps seven billion; by 2030, sixteen billion; and by 2060, twenty-nine billion. You note that these are not slight increases; they are doubling ratios, with less and less time between doublings. So while we will have "only" one billion more bodies between now and 1980 (ten years!) we'll have doubled our present population within thirty years, and will have five times our present population by sixty years. So the mere problem of where we're going to put all these people is serious enough. I've just discussed the difficulties of human waste disposal, that we haven't really solved the problem of what to do with that waste now. What happens when we have not three billion but twenty-nine billion people? Where are we going to put the garbage?

That's only part of the difficulty though, because the really serious problem to be faced in increased population is the ratio between the number of existing human beings and the available food supply. At present, we have approximately ten billion acres in the world that are currently habitable and cultivable; ten billion acres on which people are living, and doing lots of things, including raising food. It's possible with present and immediately foreseeable techniques to increase this land to about twelve billion acres — that's only two billion more acres; not a whole lot.

In addition to this "extra" land, there is the so-called green revolution including our ability to produce new or synthetic foods — foods that we don't now have, methods of cultivation or synthesis that are not now used, and so forth. These might increase the available food a little more. And if we don't destroy the seas, perhaps they too can be used as a major source of food in ways that are not presently being used. But still, it is widely felt (and here one gets essentially the same three lines of argument mentioned before) that nothing can be done to solve the imbalance between population and food. There's a very sober and very realistic prediction of worldwide famine by 1975, by William and Paul Paddock. I suspect that possibility makes some difference to us living on these islands, where a great deal of food must be imported.

The United States is not now producing enough food to feed itself. Eventually, the reserves we are now living on will be depleted, and I suspect we will have serious problems.

The second major reason why futuristics is necessary is to deal with the population explosion. Let me just hint at some of the things we can do. One of the reasons I feel that something can be done is that we are not restricted to "mere" environmental manipulations, as we were in the past. We can, or soon will be able to, do things biologically that have never been possible before. As a "fantastic" suggestion: we can breed men who are half our present size, so that they'll take up less space. A foolish suggestion? Very well, but if you're going to have to put twenty-nine billion people in the space that presently has three billion, then we're going to need some pretty fantastic suggestions. In any event, there are many ways to solve problems, and I want to encourage you to think of as many ways of solving them as you can, and not to throw your hands up in despair and say that nothing can be done. Remember the earlier quotes: any-thing *can be done.*

The third general reason that futuristics is necessary is because of the field called cybernetics, which is, in general, the replacing of human activities by some sort of mechanical operation. We are all familiar with the fact that automation is replacing human labor. One of the major problems this group is going to have to face is: What are the human implications of automation? Especially we must question whether we should continue centering our social institutions and values around the assumptions of the necessity and desirability of work, or whether we are going to be willing to make the very great leap that

*is necessary towards developing a society in which most
of the people are not engaged in labor. Grapple with that
for a while.*

*But that's really the "easy" question about cyber-
netics. The more important and serious question concerns
the development of truly creative artificial intelligence.
We're on the threshold of such a development; perhaps
we've already crossed it. Already any computer can think
faster than any of us, already some computers can think
better than any of us. And there are computers now on
the verge of development that are also self-reproducing.
In fact, the next generation of computers is being designed
not by men, but by computers themselves, and these computers will be creative. That is, they will be able to do
things, think of things, to make connections that have
not been programed into them. The old days, during which
the computer was restricted to performing the programs
of human beings, is passing out of existence. Some people
have suggested that man can always pull the plug; well,
on contemporary computers you can pull the plug, but
soon there's likely to be a computer that will stick the
plug back in. We need to think seriously of the implications
of such a continuously generative technology.*

*Bear this in mind as I move on to the fourth reason
why futuristics is necessary, because I will relate the two
in just a minute. The fourth reason is something called
broadly "biological engineering," sometimes called
"genetic engineering." Biological engineering is "the conscious, potentially radical, reconstruction or new construction of human and nonhuman organisms." We are already
well down the road to creating new beings, new organisms,
or of radically altering existing ones. Heart transplants and
the use of borrowed parts from dead organisms are only
one step in the development of artificial organs which
eventually offer the possibility of continual generation and
eternal life to each individual.*

In addition to that, though, the discovery of how

genes operate, which chromosomes determine what behavioral characteristics of an organism, and so forth, means that it is possible to design human beings and other organisms the way you want them to be, or to prevent them from being the way you don't want them to be. That is, through some sort of genetic manipulation we may be able to interact directly with the reproductive process to prevent aggressiveness, for example, or to prevent anything else — the sexual urge, feelings of benevolence, or whatever. Before this, however, we will learn to alter humans physically, so that if we think it is helpful to have an eye in the back of our heads, it can be designed into the organism. Now this is why I have said quite seriously that rather than abolishing the internal-combustion engine, we can consider designing human beings that breathe carbon monoxide and give off oxygen. We can't do it right now, true, but there is no reason to assume that if we want this capability we will not have it by 2000.

Our real problem is that we have an infinitely large number of variables to consider. In the past, the major restraints on planners were the limitations of human nature — of the human organism. We were not able to operate directly on "human nature," but now, whether we like it or not, we have the potential. The question then is, how do we want to use this power?

Now if we combine these two things — truly creative artificial intelligence, and modified or new organisms, we have the development of a radically new being: a cyborg, a cybernetic organism, which is part machine and part new organism. For example, instead of using electronic computers, why not design organic computers which are able to fuel themselves and do other things which electronic computers can't? Gigantic brains, if you will, which live, which have life. Or — well, there are many other examples of ways by which these two things can be designed together. You may, for example, plant an electrode in your brain and use your brain simply as a recall device for your memory: store your memory in the university's computer and use your brain as an input-output terminal. Education in such a situation would be an extremely simple thing. All you would have to do is turn yourself on to the computer, and all the knowledge stored there would be zapped into you. Fantastic? No, not fantastic — potentially real. Thus the educational system of Hawaii in 2000 may be simply a matter of turning on a switch at an appropriate age — whatever the appropriate age is. Don't you agree that we need to consider this?

The fifth thing that makes futuristics necessary is the developing awareness of the fact of worldwide interdependence; the recognition of the world as a single ecosystem. I've heard complaints about a commission on Hawaii 2000, saying that the future of these islands can't be separated from the future of the entire world. It is true that it can't. What then can we do if we are interdependent with the rest of the world? We may save our own souls and lose the whole world. I think that we should explore this problem. I believe we can justify our enterprise only as an example for futuristics; a bad example if we fail, but nonetheless an attempt.

In any event, the recognition that the world is a single ecosystem is most evident in nature. For example, DDT has been discovered in seals in the Antarctic, where there never has been any DDT used. A nuclear battle, especially after we deploy our insane ABM system, would destroy the world. Even economically and politically, the world is one system, where a change in one part produces a generally unanticipated change in all others. For example, even if we solve our smog problem in Hawaii it may not be very long before we will be enjoying Los Angeles' smog. Now what do we want to do about that? Should we just increase the tradewinds and blow it all back? Whatever we do, the fact remains that a change in one part of the

29

world system produces an unanticipated change throughout the rest — in all areas of life — and the increasing
population intensifies the interactive effect.

A sixth reason why futuristics is necessary is the existence of the revolution of rising expectations in the world,
the United States, and these islands, on the part of large
numbers of people who were politically invisible before,
and whom therefore there was no need to satisfy. There
is a profound and growing feeling of powerlessness in
the face of desperately needed change on the part of the
young, the local people, the blacks, the poor, women,
and many other so-called minority groups. They feel they
can't do anything about change except raise hell. I think
it should be the job of this commission to act on their
very legitimate demands. In so doing, we will have to
encourage the development of a social system quite different from the present one.

For the seventh reason why futuristics is necessary,
let me go back to the first quotation I gave you: "We
shape our tools and thereafter our tools shape us." I am
convinced of the validity of a modified form of technological determinism of a society's values and institutions. That
is to say, I believe that a society's values and institutions
are determined in large measure by that society's level
of technology (unless conscious effort is made to prevent
this, though even here there are limits to what we can
do appropriately). Thus the range of social values and
social institutions possible in a society that hunts and
gathers berries for its food is quite different from the range
of institutions and values appropriate for a society such
as twentieth-century America. My point is that the values
and institutions we are perpetuating at the present time
in the United States and in these islands are for the most
part those that were appropriate (if at all) for the late
eighteenth- and early nineteenth-century America; that is,
values that were appropriate for an industrializing rural
society. We are no longer such a society. We are, among

other things, a postindustrial urban society, and hence most of the values and institutions we have are, I feel, largely inadequate for the present.

So this leads to reason number eight: the obsolescence of almost all present values and institutions. If you don't want to buy that, I ask you to be willing at least to examine all values and institutions, seriously and thoroughly, to see whether they are indeed functional for the world we are entering. In other words, there is nothing, as I see it, that we have in the present that we need assume should be around thirty years from now.

Here's just one example: our national form of government under the constitution of 1789. That constitution may be considered basically to have been a rather satisfactory response to eighteenth-century technology in America. Imagine that you were a founding father in a preindustrial country, composed 90 percent of farmers, and had no experience of internal communication or transportation. If you were a democrat, that is if you wanted to have the widest possible popular participation, what sort of government would you design? Something like the 1789 constitution probably. But how similar is U.S. society in 1970 to that of 1789? Not very. If you were to sit down and design a constitution for the present, would you really want to take the technology, the structures, the methods, and the philosophies of the eighteenth century as a basis for designing for the twentieth century, or, in this conference, for the twenty-first?

A second example of what may be an inappropriate system for the future is the nuclear family. This family system under which we presumably all now live, was also a relatively appropriate response to nineteenth-century technology, but I'm not sure that it is especially appropriate for the twenty-first century. I'm not even sure it's appropriate for the twentieth, but this is obviously a specific point that can be either accepted or rejected, and that, I think, doesn't destroy the basic position I'm taking. If you

*look at the manifest and latent functions of the family —
procreation, regulation of the sexual urge, raising and
socializing children, the economic functions of the bread-
winner who goes out and earns the food and thus helps
keep half the population employed in the home, the provision for adult companionship, and so forth — all of
these functions can be taken over, indeed are being taken
over, by other institutions in our society. Should we encourage this? Should we try to perpetuate the nuclear
family? Or should we encourage or at least permit homosexual marriages, group marriages, and no marrying at all?
Well, this is getting down to controversial specifics, but
nonetheless I wanted to do this in order to give specific
examples of the necessity of our examining all institutions
and values on the basis of their appropriateness for the
future.*

*So much for the eight reasons why futuristics seems
to me to be necessary. If you object to the last points,
at least go back to the threat of environmental pollution
and the warnings of the prophets who say, "If we don't
do something about it now, all is lost." The unfortunate
thing about our reaction to such prophecy is that we've
heard such things many times before. Prophets have
always been running around predicting the end of the
world, and the world "unfortunately" hasn't ended yet,
so we can always feel that it's not going to end now.
I certainly hope we won't complacently dismiss these serious warnings, but we should not be paralyzed by fear
either.*

*Let me now mention two major arenas we have avail-
able for futuristic activities by making this observation:
futuristics, as I understand it, is action oriented. That is,
most futurists want to do things. We are not interested
in just passively sitting back and projecting trends. Oh,
I suppose there are those futurists and trend projectors
who just say, "Ah, ha, ha. We will die in 2018," and that's
all there is to it. They're interested in seeing only how*

accurate their calculations are. But I think most futurists are actually concerned with preventing disasters and with helping people determine and achieve the goals that the people themselves want.

The big problem is that of values — how do we determine the values upon which we are going to design this future? Especially, how are we going to determine these values in a situation in which there are no fixed parameters? If there is no essential, unchanged human nature beyond the reach of biological engineering, then we no longer can assume, "well, humans are essentially unchangeable, and thus the range of things we can do is very narrow." Unfortunately, we are just beginning to get concerned with futuristic activity at the very time that we are faced with an unbelievably wide range of alternatives. (Some people dispute this, saying that such things as environmental pollution and the tenacity with which people cling to obsolete values seriously limit our alternatives. I hope and feel they are wrong, and I'm trying to prove them so.) Thus, we've got to be very much concerned with expanding our own minds so that we will be less cluttered with the notions that we've had in the past. That's easier said than done of course.

A problem related to this is democratic participation in futuristics activities. We have said over and over again in our meetings, and I completely agree, that we don't want to get hung up on what the experts say. We don't want a small number of people designing the future for us. I hope that we will as a group genuinely try to encourage the participation of every single person living in these islands; that we will get as much participation from as many people as possible. Nonetheless, I fear it might be prematurely inhibiting to go out and ask the ordinary individual to design the future for Hawaii 2000 because there is little, generally speaking, in the educational or experiential background of any individual now living which would encourage him to think of the future other than essentially as it is at present, with a few minor corrections. That is, our educational and social systems encourage us to think about the future in terms of the present. But if we will reflect even on our own lives, we can be persuaded, I believe, that this is certainly not the way it's going to be, unless we do very radical things to prevent change in the emerging future. So, one of the first things I hope this committee will do is turn its attention to the problem of finding out how we can encourage the citizens of the state to think in utterly new ways about the future, in order to probe their real desires and dreams. I have some suggestions for that and I solicit your suggestions as well. I think this is a very important matter, for if this were to be an elite, separatist, dictatorial operation, it would be a great misfortune. But unless we encourage the total population to be free of its overlearning from the past, then it's likely to do worse than we do, no matter how poorly we perform.

The two major programs for futuristics I alluded to before are environmental and biological engineering. In the past, I would say actually up to the past five years, as far as most planners or legislators were concerned, if you wanted to change human behavior you essentially had no choice — you tried to manipulate the environment: you changed institutions, you altered architecture, you built roads, you destroyed buildings, you passed laws penalizing people for doing some things and rewarding them for doing others. We're still going to be involved in environmental engineering of this sort, and the recent marriage of the techniques of the behavioral sciences to architecture, resulting in the science of "environmental systems," is something that I believe is very important for the work of this committee. What changes do we want to make in the environment, in the institutions, in the buildings, in the natural surroundings, and so forth? And how can scientific analysis help us?

It is the second program, though, that we are more

likely to fear, to shrink back from, to be afraid of, or to say can't be done: biological engineering. What changes do we want to make, if any, in the human body, or in other organisms? Look: we are no longer restricted to just exhorting people, preaching to them, and teaching them, on the one hand, or changing their environment, on the other. Now we can do very profound things in changing their physical and psychological structure, and their biological makeup generally.

Finally, how do we ourselves actually go about designing the future of Hawaii? I can't go into all the techniques here, but I do want to suggest some of the first steps very briefly. There are five general aspects that I'd like you to think about.

First of all, we can read, think, talk, and write about the future. I'd be glad to suggest an essential library that all of us might well read. (See Bibliography B, p. 490.) Because I think we should encourage as many people as possible to think about the future, we should try to get into the educational system at all levels. We should utilize all media. In fact, there are all sorts of possibilities to get more and more people involved in designing the future.

There are, however, essentially four types of techniques that relate to this point of reading, thinking, talking, and writing about the future. One is simply intuition, the way you feel about things, imagining the way the future might be. In order to do this, we need to engage in what I call "radical imagining." We need to think about things we have never thought of before. There are techniques by which we can get ourselves and others out of our present ruts, and begin thinking about things we have never before considered, or thought well of.

A second source for considering the future is science fiction, because in such fiction we can play around with things in ways scholarly writings cannot. An awful lot of tremendously good ideas come from science fiction.

I next suggest something that has been mentioned several times before, and I most deeply hope we do indeed engage in it — simple analysis of projections of current trends. For example, what will happen if we continue to increase the number of automobiles in Hawaii at the current rate? What will happen if we continue to allow unchecked immigration? What will happen if we continue to make tourism our major source of internal income? Even this is tricky business, for we have to be concerned not only with simple straight-line projections, but also with problems of rates of change, cycles, obsolescence, and the like. But the statisticians can worry about the problems of trend analysis for us.

Finally, there are the so-called Delphi techniques that have been developed very recently for social forecasting. Essentially this involves a board of experts who are asked to estimate when certain events will occur: When will cybernated organisms be developed? When will drugs be used normally in the educational process? When will we land on the first inhabited planet? When will immortality be achieved, and so forth? We ask groups of experts (the technique is actually more sophisticated than this) to estimate the occurrence of these events, and next get an average estimation of when they think these things will occur. Then we design a future appropriate for these estimates. All right, that's one range of ways in which we can prepare to design the future.

The second range is in the design and playing of games (some of which might be like Monopoly) in which we make cards and throw dice and so forth, so that we can imagine what living in the future might be like. We "live" in the future during these games, and we see how we react when certain things happen — that's one type of game. Another type is role playing, in which we imagine that we are some person other than what we are. Let's say we imagine that we are immortal — which is a little difficult to do because if there's anything inevitable, aside from taxes, it is death. Well, like it or not, death may no longer be inevitable. And if it isn't, what's it going to be like living forever? There are lots of other things, including the possibility of making infinite duplications of yourself, so that there could be many copies of you in existence at the same time. If you have difficulties relating to yourself now, can you imagine what the problems will be then? In any event, begin living in imagination in new situations and see what difficulties, hopes, expectations, and fears are there.

Third, is the design and execution of computer simulations of the future. The University of Illinois has a teaching system, called PLATO, through which students interact with a computer in designing a future for the year 2000. The U.S. Department of Defense is also continually using computer simulations of military futures.

Fourth, is to design and/or to live in alternate-life-style communities. That is, we as a group could join the hippies on Maui and find out what it's like to live under different rules from our present ones. If you don't like that, then tell me what sort of society you would like to imagine our living in. Then let's not just talk about it, let's go do it. Even if we ourselves don't want to live differently, there certainly are other people in the islands who would like to live under different rules, and I seriously would like to see the State set up areas where groups of people who want to live differently from the rest of us can go live that way, freed temporarily and as an experiment from the rules and regulations of ordinary society.

More than that: instead of rewarding people who are most like everybody else, I would like to see the State reward people who are most nonviolently different. At least reward people who come up with "strange" ideas, who want to live in "strange" ways. Give these people medals, put them on television, put them on the front page instead of featuring those people who are most like the average American, or else who are different only by virtue of being more violent. The reason I want to do this is partly to have them serve as models for the future; to give the rest of us examples of what it might be like to live as an individual or as a group under different rules. I think there are plenty of people who want to do this, and I believe the State ought to support them if for no other reason than for the survival of the whole.

Donald Michael in his book The Unprepared Society (New York: Basic Books, 1968) doesn't quite go this far, but he does talk about what he calls "interstitial societies" — groups of people who now live in the "cracks" of existing society. Maybe this is one way we might try it. Let some people live in a new way a certain portion of the time and then live in the "straight" world the rest of the time. In any event, there are all sorts of ways in which this can be done, and I think we ought to consider generating admiration rather than condemnation for these people. I don't want to go into an anthropological justification for this, but while it made sense in a tribal society to condemn people who didn't go along with the group, it doesn't make sense for the evolving future to condemn people who want to try doing things differently — instead we should encourage them.

And finally, we can join a political action group and work directly for change. The Communist party, the SDS, the Young Americans for Freedom — at least these have types of people who don't want just to talk about change, or think about change, or play around with change: they want to make these changes now. "Black Power," "Students for a Democratic Society," whatever the groups might be — it seems to me that we are obligated to participate sympathetically in what they are feeling and doing. These are groups that want to do things differently. What can we learn from them? How can we incorporate their visions of the future, their desires for change, into a livable future for all?

The citizens of Hawaii and the members of this com-

mittee have an unusually bright challenge before them; an opportunity no other officially organized group of people has, so far as I know. Many people in much of the rest of the world are either ignorant of or apathetic toward the necessity of planning their future. Many Americans seem to assume mistakenly that we can satisfactorily prepare for the future simply by believing and acting as we have in the past, by looking into the rear-view mirror.

It's a great privilege to be associated with the citizens of Hawaii who are brave enough to try to do something new. Let's get to it.

Today We're Starting Something
Robert Theobald

Robert Theobald, British socioeconomist, was born in India, educated at Cambridge University, and worked in Paris before coming to the United States. He is the author of *Teg's 1994* (1972), *An Alternative Future for America* (1970), and *Free Men and Free Markets* (1963). He edited *Social Policies for America in the Seventies* (1968), *Committed Spending* (1968), and *The Guaranteed Income* (1966). Theobald lives in Arizona, partly because he likes it there, partly because he thinks Arizona — like Hawaii — is one of the places able to deal with the future.

T oday we're starting something, not finishing it. My role, therefore, is not to give you a nice, neat set of ideas and concepts that you can go home with, but rather to start us out on a route which will take you and me in directions that we don't yet know.

This says something about the way I speak and something about the way you should listen. I suggest you don't try to understand everything I say in detail, but that you try to get the flow and feel of it. It's not the way to listen in normal academic situations, but then, I'm not a normal academic. I would also suggest that you try not to get hung up on the first thing you dislike. I can guarantee you that some more is on the way.

Let me share with you two visions. The first one I had when I was here a year ago. I went to sleep and had a sort of time-lapse photographic picture of the island. And each year I watched the houses climbing up the peaks, until in 2000 the last peak was crowned with the last piece of concrete and the island had vanished completely but for these houses. When I came back this year, I had the same dream — at least, I thought I did. It seemed real and lifelike to my imagination. But, no — in the end, I looked around and discovered that what was left behind was Diamond Head, all by itself as a nice green area. In other words, one victory is not very important if you believe that you really haven't changed anything. What you managed to do was to turn people's attention elsewhere for the time being. It's a much bigger question.

The bigger question, I think, is suggested by a conversation I overheard the other evening between two Martians. One Martian said to the other that he had just run the latest data through the Martian computer, and that he regretted to inform the Martian observer on Earth that the odds had now risen to 99.9 percent that we would not be here in 2000. You notice that the Martian race is a much nicer one than we are. They would like us to be here in 2000. And I think that the Martians are perfectly right. Any rational analysis of the state of the world must lead you to conclude that the human race will have wiped out the carrying capacity of this world within thirty years.

I think there's an interesting example of this: In your employment picture for 2000, you have 53,000 people in the armed forces. I can assure you that if we have armed forces of that magnitude in 2000, we won't be here. In other words, if we haven't learned in thirty years that we cannot use violence, the chance of survival of the human race is minimal. I could show you the same conclusion in certain of the employment data which doesn't take any note of the fact that pollution and ecological issues are going to force massive changes in employment patterns. But you see, having said that once, I now forget. In other words, I say that things could not be worse. But you don't brood on that. You simply say okay. Then, in a very real sense, we will be justified in doing anything we can to change the situation. Because the future, if we continue in the same direction, will be disastrous. Now, why do I say disastrous? Well, I think it can be proven pretty quickly and simply. Man, in the industrial era of the last two hundred years or so, has been trying to get power over the environment, power to do what he wanted to do. Within the last thirty to fifty years, he has become incredibly successful because he has developed essentially four tools.

One of them is energy — the availability of as much energy as he needs. And energy can do anything you want. It can create fresh water out of salt water, it can turn marginal land into productive land, and so forth. It also has secondary consequences, as we are now beginning to understand.

The second thing we have invented is what I like to call alchemy, but what I should really call manipulating the microstructure of nature. In other words, we can produce materials with any set of qualities we wish. We can simply say to a chemist or physicist or whomever, "produce me so-and-so," and it will get produced, if it matters enough. That's what the space program should be taught.

The third thing we have is the computer. The computer is a calculating machine of vast power, that will answer the question you ask it. Of course, it remains true that if you ask a computer a stupid question you will get a stupid answer. But then, of course, that's true of human beings as well.

The fourth thing is that we have become very expert at training. The presence of your university here is a living proof of that fact. I use the word "training" very deliberately, because very little education takes place on university campuses. The distinction between education and training is that training teaches you a set of data that somebody else has already learned, and education teaches you to think for yourself. People don't like people to learn to think for themselves in general, and education is therefore a very different animal to train.

But the combination of energy, alchemy, the computer, and training made it possible to do an increasingly wide range of things. Then we found we had a problem, because we had no criteria for what we should do, except one very simple one. If it can be done, do it! If you can fly a supersonic aircraft, fly it! If you can go to the moon, go! Anything technical that can be done, should be done. And then suddenly we found out it wouldn't do. And that is this incredible problem we have suddenly got into — which is that everything we do that is important has secondary, tertiary, and continuing consequences. If you knock down the forest you change the climate; if you fly SSTs, you may have high-level pollution of the atmosphere, which you simply cannot get rid of. And so on.

Now we have a new problem, which is that man must choose what he wishes to do. When we get into that one, we suddenly discover that we have no techniques we can trust — and that is why the task you have accepted is so incredibly difficult. Because what you have said is that you're going to get together and you're going to discover how a community makes choices about its future. Let it be very clear that as a culture we don't know anything about this issue. I think we know some things as individuals, because a few of us worked on this and had some ideas, but as a culture we know nothing about it. Now our situation is not new. Many cultures have perished. Toynbee points out that there are a lot more dead cultures than live ones. Cultures confronted with total change in their environment have usually — in fact, I should say, have always — failed. That is why I said that we will probably fail. There are two reasons I will cite.

One of them, I suppose, is purely selfish and personal: I'm engaged in this thing and it's probably going to be pretty messy if we fail. Well, there's another reason: there is a critical difference it seems to me between the situation in which leadership could pass from one culture to *another, as it did, for example, from Spain to Britain on the defeat of the Armada, or from Greece to Rome, or whichever cultural change you like, and the situation in which, at least as I read the picture, nothing will be left unless you wish to count rats or insects, who are resistant to whatever it is we do on the Earth. Because, for the first time, man has the power to prescribe a total world, and I have no doubt that we will do so, either positively or, much more likely, through failure to make the required decisions to deal with the ecological issues. So in a very real sense we have a peculiar situation, a fundamental historicality of situation. In other words, what we are trying to do has never been successful. I don't know enough history to know if it has ever been tried, but it has certainly never been tried successfully. And probably, it never could have been, because without our communications and without our abundance it was likely never feasible.*

Now, how do we make choices? As I said, I think we know something as individuals although we don't know anything about it as a culture. I think, basically, that change occurs when two conditions are met. (There is someone here from whom I've learned much of this: Gregory Bateson.[1]) Basically, decisions have to be effective and feedback has to be accurate. Now, this sounds very simple. All you have to do is get correct information and then somebody has to make intelligent decisions. Well, don't we run the culture that way, at least in theory? No, we don't! We run a culture which is designed to produce inaccurate feedback and ineffective decision-making in terms of reality. That may sound a bit shocking, but let me try to explain what I mean. If you have a boss on whom your career and livelihood depend, you do not bring him bad news. Not if you have any sense, you don't. And as our culture is based predominantly on structural

---

1. Anthropologist currently at the Oceanic Institute, Honolulu. — Editors.

authority, on bosses, we have built into our culture an immediate distortion of feedback patterns.

Not only that, but our culture justifies lying at all levels. Whether we call it public relations, which is business' and the church's term for this process; management of the news, which is government's name for it; or advertising, which is the businessman's name for the commercial side of it — they're all lies designed to bring about what you wish to happen. Telling the truth is a very obsolete concept in our culture. If you think I'm being unfair, look at the events around you, look at what really happens. The second requirement for effective decision making is some responsible people. Well, I think that Kafka is almost our best author. You go to somebody and you say, "I don't like what's going on," and assuming he is a nice person, he says, "Yes, it's very sad, but, of course, it's not in my office. Why don't you go and talk to B." And assuming you meet more nice people, you get shunted from B to C to D to E; eventually, you end up back with A again. And nobody's responsible. Because nobody has any feeling that the law or the rule or the pattern needs to be changed.

It's just too bad; it would be nice if it were different, but it's difficult to change anything around here. I think this isn't as bad on the islands as it is on the Mainland in some ways, but I think you have some of your own patterns which compensate. Now, if you want to change this, which way do you go? The extraordinary thing is that political scientists tell you to go over to a dictatorship. You listen to them, and they say that democracy hasn't worked. Obviously, if we're going to deal with the massive problems that now confront us, we are going to have to move into more centralized authority, which, in light of this analysis, is extraordinary, isn't it? Because what was wrong was that we already have too much centralized authority. At least, if I am right, we have to move in exactly the opposite direction; that is, away from a situation in which people have structural authority toward a situation in which people have sapiential authority — authority based on knowledge — over the way you run your culture, in terms of the capacity for people to talk, to plan, to think, and to create with each other. You run back to two old virtues, which some of you will remember from religious traditions: honesty and responsibility. There are two others you may remember: humility and love. But they all fail in the systems theory which says that, basically, if the system is going to survive, you had better be certain that you don't try to take over too much. Gregory Bateson has an appropriate comment, which goes this way: "The worst thing that can happen to a parasite is to find a perfect host." You see, if it finds a perfect host, it eats him, and when the host has been all eaten, the parasite dies. Well, that's mankind and Earth at the moment. You'd better learn to be humble and in a hurry!

And love? I'm still not happy about the parallel, at least as to how I can explain it, but basically, I think systems theory says that for a system to work you must have spare capacity. In other words, the system must not be so overloaded that when something unexpected takes place the system cannot cope with it. Maybe, that's what love is all about. Because what love says is, "I will support somebody when he needs support." That may be an odd definition of love, having gotten used to Hollywood. But love, I think, is not swarming all over a person, not supporting him at all times whether he needs it or not, but being there essentially in emergencies. My definition of an emergency is very wide — physical, moral, spiritual, whatever it may be. Therefore, I think we have a strange problem in that religions were right and the industrial age was wrong. The industrial age is going to turn out to be a gigantic aberration, but an aberration that brought us to a point where we could do something that could never have been done before. Therefore, in the long sweep of human history, it may, if we survive, make sense. It brought us abundance. It brought us the capacity to feed, clothe, and shelter every human being as long as he is willing to be fed, clothed, and sheltered at reasonable levels, not to demand three yachts, four cars, five airplanes, and six television sets. It also brought us something else: the language by which I believe we can understand and be logical about our future. We'll come back to that a bit later.

So what I think we have to do now is, somehow, imagine a democratic world. I think there's nothing wrong with democracy, except that it's never been tried. Don't let us kid ourselves — we don't have a democratic system. Anybody who thinks we do hasn't analyzed the entire political system under which we all live. A democratic system is one in which people are involved in their own self-government. It takes an awful lot of face to suggest that many significant proportions of our population today are either interested in or involved in their own self-government. I don't care whether you take the city of Honolulu or the University of Hawaii or the state of Hawaii or even the nation of the United States. In fact, the extraordinary thing is that it usually turns out that the further away from something you are, the more power you have. And people get most upset when you want self-government near your own locality. You talk about having a right to decide what goes on at the university. People get much more upset about that, because it's actually real, when they do it without your pretending to be involved in foreign-policy determination, which you're not anyway.

Now, there's a problem here — it occurs when you sit down in groups and start talking. Because there are two ways to tackle any question. One is to say we know what the question is and let's find the answers. In other words, we have a transportation problem. What's the transportation problem? Well, I can't drive my car from here to there in five minutes. I used to drive my car from here to there in five minutes. Not now, I can't any more. Or, we have another problem. We need to educate not thirty-five thousand, but seventy thousand people. By educate, we mean the same care. Okay, what do we have to do to get seventy thousand people into the same educational pattern as thirty-five thousand? But then there's another path of discussion that says, let's decide what we mean by the word "transportation." Or, even worse, let's decide whether we really want to transport ourselves or whether we want to communicate messages instead. Or, let us decide whether education is what is going on in our schools and universities.

People who talk these two totally contradictory languages cannot hear each other. They really can't. The basic trouble here is, first of all, a generation gap. It is, in general, not entirely, but in general, the young who say, "We do not know what the questions are," and the old who say, "Let us solve the existing questions." Now, second, it is, I think, basically a gap in technique between the sexes — men who will quite surely know how to structure arguments and women who will say, "Look, things are a lot more fluid than that somehow," and find out that patterns by which men insist on discussing simply cut out too much of the possible styles of discussion and argument. And third, under no particular context, I suspect that it is profoundly a cultural question. I think that the Western style of certainty is probably, to a degree and an extent, alien to the Asian style.

I'm going to have some suggestions when I sum up and when I've seen reactions as to some practical ways of handling this. All I want to do at the moment is sensitize you to the issue. If you think that's easy, forget it. Go home. And if you aren't willing to spend an awful lot of your thinking, your motivation, and your commitment over the next few months, trying to discover what this all means, go home. Because there is no way to get into this issue without, basically, tearing up an enormous amount of who you are, and I say "who you are" quite *deliberately. Your words, your patterns, your ideas, have to change if you take this seriously. If you're not willing to watch where you're going, you will be destructive to yourself and to everybody else in the group. We had a long discussion about this when I was meeting with people to talk about how this should be handled. I said that the first thing we have to say to people is, "If this doesn't make sense to you, if you think it's all crazy, don't stay because of a sense of commitment. Get out! Because you're not good for yourself and you're not good for the other people in the group. I'm not asking you to know how to handle it; I'm asking you to want to know how to handle it."*

One of the strange things, as we move between eras this time, is that in the industrial and intellectual eras, first we understood them and then we acted. And now suddenly, it's gone the other way. Now we have to want to act first and then we can find the commitment to understand what it means. What I'm asking for, and what we have to find out is, "Does it matter to you? Does it matter profoundly, what this island is going to look like?" And by extension, I think quite possibly, what this world is going to look like in thirty years. If it doesn't, you shouldn't be here. I think it should matter to all. But that's another question. I can't imply, I can't put my shoes on you — and anyhow, I shouldn't. But don't stay unless you want to. Don't stay out of a sense of duty, don't stay because it isn't fair to the chairman not to be around. And when you do stay, watch your attitudes to other races, other sexes, and other ages. Realize that we have some deep built-in patterns in terms of how we think young people should be related to — and it's fascinating. You begin a group discussion, and the older people talk and everybody listens quite quietly; then younger persons start talking and suddenly they get cut off. Well, they get cut off because, obviously, younger people have less to say. That goes without saying. Women have lots to say, and this you see, is the point where one of the Asian culture patterns, I think, is going to be very rough. Because Asian culture patterns still emphasize the fact that young people must, can, and should learn from their parents far more than Western culture patterns do. What I'm saying is what Margaret Mead has said, that, basically, everyone of us over thirty is a pilgrim into a strange land. It's a difficult reality to live in.

I wish now to briefly throw out a theory or concept about the whole issue here of the various task forces you've been asked to serve on. Everything I've said up to now I feel pretty convinced about. I may be wrong, but these are ideas I've worked on for a long time, and I'm pretty sure that they're at least in the right ballpark. The issues I'm going to raise now are deliberately provocative, things that I think are important. I do not believe in shocking people for shocking's sake, and I will never tell a lie from a platform. But I will not want any or most of these things to come out until I have had a chance to talk with the task force or somebody else.

Well, let's take first the task-force topic "Hawaii's People and Life-styles 2000." I suggest that if you are going to talk seriously about the year 2000, you are going to have to consider extrasensory perception, which I believe will have been understood and clarified as a perfectly physical phenomenon by that date. Now what does that mean in terms of how a society operates? I don't imply that I know the whole answer to that question, but I am clear in saying that by 2000 we will have more effective means of communication, based on factors that we do not presently understand. We will not use words, which are an extremely inefficient way to communicate, in the same way that we do at present.

Another issue, of course, is the one you're already into: abortion and sterilization. What does that mean for life-styles? And above all, what does it mean for women's life-styles? You see, we still really are assuming that women should bear X number of children, that that is their lot. When you get right down to it, that's where we are on the woman issue. Well, if we say that we aren't going to have more than two children per woman, and even if you leave out the issue of the dramatic lengthening of the life span, that isn't a life for a woman. Leave out, of course, as well, the question of whether you're going to have test-tube babies. But even given just no other changes except the need for population control, you're going to have to alter dramatically your view of what women are, who women are, and what their role is.

Regarding the topic "The Individual, Privacy, and Mental Health,"[2] these are two things at totally different levels. One, I suspect, is that we're going to have to pass a law on computers in a very short while. I'm quite serious. The computer, or rather the person running it, is going to have to be legally responsible for the actions with that computer, including loss of credit, loss of jobs, and the like, by credit or other services which bring incorrect information to the public. That's a nice thorny thicket for somebody to get into, but it's a short-run issue. The long-run issue is, "Does the computer get your information whether you want it or not, or do you decide what goes on the computer?" A moment ago, I suggested that there's no doubt that you must have the right to decide what goes into the computer about you and your life. And that's where the whole issue of privacy has to be considered at a totally different level. As I said, these comments are teasers, simply to raise the range of issues in various ways.

Now, with the topic "Natural Environment — Land, Sea, and Air": I recently read in a newspaper that California is considering taking the profit out of land speculation — by taxing. Now there's another pretty kettle of fish. What sort of laws should you or could you pass? If you decide that basically the land belongs to the people,

2. The task-force participants later changed this preliminary designation to "The Quality of Personal Life." — Editors.

because that's really what it comes back to, if you say you're not going to allow people to speculate in land, what it really means is that you say that increase in land value is due to the total population and not to the individual owner. And I think that's a lot closer to the truth than the way we're operating at the moment. I'm not saying it's all the truth, and that's part of the trouble. But basically, the way some people get rich out of land speculation is not because they do anything, but because a lot of other people do something. Why should the speculators make money out of it?

I suspect that for you who are still here in 2000, there will be at least one underwater city, somewhere around Hawaii. Where do you want it? How do you want it? Do you want to be involved in undersea research at the level that somebody's going to have to be. And if so, what happens? And if you're not going to be doing that, I suspect you're certainly going to be fishing with totally new means, using electric barriers, and so forth, for keeping schools of fish in particular places. If you want to get your imagination stretched, read some science fiction. It's not all good, but perhaps we can put out a list of a few science-fiction books which will simply make you stretch your imagination. There's one I've read recently about how to get a large amount of our food from deliberately farming waste. It's a way to shift out of your present thinking, which is all I'm trying to do here at the moment. In a recent book my wife and I did, set in 1994, one of the locations was an underwater city. [3]

But while we're on transportation and housing, let me put in another word which I think ought to belong there — communication. You see, it's very odd that we think everybody has to travel to work every morning and travel back in the evening. Now, why shouldn't you work in you home? And why must we have office buildings

3. Robert Theobald and J. M. Scott, *Teg's 1994* (Chicago: Swallow Press, 1972).

which are empty sixteen hours a day when we go home. It's ludicrous! It's the most incredible waste of space that one could imagine. Now, when you have to have factories and offices, and people have to have visual contact — yes travel is necessary! But with computers? It's nonsense! I'm not saying we could have done it yet, but I can tell you that we can do it faster than we're going to with our planning. Most people don't need to travel nearly as much as they do. The way to solve the traffic jam is not, I suspect, to try to get more cars on the road, but to stop traveling to work at nine o'clock in the morning. On the short run, what about looking seriously at some of the other transportation patterns in the world? The people of Ireland run jitneys, which are cars running on a very loose schedule between various parts of the country. You don't have to run large buses as the only way to move people. You can set up systems which will move small numbers of people conveniently. Look at different sets of cultural patterns to solve issues. For example, do you know what the Japanese police recommended you take if you decided to drive to Expo '70 on a crowded day? Two meals and a portable toilet.

"The Economy" topic: This is where I'm going to lose the task-force leader on economy, but too bad. I believe that we should have abolished money as a method of controlling purchases and sales by 1985. Money is a method of moving information. Once you have computers, you can move information more effectively. And money becomes an inefficient means of doing the job. Now, if you think that's far out, I suggest you simply look at the alternatives, one of which is the credit-card system. This system is really far out when you take it seriously. Because what is happening is that if you are well off and have a job, you can be better off and get as much credit as you want. You're getting a split now between the credit-worthy and the noncredit-worthy, with some pretty scary results, let me tell you. Now, to reiterate, in an abundant

occasion. I think we're going to split back down again into these two levels.

Now, the topic "Education": I think that the university and the school as now known will not exist in 2000. I think they can go in only one of two directions. They will either be absorbed back into the community; in other words, become once again an integral part of the community, and will not isolate eighteen- to twenty-four year-olds, who are also quite integral to the community. Or, alternatively, they will become places where particular problems are studied, so that you will have groups working on ecology, others working on poverty, and still others working on communications, and so forth. But I believe that this path, which grew without any thought, and which has ended up cutting off our brightest, most imaginative people, at the peak of their energy, from anything significant to do with their lives, simply has to end, and end very rapidly. I am very nearly convinced that we will see large-scale collapse of colleges and universities in the seventies, partly because legislatures and private agencies will not fund, and partly because students will not go. I think there is a particular need to look at the relevance of this topic in Hawaiian terms. Because there is a difference in this university, one that is quite palpable when you come from the Mainland. But my main conclusion does not change: the university as an isolated place, unless it is dealing with a specialized problem possibility, is obsolete.

Next is "Political Decision Making and the Law": Oh well, I've got into trouble everywhere else — I'll finish off clean. The law justifies lying, like every other institution. Besides, what is the lawyer's role, except to lie as efficiently as he can? I use lying in the broader sense of the word — to distort the truth as seen by the jury. The judiciary system is a justification for the brightest adversary to win, not a design to elicit the truth. But, you say, it works. All right, it works better than anything else — but that isn't enough anymore. I've worked very hard at trying to imagine a world in which people are irresponsible, dishonest, hating, and proud, and I can't do it. But the law is in that context, the context of the evil of man. It says man is inherently evil, let us set up the best system we can to deal with evil man. What man's law is saying isn't the way to look at man. The only way to look at man now is as a creature striving for self-realization. And then the laws that handle this creature won't do. The other reason the laws handling it won't do is that if you as a judge want to put out a new ruling, you've got to find a precedent. It doesn't matter if the precedent isn't any good, you've got to find one somewhere. It's a hell of a way to run a future-oriented society, if I may be so blunt. It makes it awfully difficult to keep up even if you want to.

As for politics — same problem. The role of the politician is to get elected. To get elected, you must get the most votes. How do you get the most votes? By finding out where the population is and by standing for that. That may be a little bit cynical, but not very. So an election, in a sense, drags you back — to where the population is, not where it ought to be. I'm not knocking politicians; I hope nobody's getting an idea that I'm knocking any particular group. If you have, you've missed the whole point. We are all caught in our own traps, and we are all responsible. The best line is Pogo's: "We have met the enemy and he is us." If you can't believe that, I suspect you shouldn't be in this futures activity. In other words, if you've got some untouchables, whether they be lies or tales or politicians or businessmen, get out of this game. Nobody is to blame in that nice convenient specific sense. Only all of us.

I'm not going to talk about "Hawaii and the Pacific Community." Not because I don't want to, but the present,

*I think, is going to grow out of what you're going to dis-
cover. The reason, in a sense, that I'm disqualified from
talking about this, at least at the moment, is that I have
a rather specific dream about Hawaii and the Pacific
community.[4] And I don't want to impose it upon you.*

4. This is of Hawaii as a world communications center. Theobald and
Scott, *Teg's 1994*, pp. 101–108. — Editors

3 THE CONFERENCE

Overview
Editors

I n the midafternoon of Wednesday, August 5, 1970, to the accompaniment of a classic Hawaiian chant, "Water of Kāne," performed by the authoritative interpreter Ka'upena Wong,[1] the Governor's Conference on the Year 2000 began. This ancient song, like the stylized Hawaiian petroglyph figure chosen as the conference symbol (and reproduced on the title page and jacket of this book),[2] symbolizes our belief that some elements of the deep Hawaiian past had a timeless beauty and futuristic relevance from which all could draw inspiration. The chant reminded us of the intimate bond between man and nature and of the profound question of the meaning of human life.[3] Close as we still are to dramatic volcanic mountains, the warm sun, the incessantly restless sparkling sea, soaring billowy clouds, gentle to forceful movement of wind and rain, glorious sunsets coloring skies beyond imagina-

1. A recording of this specially performed chant has been placed for future reference in the official archives of the state of Hawaii, the Bishop Museum, and the Department of Music of the University of Hawaii. We wish to acknowledge the assistance of Mary Kawena Pukui, leading authority on Hawaiian culture, who guided us to this chant and a suitable translation of it.

2. Drawing by Joseph Feher. From: Joseph Feher, comp., *Hawaii: A Pictorial History* (Honolulu: Bishop Museum Press, © 1969), p. 131. By permission of the artist and the Bernice P. Bishop Museum.

3. Superb contributions to this theme were later made in reflective remarks by the Buddhist Reverend Yoshiaki Fujitani, Catholic Monsignor Daniel J. Dever, and Protestant minister James Swenson when we gathered together in plenary sessions of a social nature.

tion, twinkling starry nights, and love of life, this ancient
song continues to strike a resonant chord within us.

THE WATER OF KĀNE [4]

A query, a question,
I put to you:
Where is the water of Kāne?
At the Eastern Gate
Where the Sun comes in at Haehae;
There is the water of Kāne.

A question I ask of you:
Where is the water of Kāne?
Out there with the floating Sun,
Where cloud-forms rest on Ocean's breast,
Uplifting their forms at Nihoa,
This side the base of Lehua;
There is the water of Kāne.

One question I put to you:
Where is the water of Kāne?
Yonder on mountain peak,
On the ridges steep,
In the valleys deep,
Where the rivers sweep;
There is the water of Kāne.

This question I ask of you:
Where, pray, is the water of Kāne?
Yonder, at sea, on the ocean,
In the driving rain,
In the heavenly bow,

4. Taken from Nathaniel B. Emerson, *Unwritten Literature of Hawaii;
the Sacred Songs of the Hula Collected and Translated with Notes and
an Account of the Hula* (Washington: Government Printing Office, 1909),
pp. 257–259.

In the piled-up mist-wraith,
In the blood-red rainfall,
In the ghost-pale cloud-form;
There is the water of Kāne.

One question I put to you:
Where, where is the water of Kāne?
Up on high is the water of Kāne,
In the heavenly blue,
In the black piled cloud,
In the black-black cloud,
In the black-mottled sacred cloud of the gods;
There is the water of Kāne.

One question I ask of you:
Where flows the water of Kāne?
Deep in the ground, in the gushing spring,
In the ducts of Kāne and Loa,
A well-spring of water, to quaff,
A water of magic power —
The water of life!
Life! O give us this life!

In his welcoming speech, Governor John A. Burns challenged the conference to "dream large dreams"[5] and seven hundred of us were off on an adventure that gripped our attention for four days from the afternoon of Wednesday, August 5, to noon of Saturday, August 8. To report adequately on this conference would merit a volume of its own, but here we can only explain its general principles, chronicle the sweep of events, and single out a few points for special attention.

In any case, we hoped that the conference would

5. As Senator Nadao Yoshinaga has commented, "Few people know the Governor as a dreamer, but more as a realist — a real practical guy" (*Honolulu Star-Bulletin*, January 21, 1972, p. C–6). Senator Yoshinaga further explained, "The Governor is an idealist, a dreamer . . ." (*Honolulu Advertiser*, January 21, 1972, p. B–1).

stir imaginations, bring constructive creativity to the draft task-force reports, and broaden the base of participation.

The conference was held in Waikiki's Ilikai Hotel, favored for its large-scale conference facilities. The conference committee considered some imaginative alternatives before settling upon this more conventional solution. Among alternatives were: an open-air conference in a park, an on-site conference at the location of task-force concern of the moment (for example, a blocked-off street in a low-income area, a highway overpass, or a hillside overlooking a housing subdivision) or a mobile conference (for example, some combination of on foot, bicycles, automobiles, radio-connected buses, chartered ship, airplane, and helicopters). In partial satisfaction of our desire for situational relevance and mobility we held our final conference session on the open grounds of the East-West Center at the University of Hawaii.

We began in plenary session, following the governor's welcome, with a ten-minute filmed talk, made especially for Hawaii 2000 by the busy author, Alvin Toffler, whose book Future Shock, *soon to become a national best seller, was being published that week. His remarks are presented in Part Three. This was followed by a forty-five minute multimedia evocation of future-oriented thinking. The multimedia presentation was a chronological statement of Hawaii's environmental and social development from its volcanic origins, through some of its most celebrated historical occurrences, to the present, and onward to a consideration of the varieties of two types of futures. One was that of the dismal futures of continued, unplanned, and unsystematic growth. The other was composed of images of bright futures which might result from the foresight of the conference. The presentation employed both rear- and front-screen projection of 8mm and 16mm motion pictures and 35mm slides on a specially constructed screen. A four-track sound system integrated voice, narration, music, and special effects.*

We next presented an hour-long panel of seven young people who provocatively voiced their aspirations for Hawaii's future. They had been given copies of the draft task-force reports and were asked to say anything they wanted about them in a five-minute presentation. No instructions other than this were given; and no effort was made to introduce them to various modes of thinking about the future. They were chosen in part to represent examples of "right," "left," "middle," and "nonpartisan" young political thinking.

The panel was chaired by Linda Luke, president of the Associated Students of the University of Hawaii. George Hudes, twenty-seven-year-old political-science graduate student, and a leader of Students for a Democratic Society, criticized the lack of concern for the present in the preliminary task-force reports. "This is characteristic of the futuristic fog machine which pollutes clear thinking about the present. Future shock? If we have any sensibilities left, present shock should be more than sufficient."[6] "I ask you to be people of the year 2000 today," he urged. "Be neurotic, for in this society neuroses may be our only indication of health. Break the rules — it is proper to break rules that break people. Be obscene — to be obscene to obscenity is to negate obscenity." Hudes argued that until Hawaii ceased to be a military base to support suppression of "national liberation movements" abroad it could have little hope of ensuring human dignity at home. He further urged attention to problems of food, housing, and Hawaii's economic structure. Allan Hoe, twenty-five, part-Hawaiian veteran of the war in Vietnam, and president of the student body at Leeward Community College, called for future efforts to preserve the Hawaiian race and culture. "I have doubts about our ability to change now or to change within the next five years so we can reach 2000," he explained.

6. *Honolulu Advertiser*, August 6, 1970, p. B–2.

Lehua Lopez, a twenty-one-year-old family social worker, said that it may already be too late to save the Hawaiians "because there are no Hawaiians left." [7] Calling attention to the dependence of local welfare on federal government support, she criticized what she believed to be the position of the SDS speaker on the venality of present institutions. "Mr. Hudes, if there is any way you can make your world come true, do it," she said. "But for us who have to work to get food now, it is a bummer." Barbara Stewart, a fourteen-year-old leader of the high-school division of the Young Americans for Freedom, defended the capitalist system for the future as "the best we have." She complained that certain task-force recommendations would "saddle overtaxed citizens with a multimillion dollar burden," and urged that we "not improve ourselves into a state of bankruptcy." Gail Harada, a seventeen-year-old member of the Pacific and Asian Affairs Council futures study group, said that young people do not want a "hand-me-down world." "The future is something that still can be influenced," she said. "We should have an idea of where we are going and how we are going to get there." She criticized the task-force reports generally for assuming that "the military and economic status of today" would be extended to 2000.

Tim Leedom, a twenty-four-year-old aide to then Lieutenant Governor Thomas P. Gill and former chairman of the University Young Democrats, said that the real problems on the way to 2000 were pollution, overpopulation, and the threat of nuclear war. He urged, "The American way is going to have to change and it will have to change now. Tomorrow will be too late." The chairman of the University Young Republicans, Robert Replogle, twenty years old, speaking for himself, suggested that Hawaii se-

7. In 1964–1967 there were an estimated 7,540 pure Hawaiians and another 118,640 part-Hawaiians in Hawaii. State of Hawaii, Department of Planning and Economic Development, "Estimates of the Hawaiian Population of Hawaii," Statistical Report 83, August 27, 1971.

cede from the Union because "in Hawaii we are too dependent on everyone, especially on the United States." He predicted ecological disaster for Hawaii, and the end of the world in fifty years. He concluded, "I am concerned about now. I can see no real purpose in this conference. Nothing can really come of it."

John Witeck, twenty-five years old, coordinator for Youth Action and an organizer of the June youth congress on the future, said, "Selecting Tom Hamilton [8] as a chairman of the task force on economy is like asking Al Capone to chair a task force on crime control." The audience roared with laughter. "It's not that Tom is a bad guy or a crook — but he is part of the problem," Witeck explained. "The task-force reports are boring — that's the opinion of every young person I've talked to," he said, adding that the task-force attempts to be apolitical merely reinforced acquiescence in the state of present society. Witeck noted a "rising level of bitterness" in Hawaii and predicted, "I'm not trying to scare you people, but I think bloodshed will come here." He explained that the only way to avert it would be widespread nonviolent political participation. Witeck urged, "Let's all work together. If it doesn't happen, it is silly to talk about 2000."

David Asai, a seventeen-year-old high-school leader from Maui, who had just been named Hawaii's teenager of the year, stressed tolerance and love as the basis for Hawaii's future. Drawing upon biblical imagery, he reminded the conference that many of today's "hippies" had the physical and economic attributes of Jesus Christ: beards and rejection of material values. He struck out at ethnic prejudices in Hawaii, asking, "How many times have you heard 'damned haole', 'stupid Japs', or 'dumb Samoan'?" He asked each participant to look at the person seated beside him, and say "I love you," and mean it.

8. Thomas H. Hamilton, political scientist, former University of Hawaii president; in 1970 president of the Hawaii Visitors Bureau, and later consultant to the trustees of the Bishop Estate.

The audience complied, with laughter. Asai responded, "It's funny. It's pretty funny to a lot of people. But without love, this country, this world . . . Hawaii is not going to see the year 2000."

After this provocative beginning we devoted an informal social hour to reflection and exchange of reactions. Then we gathered for dinner and a keynote address by the world-famous science-fiction writer Arthur C. Clarke. His remarks are shared here in Part Three.

The next two days were devoted mainly to thirteen separate workshop sessions in which were discussed the preliminary task-force and neighbor-island reports. The draft task-force reports had been distributed about two weeks prior to the conference to all expected participants.[9] Conference participants were there to do just that: participate actively in workshop discussions. Up to about fifty persons were expected in each group. Over half of them were not members of the original task forces, so that there was a potential for many fresh ideas as well as a critical clash of understandings. About one-quarter of the participants were students and young people.

Realizing that the structure of separate task-force working sessions would present a fragmented view of Hawaii's future, we provided a one and a half hour period near the end of the conference for a plenary session to hear brief reports on the task-force discussions. We called it "Hawaii 2000 Overview." We hoped that this integrated panel of task-force chairmen might stimulate some more holistic views of Hawaii 2000. We will later comment further upon the results of this integrative effort.

A sequence of speakers from outside Hawaii was designed to provide additional stimuli to the workshop discussions and to contribute to the eventual revision of the task-force reports that are presented here in Part Four.

9. State of Hawaii, Governor's Conference on the Year 2000, August 5–8, 1970, *Preliminary Task Force Reports (July 1970)*, mimeographed, Honolulu, 1970.

Arthur C. Clarke brought a mind-expanding world view; the writer Robert Jungk movingly contributed a humanist's imagination; and policy scientist Yehezkel Dror directed our thinking toward the tough tasks of translating future imagination into present action.

Two additional speakers were intended to give us perspective upon Hawaii's future in relation to the United States as a whole and to the Asian and Pacific region. The first speaker was Charles W. Williams of the national goals research staff in the Executive Office of the President in Washington.[10] On the basis of a wide national survey of scientific research and technological developments he then knew to be in progress, Williams conveyed to us a profound sense of an anticipated gigantic leap forward in technology expected to emerge during our thirty-year journey to the year 2000. There would be, he predicted, "a tremendous number of new trends as a normal part of life by the turn of the century, far more than has been experienced in my judgment in the last thirty years, perhaps in the last several centuries." Thus, he explained, "we are entering a situation in which the cause-effect relationships, in which the interdependency of activities, in which the way action in one area affects action in another area of life, in another part of the world, is simply different than it will ever have been in the past."

Our final outside speaker was the distinguished Japanese economist Saburo Okita, president of the Japan Economic Research Center, who reminded us that Hawaii would move toward 2000 in the context of a dynamically developing Japanese economy with worldwide effects and a wide gap between the economically advanced and the less-developed countries of Asia and the Pacific. However, he shared with us the thought that Japan's unprecedented

10. This future-oriented staff, subsequently disbanded, had just finished its report at the time of our conference. National Goals Research Staff, *Toward Balanced Growth: Quantity with Quality* (Washington, D.C.: U.S. Government Printing Office, 1970).

rate of economic development might not continue indefinitely. In his explanation of the situation in Japan, we thought we saw much in common with our own experience:

We made some calculations recently comparing Japan to the United States in terms of GNP (gross national product) per acre, not per capita. We found out that we already have five times as high GNP per acre as that of the United States, and if you take the flat area only we have about 10 times as high GNP per acre as the United States. So Japan is very vulnerable to the deteriorating environment. . . . This will get more and more serious in coming years as industrial output keeps on expanding. This may result in a lower rate of economic growth because we will have to divert the resources to prevent deterioration in the environment.

Also there may be some changes in the mentality of the Japanese. We were brought up from poverty. Most of the present leaders in politics, business, and government were born in a low-income society. And one of the highest virtues in the minds of current leaders of Japan is to work hard and to save more, to invest more, to expand rapidly.

But this may gradually diminish or weaken when the next generation of Japanese come to power. They were born to somewhat better economic conditions. Many of them were born to a society which was becoming affluent. They may like to have more leisure; they may like to work shorter hours; and those things may affect the future course of the economy. Anyway, a country must live harmoniously with others. One country cannot continue an extraordinarily high rate of expansion forever. The continuation of such an extraordinary rate of growth may disrupt the harmony of the world economy. Moreover, the people may lose interest in economic growth eventually.[11]

11. Transcribed from tape-recorded remarks.

Finally, Mr. Okita noted that the future of Hawaii would be affected by three factors: American prosperity, Asian prosperity, and the nature of United States–Asian relations. He predicted a diminishment of American military involvement in Asia and the probable growth of closer relations in the economic and cultural fields. He explained, "If a closer relationship develops between Asia and the United States, then there is a very good chance for Hawaii to become more prosperous." He concluded, "I hope the influence from these three factors will be in a favorable direction."

In keeping with the participatory and flexible society envisioned by many for the future, we attempted to express this in our conference design in two ways — in providing opportunities for alternatives and in the way we "ended" the conference. First, during the conference we provided a blackboard in a central location for anyone to announce his own conference program, and we arranged to have open meeting places constantly available for groups with shared concerns. We had no illusions that we could satisfy seven hundred diverse individuals with our conference program — and we were right. Among the first to avail themselves of this opportunity was a group of young people (some connected with the June youth congress that stressed action now on present ills as an approach to the future) who wished to discuss how they might more effectively influence the conference proceedings. There was by no means consensus among the young, but there was a frank exchange of feelings. One result of this countercurrent to the conference mainstream was an effort to extend the next-to-final plenary session of the conference — in which all task-force chairmen reported — into a citizens' meeting to condemn the evils of present society and to pass resolutions for immediate corrective action.

Among the ideas presented for action during a fifty-minute period were: to call a moratorium on school

attendance in all areas deemed bereft of "human develop-
ment"; to create experimental communities on Oahu and
Maui for new life-styles; "to make land developers legally
responsible for their actions if not based on full public
disclosure of all details"; to call for unconditional with-
drawal of all United States troops from Southeast Asia
and to use the savings to feed the world poor; to limit
Hawaii's population; to raise electricity rates to discourage
its use; to match the cost of the conference ($65,000) with
a program to feed hungry children; to create a Pacific
futures research center; and to continue the work of the
conference through a State department of futuristics. For
some, the experience was an emotional one. One partici-
pant cried out angrily, "You don't start a dialog by insulting
us." [12]

Here again, tensions surfaced that had marked the
Hawaii 2000 effort from the outset between action now
in a present- or past-derived mode (or radical critique of
the present) versus creative thinking about the future as
an approach to solving present problems or to redefining
present problems in ways to facilitate their solution with
the least disastrous effects upon future life. We shall dis-
cuss further what we learned from this experience in the
final article in this book.

On the last morning of the conference these tensions
contributed to a dramatic experience. To symbolize the
linkage between the Hawaii 2000 conference (August 5–8)
and an immediately following conference on the future
of Asia and the Pacific at the East-West Center (August
9–15), we decided to hold our concluding plenary session
in the John F. Kennedy Theatre of the East-West Center
on the University of Hawaii campus. Two presentations,
designed to be complementary, were given: the summary
report of the task force on Hawaii and the Pacific commu-
nity in 2000, and an address by an outstanding Asian leader
on Hawaii 2000 in Asian and Pacific perspective.

12. *Honolulu Advertiser*, August 8, 1970, p. A–11.

During the preceding workshop sessions on the Pacific-oriented workshop report, strong objections were raised to what were regarded as militaristic, imperialistic, business-dominated, and American superiority assumptions, of the preliminary task-force report. (It must be recalled by those who read this book far in the future that our conference took place at a time when there was heated dissent against American involvement in the Vietnam War and when virtually every aspect of American society was undergoing scathing criticism, by young people and others.) This mood, combined with a not wholly satisfactory effort to redirect the conference to present-action concerns by several young people the previous evening created an atmosphere of anxiety, tension, and widely shared expectations of the possible eruption of angry confrontations during this plenary meeting.

In his opening report to the meeting, the Pacific community task-force chairman George Kanahele demonstrated that he fully understood and had benefited from the criticisms that had been leveled at the earlier draft report. His report was well received, but during the following discussion period, tensions began again to build up. Finally, a question led to the expression by a newcomer of frustration over the meaning of the aloha spirit in Hawaii. At this point, spontaneously, Mrs. Pilahi Paki, a Maui-born Hawaiian culture consultant and Hawaiian language teacher, rose at the back of the theater in a long red-and-white flowered mu'umu'u. She said, with overtones that no printed text can convey

I would like you all to understand that the "Aloha Spirit" is the coordination of mind and heart . . . it's within the individual — it brings you down to yourself. You must think and emote good feelings to others.

Permit me to offer a translation of the word aloha:

A   **stands for** *akahai*, **meaning kindness, to be expressed with tenderness,**

L   **stands for** *lōkāhi*, **meaning unity, to be expressed with harmony,**

O   stands for *'olu'olu*, **meaning agreeable, to
be expressed with pleasantness,**

H   stands for *ha'aha'a*, **meaning humility, to
be expressed with modesty,**

A   stands for *ahonui*, **meaning patience, to be
expressed with perseverance.**

**These are the traits of character that express the charm,
warmth, and sincerity of Hawaiians. It was the working
philosophy of my ancestors. . . .**[13]

*"They handed it down to me and I wish to give it to
you," Mrs. Paki concluded.*[14] *There was a momentary hush
in the theater and then several hundred of us began to
applaud and to stand together in a prolonged ovation.
Tears welled up in the eyes of many; some of us actually
cried.*

*At the end of the session many persons crowded
around Mrs. Paki. One woman from Australia rushed up
to give her a hug, explaining, "I just came because she
made my husband and me cry. . . . What she said was
beautiful — my husband still has tears in his eyes."*[15]
*Another man said, "We've been muddling around for four
days trying to find directions for Hawaii's future. . . . No
one else even thought of what that woman said. She's
got the answer."*[16] *It was a deeply moving experience and
remains in the memory of participants as the emotional
climax of the Hawaii 2000 experience. We hope that social
psychiatrists will some day provide us with a scientific
explanation of this important event because we sensed
that no religious creed, no ideological doctrine, no appeal
to the purely intellective or rational aspects of human
experience could have united such a diverse group of*

13. *Honolulu Advertiser*, August 9, 1970, p. 1.

14. This sentence was somehow omitted from the newspaper account,
but we recall distinctly that she made it.

15. *Honolulu Advertiser*, August 9, 1970, p. 1.

16. Ibid. In the conference opening session, of course, David Asai,
student leader from Maui, said the same thing in a Christian context
but without the same effect. At that time a sense of community and
tension had not been developed among the participants.

Americans who had gathered for several days to call every aspect of their present way of life into creative question. Perhaps only a shared love for Hawaii, a shared dismay at the injustices suffered by the Hawaiian people, and a shared willingness to search together toward a new society devoid of racism, exploitation, and insensitivity to human feelings — plus the beautiful concept of aloha personified in a wonderful Hawaiian woman — could have combined to create the spirit of group harmony that followed Mrs. Paki's speech. We await comparison with the experiences of other large-scale experiments in anticipatory democracy elsewhere in America and throughout the world that may further clarify for us the unique importance of aloha for Hawaii.

We concluded the conference in a way that stressed open community participation. It was also intended to convey the idea that the conference could not possibly "end" in some formal way but must diffuse in various ways as a creative influence upon normal community life with then unforseeable consequences. Outside Kennedy Theatre, on the open grounds of the East-West Center, we designated twelve locations (ten for task forces, one for neighbor-island groups, and one for general discussion) where any person in Hawaii could come to engage in an "open dialog" with the chairmen and other members of the conference task forces. We began to "end" the conference in this way at eleven o'clock on Saturday morning, August 8, 1970. Unfortunately the opportunity was not well publicized and virtually no one appeared from the community to take advantage of it.

Instead, there emerged spontaneously in the place planned for a general discussion of Hawaii, a group of about one hundred fifty participants, including many young persons, who were eager to take some kind of action to ensure that the work just begun would continue. A student, Paul Sullivan, expressed the feelings of many, "There's no reason why the futuristic conference on Hawaii in the year 2000 should die today. If my children are to have a good life, this thing has to go on. It cannot die here, or there won't be a year 2000." [17] *State Senator John Hulten, former president of the senate, who had been one of the original supporters of the conference, assured the group that a permanent State Commission on the Year 2000 had been provided for by the legislature to continue the work of the conference and urged them to organize in some way "to work with and feed the commission. . . ."* [18]

After several other suggestions were made, including the establishment of a futures research center and a group to specialize in intergroup communication, a group of nineteen volunteers and nominees was created to plan further meetings and to consider specific projects. This group met for lunch in the East-West Center cafeteria and elected a five-person steering committee. [19] *Out of their deliberations subsequently grew an independent group called "Hawaii's Future."* [20]

Against this background of the conference as a total process, we now recall the contributions to our thinking then that were made by four of our internationally famed speakers: Alvin Toffler from New York, Arthur C. Clarke from Ceylon, Robert Jungk from Salzburg, and Yehezkel Dror from Jerusalem. Following them, in Part Three, we have included an interview with Hawaii laborer Alfred Pasamiento, Sr., who made a major contribution to the group discussion of Hawaii's people and life-styles.

17. *Honolulu Advertiser*, August 9, 1970, p. E–3.

18. Ibid.

19. James Dator, Paul Sullivan, Tom De Waele, Clorinda Low Lucas, and Marie Stires.

20. Chairmen have been Gerald Sumida and Chapman Lam. Although the members of this group have not yet been able to develop programs to carry out their initial expectations, the process of its emergence has been described briefly here as an example of the kind of spontaneous organizational activity that may accompany experiments in anticipatory democracy.

Anticipatory Democracy and the Prevention of Future Shock

Alvin Toffler

Alvin Toffler is the author of *Future Shock* (1970) and *The Schoolhouse in the City* (1968). His course on the sociology of the future offered at the New School for Social Research was one of the first of its kind. Toffler lectures widely and is a consultant to foundations and major corporations.

Last April at an international meeting of futurists in Kyoto, Japan, I met Jim Dator and Keiji Kawakami [1] who told me about an exciting, perhaps historic, experiment that was about to take place in Hawaii this summer. They explained to me that the governor of Hawaii had brought together large numbers of people from all sectors of the State to discuss a rather unlikely subject — the future. And I was delighted when George Chaplin asked me to come to Honolulu to join in this experiment. The reason I was so enthusiastic about this and the reason why, in fact, it turned out I could not come to Honolulu, was that I had just completed a book called *Future Shock*, [2] published this week and in which, among other things, I called for or urged the case for doing precisely what Hawaii is attempting to do.

1. A member of the conference advisory committee and president of Iolani Sportswear. — Editors.
2. *Future Shock* subsequently became one of the most widely read books of the time. Toffler's contribution to the present volume has been transcribed from the sound track of a ten-minute color film that he made for us as a substitute for his direct participation in the opening ceremonies of the Hawaii 2000 conference. — Editors.

Future Shock *is based on a revolutionary thesis. It argues that what is happening in America, Japan, Germany, Italy, Sweden, England, and in all the other high-technology nations today, is not a simple extension of the industrial society all of us have been brought up under or are familiar with, but rather the birth, the explosive birth, of a new kind of civilization. I call it a superindustrialism — you may call it something different. The important thing is that the new society is in fact new and that the guidelines of the past, whatever we've learned about industrialism, no longer necessarily prepare us for the kind of civilization we will have to cope with tomorrow. Superindustrialism is a new kind of society with new values, new conceptions of time, space, beauty, sex, religion, God, whatever. It's a new society and it demands new kinds of personal coping with change. It demands total reorientations, new life-styles, new attitudes. And this new society is springing up in our midst at a rate that is staggering.*

In effect, what we are doing is superimposing a new culture on our old one. And compelling people who are ill prepared to travel into the future to live in this new society. Now, anthropologists use the term "culture shock" to talk about what happens to a traveler in the Peace Corps, or just a businessman, or just a visitor, who suddenly finds himself plunged into a strange, alien culture where all of the cues he relies on for psychological orientation have been withdrawn and replaced by other strange signals of the environment. Words don't mean the same. Gestures don't mean the same. Even time takes on new meaning, so that being asked to wait outside a man's office for two hours is not cause for insult, but just the normal way of doing business. When we take people and plunge them into a strange culture, the effect sometimes is culture shock, which is a condition characterized by anxiety, irritation, fatigue, sometimes what seems like senseless apathy, and so on.

I would argue that what we are doing in our society,

by imposing a new culture on the old one, is exposing millions of Americans and Japanese and Germans and others in the high-technology countries, exposing them to culture shock in their own countries. We're asking them to step into a new society and to quickly, instantaneously as it were, learn to cope with the new environment emerging around them. The difference between future shock and culture shock is that the traveler to a strange country frequently has the sense that he can go back where he came from, to a more familiar territory. But the traveler into the future cannot go back — there's no way to return. And the consequence is that he must learn to cope with tomorrow.

Future shock — the inability to cope — is what happens to people when they are overwhelmed by change, and this inability has profound psychological implications for the individual. It's related, I believe, to much of the confusion, the panic, the violence, and the deadly apathy we see around us in our society. But, it has equally deep implications, not just for personal life, but for our political structures as well. This isn't the place to explore, as I suspect you will at your conference, the intensifying symptoms of national, even international, nervous breakdown that we see around us. Nor is this time for me to try to describe some of the adventurous, imaginative new ways of coping with either personal or public problems that I've discovered people experimenting with all over the world, such as crisis counseling, situational groupings, new styles of planning — all the fascinating developments that go under the heading of futurism in general. And the attempts to look at the future not just from the point of view of attempting to make straight-line projections from the past, but rather imaginative explorations of possible futures. This means scientific probes into probable futures. And, more important perhaps, an attempt to get at the question of preferable futures.

And that, I take it, is what this meeting is all about.

Because I believe one of the most important strategies for social survival is what I call in the book "anticipatory democracy." [3]

Anticipatory democracy is, I believe, absolutely essential in a society that is in danger, as a British friend of mine puts it, of "going random." We see today great systems, governmental, business, and personal, going askew. A city faces pollution, it faces power shortages. I'm speaking from New York City where this is a daily life experience for us. And we find an attempt to cut down on pollution by banning automobiles. The result of that is overloading subways, or vice versa. We see a breakdown in the rationality of the very systems upon which our livelihood, our environment, and our health depend. This, I believe, grows out of one of the failures of planning in the last half-century, because we have had attempts at what might be called technocratic planning, top-down planning. But little attempt has been made to involve masses of individuals in exploring and shaping their own futures, their own destinies. And this is why I think that what you are attempting to do in Honolulu is so vital.

I view it as a pioneer experiment with anticipatory democracy which will be watched closely by other people in London, Tokyo, Stockholm, and in other centers in the United States. In Future Shock, *I argued the case for the creation of what I called social future assemblies: attempts to bring large numbers of people together in their communities, on the job, in their professions, and elsewhere, to discuss and to contemplate alternative futures. But the pace of change is now so rapid, so breakneck, that what I wrote as an idea in a book not long ago, I find even before the book is published is being done and it's a delight to know that somebody is in fact attempting this.*

3. When we were first introduced to this concept in an advance copy of *Future Shock*, we recognized it as aptly expressing what Hawaii 2000 was trying to do. It continues to guide our efforts, as symbolized in the subtitle of this book. — Editors.

I find it particularly appropriate that the first dramatic experiment with anticipatory democracy should take place on an island that lies between Japan and the United States, the two nations thrusting most rapidly into tomorrow, the two nations whose people, I suspect, are likely to suffer the brunt of future shock before other nations do. And so, I regret not being there to join you. I believe that we must come to understand future shock, that future shock may turn out, unless we're careful, to be the most important psychological, political, or cultural disease of tomorrow. And more important than learning simply to diagnose the symptoms is learning to cope with it, and even more important, to prevent it. What you are doing, I regard as an experiment in the prevention of future shock.

The Future Isn't What it Used to Be
Arthur C. Clarke

Arthur C. Clarke is a distinguished scientist and science-fiction writer who lives in Ceylon. An expert on space travel, he won the Franklin Institute's Gold Medal (1963) for having originated the communications satellite in a technical paper in 1945. He has authored forty books which have sold ten million copies in thirty languages, and is coauthor of the film "2001."

hat do we mean by the future? Well, a philosopher could probably prove that it's meaningless to talk about the future. This the first age that's ever paid much attention to the future, which is a little ironic since we may not have one. In the past, to most people, the future just didn't exist, even as a philosophical concern, because it seemed obvious that it would be in no fundamental way different from the past. A man could be pretty certain that, apart from accidents of war and nature and so forth, his life-style would not change appreciably from that of his grandfather or his great-grandfather, as far back in time as anyone could look. Nor was there any reason to suppose that it would change in the future. Well, we know rather differently.

Before it's too late, I would like to explain what I'm trying to do now. I'm not trying to predict the future. That's impossible, despite any claims you may have read in the astrology columns. All I'm attempting to do is to outline futures which could exist. And I'm also restricting myself very largely to a single aspect of the world-to-be — the technological future. This is perhaps the only area where something useful can be done, because coming inventions cast their shadows before them, and technological forecasting plays an ever-increasing part in the modern world.

However, even this restricted type of forecasting is very difficult, because even inventions which can be quite clearly foreseen may have an impact which nobody could have imagined. I'd like to give a couple of examples of this which may strike you as being rather amusing, but which do contain a very good lesson.

About a hundred years ago, a parliamentary commission was called in England to deal with the extremely alarming news from the United States that a Mr. Edison had invented an electric light. This was very alarming to the gas companies. And as we British do in emergencies, we called a parliamentary commission which heard expert witnesses. They duly assured the gas companies that nothing further would be heard of this impractical invention. One of the witnesses called was the chief engineer of the post office, and somebody said to him, "What about the latest gadget these ingenious Yankees have produced, the telephone? Do you think it will be of any use in England?" Whereupon the chief engineer of the post office replied, "No sir. The Americans have need of the telephone, but we do not. We have plenty of messenger boys."

Now, this is what I call a failure of imagination. This very able man who, a couple of decades later incidentally, backed Marconi in his early "wireless" experiments (I guess he had learned his lesson by then), failed to see in the telephone more than a substitute for messenger boys. He could not imagine that the time would come when the telephone was the basis of commercial and social life.

The other example is in our own century. When the first automobiles started running around, in clouds of smoke (as, of course, they are still doing) it was pointed *out that even when they'd got the bugs out of them and they could travel for a whole hundred miles without breaking down, they would still be very limited in their application. You could not use the automobile outside the city for an absolutely fundamental reason: there were no roads outside the cities! Who could have dreamed that, within a lifetime, most of America would be road?*

So here you have examples of two inventions that already existed, staring people in the face, and even then it was not possible to anticipate their impact on society. And then, of course, there's the totally unexpected invention that nobody anticipates — not even the crazy science-fiction writers. If I were giving this talk in 1800, I would probably expound at length on the marvels of the new steam engines. I wouldn't say a word about electricity. If I were giving this talk in 1900, I'm sure I'd say a lot about electricity and radio; I doubt if I'd mention atomic energy. I wonder what I'm overlooking now?

Well, I'll tell you two things which I'm not overlooking, but which I shall have to look at hastily and pass on, because they're so big that they make any attempt to predict the future impossible. The first is contact with extraterrestrial beings. This may not happen for a thousand years; it may happen tomorrow. Contrary to the belief of some people, it hasn't happened yet — at least not in recent times, though maybe it did a few million years ago, as I suggested in 2001.[1] The other is the rise of the ultraintelligent machine. This is inevitable and will probably be occurring around the end of the century. When this happens, all bets are off.

You may think that I am attempting the impossible in saying anything useful about the future. Perhaps I am, but it's still worth trying for several reasons. One of the best: it's good fun. That's all the reason one needs for doing anything. But it's also useful because, if it does

---

1. Arthur C. Clarke, *2001: A Space Odyssey* (New York: World Publishing, 1968). Based on a screenplay by Clarke and Stanley Kubrick.

nothing else, it develops flexibility of mind. We've seen in the past the chaos produced when some new invention impacts upon a society that is not prepared for it. By sketching possible futures, we can decide which ones we like — and, hopefully, work towards them. But I admit that science-fiction writers are fonder of the alternative — sketching perfectly horrible futures. Even this, of course, is useful because they may serve as a warning.

I had perhaps better give another warning to the practical businessmen and politicians in this audience. I have never been very interested in the near future; my sights are usually set fifty or so years ahead. So the warning I'd like to give is this: if you take me too seriously, you'll go broke. But if your children don't take me seriously enough, they'll go broke.

Incidentally, I'm rather sorry you called this "The Conference on the Year 2000" because I've been rather oriented towards 2001 — and there is some confusion here. You know, an awful lot of people don't realize that 2001 is the first year of the new century, the new millennium. Two thousand belongs fair and square in this century, because there is no year zero in our calendar. So you've got to wait until 31 December, 2000, as the clock strikes midnight and ushers in the first of January 2001, before you start your celebration. I know the psychological effect of those three zeros going up on the calendar is going to be so great that people will jump the gun by a year. So I suggest that we declare the whole of 2000 a holiday. If we make it to there, we'll be fully justified.

Anyway, 2000 or 2001, that's thirty years ahead. When we look back into the past, thirty years ago to 1940, how our technology, how our society, has changed since then! But you know, chronologically, the distance between now and the year 1940 is not a fair measure of the changes that we may expect by 2000, because the rate of technology is doubling approximately every ten years. This means that 2000 is really as far off as the 1890s in terms of the technological changes we may expect. So you have to think back to the 1890s, the end of the last century, to get some idea of what we may see at the beginning of the next.

Well, 1890 is quite an interesting date, because it was about that time that the great revolution took place in our homes, in our way of living — a revolution which changed our life-styles more than anything that had happened in all the ages before. The elements of that revolution were very few — you can count them on the fingers of one hand. They were: piped water, indoor plumbing, gas cooking and heating, electric light, the telephone. Those were all coming in around that period. I think the only comparable advance in the thousand years before was the introduction of glass windows — which may not impress you as much as it does people farther north. But to appreciate the importance of glass windows, try to imagine a typical winter night in Camelot, with the gale howling through the great hall.

So when you consider what those few changes, which you now take completely for granted, meant in comfort and convenience and health, can we expect to see — in our homes, at any rate — equally great technological changes?

Well, let's see if we can. Once upon a time, all family units had to be virtually self-contained, producing everything they needed. If you ever go to Mount Vernon, you will see rooms full of strange gadgets and machines which today nobody can use and few people can even recognize. I'm sure that General Washington would have been very surprised to know that the time would come when his successors' homes didn't contain a single spinning-wheel or hand-loom; they have been swept away by mechanization. The preparation of meals is the last manufacturing process left in the home — and, of course, the kitchen's already doomed by the Deepfreeze and the TV dinner. In another decade, you'll be able to buy a "home automat" in which the month's meals will be delivered in a package weighing about a hundred pounds for the average family. You may think that a hundred pounds is rather a modest weight, but let me remind you that ninety percent of most food is water. Ninety percent of you is water. (Nothing personal!) Why should you pay for that, when you can add it from the tap? So you see you'll get your month's meals as the astronauts do — dehydrated and packaged. You'll just have to dial the meal you want; water will be added automatically, it will be reconstituted and emerge perfectly cooked in about ten minutes.

Or else a sign will flash on saying, "Sorry, filet mignon out of stock." And if it is in stock, it will never have been near a cow. (One day I'm going to give this talk in a farming community and will probably be lynched.) But we've got to face the fact that natural meat production is so inefficient that it may be impossible on purely economic grounds by 2000, if indeed it isn't prohibited by law. It takes about ten pounds of fodder or vegetable matter to make one pound of meat. This means that for every man who eats meat, ten men have got to starve. Cows and sheep are mobile processing plants, mobile food factories, with an efficiency of less than ten percent. We can't continue to waste good agricultural land on them.

Now I happen to be a carnivore who hates vegetables and thinks that salads are rabbit food, so I regard this situation with some dismay. Maybe we can continue natural meat production on marginal land, using animals that can exploit such land, for example, antelopes, tapirs, the hippopotamus. And, of course, there's the sea.

I wrote a novel fifteen years ago about whale ranching, called The Deep Range,[2] in which I worked out some of the technology of herding whales. You know, whales are very intelligent mammals. Anyone who has herded cows will probably agree that it'll probably be much easier

2. Arthur C. Clarke, From the Ocean, From the Stars; an Omnibus (New York: Harcourt Brace, 1962).

to herd whales. They have a language which we may learn. We could certainly control them — and a fifty-ton cow producing half a ton of milk a day is an interesting economic proposition!

But there are some problems here, one of which is that by the time we have the technology, there may be no whales left. The other problem is, I think, a more interesting one. And that's the problem of morality. Are we justified in killing animals which have brains as large as ours? But I must confess that I'm getting a little skeptical about the intelligence of whales and dolphins, for a rather fundamental reason. They seem much too friendly to man. Nevertheless, recently I was delighted to discover that it's now a crime in the USSR to kill a dolphin. If this legislation can only be extended to human beings, we'll be in great shape.

Anyway, maybe we will develop whale ranching, and I was reminded today that I had set the headquarters of the whale-ranching organization here in Honolulu, about a hundred years from now.

But whatever happens, I think that the main food production of the future is going to be from nonliving materials, direct from the basic resources of coal and oil, limestone and water, and the carbon dioxide in the air. There's a great deal of work going on in this area right now. I'll mention only one of the more fascinating current possibilities — microbiological engineering. This is the development of special strains of bacteria or microbes that can process wastes and, in particular, petroleum products, and turn them into edible food.

This sounds pretty revolting, but may I remind you that microbiological engineering is the way mankind has always made its most exquisite and expensive luxury foods. This is the way we make cheeses and wines and spirits. But now we are applying this, not to the traditional materials, but to things like oil, and large pilot plants are being built right now. There's one plant going into production in England, which hopes to produce steak for about fifteen cents a pound. And about three percent of the world's petroleum production could provide all the high-grade protein needed by the human race. So I think that agriculture as we know it is going to be phased out in the coming century.

This process may be accelerated by another development which is a by-product of space research — the development of closed-cycle ecologies, needed for prolonged-duration space journeys and bases on the moon and planets. Here, we've got to reprocess and reconvert all wastes back into food. The equipment needed to do this is going to cost quite a few billions before it's made, but once it is available, our food problems will essentially be over. In a way, we'll be back to the primitive agricultural village where there was an endless cycle from the field to the kitchen to the compost heap to the field to the kitchen, a cycle powered by the energy of sunlight. In the future, it will probably be powered by atomic energy. This means that any small community — perhaps, one day, even single households — could be virtually self-sufficient in terms of food. And this is another reason why I think agriculture will be phased out and enormous quantities of land will be liberated for other purposes. I hope much of it is allowed to revert to wilderness, which we need badly for psychological as well as physiological reasons.

I'm much indebted to Buckminster Fuller for many of these ideas, and particularly the concept of the autonomous or self-contained house which would have no roots tying it to the ground anymore, because it would need no water pipes, no drains, and hopefully one day, no power lines — because, surely, sometime, we're going to invent a compact way of storing or producing electricity. So Bucky Fuller's autonomous house could even be completely mobile, especially if it's made of the new materials that are coming in, which are stronger than steel and *lighter than aluminum. It could be picked up by even one of today's helicopters or flying cranes, and taken anywhere you liked. Maybe one day it will even have its own propulsion system built in.*

Another particularly delightful idea of Bucky Fuller's is this. You know his beautiful geodesic domes? In fact you have one here,[3] and you may have seen the famous one at the Expo in Montreal. These can be built to any size; Bucky wants to put one over New York to keep the weather out. It'll be a fine idea — until a jumbo jet goes into it. Well, when these domes, or these bubbles, get more than about a thousand feet in diameter, something rather interesting happens. The structure is so efficient, so light, that the weight of the air inside it becomes more than the weight of the structure. This means that if the temperature rises a few degrees, it becomes a hot-air balloon and can take off. So you see, you could have mobile towns, migrant cities, flying south in winter or north in summer, or whenever they wanted a change of scenery. You know, one of your great problems in Hawaii, one of your most serious single problems, is the fact that very soon you're going to be only two hours from Los Angeles. Just suppose the time comes when Los Angeles decides to visit you every winter!

Well, what I'm driving at is that the world of the future is going to have far greater mobility than we have in this age — and we think we're pretty mobile. Luckily there are still enormous areas of this planet which are totally empty, but which could be occupied. They're very picturesque, very beautiful, and the reason they're empty is that no one can live there at the moment, because no one can raise any food there. Every year I commute two or three times from my home in Ceylon to the United States. I go through Europe, so I fly right across the Middle East and you know, even in a jet, you fly for hours over

3. The Hawaiian Village Dome, constructed by the late Henry J. Kaiser. — Editors.

the most picturesque wilderness. And millions of people could live there temporarily, part of the year, and then move on somewhere else if they wished.

Now a mobile, planet-wide culture demands cheap, instantaneous, and universal communications. The telephone revolutionized life in the past, but that's nothing to what is going to happen in the future. And this is something which concerns you on these islands very much indeed.

The coming revolution is based on two developments. One is the solid-state electronic devices, of which the transistor was the first. Of course, you've all seen the transistor radio come — it gets smaller and smaller. But perhaps most people don't realize the full extent of the solid-state revolution. The computer which would have filled a room twenty years ago is now no bigger than a desk. The Hamilton people are putting the first wrist computer-watch on the market next year. It shows the time in luminous numbers, so that you can read it directly; it contains, I think, the equivalent of two thousand transistors. But it's no larger than an ordinary watch. Further, Dick Tracy's wrist radio has been possible for some time.

This means that almost any type of electronic equipment you can think of could be made cheap enough and reliable enough — which is just as important, if not more so — for every home. And the other thing, of course, which is going to cause this revolution, is the communications satellite. The first commercial comsat, Early Bird, could handle 240 simultaneous telephone circuits. Intelsat Three, now linking you with the rest of the world, can handle not 240, but 1,200. Intelsat Four, due to be launched next year, can handle 6,000. So in under ten years we've gone from 200 telephone channels to 6,000. By 2000, there'll be enough communications capability in orbit for the whole human race to pair off and talk to itself.

We shall need that capacity, not necessarily for this

particular project, but to handle all the other types of com-

munication, of information transmission, we'll require. Because coming into the home in the next decade — in fact, already in some homes in a rudimentary form — is a device which is going to transform society more than the telephone did, perhaps even more than the automobile did. Let's call it a home communications console. It will have a television screen, a computer keyboard, a television camera, a microphone, and perhaps a hard-copy read-out, if you want a permanent record of what appears on the screen.

Now let's see what this will do. Through it, you'll be effectively in face-to-face contact with anyone, any-where on the planet. This will replace our present tele-phone system. I think we'll have a flat charge irrespective of distance, because there are no long distances in the world of the communications satellite. In fact, I suspect that you'll not even be charged for your calls; you'll just rent this device by the month, or the year, and once you've got it installed, you can use it as much as you like. I would like to know what percentage of the cost of a tele-phone call today goes to pay for the incredibly complex electronic equipment that does nothing but calculate the cost of the call. (If the farmers don't get me, the Bell System will!)

This, I'm sorry to say, also means the end of the news-paper. You will just dial a news channel and you will see all the headlines and contents flashed on the screen. You'll decide what it is that interests you and blow that up until it fills the screen — the news, the editorials, the cartoons, the reviews, sports — anything you like will be there. The last minute's news. And not only the local news, but every newspaper in the world, if you can still use the term "news-paper." If you want the Sydney Morning Herald *or* La Prensa *or the* London Times *or* Pravda, *they'll all be just as easily accessible, because everybody will have satellites up there.*

And not only the current newspapers, but every news-

paper that's ever existed, right back to Ben Franklin and the Spectator, because this device will enable you to plug into the global electronic library — and every book, everything mankind's ever written or recorded, will be available in your living room. The time is going to come when scholars and students will find it impossible to imagine how they could have operated without this service. The communications revolution will be as great in some ways as that caused by the printed book itself. If I understand him — I'm not sure I do — McLuhan thinks it's going to wipe out the printed book, though I'm very doubtful of that.

So we'll have the orbital newspaper, and the orbital library. But this is only the beginning of the revolution. The thing I'm most interested in, in fact what I was writing about exactly twenty-five years ago this week in my Wireless World paper on communication satellites, [4] is direct television broadcasting into the home from space. In 1945, of course, no one had built any ground networks, and there were only a very few television stations. The first one was opened by the BBC in London, years before the Americans got around to it — and closed down again before the Luftwaffe could home on it. In this twenty-five-year-old article, I said it probably wouldn't be worthwhile spending much money building enormous microwave relay systems. In fact, it was done; that tremendous investment was necessary at the time. But now we're moving to the next phase, direct broadcasts from space.

This is beginning, in three years' time, in the country that needs it most — India. A contract has been signed between the National Aeronautics and Space Administration (NASA) and the Indian government to use the ATS-F satellite, to be launched in 1973 — it was due in 1972; it's slipped a bit, like everything else these days. This satellite will be sufficiently powerful for its programs to be

4. "Extra-Terrestrial Relays," Wireless World, vol. 51, no. 10, October 1945, pp. 305–308.

picked up in any village in India, directly, *without going through huge ground stations and local networks, which of course do not exist there. It can be picked up by an ordinary television set with an additional antenna, a sort of chicken-wire dish, maybe six feet across, which may add a couple of hundred dollars to the cost. The Indian government is going to provide, as a pilot project, about three thousand sets. You need only one set per village to start a social revolution. I hope this will be just the beginning, because direct broadcasts from space can open up the whole of the undeveloped world to bring education, culture, every type of information to an entire continent — to Asia, to South Africa, to Africa, to South America. It can bring whole nations out of the Stone Age, for it can help solve some of the most pressing social problems of today.*

The first purpose of the Indian satellite is instruction in family planning. The Indian government thinks that perhaps the only way it can solve its appalling population problem is by direct broadcast satellites. There are half a million villages scattered over a continent, with virtually no communications. You can't even get from one to another during the monsoon season. More than half a billion people are living in ignorance and poverty that we can scarcely imagine. So family planning and improved agricultural techniques are the things that the government hopes to put across with this experimental, direct-broadcast satellite system.

Beyond that, every type of educational material, in principle, can be put through satellites. They are particularly applicable to developing countries, where there may only be one teacher for a thousand pupils, and that teacher only one year ahead of his pupils. You may know the interesting experiment in American Samoa, using educational TV to "bootstrap" the whole educational level by spreading the good teachers over the whole community.

I've also seen studies of the effectiveness of educational TV in countries like Brazil and Mexico. It appears that you could provide twelve channels of color TV to every school in a country like Mexico for the cost of about one dollar per pupil per year — the cost of the satellite and the ground hardware. This may not be a very fair figure because the cost of the programing can be two or three times the cost of the system. All right, let's say four dollars per pupil per year. So this is why I get so angry with those well-intentioned but ignorant people who say, "Why spend money on space when there are so many social problems here on earth?" Some of those problems can be solved only in space.

Try to think of the social and political impact of direct broadcasts covering the whole world, not just a limited area like the fifty-mile range you have today with ground television transmitters. I like to remind American audiences that the United States was created a hundred years ago by two inventions. Before they existed, you could not have had a United States. Afterwards, it was impossible to avoid it. Those two inventions were the railroad and the electric telegraph. We are seeing now a repetition, on a global scale, of that same situation — but now it's not the railroad and the telegraph, it's the jet plane and the communications satellite. I think the final result will be very similar.

It's obvious that this development is going to have a tremendous impact on language. If any one nation could establish a monopoly of the direct-broadcast TV satellite, the language of that nation would become the language of all mankind. It seems to me we have a rather interesting flashback here to the point in time when all these linguistic troubles started, at the building of the Tower of Babel. Far higher than the architects of that unfortunate structure ever imagined, we may be about to undo the damage that was wrought then. I'd like to quote Genesis, because it is so appropriate to this whole subject: "And the Lord said 'Behold, they are one people, and they have all one language; and this is only the beginning of what they will do; and nothing that they propose to do will now be impossible for them'."[5]

Of course, this development — the global communications system — is going to raise many problems, as all technology does. I'll just mention one, which already concerns you to a considerable extent. That's the time-zone problem. We'll be living in a world where anybody can speak to anybody else just by dialing a number. It will be like living in a small town, where at any one time, a third of the people are asleep — but you will never know which third.

So what are we going to do about it? Well, there are two possibilities. The first one is that we simply abolish sleep. It's yet to be proved absolutely essential; the young people seem to be disproving it. It may be a bad habit we picked up in the course of evolution, as a result of the day-night cycle. Many deep-sea creatures, at any rate, don't seem to sleep or seem merely to take a catnap occasionally.

Perhaps we can find some electronic means of abolishing sleep, or at least of compressing it into a few minutes every hour. But there may be some unfortunate consequences, for there are indications that dreaming is essential. The purpose of sleep may be to get the garbage out of the computer, when it's switched off.

The other alternative is a more subtle one, but almost as interesting — that is to abolish time zones. This has been suggested half seriously, and let's look at the implications.

Assume that we synchronize our watches now. Everywhere on earth it's twenty after eight, or let's say 2020 hours. We all get up at the same time by our watches, say six o'clock. We synchronize our working hours in all the offices all around the world, say between 0900 and

5. Genesis 11:06, R.S.V.

1700. But if we do this, obviously some people will be getting up in the middle of the night and going to work, while others will be getting up at noon and going to work, and this wouldn't be fair.

So we have to make one other change. Besides synchronizing our watches, we'll have to switch from our present solar time to sidereal time, the time the earth takes to revolve on its axis with respect to the stars. Sidereal days are four minutes shorter than solar days. As a result of this, during the course of the year, the sun for you will appear to go right around the clock. If you get up in the morning at six o'clock by your watch now, and the sun is just rising, six months later when you get up at six o'clock, the sun will be just setting. So everybody has equal time in the sun.

There are some professions that will be rather badly hit by this. I think burglars may find it difficult to operate, but you can't please everybody all the time.

Now I think you will have realized that one of the most important implications of the home communications console that I mentioned earlier is that anyone, at least anybody above the executive level (and as I will explain later, there will be no work for anybody below the executive level) will be able to do ninety-nine percent of his work without leaving home. (It is at this point, usually, that I see a look of utter consternation on the faces of the wives in the audience.)

I can see the time coming — and this is perhaps as far out as I care to go — when if the world's leading heart surgeon, or the world's leading brain-transplant surgeon, decides that he likes to live in Hawaii, he can do so and operate on patients anywhere in the world without leaving home, through slightly more sophisticated devices than the ones I've described — color stereo TV together with remote manipulators of the type that are already in use in atomic-energy establishments and elsewhere. There are micromanipulators, remote controlled hands, which are *far more delicate than human hands. They can operate on single living cells, and could cut the appendix out of a bacterium, if it had one. So you see, almost any type of intellectual work, and many types of precision manual work, could be made independent of location, so that people could live practically anywhere.*

The implications of this are tremendous. One of them is that it means the end of the automobile. We are living, as you know, in an abnormal age, when all the curves are going up and obviously have to flatten out somewhere. This is the time when men started to rush around in a great hurry — we're living in the first age of long-distance commuting. This age is going to be only about a hundred years long. In the next century people will find it inconceivable that men spent a couple of hours a day sitting in two or three tons of ironware, breathing carbon monoxide, just to get from their homes to their places of work and back again.

The traffic problem is not going to be solved by covering the world with concrete. It's going to be solved by getting rid of the traffic. The motto of the future is going to be "Don't commute, communicate." Incidentally, talking about covering the world with concrete, I came across a statistic the other day that I found rather depressing. It takes twenty-five square feet of grass to regenerate the oxygen for one human being. How many men have we robbed of air by our superhighways and our parking lots and so forth?

Now another invention which will be rendered obsolete by the communications revolution is one which has been around for three or four thousand years, but which is now, as many of us have suspected, moribund. That is the city. Cities were essential when the only way men could get together and do business was by meeting face to face. This need is rapidly passing. Therefore, the cities, at least as we know them, will begin to die.

I'm sure there'll be small cities, or large towns, indefi-

nitely for industrial processes. There'll be university towns, even in the age of teaching machines and TV lectures. But the vast conurbations which have blighted so much of this planet for the last century will slowly fade away — very slowly, I'm afraid, because bricks and mortar have got such enormous inertia and represent such tremendous capital expenditure. I've little doubt that there'll be even larger cities in 2000 than there are today. But they'll be like the dinosaurs in the last age of their giantism. A century later, there will be only bones.

Unless — well, there's always a possibility that the population explosion can't be controlled. In that case, the whole world will become one seething city. But that wouldn't last for long. Though medical science might keep at bay that old regulator, the black death, there are plagues of the mind worse than those of the body, and the meaningless violence that has wracked so many communities could be a pretty mild foretaste of a psychologically overcrowded future.

You may have seen those terrifying films showing what happens to rats when they are deliberately overcrowded in the laboratory. You give them all the food they need, but you don't give them space. In a while, they become totally psychotic, showing the whole range of human neuroses. Although everyone now accepts the need for population control — but usually for other populations — very little thought has been given to the level at which we should ultimately aim, and this involves some very difficult questions.[6]

There's no doubt that, with proper organization, our planet could support a much higher population than it does today, and at a higher standard of living. But should it be done? In a world of instantaneous communications and swift transport, where all men are virtually neighbors, is there any point in a population of more than a few

6. During 1971 five bills were brought before the Hawaii state legislature dealing with population stabilization. — Editors.

millions? The astronomer Fred Hoyle once remarked to me that the optimum population of the world should be around a hundred thousand people, because that's the maximum number you can possibly get to know in your lifetime. Well, you may say that's a rather self-centered point of view, but it's an interesting one. And it's worth remembering that Plato thought that the ideal city should contain only about five thousand free men; his city also contained a much larger number of slaves. His "democracy" couldn't have functioned without them. Nor can the world of the future, especially if, as I hope, its population is eventually stabilized at a small fraction of today's. The big difference, of course, is that the slaves of the future won't be human. Most of them will be robots at all levels of technical sophistication, from things like our naïve little automatic washing machines up to much more sophisticated, intelligent robots which can run the household for you, answer the mail, babysit the children, teach them, keep your accounts, do your income tax — a sort of combination secretary-valet. You will have a central brain, just as you have a central air-conditioning system or central heating system. In the future, you'll also have a central computer. It will have sensors, eyes, and manipulators all around the house to do odd jobs.

But for this particular purpose — for mobile jobs, cleaning, looking after the garden, and so forth — there's a nonmechanical solution which offers considerable economic advantages, and I think an emotional bonus. Why should we go to the trouble of building extremely complex mobile robots when Nature's already done ninety-nine percent of the job for us? During the last decade the ultimate secrets of the living world have been revealed. The next great breakthrough in technology is going to be in "biological engineering."

Now, animals, of course, have been used for centuries, as extensions of our personalities and our bodies — for example, the sheep dog and the working elephant. The most dramatic use of animals is one no living person has ever seen: that of the war elephant. A war elephant had to understand, instantly, several hundred words of command. If it didn't, the warrior was in trouble. Then there's the Seeing-Eye dog for the blind. These are remarkable examples of what can be done with already existing animals and primitive training techniques, but it's quite a scandal that (with quite trivial exceptions) man has domesticated no new animals since the Stone Age. It's time we did something — either domesticate some new animals or create some. If we tried, in a few decades, we could develop a creature, perhaps based on the chimpanzee, with a tenfold improvement in intelligence, motivation, vocabulary, and disposition — a domesticated ape, if you like. When it comes on the labor market, the servant shortage will be over, and the housewife of 2000 need no longer be envious of her great-grandmother of 1900. Until, of course, they start to form their own unions.

You may object at this point, if you haven't already, that the main result of all these developments will be to eliminate ninety-nine percent of human activity, and to leave our descendants faced with a future of utter boredom, where the main problem of life is deciding which of the several thousand TV channels to choose from. That's perfectly true — if we look at humanity as it's constituted today.

H. G. Wells once said that future history will be a race between education and catastrophe. I doubt that even Wells realized the educational standards we would ultimately have to attain to deal with the problem of universal leisure. For while, ironically enough, we hear a lot of talk about full employment, what we're ultimately heading for is the exact reverse — full unemployment. Just as there's no function today for manual laborers, and there'll be none tomorrow for those with only clerical and executive skills, so the day after tomorrow, society will have no place for anyone as ignorant as the average midtwentieth-century college graduate. (I'm not getting at college graduates specifically — I'm just making a general point.) He'd be just as lost and helpless as one of those highly educated men — the Pilgrim Fathers — dumped in Times Square during the rush-hour.

If it seems an impossible goal to bring the whole population of this planet up to superuniversity levels, remember that a couple of centuries ago it would have seemed inconceivable that one day everybody would have to be able to read and write. I recently came across an amusing example of the way in which educational standards have escalated. Apparently in the Middle Ages, if a boy in England wanted to do arithmetic, and was content to go no further than addition and subtraction, Oxford or Cambridge could cope. But if he wanted to learn multiplication or division, he'd have to go to Europe.

Today we've got to set our sights far higher, and it isn't unrealistic to do so. Developments in teaching machines (have you heard the phrase "Any teacher who can be replaced by a machine, should be"?), investigations of the way in which the brain stores information, perhaps electrically, perhaps chemically — these may provide the new and revolutionary weapons we need for the war against ignorance.

The greatest single industry of the future will be education. The second greatest is going to be entertainment. Contrary to the belief of some academics, the two are not necessarily incompatible.

For every man, education will have to be a process which continues all his life. We've got to abandon, as swiftly as possible, the idea that schooling is something restricted to youth. I think it was Shaw — it usually is Shaw — who said that education is too good for the young. How can it be confined to youth, in a world where half the things a man knows at twenty are no longer true at forty, and half the things he knows at forty hadn't been discovered when he was twenty? If I had to sum up the single greatest social problem of the future in one sentence, it's going to be that of raising the school-leaving age to approximately one hundred twenty.

So perhaps the greatest change at the turn of the millennium will be in the mental attitudes of our descendants, rather than in the physical backgrounds of their lives, although those too will have changed profoundly. We'll have to develop a flexibility of mind, a capacity for organizing knowledge and an active curiosity about the universe, which will make us seem almost a new species. Anyone who's ever had the stimulating — and awesome — experience of meeting a really educated man will know just what I mean. I've been lucky: twice in my life I've met an educated man.

In the race against catastrophe of which H. G. Wells warned us, the last lap has already begun. If we lose it, the world of 2000 will be much like ours, with its problems and evils and vices enlarged — perhaps beyond endurance. But if we win, 2000 could mark the great divide between barbarism and civilization. It is inspiring to realize that, with some luck and much hard work, we have a chance of living to see the final end of the Dark Ages.

Three Modes of Futures Thinking
Robert Jungk

Robert Jungk, humanist-philosopher, initiated the first International Future Research Conference (Oslo) and cofounded Mankind 2000, both in 1967. He has written and edited many books about the future, starting in 1952 with *Tomorrow Is Already Here*. Born in Berlin, he was arrested for underground anti-Nazi activities, but escaped. After World War II he became a newspaper correspondent in America and Europe where he now lives.

Dear friends, dear beautiful girl — I met you only last evening, introduced quite properly, and all last night I couldn't sleep because of you — not for the obvious reason, but for another one. Because in our dinner conversation you mentioned something that had happened to you when you were in Washington, D.C., this year. You had gone to attend a meeting of students which was supposed to be devoted mainly to singing, fun, and mutual enjoyment. The police thought bad of it; the people in that building were asked to leave the building. And as you know, the police are impatient and prone to use violence all over the world: they began to fire tear gas. And so you experienced that outrage: the brutality of our time.

Now why didn't I sleep? I didn't sleep because you said, "The only people in Washington who talked sense to me, the only people on the mainland who talked sense to me, were the Black Panthers, who said, 'We have to train you for counter violence, we have to train you for shooting, we have to train you for arson — this is our only way to fight back!'" I feel this is a very dangerous *way. I feel from the experience of my life that violence can never be a way to change the world. Violence tends to escalate. And the fact that so many of the people who, like myself, want to change the world, want to do away with old, obsolete structures, are now turning to violence, is, in my opinion, actually playing the game of their opponents. In the method of violence, I feel that the police and the military are actually stronger: they have been prepared and trained for it. Now you ask, and many of the young people and many of my students ask, "What can we do? Nobody is listening to us, nothing is changing, we are tired of rhetoric, we are tired of being led astray, we are tired of being cheated."*

I feel that if you want to open the door and the key you have used so far doesn't fit and doesn't do the trick, then you have to find another key. If you insist on breaking down the door, you will have a momentary success, but not more. They are going to build another door; it will be a stronger door; it will be clad in steel. Next time, you use dynamite and they will come back at you with dynamite. I feel this is actually descending to the style of the cavemen; and I feel that we, the people who are responsible for the future of the world, shouldn't descend to that, a style of prehistory. We should find new ways.

I feel that futurism is actually such a new way; that is the reason I've turned to it. I feel that futurism is the modern weapon. Favoring change, it presents a permanent challenge to the people who actually bar the way, who hinder us from progressing, who actually stand in the way of progress.

Yesterday George Hudes[1] started his remarks with this sentence: "Let's do something about now and not worry so much about the year 2000." Words, which by the way, were almost literally repeated in one of this morning's radio programs. As I said, I didn't sleep, so I turned on

1. Political science graduate student, active in Students for a Democratic Society at the University of Hawaii. — Editors.

the radio, and heard a commentator say: "I'm worrying about the Russians and the talk about disarmament. Let's worry about the present, not all this bullshit about the year 2000. And therefore let's keep our arms." It's curious that very often nowadays, the revolutionaries and the ultrareactionaries talk a very similar language. Now, I repeat Hudes' sentence: "Let's do something about now and not worry so much about the year 2000." I would turn the sentence around and say, "Because we worry about the year 2000, let us do something now." Because without a long-range view of what could and what should not happen, what might and what ought to happen, we will certainly do the wrong thing and unwittingly hurt those who say, après nous le déluge.

I wish my father had been a futurist. I wish the generation which was empowered twenty, thirty, forty — or only ten — years ago, would have given some thought to the consequences of ever-rising production, to the excess of urban sprawl, and to the acceleration of the arms race. The present you worry about is always yesterday's future. The future is, to a large extent, the result of the present. To play one against the other is a mistake. They are both parts of the same time continuum. They are indeed inseparable.

I came here with a prepared paper, but as I tossed about all night, I thought, "Well, why did I turn to futurism? How was it?" And naturally, as has been mentioned before, my thoughts went back to Hiroshima. I spent quite some time with the survivors of Hiroshima and they have had the strongest impact on my own life, partly because I feel very much in a similar situation. They were survivors of the atomic bomb; I was a survivor of Auschwitz and the concentration camps. So we had some kind of kinship. And I'll never forget how these victims, and especially an elderly couple, who were about to die from the long-range consequences of the bomb, asked me, who came from abroad, "Didn't the people who threw that bomb think *about these long-term consequences? Didn't they* know *that this was not an ordinary weapon, but a weapon which reached out into time — which destroyed not only space, but also the time ahead of it?" And I said, "No, they did not think enough about it."*

I once wrote a story of the family of atomic scientists, and again and again, I was surprised by the lack of foresight of those whose job is really foresight. C. P. Snow has said that scientists have the future in their bones; but I must say most of these scientists didn't have the future in theirs. They really did not give attention soon enough to what might happen, what might be the consequences of their efforts; they just did their thing. They were what we now call in German Fachidioten, *overspecialized idiots, primarily after a more perfect, a more beautiful gadget. And when they finally began to have afterthoughts, it was already too late. The gadgets were no longer theirs, they belonged to the people who had paid for their efforts.*

Now, why have I become a futurist? Because I feel that this kind of attitude is actually leading us into disaster. I was tired of being the eternal victim; I was tired, like many progressive people, of running behind that cruel train of historical events, of crying out against the injustices done in the world after they had been committed. I said to myself, why can't we actually anticipate developments so that these catastrophes don't happen anymore? Isn't there a way to foresee where we are going? Isn't there a way to avoid unnecessary catastrophes and isn't there a way to induce change in a more modern and better way than by barricades, revolutions, fire, arson, and war? Sure, this has been the way changes came about for ages and ages, and again and again, but I think we have come to a point in history where we can't change that way any more. We have to find new ways, new methods of changing history. And that's when I changed from a reporter into an activist, and also turned to something we now *call futures research.*

Now, whereas futures research is enthusiastically greeted, and it has been thus greeted by many people, some very interesting and welcome doubts have been expressed about it more recently. Among them are two objections which really are quite contradictory. Some critics complain that forecasters use too much imagination and therefore cannot be trusted. Others object that they do not use enough imagination and tend, therefore, to be conservative and dull. I happen to know some superior minds who want to be on the safe side by pronouncing the accused guilty on both counts. I feel that those who think that most of our current studies in futures are much too cautious and do not produce striking perspectives really have a stronger case. Among them, by the way, is Arthur C. Clarke. Many futures researchers, in their aim to be taken seriously, are overcautious. They seriously lack intellectual courage. Many of today's scientific anticipations and predictions are indeed, as the American futures researcher Hasan Ozbekhan has pointed out, not much more than extensions of the present. It has been argued that this could not be otherwise, because the human mind, even the most inventive one, is deeply conditioned by the moods, the styles and, in the last resort, the values, which surround it. Therefore it has been said we will always be, more or less, prisoners of the present — even Einstein couldn't escape this jail — and even our seemingly most future-oriented thoughts are nothing but mirrors of our present thinking.

One RAND researcher, the sociologist Fred Charles Ikle, has written a very convincing article about that problem. He has said, "Imagine a man in the Middle Ages thinking about the future. He would have seen a future full of monasteries and churches." Now most of our utopias, most of our visions of the future, are full of technology, of gadgets, of apparatus. Maybe we are as wrong as the people of the Middle Ages would have been. Maybe we are conditioned too much by what we see now and we can't see the turn which is going to come soon, which might lead us away from the overwhelming importance of technology to different problems, to different objectives.

Technology might then still be something important, but of second order. Technology has to function well, and in the future we will talk about it only if it doesn't work. We may have a relationship with it similar to the one with our body. If something ails, we are forced to be concerned about it, but the real human being is something which is more than that body. Therefore, I feel that the next development will put technology in its place without taking it away.

But how can we, then, if we are really prisoners of the present, explain the many departures, often very radical ones, from the known and the accepted which have abounded, especially in the history of the arts and the sciences. It is almost impossible to explain them logically. They mostly happen in jumps and seem to be the results of flashes of sudden inspiration. Advanced studies of creativity, a deeper understanding of the physiology and the psychology of human imagination, will be necessary to put more light into these dark corners.

The next most important frontier of research may be found here in man. And it is in man's so far only partly discovered potential. Futures research, directed thus far mainly to technological forecasting and to a much lesser extent to social prognostics, will be wise to pay increasing attention to the studies of those scientists, whom Nigel Calder has called the "psychonauts," because so much of the future in a man-made world begins really in the depths of man's soul and mind. Waiting for breakthroughs in that area, futures research will have to use the existing body of knowledge, produced by research on creativity. Especially a new branch of futures studies, which will probably gain more in importance, namely human forecasting, *or as the Russians call it, anthropological forecasting, will greatly benefit from a closer association with anthropologists, ethologists, psychologists, and psychiatrists. I feel this, a great new area in futures research, will be the most challenging, the most interesting one of all.*[2]

In an earlier paper [3] *I noted three forms of imagination which might be of use in futures research: First,* logical imagination; *second,* critical imagination; *and third,* creative imagination. *Of these three, only the first so far has had enough attention from the futurists, a fact which has considerably narrowed the scope of their studies. The main function of logical imagination in the field of futures research will be found in the anticipation of* logical futures. *The application of critical imagination will be indispensable for the development of "willed futures," as René Dubos calls them.*[4] *The role of creative imagination is of greatest importance in the elaboration of* invented futures.

Now let me first turn a little to logical imagination. The central idea of logic is the concept of order. Logical imagination will try to develop concepts which can be built in an orderly way — stone put on stone, step after step. Now we know that history certainly is not made in such an orderly way. Sure, we can discern a number of patterns, but more often after the event than before. The role of surprise is enormous. And we have only to read "surprise-free projections" like the one developed by Kahn and Wiener to see how different reality really

2. Several papers on this subject were given at the fall 1970 meeting of the American Anthropological Association. They are presented in Magoroh Maruyama and James A. Dator, eds., *Human Futuristics* (Honolulu: Social Science Research Institute, University of Hawaii, 1971).

3. Robert Jungk, "The Role of Imagination in Future Research," *in* Japan Society of Futurology, *Challenges from the Future: Proceedings of the International Future Research Conference* (Tokyo: Kodansha, 1970), vol. I, pp. 1–7.

4. René Dubos, *Reason Awake: Science for Man* (New York: Columbia University Press, 1970). Professor Dubos served as a consultant to the task force on the quality of personal life. — Editors.

is.[5] I feel that these surprise-free projections, if they are not taken with several grains of salt, can be misread. Most people have taken Kahn's projections as valid predictions although they were used only as heuristic instruments. Because there are other similar heuristic qualities in logical imagination, let me mention a few.

One that I have developed and practiced with my students is the method of exaggeration. By logical extrapolation of an existing trend, beyond the limits of the possible, you will get results which are caricatures of the present phenomenon.[6] Imagine that the yearly rise of the GNP in the U.S. or in any other industrial power, for instance Japan, will continue for another fifty or one hundred years and you will come to the conclusion that the production of the year 2070 would weigh more than the entire planet. Extrapolate the curve of scientific papers or the number of scientists or the number of private motor cars and you will sooner or later get similar perfectly absurd results. Fremlin used that procedure in an impressive way when he demonstrated the consequences of an unchecked population explosion, by calculating how soon men would have to exist like sardines.[7] The method of exaggeration, by concentrating on one subject only and by assuming that the rates and the trends of development will stay the same, may actually serve to discover some hidden or overlooked possibilities. This may be especially true when applied to whole systems. In fact, this has been tried in the negative utopias of Huxley, Samyatin, and Orwell.

Another interesting use of logical imagination as an

5. Herman Kahn and Anthony J. Wiener, The Year 2000: A Framework for Speculation on the Next Thirty-Three Years (New York: Macmillan, 1967).

6. This has been done for Hawaii by Robert C. Schmitt, "Long Range Forecast for Hawaii: the Statistics of Tomorrow," mimeographed, Honolulu, 1970. — Editors.

7. J. H. Fremlin, "How Many People Can the World Support?," New Scientist, October 29, 1964.

instrument of mental experimentation is, and we tried it out, the method of changed parameters. It might give us new insight into the demographic developments for instance, to assume, just as a heuristic device, just as an experiment, and as a searching instrument, some improbable assumptions about the speed of population increase. What would actually happen if we suddenly had a population decrease? What would be the consequences if we actually could influence sex patterns and have more females than males or many more males than females? Here again, such a mental exercise might bring us new ideas, might turn us away from conventional thinking, might loosen one, two, or three stones of the jail of the present. Let me dwell here a moment more on the idea of mental experimentation because I feel that it might help overcome the lack of imagination some critics of futures research talk about. Though it is important and legitimate that the main accent of prognostic work should be on clearly defined goals and objects, it would be wrong to exclude a certain amount of free-wheeling speculation. Some years ago I tried to introduce the idea of pure social imagination in contrast to applied social imagination. In the first place, mental experiments obviously belong to the realm of pure imagination. Their aim is simply the opening of new horizons, the discovery of new possibilities, the relaxation of constraints in order to find ways around them.

Then, for another instance, the method of paradoxes we played with a lot might generate fruitful ideas by standing some of the basic assumptions used in logical thinking on their heads. What would happen, for instance, if technology was not geared to produce more and more at higher speed, but less and less at deliberately lower speed? The motive might be, for instance, that there should be more jobs in order to cope with the increase of surviving population. What would be the consequences of teenagers' becoming teachers, if only for a few hours *every week, and of the elders' sitting down on the school bench and learning from them?*

Among the most frequent applications of logical imagination to futures research we find nowadays is the method of contextual mapping. *Here again, an experimental use would yield interesting insight, especially by playing with a method that I call the method of invasion by other disciplines. This was really first discovered by Donald Schon, but it has so far been used by the mutual invasion only of disciplines that have one or more frontiers in common, as for instance, physics and biology. But there might be interesting cross-fertilization by applying, combining, and coupling more distant fields. For instance, think a moment about how some concepts used in the legal world might apply to electronics, and vice versa; you might then find very interesting new hierarchies in your thinking about legal matters but also in speculating about the development of electronics.*

In Berlin we had a very interesting experience when we got together a teacher of modern music composition techniques, especially of the twelve-tone method, with a professor who constructs new, numerically controlled, automatic machines. The encounter became of great importance because the concept of rhythm held by the musicologist actually changed the outlook of the machine builder: it gave him ideas on how he might program his machine to get shorter production series of products, thus allowing more variety in mass production.

These are a few ideas of how one might use logical imagination. I will finish with one last example, which I have named the method of the ladder, *so called because it might provide us with a way to climb over the walls of the prison of time. There exist at this hour hundreds of forecasts in futures research. My idea is to take any one of these forecasts and to imagine that it had come true, but only in order to proceed from this level to another forecast. That would provide us with a second level, which* might then again be used to do a forecast based on a forecast based on another forecast. And so we might actually proceed step by step on a ladder, getting further and further away from so-called reality. But there are two limits, we found out. One would be the limit of our semantic possibilities. What are we going to call the new discoveries? We actually tried to invent new words for these new things we found on different levels because the old words always brought us back to the old things, put us back into the jail of time. How could we eliminate this? Probably only by daring to leave the path of logic and turning to another method, which we may call creative imagination.

Before I turn to creative imagination, I want first to discuss critical imagination because this is also a step preceding creative imagination. Let me first turn to the uses of critical imagination, which will bring us back to earth and to somewhat firmer ground, because critical imagination is concerned neither with mental experimentation nor with speculation, but most of all with the problems of needed change. The fact that critical imagination has so far been very little used by the futurist may have to do with the historic origin and economic foundation of futures research; the fact that military establishments and industrial managements have been at the origin of many futures studies, that they were the most forceful backers and promoters, has made a mark — a mark some people think indelible. Therefore much of the motivation for looking into the future has grown from fear — fear of falling behind in the development of weapons, fear of losing out in the competitive struggle for new products and new markets, and fear of any future which might seriously put in question the existing economic and political conditions.

This seems to be true of the power structures in the West as well as in the East. They used the new developments in methods and techniques of anticipation, forecasting, and planning to a large extent for crisis management, actually for avoiding the future. Now, that in itself could be a legitimate aim if there were attempts to analyze the coming crisis without regard for those who bear a heavy part of the responsibilities for it. It would mean, for instance, that the futures study of the world food situation would no longer leave out the decisive role of commodity markets in the speculation in wheat, rice, coffee, and other "futures." It is not enough to talk about the great possibilities in ocean farming. It may be more important to talk about the distribution of existing food products and about the power exercised by those who are able to hoard them and to speculate with them. A critical futurist would not refrain from devoting a major part of analysis of the urban crisis, for instance, to the present and anticipated conditions of private ownership of real estate. Or, for that matter, to union practices in the building trades. He would, in prognosis of the further development of the socialist countries, for instance, not hesitate to put the finger on the bureaucratic rigidity and the autocratic power exercised by a dogmatic elite of aging tryants. The same lack of critical imagination, which I think is essentially very important, mars, in my opinion, the efforts of most "think tanks" in the United States, or the studies of such eminent individual futurists as Hermann Kahn, James Forrester, and even Erich Jantsch.

They see a great many changes ahead, but they apparently cannot envisage a really radical transformation of the economic and political power structures in their own countries. I have looked in vain among the published material of the RAND Corporation for any study about, let us say, a socialist United States. What would happen then? After all, they have studies about a change in Colombia, even very fundamental changes in Colombia; but not about the United States. That is strictly taboo: you don't touch it. Not even if it is only a mental game. Maybe such studies exist as classified material, but I don't think so. In fact, someone at RAND did something similar once. He speculated — only speculated — about the pos-

sibilities of unconditional surrender. Under what conditions would and could the United States ever surrender unconditionally? And this raised such a storm that nobody has ever dared to touch such a hot subject again.

However, some of the Vietnam researchers at RAND tried to do a similar thing. They prepared a list of options for the war in Vietnam, and when Nixon came into office, they submitted these options to Henry Kissinger. One of the six options was total withdrawal from Vietnam. They were told to eliminate it because it couldn't even be discussed, couldn't even be shown to the president. Then they wanted at least to mention in their revised report that they had originally discussed total withdrawal, but they were told that even that was not possible. So you see the built-in obstacles to real imagination. And it makes me ask, how could one establish some kind of sanctuary where people actually might be able to think about the future in full freedom, even if it meant that they had to challenge the very people who gave them the money to run the institution? So far no power group has had the greatness and the foresight to do such a thing. It might be exactly the rational and logical thing to do. The lesson is clear: critical imagination will not or cannot be developed by those who are too closely tied to their establishments. Its development and application will be carried forward either by critical minorities within a system or by the outside competitors of that system.

What will critical imagination do and how will it proceed? First, the critical futurist will be on a permanent search for the weaknesses, contradictions, and inherent dangers of the existing state of affairs. That will imply the study of mistakes, as well as of neglect, including those which would not be detected by an examination of things as they are, but are likely to be found only by the magnifying glass of anticipation of further development applied to the present. The lack of development of new mass-transportation systems in many highly indus-

trialized countries, the lack of planning concerning the future participation of a growing intelligentsia in the direction of the state and industrial enterprises, the impact of value change in the upcoming generations — all such would be classified as critical futures studies that would have to be done.

Another critical instrument in the evaluation of futures research will develop from very simple but rather personal questions, for instance: Who did the study? Who financed the study? Whose interest is best served by the study? If you apply such criteria you very often can assess those studies in a different way, and you find out that they are actually not as objective as they want to appear.

But future-oriented diagnosis is only the first part in the working of critical imagination. The second part will always be concerned with the invention of better futures, of desirable futures. Based on the critical evaluation of presently visible and anticipated developments, such detailed models, for instance, of more human institutions and conditions, have more experimental qualities than a concrete planning function does. These qualities should make it clear to everybody that a vastly different future might be possible, and how it could, not necessarily would, look. By such a double attack, frontal on the present by exposing its weaknesses, and from the direction of the future, by showing desirable alternative futures — the critical futurist would help to bring about that kind of deep transformation of mind, and maybe of reality, which has become the dream of those who will actually live in the future — the young generation. Therefore, critical imagination and its use will appeal mainly to the men and women under thirty.

They are, and this is a serious matter, still being kept ignorant of a great many anticipatory studies which are being treated as proprietary or private information. Many big companies and government departments are engaging in futures studies that are known only to a very small circle of people who can be entrusted with the secrets. One doesn't want to give away trade secrets nor state secrets. Therefore, the future is being treated as something essentially secret. This practice is now increasing. It's becoming more and more important because as we direct ourselves more and more toward the future, more and more ordinary facts may become part of an anticipated system you want to protect and therefore you can't talk about.

I learned of a very interesting example from one researcher who told me the following (which he put hypothetically, though I feel he probably had had the experience, but could not say so): "Our institute has been asked to work for a big company. If this company had developed a revolutionary new method of energy production, then I could never mention it, not even in any of my other forecasts. And from this moment on, I would become a liar because I would have to leave out a very vital fact in most of my anticipations of the future. So I can't go on working for the institute, I can't go on under conditions where secrecy is imposed." But on the other hand, only those firms, only those government departments that are interested in proprietary information give enough money to have studies in real depth. I feel that the growing secrecy in the futurist sciences, in futures research, is as big, if not a bigger danger for our future than the secrecy in the natural sciences. Because here, the means, the possibilities of changing history are tampered with, and very often are put on a wrong track. But there is at least one way around that. The young people who do not get proprietary information, who are kept ignorant of many anticipatory studies, have one thing going for them which may be even more important sometimes than such data. They have sharp judgment, a high degree of independence, and visionary powers, which are strongest in the first ten or fifteen years of a person's adult life, as psychological studies and eminent innovators in the natural sciences have shown. Sometimes knowledge may actually impede seeing the "new." Sometimes knowing too much may make it difficult to think in a radical way.

I turn now to the third kind of imagination I value most of all: creative imagination. My own definition of it reads this way: "Creative imagination is not content with extending, combining, or negating already existing trends. It attempts, by breaking out of the existing systems or countersystems, to strike out on a completely new cause, breaking radically with prevalent concepts. Creative imagination gives birth to a new era whenever and wherever it emerges. It marks an epoch. And very often it locates a new state of mind beyond the controversies which are characteristic of and apparently an inextricable part of the times it left behind." We experienced such breakthroughs of creative imagination, for instance, when the age of enlightenment emerged at the time the deadly struggle between the Catholics and the Protestants was ravaging Europe during the seventeenth century. That was the base for the breathtaking development of science and technology in the three hundred years to come. Is it not conceivable that there is ahead yet another change which would relegate these religions of our days — science and technology — to a place of less importance? Change may be here again, a coming third force that actually will become more important, surging forward behind all this.

The main obstacle to such an emergence of creative imagination, in my opinion, is our outmoded concept of so-called facts or data. Only data that can be defined and proved are held to be valid by present scientific standards. This approach is considered to be realistic, but in fact it negates the dynamic and ambivalent character of reality. New concepts of what data really are should recognize, in application of the style used in modern physics, psychology, and biology to the social sciences, that "data" are merely still pictures in a moving scene, that reality is much more fluid, ambivalent, and subject to constant change. So many of our predictions based on data are based on the past, are dealing only with something dead to a large extent. Unless we change our way of observing things, unless we find methods to put this fluid situation into words and pictures, then we will probably never get out of this prison of the present or of the past.

Creative imagination will not be afraid of visions coming suddenly into view from sources in the unconscious. It will patiently hold itself open for hunches, daydreams, and sudden sparks of insight. It might rehabilitate meditation and even mystic enlightenment as a source of new insight. I feel that this imagination will soon develop a new kind of laboratory, a laboratory of the mind, which will methodically find out how creative imagination might be produced by conscious effort, rather than by accident or patient waiting as at present.

Now, let me finish with a few proposals, of which the mind laboratory is one. I feel that mind laboratories, however, will be a thing of the elite, of the specialist. I feel that we have an immense untapped source in the imagination of the nonspecialist, of ordinary people — which we all are, because everybody can be a specialist only in a very tiny fragment of what can be known. I feel that we can and should open up the largest untapped source of human progress: the imagination of the ordinary person. Most of the time nowadays it is destroyed in the first three to five years of life. Later in life, if it has managed to survive a little, it is repressed with such words as: "No, you are not right. You dream. You don't stick to the facts." This is a wrong realism which thinks that something is real only if it has been proved, never something that is developing, or is new. We will have to make conscious efforts to open up this immense source in human beings. There was, just before the French Revolution, a very interesting device to get at that hidden treasure of the people: the cahiers de doléances, complaint notebooks, in which in every little community, in every little village, people wrote their complaints and proposals about their villages, about their situations. I feel that we might institute similar little books of proposals, by people, or communities, getting together and developing ideas. There could be family and professional groups, all kinds of gatherings; the members should sit together and talk about the schools, about the cities, about political institutions, and about the distribution of power tomorrow.

I myself have experienced such groups. Typically, the first few encounters are not interesting because people come up with routine answers; they repeat what they have read in the papers, what they have seen on television, or what they've heard on the radio. But if you keep on, if you have the patience, you will find that people slowly develop their own ideas. They haven't been asked for ages. They have always been on the receiving end. They have never been challenged to be creative. And if you can open them up, it's fantastic what comes out. The first man from whom I learned this is an Italian reformist-activist, Danilo Dolci, who did this with Sicilian peasants, people who were almost on alphabets. And I saw how they gained confidence, how they actually produced the most magnificent new ideas. My friends the activists will say, "We already have many good ideas in the world, but we just can't get through with them; we can't do anything about them."

I feel that maybe we don't have enough ideas about the right things. We have lots of ideas about new machines, about new power relations, about new technologies, about new international configurations; but we have very few about the development of human life, of human possibilities, of more human-oriented settlements. There is really an imbalance between the political, economic, and technological on one side and social needs on the other. And unless we develop these other goals, these other ideas, we won't get anywhere.

You have to redress a balance. This is not a short-range project; it will take some time. It will actually change the social climate; it will change the climate not only among the people who are now outside the power elite; it will change the climate within the power elite itself. I feel that many of my friends who think that you have to change the world by violent revolution disregard the time factor. They say we can't wait, and they are right. We shouldn't wait, but on the other hand, if we cannot wait, then actually by taking the wrong step, we are thrown back even more. Isn't it then better that by changing the climate patiently, you actually proceed to a new future?

Now let me finish with one special idea. I am not a scientist, though I've been cast in the role of one. This is wrong. I'm a newspaperman, and always have been. I am a newspaperman by conviction, because I feel that they are the last generalists of the world. I sometimes feel as if I'm visiting many different shops, where people work in their specialties, and I go from one shop to the next. I bring them into contact and I cross-fertilize them, and I tell one what the other is doing, and then I try to formulate — you can say superficial pictures — but at least they are pictures of a whole. They have a certain horizontal dimension, where other people try for a vertical extension. Now, as a journalist, I feel strongly about what the other media are doing. I say that especially here, because after all the idea of this conference came from George Chaplin, who is a newspaperman, and I think that what he has done is a wonderful thing. The newspapers and other media will have to change their outlook, their treatment of news. They talk about a house only when it falls down, never when it's being built. They are geared to catastrophe, not to building and construction. I feel that by giving us more information of what could, might, or should happen, they will greatly affect all of us. They have an immense educational job to do, and I would be glad if this conference became a part of that job.

Translating Alternative Futures into Present Action

Yehezkel Dror

Yehezkel Dror is a professor of political science at The Hebrew University in Jerusalem. He has lectured throughout the world on policy making, planning and administration. He heads the Israeli Future Studies Association and is on the editorial board of the journal *Futures*. Dror has written widely and has been honored by his nation and others. His books include *Design for Policy Sciences* (1971), *Ventures in Policy Sciences* (1971), and *Crazy States: A Counterconventional Strategic Problem* (1971). Born in Vienna, he has lived in Israel since 1938.

T he history of my visits to Hawaii raises some difficult questions of prediction methodology. The first time I was here for four days; this time I shall be here for twenty-four hours, so, by extrapolation, one of my next visits should take five microseconds; and I don't know how we'll manage that.

Prediction methods and indeed the whole question of dealing with the future raise many difficulties, especially when we presume to look at the future to find some guidance for the present. Guidance for the present is only one of the functions of futures studies, and not the most developed one. We engage in futures studies to escape from the unpleasant present into unknown and optimistically expected futures. We engage in futures studies as a kind of catharsis, projecting our innermost fears and hopes into the undefined time horizon of beyond 2000. We engage in futures studies in the hope of satisfying *the old human curiosity to gain some certainty on the future, to relax our certainty of death. We engage in futures studies because this provides a convenient context legitimizing the bizarre — whatever is now absurd suddenly looks respectful if predicted into the future.*

Let me leave aside those functions of futures studies and focus on a different one, namely interest in futures studies to influence the present. I use the term "influence the present" on purpose. I don't say that by futures studies we can shape the future. Hopefully, we can influence it to some degree. Anyone who says — no one says it, but some imply it — that we can determine the future is, I think, falling a victim to the ancient Greek sin of hubris, arrogant pride. It is a big jump in human fate if we can consciously influence, somewhat, the future unfolding of humanity. To presume to determine it in details is incorrect, and I guess we are lucky it is incorrect because it would be terrible to shape the future of humanity by our present images.

It is easy for me to deal with the subject of 2000 or 2001 because this provides a strict constraint on what I'm dealing with. It would be much more difficult to deal with 2100. Please let us bear in mind that the distance between 1970 and 2000 is the same as the distance between 1940 and 1970. Even if we assume acceleration of social change, really nothing fundamental has changed in society since the 1940s. If we go back to 1920 — I wouldn't mind either — we just have different technology around. The problems of conflict, for instance, are different because of the tremendous potential of nuclear energy, but the basic features of society are the same.

This is well illustrated and even demonstrated by the so-called revolutionary ideologies which are fashionable in some parts of the United States and also in Europe. The Europeans are more sophisticated about ideologies, having had more experience. What are today represented as the most advanced revolutionary ideologies — and this is not a condemning statement nor a praising one; it's an objective statement, I think — are very similar, or even identical, with the revolutionary ideologies of Europe in the last three hundred years. There may be some differences — one of them is the idea of zero population growth. Well, I think I know what Trotsky, one of the more radical revolutionaries, would have said about this. I may be wrong, but surely he would have said that this is the very reactionary attitude of a few who want to preserve the good things of life for themselves, ignoring all those condemned never to be born. Thus, we should be aware that, when speaking about the year 2000, we are not speaking about the total transformation of all that we know.

Furthermore, from a methodological point of view, there are strong contradictions in a lot of futures research. For example, you have been recommended to read Gerald Feinberg's Prometheus Project*,[1] which is just an illustration of this contradiction. He says in the same sentence, or in consecutive sentences, the following things: we are going to change the human being itself — by chemicals, by radical education, by molecular engineering, by parapsychology — in some way. And then we presume to say how the world would look with a different humanity. A complete absurdity! By definition, once we succeed in reinforcing human capacities, we enter a new stage of history. The same as a mouse cannot predict what a gorilla will do, and hopefully, the gorilla cannot predict what we will do — so are the limitations of the human ape of today to the homo superior of tomorrow. We cannot predict what a different type of humanity will do. We can easily speak about the idea that our main endeavor is to raise the capacity of humanity to shape its further future. But to say how a reinforced humanity will determine the future is beyond the limitation of our minds. Therefore, we must be careful to decide what we are talking about.*

1. Garden City, New York: Doubleday, 1968.

*That is why, knowing that other subjects are also impor-
tant, mine is a narrow one, namely how to translate futures
studies within the time span of the next thirty or forty
years into present decisions or present actions. Every
attempt thus to use futures studies to shape present
activities brings us straight into four dilemmas.*

*The first dilemma, which has been well reflected in
some of the most impressive study-group reports, is the
contradiction between dreaming and prophecy on one
hand, and planning and engineering the future on the
other. Those are different things. It is difficult to bring
about a meeting or a mix between them, but basically,
they are all essential functions. If someone would say that
prophets are more important than planners, I might agree.
I like the Old Testament and am bound by its perception
of the importance of prophecy in the very long range.
When we speak about shaping the next thirty or forty
years, we are involved in additional and other things. There
is a tension and even a contradiction between looking
at futures studies as dreaming or prophecy, and looking
at them as providing goals for social engineering — a bar-
baric term which we shall avoid after I've used it twice.*

*The second dilemma is the difference between
— what shall I call it? — debugging, and idea realization. We can approach our problem in two main ways.
What is bad about the present situation? How do we
get rid of the bad things in the present? I will call this
"min-avoidance." How can we minimize the bad things?
There is a different approach: ignore some of the present
diseases, and look at human potential for development.
We look for ideals which we want to realize, rather than
fix our eyes on present diseases. These two approaches
are not completely contradictory, because absence of
disease is a part of health; but health is much more than
absence of disease. And this is a real problem. Do we
look into the future for what we want to achieve or do we
look into the present for what we want to avoid?*

The third dilemma, related to the second one, is the opportunity cost of future activities in terms of present problems. Let me start with an illustration: space activities. One can say, how can we devote money to put a man on the moon or send a probe to Mars when children are hungry? One can say, how can we only look at present hunger and not also prepare ourselves to solve the even more difficult problems which we may meet in the future? It depends on our evaluation of time. In most revolutionary movements, one of the basic tenets has always been, "We are ready to sacrifice the present to build a better future." One doesn't have to adopt such an attitude. But the contradiction between devoting limited resources to short-term activities or to long-term activities is one of the inbuilt and unavoidable problems in any endeavor to shape the future. It is not the same to say that we want to devote our resources to get rid of hunger now and to say that we want to build up knowledge so as to improve humanity in the future. These two approaches compete to some extent, one with the other.

This leads me to the last contradiction or internal tension, related to the third one, namely the problem of limited resources. I did a study of planning on Holland about eight years ago when it was a quiet, solid country. In the meantime, it has become modernized with lots of things going on. And in this very solid country a study was done, putting together the demands of different social groups and estimating how much it would cost in resources to realize them in the next ten years.

Then a prediction was made of what resources would be available. (Not money. Let's deal with real resources; money is a mechanism of exchange — we might be able to do away with it.) How much knowledge is available, how many persons are available, how many machines are available, how many real resources are available? In this very solid country, the most restrained list of demands was twenty times as large as the most optimistic estimate of the resources available to satisfy them. If I aggregate the excellent ideas put forth in the study-group reports, as augmented by all the discussions, I think we'll reach a proportion of fifty to one. Each idea by itself is excellent, but we just can't have all of them in the next twenty to thirty years.

The foregoing are among the basic dilemmas of any effort, not to translate the future into the present, but to interconnect our hopes and desires for the future a little with present actions, to try to change the emerging futures a little with the help of present decisions.

Let me move on to Hawaii and see how far I can translate those dilemmas into problems of Hawaii — though here my ignorance will become even more obvious. Let me do so in the form of a number of principles of how to deal with those dilemmas.

First, it is absolutely necessary to be selective and to establish priorities. I am a little struck by the tendency in the task-force reports, and even more so in some of the discussions, on the one hand to want to make tremendous investments in Hawaii — transportation systems, community structures, and so forth — and on the other hand, to get rid of tourism, the military, pineapple, and sugar. What remains? Is planning based on the assumption that the volcanoes will spit out the gold required? Even if they could, it wouldn't help because the amount of gold required would reduce the price of gold on the world market. We must consider when speaking about action in thirty years, and about action now, that we must establish priorities.

In addition to establishing priorities, we can try to increase resources. Here there are big opportunities. There is an idea in some of the civil-defense literature to regard the total population as a resource, the idea being that in case of a tense international situation, simple instructions will be issued so that every person can build a fallout shelter. Why should we leave all the good ideas to defense issues? One way to increase resources is to involve the whole population in tying its present activities in with the future. This may also help in the political dilemma and the psychological dilemma between present satisfactions and future satisfactions. It involves hard and tough moral decisions. But from a technical point of view, we can try to bridge the distance between present endeavors and present satisfactions and the future by trying to get larger and larger groups to regard sacrifices for the future as wanted by them. This can be used for the better or for the worse, but it is something to be considered.

Second, whatever we do we'll have to have some mix between min-avoidance and maximum idea approximation; here we get into the substance of the problem of the future of Hawaii. Now, of course, this is a subject in which you are better qualified than I, but as I came here to discuss it, I'd like to touch upon it a little. I think that the question must be asked, what are the worst features that you want to get rid of? This doesn't have to be called futures studies. There is no need for a twenty-year perspective to say that we want inexpensive housing. It may take ten years to get it, but there's no need for extrapolation or imagination or creativity to decide that this is an issue. To solve it, we may need creativity in designing a new type of housing. But debugging, min-avoidance, is essential and does not need much help of futures studies.

We may also try to pick two or three areas where we want to go beyond getting rid of the worst features of reality, to build up the future in the present, to engage in pilot development of some new ideas. For Hawaii to decide in what areas it wants to pioneer, the specific conditions of Hawaii have to be considered, including its culture, its history (which is so well reflected in some aspects in the labor force), and I add (this is one of the similarities between Israel and Hawaii), the small size. Small size is an advantage for many things. The economists like to speak about the diseconomies of small size, but this is where they are narrow economists. From the viewpoints of community life, of social integration, and of social experimentation, small size is a big advantage. So the search must be on (and is on in your impressive work) for specific things which Hawaii will try to develop positively, in addition to getting rid of a number of things.

For instance, and here I'm purely daydreaming, what about a statewide ho'oponopono[2] — taking your traditional institution, superimposing on it the feasibility of distant face-to-face relationships, using the small population as a culture suffused with technology to try out something new. Now this is just an illustration, which may be correct or incorrect. But it should illustrate: (a) taking something manageable; (b) taking something significant, not only for Hawaii but for humanity as a whole; (c) taking something for which small size is an advantage; and (d) taking something which fits into and uniquely represents the culture and traditions of Hawaii. I would urge, for those experiments, picking things which depend mainly on devotion, commitment and human will, and not on big financial investments (so as to be independent from big money and to reserve large financial resources for min-avoidance — antipollution, anti big city or small city, transportation systems and so on). By picking such a mix between min-avoidance and idea realization, we may be able to find a few lines along which we really want to proceed, in order to build up in the present parts of our images and dreams of the future.

How can we translate those general principles into reality? The task forces didn't reach this point, so I don't know either. But there are a number of things that should

2. The possible futures relevance of this traditional Hawaiian concept is explored further in the task-force report on the quality of personal life. — Editors.

be considered. First of all, when we speak about translation of futures studies, thinking, or dreaming into present reality, there are two main ways for this translation — a diffuse one and a specific one. The diffuse one is more important in the long range, and this is what you are achieving at this conference with your activities; namely, thinking about the future, not for implications of concrete action in the present, but for educating our minds to the future dimension, or to use the very appropriate phrase of Sir Geoffrey Vickers, for developing our "frames of appreciation," sensitizing our minds to an additional dimension, and providing an emotional feeling for the future. It is not a purely intellectual phenomenon, but is an emotional feel for the future, as was so nicely attempted in the audio-visual presentation that opened this conference. But a main impact of concern with the future is that the future should be a subconscious part of our daily endeavors. Now, if tomorrow you were asked, "This conference cost X dollars, what is the output?" I would say first of all that the output is immeasurable. It is in the minds and hearts of people — and this is the most important thing.

But we shouldn't limit ourselves to that. The diffused educational impact is critical but indirect, not measurable, and it can be lost if there is no follow-up; you can't rely on it; we can hope for it, we can't be sure about it — it may disappear with the first crisis. Therefore, in addition to the educational, mind-broadening, and emotion-sensitizing effects of dealing with the future, we also want some more direct translations. Direct translations require hard work, but even more than that, they require some additional things.

First, if we want to translate future images into present action, we have to make hard and controversial decisions. One of the nice things of dreaming about the future is that we may all be able to reach agreement, in two ways: we put into our conclusions generalities which we *all agree to, or we aggregate what everyone wants and put that into one volume. This is fine, but useless, even counterproductive, if we want to apply implications. When we want to apply our implications, priorities have to be established, selections have to be made, scarce resources have to be allocated to goal A, which means goals B, C, D, and E don't get them. Clearly, for every goal that receives priority, many other goals don't. Therefore, it is easiest not to do anything. If we don't ask questions, we don't struggle about answers. But if we want to move in a given direction, let us know that while we discuss it pleasantly — action decisions on the future are a subject for conflict, as all human decisions are. We may love one another and still strongly disagree. If we agree, everything isn't love, it's hypnosis or enforcement. This is a real problem, because we hesitate to break up the harmony of speaking about the future, but if we don't break up this harmony and make decisions, we cannot translate futures thinking into present action.*

Second, dealing with the future is a long-range commitment requiring patience. We should start now, because the results won't be in tomorrow. In ten years they will be in, if we start yesterday. Therefore, impatience with present bad things is essential as a driving force to start action, but is dangerous as a hindrance to the long-range view needed to achieve impact.

Third, we must be elastic, and avoid rigid fixations on what seems to us important now. Our views are going to change not only because of external variables but also because our efforts to shape the future are the beginning of a shared learning experience. We must learn from what we are doing. We must progress by phased sequential decisions, redeciding all the time in view of what we have learned from earlier decisions. This requires a nondogmatic attitude, a capacity to learn, and, in particular, a fear of slogans. Easy slogans of whatever kind — for example, yes-population, no-population — have to be avoided because slogans hinder our thinking. And after all, what is the use of thinking or trying to deal with the future if it doesn't free our minds to think in somewhat more creative ways.

Fourth, we need some interaction between futures thinking and day-to-day decision-making. This is a tough knot, because we can easily run into situations in which day-to-day decision-makers pay their debts to the future by having the future studied and that's the end of it. We are not interested in futures studies as an output, but as a tool to shape the future and influence it. Therefore, the interface between futures studies and decision-making is essential. We need an interface between the conclusions of ongoing futures studies and the day-to-day decision-making organization. This requires three things, going from the less to the more important.

(1) It requires methodological sophistication, suitable futures studies formats, consistency between the different images of the future, scenarios tying in the present to the future, resource estimates, and so on. No one should present action-oriented, short-range, future images without costing them in terms of the human devotion, time, and resources required. But since we are not at a technological conference, let me leave this aside, and just mention that the methodologies are essential for tying in futures research with present action.

(2) Most importantly, we need a certain attitude, a certain orientation, which combines realism and idealism. I call it idealistic realism, but I will agree if you call it realistic idealism. This is a big dilemma. In fact, I have experienced it in my life in Israel, where I have been involved for many years in building up the country as a member of a revolutionary, pioneering movement which, by all criteria of feasibility analysis, was absurd and crazy. It was crazy, but it did achieve something big. And I'm

now spending some time at the RAND Corporation, where strict analysis of feasibility is a tremendous contribution. When we deal with the foreseeable future, we must achieve some kind of idealistic realism. When we speak about the long-term future, "the future of the future," when we want to invent long-range futures, we get into what Robert Jungk so inspiringly presented. Then we can reduce the role of realism and increase the role of inventive idealism, keeping in mind humanity as it is. But when we speak about the short-range implications of futures studies on reality, this tension with idealistic realism must be kept in mind.

(3) The conclusion is that we must, in part, institutionalize our concern with the future. Having some enthusiasts is essential, having some broad involvement is both essential and desirable, but we need more than this. We must institutionalize the concern with the future. How? Well, let me give an illustration. I think, with my limited knowledge, that Hawaii should have a main center on futures studies and futures research shared by the university and the state government. I can imagine such a futures research and teaching center engaging in a number of functions. Functions would include (in no order of priority): education on futures in the broad, popular, positive, democratic sense of the term; preparation of professionals in futures studies (which is most essential if we want to progress with translation of futures into reality); research on specific Hawaiian futures (building up and implementing what has been so nicely begun with this conference) and perhaps having a mission as a focus for futures-oriented research, teaching, and related activities for the whole Pacific area. I can well imagine that one of the ways in which Hawaii could pioneer, not only in advancing Hawaii but in contributing to the entire world, would be to develop means for putting the future into the present.

I tend to say that some institutionalization, in one

way or another, is a critical variable which will determine whether this distinguished and fascinating conference is only a passing episode — the memory of which will be cherished by all of us, and which adds to all of us, but which does not lead to concrete action — or whether it will result in concrete action through following the lead provided by the task forces and by the conference itself.

Can the Poor People Get a Robot, or Just the Rich People?

Alfred Pasatiempo, Sr., and Bob Krauss

Alfred Pasatiempo, Sr., serves as an outreach counselor at a Honolulu intermediate school where he talks with and tries to help students who are in trouble. He was formerly a laborer with the State Highway Department. In addition to his counseling work, he is a congressman for Honolulu Model Cities.

Bob Krauss is a columnist for the *Honolulu Advertiser* and has authored several books on Hawaii which include *Here's Hawaii* (1960), *High-Rise Hawaii* (1969), and *Travel Guide to the Hawaiian Islands* (1963). With William P. Alexander, he wrote *Grove Farm Plantation; the Biography of a Hawaiian Sugar Plantation* (1965). He was educated at the University of Minnesota and has since covered assignments in Tahiti, Samoa, Micronesia, the Philippines, Vietnam, Japan, and Europe.

What's the down payment on the work-performing robot described by futurist author Arthur C. Clarke at the conference on the year 2000? That was the question asked by Alfred Pasatiempo, Sr., the only laborer to attend the conference.[1]

"It's amazing what I learned," said Pasatiempo, a heavy-equipment operator. "I sure would like to get one robot in my house. You know, we poor people like to live it up, too. In the morning instead of going to work I just push a button, and there it is. Then I push a button

---

1. This section reproduces a news story about the meeting of participants Pasatiempo and Krauss at the Hawaii 2000 conference. *Honolulu Advertiser*, August 8, 1970, p. A–11. Reprinted by permission of the *Honolulu Advertiser*.

and I see my friend on the Mainland. The guy said you can talk to him so close like in your living room."

"I'll say, 'Hey, bruddah! How's Los Angeles?' But I was wondering, can we afford it? I mean, how much is the down payment going to be? Can the poor people get a robot, or just the rich people?"

As the conference neared its close, Pasatiempo gave his evaluation of the $65,000 project. *"Some people make sense and some not a bit,"* he said. *"I'm interested when they talk about the Hawaiian Islands themselves — what we can do for the poor people — housing developments, jobs. But, so far, nothing like that come up. In my open heart, I wanted to come. It's something new to me. It gives me an idea how to advise my kids what to expect in the future.*

"Myself, sometimes I get bored. I can't understand all the big words. Another thing, I wish there were more local people who talk instead of the haoles [2] talking all the time. I didn't see nobody else in my field. They all have titles: psychiatrist, teacher, community director, doctor. So I just feel my way."

"I never got past the seventh grade. Anyway, I didn't learn anything from the first to the seventh. My idea is, I like to know about a different type of life. I have learned a lot about sex, narcotics, human nature, how to help other people. So I lack of one thing but I gain of another thing."

"First I was all nervous. This is the first time I have ever talked to so big a bunch of people. There was that wonder if somebody would use my education on me. But once I got started talking, the words just came out of me."

---

2. A *haole* is defined as "a white person; formerly any foreigner; foreign, introduced, of foreign origin." Mary Kawena Pukui and Samuel H. Elbert, *Hawaiian Dictionary* (Honolulu: University of Hawaii Press, 1971). — Editors.

Pasatiempo was an outstanding speaker in the task force which discussed the quality of personal life.

"To tell you the truth, I didn't want to do this job if it's just stand up and be known and not have the power to do anything," he said. "If it's just talk because they want somebody to hear them, that's $65,000 down the drain. Even when I left my job to come to the meeting, the other workers said, 'Oh, it's just a waste of time. Just a campaign for somebody.' But the conference itself makes a lotta sense in a lotta ways. Because there is so many ideas come out of it. If they don't follow through and do something about it, though, it's waste."

What should the follow-through be, he was asked. "The best way I can say is the publicity in the newspaper and television. I got my name in the paper this morning. Already, two people called up and wanted me to come to a meeting. I'll explain to them the best way what I learned. I learned one thing, that they have a lotta good speakers. And I been wonder if they are going through with these things."

"Also, I have met some business people here who listened to me talk. In other words, I have told them from my heart how I feel about the Hawaiian Islands. They said they think that is the right way, and not just make a lot of money."

4 TASK-FORCE REPORTS

Overview
Editors

Despite the belated efforts of some of us to replace the military-related term "task force" with the more pacific concept of "study group," the former usage became irreversibly widespread at an early stage and is accurately reported in this book. Hopefully, future ventures in anticipatory democracy will find a somewhat better term: the coercive connotations of "task force" do not seem apt to describe a group experiment in community creativity.

Another conceptual problem facing similar futures efforts will be to select words to describe subject areas for futures inquiry. We employed rather conventional terms (for example, economy, arts, education, housing, and transportation), and made no effort to coin or employ possibly unfamiliar terms that might serve to help us make a more humane transition from the present toward a more desirable future. Probably the process of widespread futures thinking among members of a community will result in the creation of terms that will both reflect and assist the emergence of objective future realities in a way less impeded by past-bound present terminologies.

We employed a two-stage process for selecting subjects for task-force inquiry. First, we elicited from the advisory committee a long list of subject suggestions; then we finally reached committee agreement on the present ten. Experience leads us to think that perhaps a more innovative set of topics might have been selected by seek-

ing more expert futures advice and more widespread lay suggestions. Probably an assumed constraint of time for conference presentation limited the number of topics to ten. Perhaps we should have tried to encourage futures thinking on a wider variety of topics, an approach that would have confronted us with the useful but harder task of seeking to find a small set of ideas that would satisfactorily encompass the more finely articulated universe of futures concerns. On the contrary, we began with global concepts and hoped for the subsequent emergence of differentiated and more concrete futures applications.

The selection of task-force members was also a two-stage process. First, chairmen were appointed by the advisory committee; then these chairmen picked the members of their own task forces. The idea behind this was that the chairmen would work best with persons whom they themselves had selected. The chairmen's choices, however, were guided by suggestions from the advisory committee.

Very importantly, the chairmen were urged to create a diverse group that would include representatives of government, business, labor, law, arts, communications, the university, youth, women, religious and service organizations, ordinary citizens, subject-matter specialists, and others — including a member of the advisory committee for liaison purposes. It was suggested that each task force be composed of twenty to twenty-five members. To assist them in making these choices, the advisory committee chairman wrote letters to a wide range of community leaders to invite suggestions as to outstanding persons in the community who might be expected to make an important contribution. These requests resulted in bringing between fifteen hundred and two thousand persons to the advisory committee's attention, reminding us dramatically of the tremendous potential for public leadership within the people of our island state. We made a special effort to identify grass-roots or natural leaders in our vari-

ous local communities, regardless of social, educational, or economic standing. Such efforts were made partly through social workers, service agencies, and others who habitually work with economically disadvantaged individuals. Suggestions for Hawaii 2000 conference participants were solicited from political leaders; the bar association; the Japanese, Chinese, and other chambers of commerce; labor unions; ethnic associations; communications media; women's organizations; student groups; religious organizations; and a wide range of other individuals, agencies, associations, societies, and organizations.

The process of task-force organization occupied most of January and February 1970, leaving about five months for these groups to prepare draft reports for presentation to the August conference.

Five questions were suggested to guide the preparation of the task-force reports. What is the present state of the subject? If present trends continue, what would the subject be like in 2000? What alternative future states of affairs are contemplable? What present or future obstacles may block their attainment? What present or future resources may aid them? What suggestions for immediate, middle, or long-range action does the task force wish to offer for discussion? These questions provided only a crude point of departure, and chairmen were free to modify, supplement, or abandon them as experience with futures thinking grew.

Since all chairmen and task-force members were residents of Hawaii and thus familiar with local affairs, it was thought useful to provide each group with a potential for employing outside consultants as a source of creative contributions to, and critical evaluation of, their work. Thus the advisory committee suggested for each at least two consultants, leading thinkers drawn mainly from the national intellectual community, who might be engaged in task-force activities via correspondence. Such consultants could be "futurists" or subject-matter specialists. They need not be Americans and could be drawn from the whole world. Who they were and how their help would be used depended upon the task-force chairmen. Hindsight permits us to see that we were not then as aware of as many emerging world futures thinkers as we should have been. Also, now as then, we remain somewhat puzzled as to why some of the task forces failed to take full advantage of this opportunity to engage more of the world's finest intellects in thinking about Hawaii's future. Perhaps this is explicable by a combination of time constraints, limited appreciation of consulting potentialities, local defensiveness, and reluctance to expose crude initial thoughts to critical assessment. Nevertheless, some brilliant consulting assistance was sought and obtained: René Dubos for the quality of personal life; Kenneth Boulding for economics; Chester Rapkin for transportation and housing; and two consultants, Henry Pleasants and Alan Gowans, for the arts. Hawaii's James Dator served as consultant for the task forces on Hawaii's people and lifestyles, and political decision-making.

In their five months of preconference preparation, the task forces operated in ways as varied as their chairmen and participants. They met frequently or seldom, subdivided themselves or maintained unity of the whole, and varied in the breadth of creative participation. Heterogeneity within the groups, where successfully achieved, itself created challenging problems of intellectual leadership. That may have offered us a glimpse of the leadership problems to be expected in a future participatory informational society.

The problems of diversity were compounded in the conference itself when about four hundred new persons, who had not participated in the preliminary thinking, joined the nearly three hundred original task-force members. Inadequate time added a further complication: only four hours on one conference day were provided for work-

shop discussions of each preliminary task-force report. Furthermore, only one evening was provided for the task-force chairman to reflect upon the new ideas and to integrate them into his overall report to the conference on the following day. Thus, different stages of involvement in futures thinking and time pressures raised complications for evoking, critically evaluating, and integrating new ideas. One structural device we found rather effective was to have the workshops chaired by someone other than the task-force chairman, so that the latter's attention could be devoted more fully to intellectual substance rather than to group process.

Thus the task-force reports presented here in Part Four are the result of a varied group effort over a period of about ten months, from the selection of a chairman to the submission of his final written report. In the interim, task-force members were coopted, goals and procedures were established, ideas were evoked, a preliminary report was written, the report was published in advance for the benefit of all conference participants, the results were criticized and supplemented in conference workshops, a revised oral report was made to a wider conference audience, and finally a written revision was prepared for this book. It was a massive task for men fully engaged in other professional responsibilities. [1]

1. Only in writing this are we aware that we failed to make a special effort to engage women as task-force chairmen, even though women played key roles in our advisory committee and in the task forces themselves.

Hawaii's People and Life-styles 2000
Douglas S. Yamamura and Harry V. Ball

Douglas Yamamura, professor of sociology, is acting dean of the summer session at the University of Hawaii. His scholarly concerns center on human ecology, demography, and social science research methodology. Born on Maui, home and final resting place of his grandparents, educated at Maui High School, the University of Hawaii, and the University of Washington, he taught in the public schools of Maui and the Big Island of Hawaii before entering his university teaching, research, and service career. Married and the father of three children, he hopes that his children will have a "future of self-fulfillment."

Harry V. Ball, professor of sociology, was born in Missouri and educated at Washington University and the University of Minnesota. A member of the University of Hawaii faculty since 1951 his main interest is in the study of law as it relates to social experimentation.

One reason we cannot predict the future is that we are tied, more than we realize, to the past.

D. W. Brogan

hether we like it or not, to a considerable extent the Hawaii of 2000 is already here. [1] The decisions that we and others have made and are making now about our physical and social environments have and will continue to set impor-

1. Because of space requirements we removed the thirty-five pages of our initial working paper [see *Preliminary Task Force Reports (July 1970)*] that carefully reviewed the slow progress man has made in producing new social forms that increase his capacity for a full, secure, and varied life. Many persons missed our point entirely in the first draft — that the number of pages consumed represented the length of time

tant constraints upon our future options. More importantly, however, Hawaii 2000 is now here in the sense that the realities of Hawaii 2000 will be only as rich (or as sparse), only as beautiful (or as ugly), as the visions which men are willing to dream now — and, in the dreaming, create.

Given this, we as members of the task force on "People and Life-styles" feel a special burden. We honestly believe that Hawaii has a significance — even a preeminence — in the world today that is all out of proportion to its size or material wealth (or even its climate); and that this importance is due to its people and their ways of life. We of Hawaii, both those who have been born here from an act of love and those who have moved here as an act of love, are all aware of the tarnishes on our halo, the blemishes on our surface, the serious rents in our social fabric. Yet we believe that these facts, which we know and acknowledge (without passive acceptance), and our worldwide image, when taken together, only serve to document the tragic state of most of the world and the importance of what does happen to the few important beacons, of which we are one.

WHERE WE HAVE BEEN AND WHAT WE ARE

Hawaii's peculiar social organization is all the more dramatic given the fact that in less than two hundred years it has moved from being an isolated, homogeneous, preliterate stone-age society, to being one of the most modern communities in the world. During this transformation it has brought into potentially promising union some, if not most, of the major cultural traditions of the Pacific: American, Polynesian, Sino-Japanese.

---

that each step of progress in this area consumed in the past. In this version we have concentrated upon elaboration of the areas that struck us as representing the major decisions that must be made today if we are to avoid worldwide disaster, and gain substantial control over our fate by 2000. Many of us prefer our first version, for it is our firm conviction that under even the best of circumstances man will always be backing into his future.

The culture of the first Hawaiians stressed kinship, community, and harmony with nature and the gods. Property, in the sense of use-rights and access-rights to those things necessary to sustain life, was basically communal. A very high level of interpersonal security was achieved through one's kinship group and through one's membership in larger community groupings and political unions. This was so even though some warfare appears to have been chronic — some of which could be devastating to the losers. Taxes were paid in kind, that is, in work and service, and no market relationships disturbed the basically egalitarian and open relationships among men. While some privacy obtained between the sexes, there was very little concern for privacy in the modern sense. This lack of privacy, while it constituted a constraint upon individuals, was also a source of interpersonal security. Work was viewed as a necessity and not as an end in itself; it was usually executed in social settings in which the personal interaction provided the sustaining gratifications. A very high degree of ecological balance had been obtained, and it is presumed that the population was stable at roughly the size of the population of Honolulu in 1950. [2]

The first half of the nineteenth century was marked primarily by two developments: first, the decimation of the original Hawaiian population through diseases; and second, the reorganization of the society upon the basis of egalitarian-individualistic small-community premises that were produced by virtually the same social forces that produced the anticity, anti mass-manufacturing, anti-plantation, and antislavery movement in the United States. This culminated in the Great Mahele, which was to free the Hawaiian common man from feudal abuses.

The next fifty years, the second half of the nineteenth century, were (most ironically) dominated by the development of sugar plantations and the importation of contract laborers, producing a vast rural proletariat of

2. City: 248,034; county: 353,020.

foreigners, many of whom did not come to Hawaii with the intention of remaining permanently. This phenomenon proceeded at a pace beyond anyone's expectations. At least five homestead programs that were restricted to natural-born Hawaiians failed to counter the dominance of these land-factories, which were worked by imported labor and controlled by a small elite of Americans and Europeans through their privately owned corporations. The overthrow of the monarchy and annexation in 1898 by the United States secured these forms, and left the native Hawaiians with not much more than a terrible sense of deprivation and some estates dedicated to their welfare.

The next major development was the migration of plantation laborers to the cities and towns where, because of their numbers, they could establish small businesses and farms and become a newly emergent middle class with considerable autonomy from the power elite. As a divided elite increased public educational opportunities and the depression slowed immigration, concern was voiced in some quarters that the haoles were disappearing.

The continuing efforts of the elite to develop a rational-industrial type society, while still perpetuating the archaic prejudices of the nineteenth century, broke with the events of World War II. Modern industrial organization of the plantations, with the inevitable internal pressures toward rationalization that its organizational form creates, produced commensurate pressures for an individualized meritocracy and the development of organizations of wage earners as a countervailing force to organized management. World War II released these tendencies as if there had been an eruption. It brought new outside influences into the islands. Wartime experiences and the educational programs of the G. I. Bill produced a new group of trained and cosmopolitan persons who were no longer disposed to accept the previous status system and who provided the organization and much of the leadership to demand equal opportunity and full participation.

The model now became the organizationally dominated, merit-selecting, rationally oriented bureaucracy, in both the public and private sectors — which continued to be intertwined. Unionization in the private sector and civil service in the public sector carried forward these principles of bureaucratic rationality and at the same time introduced new principles of due process, justice, and job security (the vested interest in bureaucratic positions).

Formal education was seen as the new basis for preparing persons to enter into and to make claims upon these large organizations, and the same organizational models were applied to the educational ventures. Larger and larger units were established under centralized control to provide uniform treatment and equality of opportunity.

In this competition, the educationally and bureaucratically oriented descendants of plantation laborers fared rather well in the public sector, and in those previously public sectors which had become increasingly quasi-public, in contrast to the native Hawaiians, who were oriented more toward apprenticeship and interpersonal harmony.

In recent years another factor has intruded itself into the sector of the private economic bureaucracies. These have tended to become components of the largest mainland corporations and international in their operations. Thus, to be vertically mobile a person must be loyal primarily to the corporation and not to a kinship group, a community, or a locale. The personnel rotation of the military has become a powerful model in the name of the rational utilization of human resources. Yet many persons born in Hawaii are oriented primarily toward Hawaii as a place to live and as a way of life; these have been joined by many others who came here first under corporate or federal bureaucratic sponsorship and subsequently "jumped ship." As private exclusionary arrangements and public residency requirements are being declared illegal on various grounds with increasing regularity, many modern

Hawaiians of every ethnic background are beginning again to share a feeling of invasion, outside threat, and deprivation.

While these trends have proceeded, the local responses seem to have concentrated overwhelmingly upon the contradictory policies of assuring the security of every man through the private ownership of his land, while imposing controls upon land utilization (for a combination of economic and conservationist ends) which have turned the land market into a highly inflated and speculative operation. Again the cry is raised to solve this problem by opening up more state and estate land for fee-simple ownership, the late twentieth-century version of the now outdated homestead programs. The proposed answers to a speculative nightmare and to increasing outside control seem to be that everyone can get into the game, with Hawaii becoming a means to an end for an increasing number of organized interests. On the contrary, other tools are being increasingly indicated by the "law explosion" and the "justice explosion" — the awareness that in the future human security must be based upon the introduction of the rule of law into all large-scale organizations (local, national, or international) and the implementation of the worldwide demands of all for at least minimal justice. Thus, many of the challenges in the area of social organization, now faced by Hawaii, are the same as the challenges that face most of the rest of the world.

HAWAII'S SPECIAL CHALLENGE AND VALUE CHOICE

If, as indicated above, we share many of the organizational constraints and opportunities of the rest of the world, we believe that Hawaii also has its own particular value orientation that operates as its special challenge, opportunity, and constraint. In the process of living and working together, the people of Hawaii have forged a life system and orientation that reaffirms the essential dignity and integrity of every human being, irrespective of race, color, or creed. While many people are inclined to dispar-

146

age Hawaii's achievement in the field of interpersonal and intergroup relations, there is ample evidence of a fusion of racial types and a blending of cultures that is unique. Of course, the Hawaiian social structure has undergone severe stresses and at times seemed to move away from the ideal of the social equality of all men. Yet it has been possible for men of superior ability, character, and energy to achieve positions of authority and dignity without limitations as to race. Personal position and status in Hawaii has come to depend more on personal merit and less on racial or cultural antecedent. While we are far from perfect, the existence of this public code of racial equality has been crucial in promoting the ideal.

The "aloha spirit" — however it is defined — is a basic ingredient of a style of life based on the essential equality and dignity of all human beings. The basic qualities of this way of life are perhaps best characterized by such terms as openness, hospitality, neighborly concern, tolerance, general acceptance of others, emotional warmth, genuine love for other people, and friendliness. This state of mind, introduced to visitors and incoming residents from all parts of the world by the Hawaiians, nurtured however imperfectly through the stresses of successive waves of immigrants has enabled Hawaii in its doctrine and practices about human relationships to develop as a unique area of the modern world. Hawaii as an image and as a state of mind is heavily indebted to the original Hawaiians.

There is danger, of course, in clinging to outworn clichés rather than reality. Will the aloha spirit become passé? What will happen to the traditional hula? Will the giving of a flower lei disappear, or will this practice become hollow ritual? For, to remain relevant, the state of mind which we call the aloha spirit must demonstrate its viability in the terms of the twenty-first century. This guiding principle in our style of life, however imperfectly practiced, is one of the more basic elements of the identity of Hawaii.

It was only after World War II that Hawaii became the place where East meets West. Between now and 2000 our visions must be even greater in the area of human relations. We must become the place where the present leads the future, even if much of the future consists of past Hawaiian values reaffirmed and even re-created in new social forms.

In saying this we do not mean that Hawaii should impose a constraint upon its planning that others need not assume, simply because it is "Hawaiian," simply because we wish to retain an empty phrase from our past for the sake of maudlin sentimentality. Quite the contrary. We believe, with those prophetic voices of the first decade of the twentieth century (ranging from W. E. B. DuBois to W. C. Sumner) that the problem of race is the preeminent social challenge of the twentieth century, that it has not been solved, and that it poses the fundamental threat to any orderly transition to a desirable future or futures — or even to any future.

We also tend to think that the next greatest problem we face in the area of social organization generally is that of imposing personal controls over the ever larger and ever more impersonal bureaucracies. We are indebted to the great German sociologist, Max Weber, for his analysis of the power of this social form to sweep over all competitors because of its deification of the goal of efficiency and of the fact that the modern world requires such a level of efficiency. At the same time, Weber spelled out in great detail the dangers inherent in secrecy within these bureaucracies and the great contribution that this form of social organization can make to tyranny, as well as to the development of mass society, in which we find a world crowded with strangers. If we cannot survive today without the bureaucratic form, then we must also ask how we can survive with it? We suggest that the answer must lie in the seemingly paradoxical statement that we must harness the bureaucratic form to enlarge and enhance the human values implicit in our concept of aloha.

148

ALTERNATIVE FORMS OF FUTURECASTING

It should be clear by now that we have explicitly rejected some of the modes of futurecasting that have been developed by others. We have rejected any simple attempt to predict what will be. We are directed toward a statement of what we would like and what we think can be achieved with concentrated and rational effort.

We have rejected any attempt at a simple projection of trends in either of its two forms: ethically neutral quantitative projection, or horror stories. We have rejected the broadest form of science-fiction forecasting, in which any conceivable technology is assumed to have been fully developed, and in which humans are then assumed to conform to its requirements. We believe, with Lewis Mumford, that much of the application of our science in the nineteenth and twentieth centuries, that is, our technology, did not produce any increase in the quality of life or even in the long-range efficiencies it was supposed to provide. We are interested in new scientific knowledge and new technologies, but we are interested in them primarily only as they will solve, or contribute toward the solution of, the two major problems we have defined above in terms of aloha, or its absence. This is because we believe that new technologies will also bring new problems of unknown magnitudes, and we can rationalize creating these new problems and dumping them on future generations only if we can honestly say to ourselves, however erroneously, that we did it because we honestly believed we had to solve or ameliorate our most pressing and troublesome problems: intergroup relations and bureaucratic tyranny.

On the other hand, we have not attempted to visualize a world in which the problems of bureaucracy have been solved by the elimination of bureaucracy (a conceivable solution in a future in which the machines control the world and humans have become their house pets), or one in which the problems of intergroup relations have been *solved by the elimination of all cultural diversity. We believe that the bureaucratic form has some utility and that with modifications the social form can be controlled. It is the deepfelt conviction of many of the members of our task force that we should not consider any future for 2000 that would eliminate all possibility of a diversity of cultures.*

WORLDWIDE ASSUMPTIONS

But, it seems to us that our deliberations have led us to some ideas that are new to us — that even surprised us — and we gladly present them for the purposes of furthering our dialog. We have also established a set of assumptions that run into the assigned areas of every other task force. In many cases we make no attempt to argue the merits of the ideas in detail. We present them simply as propositions that appear on their faces to be almost necessary conditions for the establishment of the kinds of social relations we would like to see. Our major assumptions with respect to the world scene are given below.

1. A relatively peaceful world with, at the least, much greater arms control and political coordination among nations — and at the most, substantial development of a bonafide world citizenship.

2. A common technological foundation for a world society — this will involve extensive mechanization and cybernation.

3. Worldwide environmental and pollution controls.

4. Appropriate worldwide economic development through global bureaucracies with appropriate internal justice and external constraints, to ensure a dramatic reduction in current disparities in world standards of living.

5. A general reduction in the rate of world population growth, aiming at the possibility that the total will not exceed, or may even be less than, that of today.

6. A substantial reduction in competitively oriented achievement values and an increase in activities providing intrinsic meaning and gratification through being a con-

tributing member of one's various social groups (ranging from family to mankind).

7. A continuation of the potential stresses between one's identification with a variety of worldwide bureaucracies, and one's identification with family, community or locale, and a historic ethnic group.

8. The existence of a worldwide communication network which will make available in every community the vast array of man's knowledge and creative productions.

Concomitant with these global transformations, we assume that the dominant values now being implemented in the mainland United States and in Hawaii will have produced the following states of affairs.

1. A full implementation of the right of every contributing member of a community to the basic necessities of life.

2. A substantial reduction in the prominence of one's ancestry (racial or cultural) as a determinant in one's choice of group memberships.

Further, the fact that we have simply posited these assumptions does not mean that we have no more concern with them. While some of the global forces that affect our life-style and our survival are beyond our direct control, we, as citizens in a participatory democratic state, have exerted and should exert an influence on decisions at both the national and international levels in consonance with our goals. As a state in a federation, Hawaii's influence on national policies affecting our life-style can be exerted much more directly through our elected representatives, and perhaps even more by our example. Finally, there are narrower areas — decisions made locally bearing on plans for and development of our State — that are closely related to our life-style and welfare and in which the people of Hawaii can have a more direct voice. Such actions and decisions are subject only to the limits imposed by our legal and social values and to those constraints that derive from being a part of the social and economic networks of all mankind.

WHAT WE SHOULD AIM FOR

If our assumptions about the aspirations of Hawaii and the rest of the world are correct, then the basic issues for consideration at State and county levels are those relating to the perpetuation of individual freedom and local community autonomy in a world which will be increasingly centralized, bureaucratized, and standardized. Will the world become like an army, or will there be full freedom for the differing communities in which people will wish to live? How do we implement individual and group freedoms for citizens of the world?

Our basic answer to this question is that a person must become a citizen of each of his important social groups. Citizenship entails full participation in and commitment to each group, and also a full quota of commensurate rights and the protection of these rights.

The significant identity for everyone must be his world citizenship. To avoid the development of a colorless uniformity and to guard against totalitarianism, world organization should be limited to basic production, enlarged only as is necessary to provide for each man's basic sustenance and for the worldwide communications system. It is precisely this industry that is today organized into the greatest bureaucracy, and the one in which the bureaucratic form makes its greatest contribution to efficiency. Work in such organizations will have to be not the basis for securing special power and control over others, but a major contribution that members of the world community make, for each other and for themselves. One's commitment would have to be to the world community, not to any particular bureaucratic structure.

Participation in such organizations should have the character of a form of national service. Each person would be expected to prepare for such service, and would be provided opportunities in line with his wishes and demon-

strated abilities. No one can properly identify with a community that does not permit and demand that he contribute on a membership basis, and the world community can be no different.

It is possible — even desirable — that some manual labor will be required of all, especially such labor as maintains the humility of man in his relationships with the rest of the world. For example, it is possible that all adults will periodically engage in such activities as weeding — even if much of our future food can be raised by hydroponics. In Hawaii such basic duty might well include staffing our hotels, for it is difficult to think of any service that is more symbolic of our pride in Hawaii and of our human kinship than sharing the beauty of the islands with guests, provided the duty is voluntary (for the role of servant, especially in domestic service, is the lowest-status work we have yet devised).

Movement into and out of worldwide bureaucracies, even at the highest levels, would be mandatory, and would be the major restraint against any person's seeking to dominate the world through perpetuated control of organization. Those who control the bureaucracies would thus not be able to divert an organization to their own personal ends — not in any narrow sense of pecuniary gain, but in the broader sense of ego gratification. It is, of course, possible that such rotation might result in some loss of efficiency; however, we not only doubt this but suggest that if it did occur, the loss would be more than compensated for by the much higher level of personal security that the world would enjoy.

We readily admit that it takes considerable boldness to seriously propose a rotating structure of this kind to deal with mankind's basic resources. We can only ask that, before rejecting these suggestions, each skeptical reader examine Weber's work on bureaucracy and Galbraith's analysis of our bureaucracies in **The New Industrial State.**[3]

3. Baltimore: Penguin Books, 1969.

We do not believe that man can afford to abandon the bureaucratic form as a device for coordinating large-scale activities; we merely believe that it must be modified so that it is not an instrument of unaccountable power organized for the personal ends of permanent agents. Many who have been concerned with this problem propose socialism as the solution, but we suggest that most evidence indicates that these persons simply misunderstand the basic nature of the problem. We feel that our proposal of a randomized entrance and exit at all levels goes more to the heart of the problems.

Next we may ask if this principle of organizational openness should stop with bureaucracies? On the contrary, we seriously propose that Hawaii 2000 be characterized by a great reduction in privacy generally. It is understandable that privacy is in great demand in a world in which more people are demanding a greater range of free choice from a society that is basically constraining. If, however, constraint is less, then the demand for privacy should be less. We recognize that invasion of privacy has been equated with abuse of centralized or privileged power, but we do not believe that such need be the case. We further suggest that openness in interpersonal dealings is a major contribution of the original Hawaiian culture to our future potential. We believe that personal and interpersonal security is premised upon such openness, and that this openness is the basis of the kind of accountability that is the essence of constitutionality in any community. In a rational world the answer to private abuse is not more privacy, nor even more publicity at some levels and more privacy at others, but less privacy at all levels.

There is, of course, an additional requirement for this proposition to be behaviorally effective; that is, for reduced privacy and full disclosure to increase both personal and group security. It is that both individuals and communities be highly tolerant and supportive of individuals who are self-consciously "different," so long as they contribute to the richness of living in the society. This qualification is very important, and is an explicit rejection of nihilism. At the same time it carries the implication that, as we become increasingly open, our rule of law will move toward more inclusive definitions of tolerable conduct, just as it has in our own lifetimes.

We recognize that this suggestion to reduce privacy runs counter to the concern voiced in many quarters (a concern which we share) about the files on individuals being developed by public and private agencies. Nevertheless, we think that detailed, computerized social histories will be available on just about everyone in Hawaii 2000, and that they will also be public in the fullest sense. A step in this direction was taken by recent federal legislation requiring agencies that conduct credit investigations to permit any person about whom they have information to see his own file. Already debate is being joined about whether or not a citizen should be allowed to inspect his own FBI file. Files will be kept in a bureaucratically organized world because individuals have histories on which decisions must be made and new knowledge produced. Files are threats — or perhaps we should say, unreasonable threats — to a person in a world of secret decisions and unaccountable power, but immediately available information about persons can be a source of great security in a society with other primary principles of organizations.

Such files in Hawaii 2000 will be necessary supports for the high level of interpersonal and intra- and inter-community tolerance that are central elements of aloha. Tolerance of differences between individuals and communities cannot be achieved to any substantial degree under conditions of secrecy, unknowns, and strangeness. To the contrary, these are the conditions of distrust, suspicion, anxiety, and fear.

If, and admittedly it is a big if, such arrangements as the above can be obtained for Hawaii 2000, then each individual will face a rich variety of choices in structuring his life and can in fact exert a very large control over his own fate. In a sense that is almost inconceivable today, a person can create himself.

First of all, he will be able to be a part of several small but worldwide groupings which share one or more of his interests — the activities or ideas that excite him. This will be possible because of the system of satellite-linked communications that will be available. Already the picturephone connects Pittsburgh and Washington, D.C.; already a planning expert employed "in" Washington, D.C., works and lives in Colorado with his wife, a psychiatrist, who maintains her practice in San Francisco. With additional satellite development, persons who want to will be able to regularize face-to-face communication on a worldwide basis.

This means that place-of-residence and place-of-work, or at least some of them, will become increasingly independent decisions. However, in line with our earlier value choices, we do not believe that Hawaii 2000 should become only a collection of apartments in which almost all social interaction takes place by means of electronic transmission. Provision should be made, however, for this kind of life-style, and in time it might encompass an increasingly large segment of the population. We anticipate, however, that Hawaii 2000 will have achieved a wide range of diverse communities to constitute the social settings in which individuals carry out most of their activities. Membership in any of these communities will be by choice.

The amounts and kinds of diversity that will be possible among these communities will depend considerably upon the fullest implementation of tolerance and the necessary conditions for such a norm to be a substantial influence over behavior. We anticipate that communities may be as diverse as the most radical Israeli kibbutz on one hand, and some of our modern high-rise apartments

on the other, as diverse as the Banana Patch and Waipahu. [4]
*Some of them will undoubtedly embody counterculture
and be highly self-conscious efforts to reject the most
central elements of modern American, urban, middle-class
culture. Others will have even a higher level of sophistication and will seek a certain quality of life from various
theoretical perspectives. Some may be self-consciously
ethnic communities, but operating on a more creative
future-oriented base than at present, because all will be
aware (through the worldwide communication system)
that none of the ethnic cultures have the degree of
homogeneity that characterized even the year 1900. We
will thus find a range from unisex roles to diverse bisexual
roles at the adult level; we will have considerable diversity
in childbearing and childrearing practices and responsibilities. The creation of such communities will require
a continuation of the present trend to systematically make
our formal regulations of marriage and parenthood more
diverse.*

*It should be stressed that these communities will be
of a genuinely experimental character. Most evidence
today suggests that we do not know enough about child
development to design any single best set of childrearing
practices. In return for the support for self-choice that
each community will offer the other, all must be committed to providing systematic information to the public data
banks on the results of their practices. Thus, once again
we may return to the social experimentation, once
dreamed about in the United States, in the form of permitted diversity among the states. The possibility that each
community could be a self-correcting institution within*

4. Maui's Banana Patch attracted disillusioned young people searching
for a slow-paced life of natural simplicity in gardening, sunbathing, and
meditation. For five years owner David Joseph welcomed into his lush
valley these "children of God," who built some twenty small dwellings
and went on their own "trips" of sharing or solitude.

Waipahu is a rural town, built around a sugar mill, celebrating its
seventy-fifth anniversary in 1972. — Editors.

the range of its ideals might be given a very substantial boost by our required systematic, public evaluation. This would be possible because our reorganized bureaucratic structure and assurance of minimum necessities would enable each community to have primary values different from those of any other without fear of handicapping their children in a lifelong competition with others.

The problem then is to provide each individual and community with as much free choice in life-style and social organization as is conceivable (under conditions of high interpersonal and intercommunity security) and to provide each with a fair share of the needed resources to implement such free choice. Central here is control of educational resources and organization, so that each individual and community would have access to vast stores of computerized information and instructional materials. Such technology in itself, however, does not dictate the nature of the educational organization nor the specific content for each person. With each passing year, of course, content would become increasingly self-selected by the learner. It is probable that what we think of today as basic education (whatever its equivalent in Hawaii 2000), and some specialized education, will end at about age sixteen.

Since the stability of each community, and thus of the world, would be based substantially upon each individual's creating himself by consciously choosing his community and interest group, it would probably be necessary to have the next period of socialization by the young include a maximum of travel and participation in relatively small, and probably highly specialized, educational communities. This projection for the young is made because we believe that there is for them a very intense peer-group orientation and a need for social supports while working through their initial identity crises.

The principle of continuous learning based on self-choice would also be implemented throughout adulthood — as, for example, in that dramatic, even revolutionary experiment in twentieth-century America, the Veterans' Education Bill, immediately after World War II. One of the amazing features of the 1950s and 1960s is in the manner in which hundreds of young legislators throughout the United States, including Hawaii, experienced the choices available through this Bill and then turned their backs on it in favor of bureaucratic models in which a man is supposed to gain his freedom by having most important decisions made for him by others. The bureaucratic principle should be employed to guarantee and to provide maximum equality of opportunity, but it should not be used to dictate what should be learned and where or how it should be learned. This is the lesson we learned and then forgot or rejected in favor of secondary values. This lost principle must be reaffirmed and reimplemented; hopefully, new technologies and less intercommunity suspicion will greatly facilitate this task.

We recognize that education is today embroiled in a vast public debate. Some persons identify social, especially racial, integration with the immediate problem of placing children of diverse ethnicities into larger and larger administrative and educational organizations. The current effort to solve this problem by larger bureaucracies is not very successful because the effort itself generates a vast number of additional problems associated with coercion. So far as public resources are concerned, we could maintain at least as high, if not a higher, degree of reduction of ethnic and socioeconomic discrimination by a system using small, personal, and specialized units that provide each person with great freedom of choice.

Such choice is also necessary to provide effective education in a world with a highly mobile population. Today we worry about the manner in which we program the sequence of educational activities for our children. Because sequencing is accepted as crucial, we even talk about integrated planning for elementary, middle, and high schools in a "feeder system." But our children move all over Hawaii and all over the world. Sequentially planned education for them cannot be organized on a territorial basis, but must be organized by private organizations that offer their services in those communities among which people are moving. The nonpublic organization offers the best format for educational integration in the emerging world.

IMMEDIATE STEPS FOR HAWAII

To attain the most desirable Hawaii 2000 we propose that the following steps be taken now.

1. Support all steps to internationalize basic production on the principle of bureaucratic organization, with rotating assignment of workers at all levels. Clearly, an important step in this direction will be to support this principle in the development of ocean resources.

2. Resist all efforts to release more State land to fee-simple ownership or to break up the large estates, while initiating a program to reacquire ownership of all land in Hawaii in the name of the politically organized community. Since our land-use controls are an inflationary factor as things stand now, we should control the price of land under the principle of unjust enrichment. Reacquisition would then no longer be a hopeless dream within our constitutional constraints.

3. Begin the planning immediately of diverse communities. If a large estate really wants to donate land for a second Oahu campus for the University of Hawaii, insist, for example, that it contribute to diversity by designing a community intended to realize the goals of women's liberation. Although we are already ahead of many communities in some dimensions of liberation, let us proceed systematically to find out now what are the full implications of this movement for physical and social community planning.

4. Move dramatically to match our centralized control of educational resources with decentralization of education. Serious experiments in this area are underway, and

we should get actively involved. We should, for example, facilitate progress in our own university's work in sequential integration, at the same time as we enlarge our horizons to prepare for the day of greater variation, and nonterritorial sequential integration, within a quasi-public sphere.

POSTSCRIPT

We hope that each reader will recognize the extent to which many of us feel rooted in the past in that we believe that the basic problems of human organization will not be greatly different in 2000 than they are today.

Nothing contained in this paper should be assumed to represent the firm conviction of any member of our task force; we share only our conviction that the problems we have discussed will be areas for decision that will, more than any others, serve to determine what kinds of people we citizens of Hawaii will be in 2000, and what kinds of lives we may live. But we do share our feelings about aloha.

A last word of caution: values change. In 1985 we may prefer some other alternative for 2000 than we do in 1970. In 1985 we may see new consequences for 2030 of the alternative futures in 2000. We may look further ahead and discover that we would rather travel on a different road than the one which appeared to us preferable in 1970. Decision theory may help us with this problem; it shows us how to estimate whether we should defer our decisions in some areas until 1985, and what the social costs or consequences might be for postponing the option to change directions now. Other changes in our preferences may not be attributable to new foresights, but rather to new insights. Under these conditions, it seems essential that Hawaii, as it looks toward its future, continuously reassess its values and goals and make appropriate changes in possible courses of action.

The Quality of Personal Life 2000
John F. McDermott, Jr.

John F. McDermott, Jr., M.D., is currently professor and chairman of the Department of Psychiatry at the University of Hawaii School of Medicine. Until 1969 he was a member of the faculty of the University of Michigan. He is the coauthor of *Psychiatry for the Pediatrician* (1970) and *The Psychopathology of Childhood* (1972), and has published articles in most psychiatric journals. He is a fellow of the American Psychiatric Association, the American Academy of Child Psychiatry, the American Orthopsychiatric Association, and the American College of Psychiatrists.

INTRODUCTION

As important as our conclusions is the process through which they have evolved. It expressed the capacity of the people of Hawaii to be concerned about the future and to attempt to understand and control the forces shaping it. Our single underlying premise is that the concept of quality control is even more important to apply to our biological, personal, and social experience than it is to our automobiles and refrigerators. Quality control can be engineered into our life experience in Hawaii if we are aware of just where we wish to be thirty years hence, and if we assess the means of getting there. One principle appears clear: we must change some of our current ways of life. A linear extension of more and more of what we already have and do will bring us more and more of the problems we are finding so intolerable today. We must redirect our attention from the measure of quantity to the quality of living.*

SOME OF TODAY'S PROBLEMS

The scientific revolution of the midtwentieth century has produced a significant disruption of the balance among the individual, the family, and society. The stunning advances of technology promise to accelerate at a breathtaking pace during the next thirty years, producing an even greater gap between our scientific and our human capabilities. Technology, which once was the slave of man, now threatens to become his master, and it is crucial to consider the consequences. For example, technology has permitted man to subdue nature, but it has also made him insensitive to it, with the result that massive pollution threatens our existence. For this reason, some critical values must be applied to technology so that it is not viewed as a creature of the new environment independent of the old. Rather, technology must be viewed as an extension of man and must be in harmony with overall objectives which consider the quality of his personal life.

EXAMPLES OF TECHNOLOGICAL FALLOUT

The computer allows for instant sharing and dissemination of information stored in central computer files located throughout the country. Technological eavesdropping, recording of our vital statistics, and even more personal data giving a complete description of the outer self of every individual is argued by some as necessary for national planning. Person-to-person relationships are being replaced by more remote impersonal connections of ever-proliferating state agencies and institutions which operate less and less through identifiable persons and more and more through computers. We have been losing the race to preserve the dimension of physical and geographical privacy in our lives. Waikiki is a good example of this loss, and a constant reminder of what must be planned against. As an island state we are exquisitely sensitive to population growth, and to the limit to physical expansion which is constantly visible. The loss of physical space and beauty is particularly hard for a people who are still in union with their surroundings, and where nature, the mountains, and the sea have daily meaning to everyone. Hawaiians do not live in an anonymous concrete city. That is why development and expansion such as Waikiki arouses such intense feeling in Hawaiians. It intrudes into their relationship with a nature which is a part of their lives. We are well aware of the implications of such growth for our well-being.

THE HIDDEN CRISIS

But the problems of pollution, privacy, and even population are only the most visible parts of the iceberg. Erosion of relationships and alienation of groups have become an expected part of fallout from technological advances. It has been generally agreed that, over the past century, technological development of a modern nation has required that the values of competition, achievement, self-advancement, individualism, and independence be allowed to flourish and be promoted. These "modern" values of an urban society needed for the technological age have replaced the predominant values of the older society in which large extended families or groups pre-dominated and required the allegiance and commitment of the individual. The shift in priority away from such values as respect, a sense of responsibility and obligation toward others, and affection (aloha) can be traced in part to the shift from the old extended to the modern nuclear family with its mobility. However, it would appear that an exag-gerated emphasis on the value orientation of the technological age has exceeded the natural evolvement in which a blend of the two sets of values, old and new, would occur, and the new one is becoming pathologically destructive in its overgrowth. In one sense it is seen in the so-called generation gap, a symptom of the conflict between, and a polarization of the points of view of, young and old. The erosion and dilution of relationships between

164

groups of people, the very qualities which humans in all parts of the world developed and redeveloped over thousands of generations, discovered and transmitted to new generations, rediscovered and modified through the long history of mankind — these qualities threaten to vanish. It is questionable how man will survive if they do. Certainly the pleasant, relatively easygoing way of life in Hawaii has given way to more and more pressure, confrontation, and competitive activities, more and more distress and hostility, so that much of the warmth and genuine charm of people, the goodwill and selflessness that was once typical of many residents of Hawaii seems to be disappearing.

A SECOND MAJOR FORCE IN THIS DIRECTION

Superimposed upon the values associated with and promoted by the technological explosion of the scientific age, major powerful social movements have arisen which will unquestionably shape the relationship of the individual, the family, and society in the next thirty years. They will significantly add to the stresses on the institution of the family, which, for the purposes of this inquiry, we are utilizing as a model to be studied. Women's liberation and the youth movement throughout the nation emphasize individuality, independence, and freedom of choice, attacking the structure of the established institutions as authoritarian, and further shifting the values from the group to the individual. At present society has accepted the principle *of these movements as pointing in a healthy direction if controlled in their implementation (that is, increased freedom of choice for the individual regarding his own personal functioning). Legislative trends toward the promotion and underwriting of modern contraceptive practices, the availability of unrestricted abortion, and the liberalization of divorce laws are examples of a trend which is likely to continue throughout the next decades. Here in Hawaii recent pioneering legislation has not only recog-*

nized but further developed this important trend toward individual autonomy versus legislative control over intimate areas of personal decision-making; that is, abortion is now a matter of individual (and family) choice.

By 2000 contraception and abortion will be universally practiced, and society will likely have imposed restrictive laws or positive incentives for the control of the size of families. A series of marital models will be available, ranging from (1) trial or temporary relationships, (2) those marked by one- three- or five-year periods, and (3) those which are permanent and with which the option of bearing and raising children will be associated, perhaps even licensed. Those individuals not oriented toward a permanent, stable relationship in which mutual sharing has replaced romantic excitement will not be denied any form of sanctioned relationship or forced into a single model of marriage. Thus, while divorce will be readily available without the punitive induction of an adversary system of hostility and guilt, it will not be utilized in the sense it is today. Rather, it will be less important as the only exit because of the varying permanence and intensity of marital relationships receiving official sanction.

THE PRICE WE MUST PAY

While these trends have already begun to be implemented because of their inherent merit — for example, individual choice versus coercion — they will add further serious, perhaps even critical, stress to the institutions of the past and present, on which we depend. Marriage and the family will no longer enjoy the stability they have in the past, but rather may be fragmented, revolving, serial, partial, and semipermanent as well as permanent. The shift in the primary function of the family from the rearing of children to the self-fulfillment of the individual partners will seriously affect the new generation of children. The family has been the primary group through

*which values have been communicated to new genera-
tions and in which capacity for relationships with others
is laid down. In the past the primary group (the family)
has been responsible for the building of character and
associated values in the individual child who will become
a member of that society. The child's primary group identification is the oldest and most powerful in its imprint
on him. The secondary identifications he makes in the
outside world also shape his values, but are more recently
acquired and more modifiable by changes in the social
structure. As discussed above, the secondary group
(society) has been shifting more and more in its value
orientation and the primary group is undergoing serious
stress (and even disorganization) with regard to its major
role in character formation of the individual.*

TOWARD SOLUTIONS

*It is thus apparent that considerable attention must
be given to primary and secondary group functions, their
futures and their complementarity. To some extent the
functions of primary and secondary groups must be
blended and mixed in the future, the one complementing
the other, rather than remaining separate from each other.
For example, by 2000 society will take more responsibility
for the value system which the individual acquires both
early and later in life. In this fashion our society will attempt
to restore the balance and to blend the competing
demands of individual expression, self-interest and privacy, with those of cooperation and close relationships
with others. Because of the speed with which technological change is occurring, certain of the values of society
are shifting dangerously from those maintaining harmonious group interrelationships toward those of individual
autonomy (an overbalance which threatens to topple the
family as an institution). Society has a responsibility to
maintain a balance in its value system just as it does in
its economic system.*

A UNIFYING FORCE

Perhaps more than in any other state in the union, the citizens of Hawaii identify themselves together, bound by unique customs, music, geography, and dress. Thus, a common bond, although loose and at first glance superficial, allows the citizens of this state to consider themselves "Hawaiian," an identification with a larger and earlier culture, unique to us as a group within the United States. This, as an example of a secondary social identification beyond that acquired in the family, may provide a base upon which to build certain values and attitudes which will enhance the quality of personal life for the people of this state. It is to be emphasized that the identity "Hawaiian" is to be one that is borrowed and shared rather than taken. It may already have provided the bridge through which multiple ethnic groups have related effectively.

It is highly unlikely that by 2000 we will be a "golden people," a true melting pot free of conflicts. The dream of complete acculturation and homogenization of the various racial groups in Hawaii will not be achieved by 2000. Rather, our ethnic groups will still retain some measure, although diminished, of their own identity, providing a series of balanced contrasts, and it is to be considered that the survival of these differences may be a source of cultural enrichment to be maintained. The coexistence of several races has been a significant factor in the success of Hawaii, perhaps because of the delicate balance of all as minorities, thus denying to any race the permanent fixed position of dominance. Yet further rubbing off of the sharp edges of conflict and antagonisms will continue for the next thirty years and will provide a laboratory for study of adaptive mechanisms which enable one race to deal effectively with another, a model for ourselves and for the rest of the world to study. One essential feature, however, will be the continued giving up by each group of a certain amount of its own cultural uniqueness in order to come together in a common commitment toward a shared "Hawaiian" identity. It is obvious that we identify ourselves more as "Hawaiians" than residents of other states do with their own statehood. It is the values of this Hawaiian identity which, without idealizing any one culture, take the best from each and provide a composite from which the others may draw, and thus find further common identifications. Here then is a form of ethnic difference which the individual and his group must voluntarily be willing to dilute to provide improved and extended relationships between Hawaiian peoples, a community group spirit of sociability which becomes embedded in everybody's lives.

ANCIENT VALUES FOR THE FUTURE

The historical traditions and racial configuration in Hawaii have produced values that are peculiar to Hawaii. Many of the old values have been forgotten. They may need to be reexamined and when appropriate reintegrated into the society of 2000. This is not to say that we are to revive the old Hawaiian society and attempt to integrate its social rules and regulations into the very complex society of 2000. Rather, we should consider an attempt to reconstruct old values which can be rebuilt into newer social structures and provide newer mechanisms for relationships among people, very much as the old Hawaii has been blended into our architecture, music, and dress. For example, it may well be that we could profitably study the Hawaiian concept of 'ohana, which has been described as a highly structured system of relationships among members of an extended family living in a given geographical area. Within the 'ohana there was room for a display of considerable independence by men and women of strong character. However, in all matters of major concern, the 'ohana always functioned as a unit. For example, land or fishing grounds were not owned privately but by the 'ohana. This was a recognition that in a closed ecosystem the ownership of a resource must be secondary to the use of that resource for the greatest good of the whole. A second Hawaiian value, ho'oponopono, was a problem-solving technique evolved within the 'ohana. Ho'oponopono means "setting to right of wrongs" and provided an opportunity for problems to be brought into the open in the presence of all the people involved in the problem. Each person had a chance to speak out in the most personal terms and when everyone was aware of how each felt, the group reached a solution of the problem and that solution was binding on all parties. In old Hawaii it provided for integration of nature, the old, the young, and ancestors. A statewide computerized ho'oponopono via television might be created for the future. It would have assisted the statewide discussion which occurred prior to abortion legislation in 1970.

A third Hawaiian value, the concept of kokua, provided the foundation for an economic system based primarily on cooperation, but with considerable elbow-room for competition. Under this system it was important that one expression of kokua be repaid with another expression of kokua because such payments or gifts determined status within the 'ohana.

RECOMMENDATIONS FOR THE FUTURE

The following recommendations are made as serious attempts to begin to plan for a society in 2000. They take into account the effects of social and scientific trends that are shaping our institutions, such as the family, to a significant degree and which may topple them unless they are modernized by 2000.

Two major factors are to be considered: (1) the value system built into the developing individual (both because of the present structure of the family and society) is over-balanced toward self-interest and away from group-interest; and (2) the family as we have known it as the primary group shaping the individual's character and his *attitudes is under serious assault and will no longer exist in the same form in 2000. It is thus important that society restructure its role and anticipate sharing with the family certain of its responsibilities — that is, childrearing. Child-rearing, previously the most important function and the cement that held the family together, may not be the primary function in many families now, and may not be for most families in 2000. The control of population by the promotion of childless and one-child families, the new forms of officially sanctioned relationships between adults which are less permanent than the single marital model offered today, the mobility of families, the individuality and independence promoted among its members by social trends today, are all to be considered serious stresses. We must anticipate the problems created by these trends and compensate for them by modernizing our system. It is thus recommended that:*

1. The school experience be considered an extension of the family experience, and thus share with the family the dimensions of education in attitudes and values. It is crucial that by 2000 citizens will have worked together with the Department of Education to shape the precise values to be transmitted so that this vital area of character formation will not be ignored, or left to the idiosyncratic approach of the individual teacher. Now is the time to study the role of the school in the socialization of the child.

2. The welfare system, which has helped shape the individual personality and the family structure of so many, is universally agreed to be in need of great reform. It should be restructured to blend primary (family) and secondary (community) group functions for the future, to promote in the people it serves values, characteristics, and attitudes which are important for their development and successful adaptation. Thus economics should be the independent variable, the means and not the end.

It is agreed by most that certain personality characteristics are influenced and even shaped by a welfare system — for example, dependence versus independence. Thus a planned approach toward this issue and experimental programs seem crucial. For instance the concept of "work" may need considerable reassessment and modification by 2000. A major work within the family, especially for the mother, has been childrearing. Today it is often compared unfavorably with work outside the family, and equated with drudgery because of its tedious, unrelenting, and sometimes discouraging character. However, to insure that the highest priority of society is toward children, its greatest natural resource, it may become necessary for childrearing to be socially, legally, and economically defined as work. In this way it would achieve a status as important as other forms of careers, with extrinsic as well as intrinsic rewards.

Training for childrearing (just as for any other occupation) would be available, and appropriate pay and vacation periods would be marked off to further define and recognize its crucial importance. Not only would its importance be guaranteed as a role equal to any other career, but also society would share responsibility with parents who currently experience lonely frustration because total childrearing becomes a burden which they cannot adequately discharge twenty-four hours a day over a period of years by themselves. In sharing this responsibility, society will need actually to assume the role of parent in some cases. Inevitably, many children will be born for whom full-time mothering in the usual family structure will not be available. This may occur for a variety of reasons — for example, the wishes of the mother to work at another role, psychological interferences with full-time mothering capacity, separation and divorce, and so forth.

To provide adequate care for the emotional development of these children, a combined home-school experi-

ence, a family substitute organized as group childrearing experiences, should be available. Sufficient experience with childrearing centers in Israel has now clearly demonstrated that through planned group childrearing (provided when the mother-child bond is not available or practicable except on a part-time basis) personalities can be shaped in positive rather than negative directions. (It has been discovered that there is a particularly desirable extra dividend of enhanced outward or extended attachments, strong loyalties and sense of responsibility, developed by the youngsters toward the larger group.) Various levels and degrees of parental participation in these childrearing centers would be available, so that some mothers who were not ready for mothering could be released for different work, others involved in a partial way most satisfying to them and the children, and others devoting all of their time to childrearing, not only with their own but with other children as well.

A new profession, that of childrearing specialist, would be developed, consisting of individuals who would live with the children and serve as ongoing parental substitutes for youngsters without adequate family lives. The centers would also serve as training sites. The specialists there would serve as trainers for parents who were planning to have children, and for those who were already raising children of their own. Prevention of problems would begin to replace the rehabilitative measures of today which are so expensive, time-consuming, and only partially effective. The most important considerations would be that (a) those who are not equipped for childrearing or do not wish to rear children, would not be employed in this role, a rule of thumb that applies to other occupations; and that (b) other options for assistance in the rearing of children would be available to those families either on a full-time or a part-time basis.

3. New groups, often serving as family substitutes,

are spontaneously springing up all around us, as, for example, in communes. Often they develop for specific purposes, are sometimes semipermanent and sometimes temporary. The effect of such activities is the creation of new cultures. One would expect that a place like Hawaii, with its multiethnic population and its commitment to racial harmony, would be the most tolerant to diversity as it arises from the appearance of such groups. But we all know that Hawaii's tolerance is limited to some specific types of diversity, so that the reaction to new experimental groups, especially when they profess to values and develop living styles which are in conflict with those of established groups, are received without enthusiasm, or at best with very mixed reactions. It is recommended that experimental, naturally occurring groups be encouraged, especially those which do not harm individuals in the group or threaten directly other established groups through unwanted encroachment or profession of violence. Once experimental living groups are encouraged, we may expect all kinds of interesting communities to develop. It is most important that we study and allow these groups to communicate their experiences to us in order to evaluate possible new models for the future. The university might sponsor as a major intercollege effort the study of such groups that already exist in the military, university, yacht basin, and various other housing clusters.

4. Individual efforts by those who feel the need to establish their own new patterns of relating to others can be contagious. Large-scale community and media efforts toward improving individual relationships and improving values may be encouraged. A very basic example which achieved substantial support at the governor's conference consisted of an attempt to lessen the strained relationships between drivers and pedestrians by encouraging that hitchhikers be picked up. Some suggested that a shift in role from driver to hitchhiker would be helpful in promoting flexibility.

CONCLUSION

The consultant to this task force, René Dubos, [1] *often speaks of the "genius" of Hawaii. We must learn to define and cultivate it, for if we do, as he states, "you will be able to handle a large tourist trade without losing your soul and the qualities of life you value." The search has just begun!*

1. René Dubos, bacteriologist, has been on the staff of the Rockefeller Institute for Medical Research (now Rockefeller University) since 1927 except for three years when he was George Fabyan Professor of Comparative Pathology and Tropical Medicine at Harvard University Medical School. Increasingly during the past twenty-five years, he has devoted himself to the study of the biomedical, psychological, and social problems arising from the effects of the technological environment on modern man. He has discussed these problems in several books, including *The Dreams of Reason* (1961), *Man Adapting* (1965), *Man, Medicine and the Environment* (1968), *So Human an Animal* (1968), and *A God Within* (1972). He is also coauthor of a new book, *Only One Earth: The Care and Maintenance of a Small Planet*, prepared for the United Nations Conference on the Human Environment held in Stockholm in June 1972.

The Natural Environment 2000

Walter K. Collins

Walter K. Collins is president and principal in charge of planning with Belt, Collins and Associates, Ltd., engineers, planners and landscape architects. His areas of special competence include urban planning and master planning, project organization and administration. He has completed numerous visitor destination studies as well as resort and recreation area land-use and development studies. He has traveled widely studying resort design and operation in all parts of the world, especially in tropical and subtropical offshore areas.

F or centuries man has treated the land, sea, and air as though they were limitless. Today, especially in land-deficient Hawaii, man begins to realize that they are not. Nature's self-renewing cycles that normally rejuvenate the land, sea, and air are being disrupted, and hence the very basis of life itself is threatened.

Of the questions concerning Hawaii's future, none is more pressing in the public mind today than the matter of environmental quality. It might also be said that none is less understood. Perhaps that sense of urgency and uncertainty helps explain the interest that has given this task force on the natural environment such a large membership. Despite the seemingly complacent attitudes currently found in large segments of United States society, this degree of unexpected response by concerned citizens is striking testimony to the willingness of people to engage in meaningful community service if given opportunity and incentive. This point is essential to the fulfillment of recommendations presented by each year-2000 committee.

The assignment of this task force has been to identify and assess Hawaii's environmental attributes, to suggest environmental conditions desirable for the future and the means to attain them. These guidelines were modified by the task force as its studies and analyses came to reveal that specific forecasts are simply not possible nor even desirable in view of rapidly changing social and technological circumstances. Data concerning the causal relationships and interdependence of life systems are distressingly incomplete. What has emerged from six months of task-force sessions is a recognition that Hawaii has unique attributes, both obvious and subtle, which make it possible if not imperative for this State to lead the way in resolving environmental problems.

In the context of this conference on Hawaii 2000, then, the natural environment is understood to embrace all biotic and physical elements necessary to the physiological and psychological health of mankind.

POPULATION AND TECHNOLOGICAL OUTFALL

No consideration of the natural environment can lightly dismiss the impact of a growing population or the adverse side of technological achievements. Some people are inclined toward the view that, unless immediate and drastic measures are taken to halt population growth and to legislate against a wide range of commercial products, mankind faces imminent annihilation. Others lean to the opposite extreme, taking the more optimistic attitude that these problems have a way of solving themselves.

It does seem reasonable to assume that man is basically a rational animal who is moved to take actions that improve his circumstances and avoid those that worsen them. Yet it can also be argued that history would produce at least as many examples that illustrate the irrationality with which men and governments have directed their energies and wasted their resources.

This paper takes a middle position that acknowledges the urgency of these problems of population and the detrimental effects of technology, but also agrees that man can resolve these issues if he makes conscious effort to inform himself of the consequences and to accept the compromises necessary to their solution. First steps can certainly be taken immediately toward longer goals, as indeed they have been. But if man is to survive and progress toward a higher destiny, he must look ahead with a reasonably positive attitude tempered with a greater degree of caution than he has exhibited in the past.

Let us focus briefly on these problems as they relate to Hawaii. There are some who strongly urge that there should be a maximum limit on the number of people allowed to reside in these islands. It is difficult to quarrel with that objective as one grows increasingly aware of the impact our relatively small population has already had on Hawaii's natural environment. The problem is to determine what that ceiling should be.

Estimates of Hawaii's native population at the time of Western discovery in 1778 range upward to 400,000 souls, with a fairly proportionate distribution among the populated islands. Today, in excess of 750,000 persons reside in Hawaii, over 75 percent of whom are concentrated on Oahu, third in size of the seven inhabited islands. It is entirely possible that Hawaii could support a much greater resident population without unduly straining the islands' natural resources or fatally upsetting their ecological balances. In this connection many factors come into play that only future generations will be equipped to weigh. As examples, we are told that man's work habits are changing; that it is distinctly possible that poverty, as the term is understood today, will not exist in the future; habitation patterns may alter radically from those to which past and present generations have become accustomed;

more efficient uses of urban zones, even today, might comfortably accommodate a more sizeable population.

Contrary to many earlier forecasts, recent census figures show that the neighboring islands have not experienced significant population growth during the past two decades, while their largely agricultural economies show signs of decline. These factors could support an argument favoring a greater population, dispersed more evenly throughout the islands.

While the foregoing position focuses heavily on available space and its most efficient use for human habitation, the heart of the issue concerns not so much the space factor as it does population's impact on the continuing life-giving resources of the islands and their adjacent waters. Contamination of Hawaii's presently clean and abundant water resources may grow excessive as larger numbers of people in an increasingly technological era generate greater volumes of waste and use more detrimental pesticides and other poisons that find their way to Hawaii's subterranean and surface-water stores. In proportion to size, population also contributes pollutants to the air from vehicle-exhaust emission, burning of consumer debris and industrial residue, as evidenced on those infrequent days when the predominant trade winds are stilled. Reef and sea life have a capacity to survive only an optimum amount of foreign substance discharged into their midst, and that is influenced almost exclusively by population numbers and the degree to which measures are taken to restrict deposit of their wastes into inshore and offshore waters. Unique plant, animal, and insect forms that have adapted and evolved in the isolated Hawaiian environment have disappeared, some beyond salvation, through the clearing of land and introduction of exotic, more dominant species; unharnessed population growth only aggravates the trend and speeds their demise.

Hawaii's aesthetic qualities, her most visible

attributes, continue to undergo dramatic change as population growth makes ever increasing demands on the islands' resources. Quiet serenity, once a distinctive feature of Hawaii, is now punctuated with the piercing sounds of jet aircraft, the roar of high speed traffic, and the drone of heavy diesel machinery. Views from urban areas are obscured by the next high-rise structure, and the mountain slopes beyond are ribboned with residential subdivisions as the forests recede ever further. In the zeal to build and profit from population expansion, remnants of the ancient Hawaiian culture are indiscriminately bulldozed and destroyed to serve the interests of speculation and exploitation, in the process destroying irretrievable chapters of Hawaii's untold history. In the most remote and seemingly untouched spots, one can seldom escape evidence of man's presence in growing numbers: the ubiquitous aluminum beverage can in an undersea eden, cigaret filters in a hidden valley paradise, and styrofoam jugs discarded with abandon.

The population capacity of Hawaii's islands appears directly related to the degree and skill exercised in controlling the by-products of man's technological achievements, the extent of the community's general understanding of environmental fragility, and the ability of the populace to accept radically new attitudes toward the uses of the land and sea.

Great strides have in fact been taken by Hawaii's legislative bodies to create the type of legislation that would regulate the impact that man and his tools have wrought on the Hawaiian environment. The enforcement agencies, regrettably, have been slow to utilize the powers now available to them. An office of environmental quality control responsible directly to the state executive is in process of formation, supported by laws that bestow far-ranging authority. Statewide statutes relating specifically to air and water pollution and noise abatement now number over thirty. Measures that establish and administer conservation zones, wildlife preserves, forest and watershed management programs, beautification, parks and open space, land use, historical sites and relics, are now law. Again, however, there is all too little visible evidence that the regulatory and enforcement agencies charged with implementing these programs are exercising their respective powers and responsibilities.

In response to community concern, the members of the 1971 legislature drafted bills to improve present statutes and add new ones to deal with an even broader range of environmental concerns. Thus, the issue of whether Hawaii's population should be larger or smaller than at present cannot be resolved until our successors can evaluate the results of Hawaii's legislative efforts to reach an accord with nature. It is reasonable to project, however, that science and social consciousness will have found acceptable means to control population in relation to Hawaii's natural resources and the life systems of which man is only a part.

CHANGING VALUES

Other factors that must not be discounted when evaluating Hawaii's natural environment are the distinct tendencies toward changing values in an increasingly affluent society. Analysts versed in these matters point to evidence that seems to support a trend toward guaranteed income; increased leisure that will leave people more free time to pursue individual and community interests; a growing respect for authority of knowledge rather than authority of position; and a continuing process of reallocation of government functions between federal and local governments. These trends, as we are beginning to put them into perspective, tell us that the future outlook for mankind and his natural environment can be bright and exciting, although many would just as soon complete their lives under conditions with which they are familiar and to which they have grown accustomed.

Change is accelerating at such a pace that some

experts feel universal trauma would be inevitable if that pace becomes extreme. But, by and large, most change, while unavoidable, is subtle. And, before one realizes it, that which was revolutionary in concept has become commonplace in practice, and that which was dear has been discarded or forgotten. Thirty or forty years ago the prospect of television in the home, flights on jumbo jets, or ventures to the moon were inconceivable to most people. Today their acceptance verges on complacency. So let us not close our minds to future innovations which may seem impossible or impractical when measured against our ingrained habits and past experiences. By future standards, 1970 may look primitive.

THE NECESSITY FOR OPTIONS

Today's observer is newly conscious of the dynamic and subtle changes in his environment, and he senses that there are forces at work that might have adverse implications for the human species. But for the most part he does not know the full impact of those forces on his own life and his life-support system because science, if it does already know, has not made such knowledge universal. Man can, however, see enough warning signs to stir his concern. Lacking the necessary knowledge and comprehension, he is led to speculate on the potential effects of such phenomena as population trends, pollution, depletion of nonrenewable natural resources, ecological balances, and social institutions. The very art of forecast or conjecture under these conditions, at best, is imprecise.

Recognizing these variables as limiting factors in conceiving environmental goals as distant as thirty years, it would be shortsighted to offer any specific recommendations regarding Hawaii's natural environment in 2000 that would have the effect of restricting future actions. Rather, it is the purpose of this paper to suggest some measures that might be taken to insure the widest flexibility in dealing with the environment as man's knowledge, needs,

and aspirations change — leaving open to future generations the largest number of options for shaping environmental conditions as they become more clearly understood in the light of scientific data and technological
capabilities existing at that time.

If man today had infinite knowledge of the workings
of his universe, he might be justified in prestructuring
the entire life-support systems for future generations
because his powers of foresight and prediction would be
nearly complete. In the absence of that knowledge, he
must accept responsibility for the future by not depriving
the future of the resources it may need for its own existence. Nor should man burden the future with the residues
from his own attempts at solving present problems. Much
of man's current action results in accumulation of rubbish
for disposal by the future. Consequently, we must allow
our children and grandchildren and their progeny as many
possible alternatives for dealing with environmental matters as their greater knowledge and different values will
dictate. These options, then, form the nucleus of this
paper.

IMPERMANENCE

Man seems instinctively to think in terms of permanence: a lasting structure or monument, a business
empire, a political or social institution, a perpetual trust,
certain customs and traditions. While such things can have
certain lasting qualities, in reality they are truly temporary
because they either have a life span or can be terminated.
Only death or extinction seems to have the capacity for
endless duration, and the natural environment is peculiarly
vulnerable to that form of permanence. A species of bird,
fish, or reptile, once extinct, cannot be regenerated by
man. Plant species are equally susceptible. Were man himself to expire as a species, as some think imminent, it
is doubtful that evolutionary processes would ultimately
re-create him in his present form.

Recognizing that all life forms are intimately dependent on one another and respond to the basic normal processes of Mother Nature, it is to mankind's undying benefit that nature's system of operation be thoroughly understood, and, until such knowledge has been mastered, to cease interfering with her methods to the extent possible. Thus, "impermanence" becomes essential in our treatment of Hawaii's natural environment if future generations are to have an opportunity to apply their better tools, in the form of knowledge and skills, to fashion their natural environment. The value of options assumes greater relevance.

AN ENLIGHTENED COMMUNITY

If one thinks of goals as broad aims toward which effort should be directed, then the ultimate goal is to return as much of Hawaii's natural environment as possible to its most beneficial state: cleansing the air and water of harmful substances and their sources, and maintaining an abundance of oxygen-producing plant life; keeping water in a desired state of purity, recycling wastes, utilizing biodegradable materials, and preventing release of poisons into the sea and air or onto the land; reclaiming shorelines and marshes from urban invasion and returning them to uses least likely to inhibit natural ecological functions; and to restrict the large-scale introduction of new products and practices into the environment until their full impact on natural life systems is thoroughly tested and understood.

It would seem that the fundamental obstacle to achieving these objectives is man's uncertain knowledge of the environmental processes. This shortcoming should be corrected because it has profound implications with respect to man's values and aspirations, his political system, economic growth and stability, education, social institutions and even his life-style.

Taking the political aspect as an example, today's electorate is not adequately equipped to deal effectively with environmental matters. It is not sufficiently informed to *recognize what constitutes a pollutant, its effect on mankind, or the nature of the pyramiding interdependence of all life forms. Thus, the voter is handicapped in his efforts to translate concern into political action until a crisis situation develops. So that the electorate can become more adept in selecting and thinking on a level consistent with its representatives to improve and sustain a healthy environment, it is necessary to instill a sense of community service and to involve many more citizens in the process of community problem-solving. In turn, this requires continual relearning to keep pace with new knowledge produced by science. The practice and motivation for community involvement, if instituted as part of the educational system, could be self-inducing within a single generation, particularly if deliberate provision is made for continuing the practice into adulthood. The conference task forces can attest to the surprising eagerness of people to participate in community service. The time and effort spent in self-education, attending lectures and group discussions, at varying degrees of financial sacrifice, is a clear indication that there exists in our society a latent interest in participation in community decision-making and problem-solving that should be encouraged instead of suppressed. An involved citizenry is more likely to keep itself informed of the consequences resulting from the sins perpetrated on its natural environment than one which depends solely on the wisdom of its political representatives whose primary objective is often self-perpetuation in power.*

Studies indicate that there is a distinct trend in America today toward a realignment of governmental functions that will have the ultimate effect of returning many problem-solving activities from the federal government to the local level. Among the several causes for this phenomenon is a growing realization that local problems and their solutions are best understood by the community most closely affected. This would serve to support the contention that greater individual involvement should be encouraged in community matters. Hawaii, as an isolated geographic region, is in a unique position to promote community participation as an eventual way of life. Its governmental jurisdictions are simplified, unlike many mainland areas where counties, municipalities, districts, boroughs, and service zones, frequently overlap with duplications of authority and function. Furthermore, Hawaii is free of the type of ethnic and social segregation which tends to induce the inflexible attitudes found elsewhere. Together, these two factors make it considerably easier for Hawaii's people to think, plan, and act on a regional scale.

Another factor that contributes to the renewed concept of citizen participation is the trend toward more leisure and changes in the attitude of work for work's sake. As more and more human occupations are taken over by mechanization and other technological products, and if disposable incomes continue to grow as forecast, people will have considerably more time to pursue less material objectives that have greater personal meaning and more relevance to their ideals. This may mean continuous, lifelong pursuit of knowledge in any chosen field, whether it be art, design, music, government, philosophy, craftsmanship, or any other area of self-fulfillment. Knowledge relating to any of the infinite aspects of natural processes and the environment will likewise be sought. As people find more time and incentive to gain the knowledge necessary to shape and control their natural environment, one can foresee the day when environment can truly be considered a regional trust administered by an enlightened community.

COOPERATIVE PLANNING

Governmental structure and ethnic compatibility are not the only unique factors that can permit Hawaii to lead the way to environmental enlightenment. A major asset favoring the correction and maintenance of nature's environmental balances in Hawaii can be found in the existing form of land tenure and the State's pacesetting land-classification system. What to many people has been a restrictive and inequitable practice in land ownership in Hawaii can actually be turned to enormous advantage as one contemplates ways and means to insure that future generations will inherit a clean and efficient environment.

The State and federal governments, together with the major landed trusts and principal agricultural concerns, own over 80 percent of Hawaii's land. Because the great bulk of land is held in so few hands, there is growing motivation for public and private landowners to join in cooperative planning efforts that effectively subordinate property boundaries to the greater interest of coordinated regional land-use patterns. Such cooperative ventures have been attempted successfully in several instances, particularly on the islands of Maui and Hawaii. From the viewpoint of environmental quality, this harmonious approach to land-use planning is especially significant in that (1) it encourages a broader evaluation of environmental resources in relation to human needs, and (2) it brings together the expertise of both government and private interests to solve environmental problems in concert.

Even where public land is not involved, private landholders are finding it increasingly expedient to work with government on both the State and county levels in planning uses for their properties. Unfortunately, it is in this situation that government is most vulnerable to organized pressures from private interests whose forces are well marshaled. In some glaring instances, government has shown itself on occasion to be susceptible to such pressure tactics and has knowingly permitted commercial development and private speculative ventures to encroach on prime agricultural land, on habitats of endangered wildlife species, in volcanic rift zones, and in areas of rare archaeological significance. Ponds, marshes, lagoons, and reef areas have been allowed to be filled and covered

187

in the name of reclamation; and residential subdivision permits have been sanctioned on steep mountain slopes, resulting in extensive erosion and visual blight.

LAND-USE LAW

Hawaii's land-use law is a singular vehicle for promoting joint planning efforts on a regional or subregional basis with a view to protecting environmental qualities consistent with human needs. To have greater effectiveness, the land-use law should be revised periodically to improve its application. Serious thought should be given to refining the land classifications, particularly the agriculture and conservation designations. For ecological purposes, the two zones serve similar roles, and could be subcategories under a general open or nonurban classification that is expanded to embrace offshore areas.

As presently defined, the conservation district is a misnomer in practice because varied urban and commercial uses are permitted at the discretion of the land-use commission. Private interests can thereby be tempted to apply leverage to gain permits for urban uses within a conservation district to the detriment of the nature communities, water resources, and historical and recreation sites that are otherwise preserved there.

The shoreline areas of Hawaii's territorial waters, including bays and lagoons, ponds and reefs, have been especially neglected from the time that urbanization and technology have reached critically influential levels. The decay of marine communities near urbanized and recreational areas has reached alarming proportions. To reverse the deterioration of Hawaii's shoreline assets and restore ecological balances, a major step could be taken by classifying and regulating all shoreline areas under the State's land-use law.

TIME ZONING

The land-use law provides for periodic review and modification of boundaries for all land in each of the four existing classifications in relation to then-current needs. That provision has special significance for correction and preservation of environmental balances because it allows recurring change in the treatment of land, and even of the offshore areas if the law were so amended.

As stated, the fundamental premise of this paper is the necessity for leaving open the options for future generations to control their own environment, and it is only through a system that provides for change that this can be guaranteed. Review and change of land-use boundaries can insure such impermanence, and is the forerunner of the concept of time zoning as distinguished from use zoning.

Zoning for a designated span of time is a radical departure from the customary practice of zoning for specific uses that are intended to be more or less permanent. Virtually all contemporary zoning ordinances are designed to discourage change, committing land to its established uses almost in perpetuity. Thus, once an industrial complex becomes established, say along a shoreline area, it is practically inconceivable to attempt its removal or relocation should it be determined that the region is needed for recreational space or that industrial effluent in the flow of the shoreline current has caused severe damage to marine communities. Similarly, once agricultural land is committed to residential or other urban use, its future agricultural potential is written off forever.

Time zoning, on the other hand, assigns deadlines to all land uses so that, as technologies, life-styles, and consequent needs change, obsolete or incompatible uses can be progressively erased and converted to other uses more beneficial to the community. Buildings and other structures would be designed and planned for an intentional life span limited to the lease and zoned periods which could be identical. This method of zoning has encouraging implications for the future health of Hawaii's natural resources. As a zoned time period approaches expiration, that section of land or sea can be reevaluated for its better use as determined by prevailing needs and conditions. Thus, a constant renewal of environmental balances could be assured.

TAXATION

Brief mention should be made of the inequities of Hawaii's land-taxation practices, and their net effect of lowering environmental quality. The State has long been mindful of the need to preserve Hawaii's very limited agricultural land, and the pioneering land-use law was devised essentially for that purpose. In more recent years, a concern for open space, sound long-range land planning, recreational areas, historical sites, wildlife refuges, and uncontrolled urban growth has become increasingly evident. Legislation has been passed and public policies announced toward those ends.

Property assessment and land taxes can be especially effective tools for encouraging desired land practices and discouraging those land activities considered detrimental to the general interest. But in Hawaii where real property tax rates are established by the respective county jurisdictions and assessment valuations are determined by the State, government taxation practices are often in direct opposition to and negate the very objectives the various land laws have been designed to accomplish. Taxes on agricultural land, particularly ranches, have forced owners to sell marginal acreage to speculators and developers or to move into urban land development themselves. Properties that are zoned for agriculture or open space, which may be shown on a county's long-range general plan for eventual urban use, are given a designation called "unimproved residential," assessed and taxed accordingly. Thus, the landowner is often forced to proceed with urban development, although the economic climate, community need and public land policy are against it. This inconsistency, which can be blamed for many of Hawaii's environmental problems arising from urbanization, must be rectified and greater communication and coordination established between the State departments of taxation and of land.

Furthermore, serious study should be given to the tax board's definition of "highest and best use" of land. Shoreline areas are universally assessed at the highest rates, which only promotes greater urbanization of one of Hawaii's most environmentally and ecologically vulnerable regions.

RESOURCE PLANNING BOARD

To aid in periodic evaluations of uses affecting land and sea, it is urged that a statewide resource planning board be established to undertake and constantly update a detailed inventory of natural and human resources in Hawaii as a permanent store of essential information. This should also be the agency to collect historical and cultural data. The resource planning board should be staffed primarily with environmentalists and other technicians who are even now being trained in universities for this purpose. Provision should be made as soon as practical for an ecological computer bank to store the resource data. The computer bank would be of infinite value in governmental decision-making, and would likewise serve community service groups and others involved in educational and problem-solving pursuits. Succeeding the computer bank will be computers whose store of data will be supplemented with a capability enabling it to analyze a proposal and register an objection if it detects some potentially harmful effect on the natural environment.

The resource planning board could also serve to determine population questions.

POOLING OF LAND, SEA, AND AIR RESOURCES

Another technique for managing environmental quality could evolve from a successful cooperative approach to land planning, or from an extension of land-use law refinement, or even become a direct objective in itself if circumstances in the future were so tailored: the actual pooling of private and public lands, together with offshore waters and air rights, into custody of a central trust. However, the concept of relinquishing private ownership of land and air rights is one that will bear intensive investigation. The traditional Hawaiian practice of owning sea rights as extensions of the land was abolished officially by the courts in 1968.

It should be noted that the concept of individual land ownership is a relatively recent phenomenon that historically follows the decline of feudal institutions. Today, especially in the Western world, land has come to be treated as a commodity, rather than the resource it actually is and has been in terms of preserving environmental, and hence human, health. As a commodity, it has been seen to give rise to speculation for personal gain which can have the ultimate effect of pitting private benefit against public need in matters of zoning, public services, recreation space, and the other areas inherently in the public interest such as air and sea contamination along with other ecological concerns.

Land ownership served well as an incentive in the colonizing and growth of pioneer societies that were largely agricultural, and still serves to provide some of the diffusion of political power that is a basis for representative government. It also serves to satisfy the "territorial imperative"[1] that seems instinctive in most animal life to one degree or another.

The most recent trends toward increasing mobility of the population, and less political dominance by rural-based populations, in the United States seem to indicate that the younger generations are finding less significance in land ownership. These generations and the ones that follow will inherit the environmental problems created today, and, if they place greater emphasis on environmen-

1. Robert Ardrey, *The Territorial Imperative* (New York: Atheneum, 1966).

tal quality than on material gain, it can be expected that land ownership may very well decline as a fundamental goal in life. Increasingly, as is evident even today, land ownership may be seen as merely another income-producing investment for expected future income.

Speculation in and of itself is not inherently evil, to be sure. But no matter what one's sociopolitical persuasions, the practice of land speculation ceases to be an individual's inalienable right when a point is reached that the practice works to the overwhelming disadvantage of the populace at large in the face of mounting population pressures and growing disruption of nature's essential functions.

Again, the fact that the greatest portion of Hawaii's land has so few owners makes it possible to consolidate all that land and adjacent waters into a giant foundation with shares held proportionally by the contributing owners, similar in manner to a mutual fund investment or condominium. Administration of such a foundation's assets might be conducted by trustees drawn from a cross-section of the community, separate from government, and reflecting a broad range of skills. Criteria for selection or election of trustees, description of their duties, terms of office, could be set forth in a charter or deed of trust.

Following transfer of land to the resource foundation, land would be leased back to its previous users on a franchise basis for varying periods, determined by a system of priorities designed to maintain a balance between urban use, agricultural requirements, and other needs as they change from time to time. Sea rights could be handled similarly. Lease income from the combined assets of the resource foundation might pay dividends to its shareholders. In this way, the various trust estates, especially the charitable trusts, could be assured of continuing fulfillment of their commitments to beneficiaries without being forced, as they are now, to put their respective holdings *to urban or other commercial uses that may prove incompatible with the long-range community interest.*

Trusts, by their very nature, are mandated to maximize income from their assets. This aim could still be accomplished under the resource-foundation concept, or the trusts might be allowed to convert their lands into other assets. Those trust estates whose lands were not productive due to location would be relieved of the necessity to find productive uses, however marginal.

Shares might be determined by acreage, by fair market value, or by some other measure combining those factors. By pooling their landed resources under some formula, all could benefit and the estates would be relieved of certain critical administrative pressures.

Some resource-foundation income might be set aside to eventually acquire the remaining land outstanding in fee-simple ownership. To discourage interim speculative sales of such land, there could be a severe but graduated capital-gains tax imposed on the profit from such sales. In any case, a reasonably long period such as fifty to seventy-five years should be set for all land acquisitions so that the current land owners would not be unduly penalized and would have ample opportunity to reconcile their estates. All land in Hawaii could gradually come under control of the resource foundation so that leasehold, to which Hawaii has long been conditioned, would become the sole mode of private land holding.

In addition to removing land from the realm of speculation, the notion of a land pool could reinforce the concept of recurring options through the structuring of lease terms to coincide with a time zoning program. As leases and zoning periods approach simultaneous expiration, each parcel's use could be reassessed in relation to then-current needs and conditions, drawing on data housed in the ecological bank. This flexibility in land and sea policy could then assure the constant renewal of Hawaii's natural environment.

ENVIRONMENTAL BENEFITS

The quality of Hawaii's natural environment can be immeasurably enhanced and sustained by the adoption of some of the ideas set forth in this paper, and it is interesting to project what changes might occur.

For example, existing neighborhoods might in time be relocated entirely. It is not inconceivable that Honolulu's urban concentration would eventually shift away from the shore and the mountainsides to selected valleys, where self-contained communities in compact vertical structures would line the extremities. The valley floors would remain as great natural parks, with all human amenities and services confined within the perimeter structures. The waterfront that is presently occupied by commercial, residential, and industrial buildings would be reclaimed. The neighbor islands, not so densely urbanized yet, could be developed similarly as future conditions dictate. The city of Hilo, in the process of relocating itself away from the waterfront as a result of the 1960 tsunami devastation, gives a contemporary example of how shorelines, for instance, can be reclaimed from urban use if deliberate measures are initiated.

Land that is presently in commercial agricultural production might also be returned to a natural state as the techniques for more efficient production of crops and livestock in enclosed multilevel structures become refined. This practice, already in use in the midwestern United States, could easily become a compatible use within residential zones. The same holds true with utility systems and certain industries as they become increasingly contained within structures that recycle and otherwise dispose of their residue in a manner nondetrimental to man and his environment.

The implications for the natural environment, from the viewpoint of water resources, wilderness, recreation, aesthetics, and the natural processes of the sea, air, and
land could be eminently favorable. By making more

efficient use of our urban land through different density patterns and new concepts of urban design, the amount of land in urban and agricultural use might actually decline over the long run, while supporting much greater population demands if the future deems that acceptable. More land can be allowed to revert to some natural condition, to remain so in perpetuity at the discretion of future generations.

CONCLUSION

In ancient Hawaii, the sea was considered an extension of the land for purposes of control. Tidal areas, inshore and offshore fishing areas, were linked. And conservation was practiced both on the land and in the sea.

The last of anything was never used. Marine creatures were never collected when spawning, and birds caught for their feathers were always released. Species of plants, birds, and fish were placed under kapu *(tabu) at various times to insure their regeneration for future abundance. The fertility of the land was replenished following harvest, and measures were taken to stem erosion when natural water courses were diverted.*

What has been described in this report is in reality a return to an ancient Hawaiian pattern of land and sea management under the aegis of an enlightened community rather than of an absolute monarch.

Housing and Transportation 2000
Aaron Levine

Aaron Levine has been a professional city planner since 1947, and since 1962 has served as president of the Oahu Development Conference. He is a graduate of the universities of California and Pennsylvania and is a past national president of the American Society of Planning Officials.

ur task force had three assigned goals: to assess the future housing and transportation characteristics of Hawaii, both with and without change in trends, attitudes or public policies; to identify the goals, objectives and character of the state we desire by 2000; and if time permitted, prior to the governor's conference in August 1970, to suggest the implementation measures required to achieve those goals and objectives. Regrettably, there was insufficient time to accomplish this third task.

The task force concluded that by 2000 Hawaii will succeed, unfortunately, in looking and feeling like any other state in the nation, or perhaps even worse, since so many of its original qualities may be lost. For with the limited land area and an increasing resident/visitor population, there is little reason to believe that the negative trends evident in Hawaii during the past thirty years will not continue for the next three decades. In fact, they may even accelerate unless major shifts in public policy drastically alter the character of growth and change throughout the state.

The rationale for the task force recommendations follows.

TECHNOLOGICAL INNOVATIONS

Dramatic technological advances will be seen by 2000. For example, from a longer list compiled by Kahn and Wiener [1] *of the technical innovations likely to be realized by that time, the following will probably be available:*

- *more sophisticated architectural engineering*
- *improved materials and equipment for buildings*
- *very low-cost buildings for home and business use*
- *home computers to run the household and communicate with the outside world*
- *automated housekeeping and home maintenance*
- *automated grocery and department stores*
- *greater use of underground buildings*
- *permanent inhabited undersea installations*
- *general use of automation and cybernation in management and production*
- *recycling technologies for raw materials and wastes*
- *new sources of power for ground transportation*
- *new uses of underground tunnels for private and public transportation*
- *individual flying platforms*

How these innovations will affect Hawaii remains to be seen. Of greater importance is the question, "What kind of Hawaii do we want them to help create?" A State that conceived the first land-use law in America [2] *should be capable of harnessing the advancing technology of the future to assist it in achieving its community goals.*

POPULATION GROWTH AND EFFECTS

Repeatedly the question arises of population growth in the state of Hawaii. Do we require 1,500,000 people

---

1. Herman Kahn and Anthony J. Wiener, *The Year 2000* (New York: Macmillan, 1967), pp. 51–57.

2. Hawaii's State Land Use Law, passed in 1961, placed all private, State, and local government-owned land under the zoning jurisdiction of a nine-member Land Use Commission, which determines whether the land shall be classified as urban, agricultural, rural, or conservation. — Editors.

in the state, with 1,100,000 of them on Oahu by 2000, for the well-being of the total population? Is there a different set of target figures that should be the goal for future growth? It is apparent that a population goal within a reasonable range for 2000 should be established as soon as possible for each island, with public policy adjusted accordingly.

From the comprehensive land data presented to the task force by one of its members, planning consultant Donald Wolbrink, it certainly appears that sufficient land is available on Oahu to accommodate a projected year 2000 population of 1,000,000 to 1,100,000. However, simply having the land area is not sufficient. There must be much stronger public policy to ensure more livable development and a far higher level of planning and urban design than the state has experienced during the past three decades if the future population is to be accommodated in a manner that provides for prudent land use and decent environmental character.

PLANNING GOALS

What kind of Hawaii should we plan for?

In considering this question, the task force noted the range of alternatives that might be feasible, and concluded that the future Hawaii should be developed around the three fundamental factors that make this state unique. These factors are: the spirit of friendliness and understanding among our people and the spontaneity of its outward expression — the aloha spirit; the beauty of the natural environment; and the gentleness of the climate.

No one can disagree that aloha spirit, natural beauty, and climate are the most important qualities of our Polynesian setting. If they are most important, then they must not only be preserved sensitively, but also be enhanced through a proper blending with each other.

All too often, the rush of urbanization has destroyed all three of those qualities. The sprawl of monotonous subdivisions into fertile lands and watershed areas, the sudden transformation of small homes with gardens into impersonal slumlike apartment buildings surrounded by blacktop and no greenery, the jamming together of unattractive high-rise structures with lanais almost touching each other, have all combined to erode the natural beauty of Hawaii in far too many places.

The resultant destruction of the natural foliage, combined with the air pollutants emitted by automobiles and industries, has generated heat and smog that the trade winds find increasingly difficult to dispel. Finally, the haste and separation that is characteristic of individualized automobile transportation has contributed to a depersonalization of the urban Hawaii resident and to an erosion of the traditional aloha spirit to a point dangerously close to the facelessness of so much of urban America.

The role of the social sciences in designing our communities has been generally overlooked. The interaction of social and physical factors must be comprehended fully if we are to have good cities. For example, how can the house or neighborhood be better designed to satisfy the varied social and psychological needs of its occupants? How do different designs influence the relationships among families? How can we utilize the physical environment to enhance the opportunities of deprived groups? What changes in man should be anticipated?

There is little doubt that the increasing sophistication of medical technology is even now modifying man. He is living longer and is improving his body functions and even his body repairs. In the next thirty years there will be countless discoveries that will further alter and improve his body and mind. Man in 2000 can be expected to be more perfect than his counterpart of today.

The ramifications of these advances for housing in 2000 are obvious. The physical and even the social meaning of the home could change. It might have to assume new functions. No longer may we have to spend our nights sleeping, if sleep becomes unnecessary. Individual kitch-

ens would certainly become less important, if foods and food preparation are greatly different. New types of dwelling units would become necessary if communal living and new family patterns become more prevalent.

But no matter how drastic the transformation may be by 2000, we will still require the intervening decades to accommodate to change and to adjust our communities and our housing supply to the future life.

A sense of place and an identification with neighborhood and community will remain a powerful influence for stability. In fact, as our lives become more complex and our state more populous, the need for that personal identification becomes increasingly critical. Many of the qualities that could lead to that identification with locale can be planned far in advance.

Facilities should be provided in each neighborhood for many types of family and community activity. Facilities for educational, cultural, religious, and leisure pursuits should be readily accessible. Within the same neighborhood there should be several options for styles of living; that is, for those who desire anonymity, or independence, or a mixture of age groups, or communal living. Through sensitive siting of buildings, design of structures, density variations and distribution of open space, those options can be achieved. Homogeneity in housing types must be avoided; variety and diversity, encouraged. The British and European new towns demonstrate how variety in dwelling types and mixtures of land uses in close proximity can produce a diversity of activity and a maximum of open space around and within each development.

ALTERNATIVE PATTERNS

Alternative forms of future community development were considered. These included: (1) The desirability of greatly increasing the density of population and structures in Honolulu — that is, a "little Manhattan" type of growth. (2) The retention of Honolulu along the medium- to high-

density pattern of the present general plan, with an increase of densities in Kailua and Kaneohe — a pattern likely to occur eventually if no major shifts are made in current public policy. (3) A reduction in density throughout Honolulu and the scattering of small new communities on the plateaus and isolated shoreline points. (4) The establishment of an entirely new city elsewhere on Oahu, leaving Honolulu to remain the "old town."

Each of these alternatives has some benefits and some disadvantages. But to achieve the community-planning goals, the most preferable solution would be to organize Hawaii's neighborhoods into clusters. To these could be added the establishment of new neighborhoods at appropriate locations served by public transportation corridors that would tie together the entire community.

This conclusion on community form was arrived at after establishing three basic objectives:

(1) to restructure the urban land-use patterns in Hawaii to achieve more human neighborhood life-styles, with each neighborhood probably more dense and more compact than at present, yet surrounded and interspersed with parks and open space;

(2) to develop a network of fast, convenient, and free public transportation services connecting all the neighborhoods; and

(3) to eliminate whenever possible the future necessity for the individually owned automobile.

It is important to recognize that the public transportation system would be the critical element in 2000. It would shape the form of future urban growth and make possible land-use patterns hitherto not attempted in Hawaii.

For although technological advances in communication and automation will reduce the need to leave home to perform work, obtain an education, shop, attend the theater, or have face-to-face contact in business, the human need and desire for direct personal relationships in our daily activities will still persist to some degree. Therefore, although the number of trips for certain purposes may decline, there will still be need for a high level of transportation service.

INTRAISLAND TRANSPORTATION

In developing the concept of the public transportation system, the primary consideration should be to ensure that no member of the community is deprived of its use because of low income. This can be achieved only by the elimination of fares, meaning that the cost of the system would be defrayed not by the fare box, but by some form of tax.

It is suggested that the public transportation system be considered as a "horizontal elevator." Just as high-rise buildings do not charge each passenger for the elevator service needed to make all floors equally accessible, our communities should not charge for the transportation service necessary to make the various districts accessible in order to perform the urban functions.

It should be noted that a monorail or any other particular type of transit hardware is not being suggested at this time. Several types are already in existence and others in research and development will undoubtedly be capable of serving the transportation needs at the time. The specific type of transit equipment is relatively unimportant now. Fundamental is the concept of establishing a network of neighborhoods served efficiently and pleasantly by a high-quality public-transportation system traveling along a limited number of transportation corridors.

The corridors would be landscaped and integrated in design with the parklike open spaces separating the neighborhoods. The journey would be pleasant, rather than irritating and stress-inducing, as is now the case with most automobile travel.

203   Movement of goods could be accomplished over the

same network of transportation corridors using separate conveyances or a related mechanical system, such as a computerized belt system located subsurface, just as the delivery of water and the disposal of sewage has been accomplished for many decades.

If individual vehicle travel still remains a necessity for certain purposes after the public transportation system is available, convenient rent-a-vehicle operations could serve those needs. However, the road system for those vehicles should be carefully integrated with the transportation corridors.

CLUSTER NEIGHBORHOODS

Utilizing a cluster neighborhood concept, Hawaii's urban areas could enjoy the best of both worlds — the warmth and intimacy of small communities, along with the wide variety of cultural, commercial and social opportunities of a large metropolitan center. Neighborhoods could be varied, replete with distinctive character. Some might be oriented to education, around a community college or university; others might focus on single business activities, such as finance, research, or crafts. Due to the speed and convenience of public transportation, as well as the elimination of fares, people would be free to choose among many neighborhoods. Some might prefer to live and work in the same neighborhood; others might not. Some might wish to be close to downtown Honolulu; others might select the outlying districts. Transportation would not be the deterrent to that freedom of choice, particularly among the less affluent members of the community.

The cluster neighborhood would offer many opportunities for social interaction. It would have its own commercial and social center, a place where the community would be encouraged to congregate and participate in social and cultural activities as well as shop. The neighborhood center would also serve as the main station location for the public transportation system.

Each neighborhood would be compact enough so that everything in it would be within walking or, at most, bicycling distance. There would be no streets penetrating it for automobile intrusion. Instead, each neighborhood would be served by shaded walkways and bicycle paths. The pedestrian atmosphere would contribute to the development of healthier human beings by providing them with a light form of exercise so lacking in our sedentary automobile-oriented existence today. Handicapped or aged persons could use small electric vehicles. The neighborhoods would be connected to each other and to more distant parts of the island by the public transportation system.

Many parts of our state have the topographic features to structure this type of cluster neighborhood and transportation network. For example, Honolulu is a linear form of city separated naturally into distinct neighborhoods. Its ridges and deep valleys offer strong natural boundaries within which the cluster neighborhoods could be developed.

All but two of the other islands are characterized by rugged topography that restricts urbanization to a narrow corridor between mountains and the sea, or to the saddle plateaus between the ridges. The two smaller islands of Lanai and Niihau are probably not of sufficient size to encounter problems caused by individual vehicular transportation. Some form of self-powered vehicle would probably remain the preferred mode of travel there.

Due to the rough terrain on Hawaii, Kauai, Maui, Molokai, and Oahu, the principal transportation routes have already been limited to a single highway encircling most of each island, occasionally with a saddle road bisecting the circle. The future public-transportation corridors could follow that established highway network. A secondary mode of travel could be furnished by a transportation system by water, taking full advantage of the inland waterways and offshore waters. But it should not encroach on the water-recreation activities that are so distinctively a part of Hawaii.

INTERISLAND TRANSPORTATION

Interisland transportation will probably continue to be furnished primarily by aircraft because of their speed and convenience. But interisland ferries do offer considerable potential because of their compatibility with the island atmosphere. Although watercraft will become more sophisticated, travel by ship will probably remain slower than by aircraft. But lower cost and a more leisurely appreciation of the islands as viewed from the sea could remain outstanding advantages of water travel.

Although the elimination of fares on interisland carriers is not proposed, ferry system fares should be reasonable enough to permit interisland travel by persons of all income levels. The basic premise of these proposals is that the necessary public transportation on each island should be free to everyone, with any higher level of transportation service requiring payment of a fare.

In this connection, the task force discussed the possibility of people's working on Oahu and living on a neighbor island. Should special consideration, such as public subsidy, be offered to interisland commuter travel specifically for that purpose? The task force believes that it will not be necessary to do so because the improved environment of Oahu by 2000 should lessen the desire for living distant from a place of employment. Also, the interisland separation of residence and employment may be possible only for the upper-income groups that can best devote the time and money required for that form of commuting.

CONCLUSION

It must be emphasized that the proposal for restructuring the Hawaiian communities into smaller neighborhoods is not a retrospective nostalgia for a return to "the good old days" of small town life. Rather, it is an expression of the belief that man will increasingly need a sense of belonging, a sense of neighborhood, to allow him to develop as a cooperative human being, willing to assume a responsible community role and interact with his neighbors, instead of withdrawing into the isolation of a fenced-in yard and an enclosed automobile. For by losing our sense of neighborhood, we have become depersonalized, apathetic, and even suspicious of people who live nearby but are unknown to us.

The drawing together of communities into cluster neighborhoods would make it possible to set aside large areas for open space where neighborhoods once sprawled in single-family-lot fashion. This will reflect the fact that park and agricultural land are certain to become more precious in the future, as the population of Hawaii and the nation expands. Those lands can be a perpetual resource, if they are preserved. Also, after future conversion of beachfront neighborhoods to the cluster form, shorelines could again be opened to public use where today they may be inaccessible. In many cases, the transportation corridor would serve as the buffer between the neighborhoods and the beach parks.

It is apparent that certain major complexes already in place will probably retain their functions and locations when 2000 arrives, even though many of their structures will be replaced by then. On Oahu, Waikiki will probably remain a major tourist and recreation district; the Honolulu civic center may be expanded, but will essentially be in its present location; downtown Honolulu, with its diverse activities, will still be at the same place. The dramatic changes in land use will occur in the areas presently undeveloped and underdeveloped. By 2000, instead of debating the use of land we will probably be discussing the use of space. For there will be even greater premium on land space as well as underground space, airspace, and water space.

207   Housing and other land uses will have to consider

more efficient use of underdeveloped space. Increasingly, we will see communities composed of layer upon layer of various uses. Now we utilize the space beneath our communities only for utilities and an infrequent structure. In the future, we will use both that subsurface space and the airspace above our streets and structures. Buildings will serve multipurpose functions for greater efficiency. Designed properly, they could leave considerable open space for nearby parks and trees.

The transformation and development of our communities into cluster neighborhoods will not be an easy task. People will have to comprehend the benefits of compact neighborhoods with mixtures of attractive multifamily and single-family dwellings and the disadvantages of the traditional sprawling subdivisions contributing to the isolation and separateness of the present American life-style.

The development of cluster neighborhoods will also require a change in public attitude toward private land ownership. Renewal and development might be carried out in some districts by creating a neighborhood-wide condominium association to enable property owners to pool their properties for the common good and to share in the benefits of consolidation. It will require a level of government leadership, private initiative, and financial resources seldom available thus far in American communities. Interestingly, the Financial Plaza of the Pacific in downtown Honolulu demonstrates how one type of conversion, wherein several major commercial establishments were involved, was accomplished successfully on a completely private basis. They solved the complex problems of combining diverse land ownership and sharing a dramatic increase in building density.

There was not sufficient time for the task force to explore the implementation measures required to accomplish these proposals. It was essential first to define the Hawaii we desire. But it must be stressed that now is the time to arrive at the public policy decisions pertaining to priorities and the interrelated matters of planning for the best use of land, improved urban design, planning for densities of use, and coping with land costs, particularly in relation to housing. The decisions of this year and next will determine the character and the form of the state we will have in 2000. Establishment by the State of a permanent and meaningful commission on the year 2000 to guide and to monitor those decisions would be an effective method of institutionalizing our concern for the future.[3]

If the neighborhood/transportation concept and the housing choices suggested here are accomplished, Honolulu and the smaller cities and towns on the neighbor islands would become communities of parks. Technology would be harnessed to mold and to achieve the type of neighborhoods our citizens desire. Communities would not evolve by accident or haphazard conglomeration. As a student member of the task force wrote, "We must begin to look at our city as a work of art, a people's sculpture which we are presently sculpting."

If this is done, Hawaii would again provide equally to all its residents and visitors — no matter what their economic level — the total enjoyment of its assets: the beauty of its natural environment, the luxury of its climate, and the aloha of its people. They are the three unique qualities on which these housing and transportation concepts are based.

POSTSCRIPT BY CONSULTANT *CHESTER RAPKIN* [4]

The task force on housing and transportation has expressed its objectives for Hawaii 2000 in terms of essentials. It seeks to preserve and enhance the aloha spirit,

3. A permanent Hawaii State Commission on the Year 2000 was established in November 1971. — Editors

4. Chester Rapkin is director of the Institute of Urban Environment and professor of urban planning at Columbia University. He is also a member of the New York City Planning Commission, which is responsible for the guidance of growth and development of the city of New York. Dr. Rapkin has been consultant to municipal, state, federal, and foreign governments, planning commissions and civic associations, banking institutions, builders, developers and architects. He is the author

the natural beauty, and the softness of climate of the state. Toward these ends it has considered several different types of development patterns and their social implications that could serve as a framework for guiding the future growth and development of the state. While many other sections of our country at present are seeking ways to stimulate growth, Hawaii is in the fortunate position of planning for the most productive and pleasant configuration of its inherent vitality.

The task force feels that the principle of urban organization that will preserve the spirit and ambiance of Hawaii is best summarized under the term "cluster neighborhoods." Continued expansion of Honolulu and other urban areas would be permitted, but instead of uninterrupted growth on the periphery, the development pattern would consist of small integrated communities that possess a variety of types of residential accommodations and community services. They would be distinguished from the typical suburb in several ways, of which the most important is that individual clusters will possess the types and concentrations of uses that are ordinarily found in the central district, recreation centers, or in other nonresidential areas. Each community would be physically distinct, separated from its neighbors by bands or fingers of greenery, bodies of water, mountain ridges, or other natural boundaries. This combination of integration and separation will serve to keep the identity and neighborly scale of local communities and at the same time assure a reasonable degree of interaction among the residents of different communities by virtue of the dispersion of some of the central urban functions.

Perhaps the most intriguing aspect of this idea is that it is innovational without flying in the face of history. In

---

of some fourteen books and monographs on housing economics and mortgage finance, race relations, real estate, urban planning, and urban sociology. He has also prepared over thirty major reports and plans and a similar number of articles and technical papers.

fact, many a large city grew by expanding, overtaking, surrounding, and absorbing existing small towns previously located outside its borders; that is, by converting the interstitial green spaces to urban use. Often the names of these towns persist today as local subarea designations in such cities as London, Paris, and New York. In this process the individuality of the towns was blurred and the personality of the large center superimposed on the entire area. But the old uses or local characteristics sometimes linger on and intermix with the reconstituted urban districts, contributing to the continuity of the city. What the proposed cluster neighborhood concept tries to do is pull these areas apart again, to reintroduce the balm of nature and to restore small scale and identity in the process. In this manner the planning process does not resist change, but rather rolls with the trends by attempting to shape them along socially desirable lines.

Many planning theoreticians, including Ebenezer Howard, Clarence Stein, and Lewis Mumford, have tried to develop an urban system that would incorporate town scale and city variety, but most worked with the idea of separate but interdependent towns with or without a larger city. Growing in prominence and acceptability in recent years are the concepts of cluster zoning and planned-unit development, which seek to preserve open space in new urban residential construction by pooling part of what would have been private yards into small common parks. The idea of a coherent urban settlement, consisting of a group of related but physically separate and integrated subareas, is indeed a fresh and sophisticated continuation of this forward view of urban organization.

The smooth operation of the proposed new pattern of land use is dependent upon an extensive transportation network. Instead of relying heavily on the private automobile, the task force has recommended a free public-transportation system, supported by general tax revenues. Moreover it suggests that effort be made to discourage the use of the private car because it is a generator of pollutants, because traffic congestion makes driving nerve-wracking, and because the encapsulated vehicle serves to separate people physically and psychologically. The task force recognizes that the success of such an effort will depend upon technological innovations in the making or yet to come, and that in a very real sense the feasibility of the entire concept turns on the ease and cheapness of communication.

In view of the American's affection for his car, public transit, even if it is free, will have to be pleasant, frequent, and ubiquitous in order to compete effectively with the automobile. Even so, the car would be preferred for special trips, such as those that involve transportation of baggage or other goods, those in which the entire family, including infants, travel together, those that are late at night or those that involve many stops. Rather than strive for the elimination of the private vehicle (although the gas engine may go), it would be well to try only to reduce the frequency of its use by discouraging routine driving. The goal would be a global practice of using the car on special occasions, and then only if public transportation were not adequate.

The idea of making public transportation a free good is gaining in popularity. Costs can be reduced appreciably by savings in fare collection and accounting. Safety and service can be improved if the bus driver or conductor can devote full time to tending to the vehicle and the passengers. Moreover, cost would no longer deter poor people from traveling and would thereby enlarge their opportunities for employment, education, visiting, and other constructive experience.

Even though the free transportation proposal is still at an embryonic stage, some second thoughts have begun to emerge. Transportation specialists are worried about short-trip overload and peak-hour problems if the rationing of service by fare charge is eliminated. They are concerned about excessive use by adolescents and the elderly, for whom riding up and down in a windowless elevator is a bore, but for whom traveling in a bus or train can be an interesting way to spend a day. Specialists in urban finance are concerned about a reduction in municipal revenues at a time when cities are feeling the pinch of rising costs and increased obligations. And warriors in the battle against poverty insist that the poor need more than free transit to enhance their economic opportunities and social outlook.

The implementation of a program to develop cluster neighborhoods and their rapid interconnections will encounter many problems because it will involve not only a redeployment of population and land uses but also a shift in land values. In the traditional community, land values are a function of the savings in transportation costs that can be realized among points of differential accessibility. With a diminution in the amount of necessary travel and a reduction in the time and cost of travel, land values in general will decline, if classical theory holds true. This development will be offset by a rise in demand if population and income continue to increase as expected. These transportation changes in general will tend to level the spatial distribution of land values. The clusters will also influence the distribution of values by altering the major patterns of settlement, use, and density. Some way must be found to resolve this consequence of planning intervention equitably in order to prevent some from suffering serious losses while others, in fact, may be among the easier to handle because they involve quantifiable elements.

It is well that realistic and attractive plans are considered today to help protect Hawaii from further incursions of the great pressures and temptations of traditional urban life. Hawaii is more than the most beautiful state in the Union — it is the nation's symbol of beauty and harmony. A plan that helps preserve these elements serves not only the Aloha State, but also the rest of the country as well.

Political Decision-making and the Law 2000
Ralph M. Miwa

Ralph M. Miwa, political scientist and provost of Leeward Com-
munity College, was formerly dean of the College of Continuing
Education at the University of Hawaii. Educated at the University
of Hawaii and Johns Hopkins University, he has taught at St.
Johns College, Annapolis, the University of Missouri, and the
University of Nebraska. In 1966 he served as chairman of the
Oahu County Democratic Party and from 1970 to 1972 he was
vice-chairman of the Hawaii State Democratic Party.

I t was painfully apparent during the early stages of our
task-force discussions, especially with professional futurists, that my particular "mind-set" was not especially conducive to futuristic stargazing. Being both a trained political theorist and an active political participant, two seemingly incongruous and sometimes overtly conflicting roles,
I was uneasily aware of certain difficulties even before
my confrontation with futurists.

As a professional political theorist, I knew that the
history of political thought, at least in the Western mold,
was basically a history of individual expressions of preferred means and ends. From Plato's Republic to the
heavenly city of the eighteenth century philosophers,
various theorists had posited what were essentially subjective notions of what mankind's goals should be and
then arrayed alongside even more subjectively, if that
were possible, means for their attainment. I saw futurists,
no matter how "scientific" they purported to be, as essentially no different. Perhaps the difference was that

political theorists knew they were subjective, but professional futurists claimed themselves to be otherwise.

Although academically interested in and involved with the development of intellectual and political history, I have always harbored a gnawing suspicion, especially since Hegel was turned on his head, that political and social values are essentially products of conscious — but more often unconscious — rationalizations of environmental determinants, not the least of which are economic in nature. And I certainly would not be caught with my dialectical slip showing.

Far be it from me to heed the futurists who were saying that we need to select from an array of political goals for the future and then posit alternative means of accomplishing them, for that was precisely what I had spent a lifetime studying and found seldom leading anywhere except to questions about what influences value selection in society. (An interesting, and perhaps not too insignificant, observation I've made is that professional futurists very, very rarely manifest any awareness of previous political philosophies and philosophers in history although they often cover much the same ground and very frequently even use the same terminologies.)

As an active political participant, which state of development might have been the direct resultant of frustrations encountered in my professional experience, I am a bit wary and suspicious of grand schemes which purport to lay down incontrovertible goals, or if's and even more incontestable means, or then's.

I also suspect these reservations may have come about as the result of being exposed to easy overgeneralizations and simplifications of the political and decision-making process by those who had never so much as joined the political party of their choice.

But perhaps even more significantly, I often found through empirical experience that professed detractors of the "system" never even bothered first to understand the reasons for institutions, and second to analyze carefully the relationship between society's causal agents and the institutional means devised to accommodate, to ameliorate, and often even to oppose them.

In short, I had a really large temperamental block against what I considered to be the basic philosophic commitment of any appreciable long-range planning like a span of thirty years. Speculations in futures must, I thought, at worst reflect an extension of some subconscious desire to play the omnipotent seer of values and variables yet to be formulated, and certainly yet to be accepted by any segment of consequence in society. At best, such speculations seem unaware that we may be dealing with unknown factors in human and technological development in the next thirty years, not to mention the next five years. (William Whyte's prognosis of the organization man[1] has been seriously upset within a decade by Alvin Toffler's future shock and his very flexible man, for example. A great part of the reason for the development of Toffler's man is the fantastic technological and knowledge revolution since 1960, the consequences of which were unseen by Whyte.)

But what really "turned me off" was the tendency, in at least some of those who can see further into history than the rest of us, toward what I surmised as rather arbitrary and sometimes even antidemocratic means either to attain a preferred objective or to deter an inevitable cataclysmic catastrophe. (The doomsday saviors who suggest the covert development and dissemination of a virus to be inhaled by all to preclude any possibility of further human fertility, in order to ward off the impending population bomb, without either the knowledge or consent of society, is a case in point, if it was accurately reported.)

In any event, I recount the above because they are not only my concerns but generally reflective of a few

1. William H. Whyte, Jr., *The Organization Man* (New York: Simon and Schuster, 1956).

others who were on the task force. I don't think these attitudes are necessarily descriptive only of theorists or of activists, or even of those with large temperamental blocks. I think that in some measure most of us have such reservations to a lesser or larger degree. I must have had more than the usual share. Perhaps that is the primary reason why I sought surcease and comfort in aligning myself, more than unconsciously, with one position on the task force that claimed futuristic thinking about political decision-making should confine itself to procedural questions and guarantees and desist from any pontifications about goals and objectives.

But I should also mention, now that I've lodged my demurrer, that further discussion with futurists and those futuristically oriented dispelled some of the fears that I have long nurtured, though not all. As best as I can understand the argument, it goes something like this:

Political futures thinking need not arbitrarily decide goal orientations and procedural means. Rather, there should be an array of goals and objectives and a similar listing of the most appropriate means to attain them. In other words, "If the goals are X, Y, and Z, then the political structures and procedures might be A, B, C, and D. If, however, the goals are Y, F, and G, then the political system might have A, D, H, and I structures and procedures."

Thinking about future goals and objectives, whether they be ten, twenty, or thirty years in the offing, is not simply speculation, but a very practical necessity. It forces us to think creatively about the kind of world we would like to have and it also gives us a standard to measure the efficiency for what we are doing right now. Futuristic thinking, in other words, has both a long-range and an immediate practical application.

I must confess that the pervasive catholicity of this approach presented by James Dator was disarming. On the first point, I read him as saying that political futuristics need not arbitrarily posit hierarchical systems of goal orientations. Let every reasonable statement have its say and permit every rational means its day in court. In other words, let's not select one political theory but have several political theories (in my own frame of reference).

On the second point, I see the implicit strains of Aristotelianism, which is simply another name for practical empiricism. I can hardly argue against a position which says that one can best judge current efficiency if one has some notion of eventual purpose. If one wants to know what he can accomplish with any given tool, he has to have an idea of what he wants to do with it. The idea of what he wants to do with it provides the standard of measurement of the effectiveness of the tool itself, a Hellenic conception called teleology which predates futuristics and PPBS. [2]

In any event, I then suggested to the task-force members that they propose some simple social-system designs. In essence, this meant that they could posit certain preferred goals and objectives regarding procedures and institutions on political decision-making and the law in Hawaii and then suggest various alternative means designed to accomplish such ends. Meanwhile, I tried to devise some designs from the preconference task-force discussions to serve, if only as catalysts for more operable models.

The task was not a simple one, especially for a partial convert. The selection of goals and objectives, no matter how comprehensive and catholic, assumes that there is necessarily some system of priorities about those we select. That was the first difficulty. The second and perhaps even more crucial difficulty was that the positing of alternative goals for decision-making and the law presumes there

2. On PPBS, consult, for example, Association of School Business Officials of the United States and Canada, *Program Planning-Budgeting-Evaluation System: An Annotated Bibliography* (Chicago, 1968). — Editors

is some agreement about those aspects of our current machinery which are wrong, ill-working, or anachronistic. That's a rather large presumption, I found out. Take for example the supposed ills of "overcentralized" State government in Hawaii. Grant that such a situation lends itself to problems of dual taxation, or at least overlapping taxes. Grant also that it may lead to unnecessary layers of governmental bureaucracies. Nevertheless, for example, there are those who can legitimately argue that it has been centralized government which has guaranteed the same level of educational standards throughout the state regardless of a region's ability, or inability, to pay. With decentralized government and its corollary, the local school districts, the results on the mainland have not been exactly salutary. Economic development can also suffer from decentralized government with its problems of inadequate developmental revenues among local, county-level governments.

Thus, to posit decentralized government in Hawaii as a preferred end goal because of presumed or assumed ills is not as simple as one might suppose.

Even if it weren't so simple, perhaps we ought to try. The beauty of the democratic system of decision-making and the law has been that no one in his right mind has ever said that it is above reproach. Before and after Jefferson, the observation has been that what we have is basically often an exasperating, frustrating, and inefficient means of translating congregate wills into laws and action. But that it's the best yet devised, is often the postscript, from de Tocqueville to Churchill.

But the best yet devised may not be enough, is what I read the futurists as saying. Especially is this so when there are mounting problems of ecosystem imbalance, pollution, and unplanned urban and industrial development which require a far more rapid, efficient, effective, and equitable system of governance. The best yet devised by the minds of men has often been terribly ineffectual, and unfair, in permitting the present situation to exist, let alone what might possibly, or probably, happen in the next thirty years.

As far as I could gather, the following were some representative problem areas discussed in the preconference sessions of the task force, or extrapolated from them. By enumerating and analyzing them further, I thought that we could arrive at a listing of certain definable goals and objectives in the next thirty years. The basic problem, as I saw it, was to agree that there were problems. If we could hurdle this first stage, then perhaps goals could be set. In turn, if the second stage could be accomplished, then we could assign alternative means of accomplishment. But first things first.

These were the "problems" that concerned the preconference task-force members.

1. The political party structure and its organization of membership in Hawaii are such that truly significant issues are not presented as embodying meaningful alternatives to the body politic. Instead, political personalities are emphasized, with the result that party politics in Hawaii essentially means party personalities. The need is to construct some more relevant system of political involvement so as to enable true choices in terms of concrete issues and meaningful alternative solutions. In addition, there are social preferences and concerns which cannot be considered the exclusive preserve of one or another political party, as we know them. Current environmental concerns fall into this category. They cut across party lines. More and more of this will occur in the future. Provision must be made to restructure party politics to take such developments into account.

2. In this age of complexity and urgency, there needs to be some form of rapid and efficient decision-making by the State legislature. The current system of bicameral legislative action is too cumbersome and slow and too much exposed to pressures from special interests for it to deal effectively with increasingly complex and urgent

matters. The bicameral system of legislation often places a premium on the abilities of legislators to "politick" and to bargain as between conflicting items of legislation, often without the exposure to public scrutiny that is such a necessary part of the democratic process. Legislators themselves are unable to understand fully the intricacies of growing technological development as well as the implications of such growth for lawmaking. Their staffs are inadequate and their resources for fact-gathering are practically nonexistent. Lawmaking in the future must deal not only with traditional principles of law but with the technical implications of computer systems, atomic power, cybernetics, and the various other developments utilizing advanced technology, not to mention the ominous problems of pollution. The present-day system as we know it cannot hope to cope with the rapidly changing situation.

3. If present-day forms of the legislature and the legislative process become anachronisms in the years ahead, there is no assurance that the executive department will escape the same fate. As a matter of fact, the present division of the executive department into certain definable functional compartments such as health, transportation, and social services departments, may not be the answer in dealing with rising problem areas which cut across formal departmental jurisdictions. Take, for example, the problem of how to handle automobile-exhaust pollution. At least two of the aforementioned departments plus perhaps the tax, land and natural resources, planning and economic development, and even the regulatory agencies departments might or should be involved. In the field of education, it might prove more functionally useful to couple the department of education with the social services department rather than to maintain an arbitrary categorization such as we presently have, for contemporary problems of education are oftentimes also problems of social and familial conditioning factors. The federal

head-start program and its clearly apparent success attest to this. [3] (It is interesting to note that although no mention was made of Toffler in these discussions, the theme here is strikingly similar to his in Future Shock in which he argues that the developing pattern in bureaucracies is away from fixed organizational lines to fluid "ad-hocracies.")

4. Perhaps even the very system of separation of state powers into legislative, executive, and judicial branches of government should be reviewed. There is nothing especially sacrosanct about the doctrine of separation of powers or checks and balances. The United States Supreme Court has already ruled in the reapportionment cases that the federal principle underlying the U.S. Congress is not the same for the states. The time may be rapidly approaching, for example, when we should seriously consider the amalgamation of at least certain parts of the executive department with the legislative. Certain executive department heads might stand for election and operate, if successful, within the legislature to help formulate laws with which they are more technically familiar. (The British Parliament is not necessarily the model here, for that institution emphasizes leadership responsibilities in policy formulation. The model suggested emphasizes the technological responsibilities of leadership.)

5. Underlying all of the above, the present election system needs to be reviewed and perhaps overhauled in the next thirty years. The geographic structure of the islands has been both advantageous and disadvantageous in the process of electing representatives to the legislative and the executive departments. The relative geographic compactness and sociopolitical homogeneity of the islands have lent themselves to easy central coverage through various media. But the very facility with which

3. The Head Start Child Development Program, sponsored by the Office of Economic Opportunity was begun in the summer of 1965 "to explore ways of intervening with early developmental processes to improve the abilities, attitudes, health, and well-being of young children and their families". — Editors

the media can cover the entire state may also have forced reliance on that type of expensive media utilization which can easily and conveniently transmit election information. The net result has been increasing costs in campaigning, thereby in effect disenfranchising those without the economic wherewithal to wage successful election campaigns. We should devise ways and means to make possible equal participation in the elective process for those who do not have the means to subsidize increasingly expensive contemporary media publicity campaigns. (Since this was written, the Hawaii Educational Television network has initiated a bipartisan presentation of candidates and issues.)

6. Information exchange between the various levels of government on the one hand, and the people on the other is getting to be an enormous problem. Increasing complexities in the decision-making process with variables often unseen by the public, and of course not understood, often lead to credibility gaps. The most prevalent means of information exchange, which in this case is really only information dissemination, is in the hands of private, commercial media. Public means of dissemination and exchange may not be the answer as the media can manage or manipulate dissemination for purposes of commercial self-interest. Nevertheless, the variables which go into decision-making at whatever level of government must be understood as much as possible by the public at large so as to preclude misunderstandings and/or unfair decision-making processes. A publicly financed but independently administered body, such as educational television, could be the beginning of an answer in this complex area. In England, the British Broadcasting Corporation provides somewhat this kind of service.

7. Information exchange among the various levels of government is also rapidly becoming an unmanageable problem. Instantaneous availability of facts and data within one level of government as well as between levels is

increasingly crucial to rational and rapid decision-making. Data exchange between the legislature and the executive department, between the judiciary and the executive department, between executive agencies, among district, circuit, and supreme courts, and so forth, must be expedited as never before. Because of the nature of the knowledge explosion as well as because of escalating information gathering, an instantaneous information retrieval system centrally coordinated must be devised. (The state of Hawaii already has SWIS, Statewide Information System, a computerized system which could be the beginning.)

8. One of the most crucial problems certain to come to a head in the next thirty years in Hawaii will be the question of relationships between the State and the various county governments. Perhaps underlying all the discussion about centralized versus decentralized government and home rule versus strong State government is the basic question of whether or not all the counties can become viable entities without help from such a leveling institution as the State government with powers to redistribute resources. But such powers, in practice, may be more "equal" for the islands other than Oahu. In short, the paradox is that while centralized government is in one sense fair to those counties with limited resources, it can be unfair to those who must in effect subsidize such counties. On the other hand, centralized State government poses a dilemma to the neighboring counties in that simultaneous with the distribution of the State's financial largesse, a measure of autonomy in taxing powers, local school control, and economic development is forfeited. It should be readily apparent that an oversimplified statement of the problem, such as to suggest that the question is one of dual taxation powers, would do injustice to those who are interested in seeking ways out of the maze. There must be a balance struck somehow between keeping the advantages of centralized government and permitting more autonomy for counties through decentralization.

9. The prevailing orientation of law as a punitive device to hold society's recalcitrants in line must be replaced by one which would instead emphasize rehabilitative and correctional aspects. The aim should be to help individuals adjust to society and to themselves rather than to mete out various degrees of punishment based on the belief that what society needs is deterrents to errant behavior. Existing laws on drunkenness, for example, are a case in point. Laws on possession of marijuana which make possession a felony regardless of quantities held might be another case in point. But perhaps more significantly, the notion that enactment, execution, and adjudication of laws is the preserve of the professionally trained legal personnel and their representatives on the bench and the bar might be a vestigial remnant of nineteenth-century legalism. Perhaps Hawaii can forge a new path by suggesting that social psychologists and medical psychiatrists should be accredited participants in certain types of judicial hearings, not only as consultants but in fact as judicial arbiters. The ruling of a judge in many cases of social aberration is not necessarily legitimized by possession of a law degree. In fact, professionally trained and experienced social workers, psychiatric social workers, social and medical psychologists, and psychiatrists may prove to possess better and more relevant professional competence.

10. Together with the foregoing, the persistent notion that the legal profession alone is equipped by temperament, training, and wisdom to deal with the increasingly complex issues of a technological society may have to undergo close scrutiny and analysis. There is no guarantee that a "legal mind" may be better able to adjudicate conflicting claims of litigants before the bench in cases involving physiological damages from the effects of air pollution, in suits involving damage sustained as a result

of technical deficiencies or negligence, and in claims arising from the toxic effects of untested pharmaceuticals. It may be that experts trained in technologically related fields would be better suited to deal with such cases.

These foregoing "problems" were presented for discussion purposes both as matters to be solved and goals to be reached. It was felt that if we could agree on some of the major points, subject to further analysis and refinement, then perhaps we could make a meaningful transition to finding out alternative means for their accomplishment, or the second half of the so-called social system design. If we could not, then it was my view that any selection of alternative means for accomplishment was not a very productive exercise.

THE CONFERENCE

The workshop sessions at the actual conference were divided into five subgroups, each with approximately ten to twelve participants, led by a chairman with minutes kept by a secretary.

Each subgroup was instructed first to read the previous compilation of problem areas and then devise the kinds of goals it would like to see for 2000. Members could either support or disavow the approach taken in the preconference discussions, or take off on completely new and different directions if they felt that was a more productive avenue.

The moderator, the Reverend Claude DuTeil, further instructed the subgroups to concentrate first on problem areas as discussed in the preconference meetings and then to construct new goals and alternative means if need be. They were cautioned not to linger on discussions of problems inasmuch as the setting of goals and the listing of alternative means of trying to accomplish them were crucial in terms of the tasks outlined for the task force.

No attempt was made either in the subgroups or in the general sessions following each subgroup session to reach accord through voting. Instead, each subgroup secretary made both an oral and a written report, which were then synthesized, insofar as humanly possible, in this report. In doing so, there was exercised a degree of editing in order to produce a coherent and organized body of thought from the welter, and wealth, of a total of eighteen oral and written reports of subgroup discussions.

The morning sessions were devoted primarily to discussion of contemporary problem areas and the definition of goals. The afternoon sessions were supposedly to concentrate on finding various alternative means of accomplishing these goals. However, as matters actually turned out, there was considerable overlapping of these assignments during the two sessions. In any event, we've attempted to sort out what appear to be goals and tried valiantly to determine what appear to be alternative means of accomplishment, a so-called social-systems design as close as we could make it.

The following appear to be the various goals, liberally interspersed with means, as seen by the subgroups listed in no particular order of priority except that I have noted especially those instances of more-or-less common agreement.

1. Maximization of the individual's right of control over his own life and minimization of governmental involvement over those aspects of individual existence and development which affect only him and do not infringe upon the rights of others. Examples cited here were such cases as reevaluation of present statutes on pornography, prostitution, and gambling. Present statutes usually define such activities as criminal even though no harm is done to the lives or property of others. The definition of crime should cover only those acts which infringe upon the rights of others, be it life, liberty, or property. This means, however, that although some existing forms of governmental control should be eliminated, certain other forms should be strengthened. In the latter category were certain types of economic controls which would ensure

the development of individual capabilities and freedoms and other types of government legislation to protect against incursions into personal freedoms.

2. There should be wider, more extensive, and direct participation by individuals in the political decision-making process. There is a lack of grass-roots participation in government which contributes to a sense of alienation on the part of the people. Some of the reasons for the foregoing may be traced to a system of education which has failed to encourage a more positive attitude towards political involvement and participation. Others may be traced to existing concepts of district representation based essentially on geographic boundaries. This is unrealistic because geographically defined district representation is merely a physical concept. Still others may be traced to increasingly large electoral districts with the same number of legislative representatives. The ratio of people to representatives increases as time goes on, thereby adding to the difficulties of communication.

Whatever the reasons, there is a definite necessity for more effective communication links between those engaged in the decision-making process and the people. A system should be devised so that decision-makers can better communicate the reasons for their decisions to the people and the people should be better enabled to convey their thoughts directly to the decision-makers. Such direct relationships and channels of communications would also ensure accountability of decision-makers — a necessary part of the democratic process.

These were the two basic goals perceived in the myriad reports. They are the result of combining several seemingly disparate major and minor objectives, sifting through a number of subsidiary and often tangential short-range goals, classifying more logically and systematically various suggestions which often overlapped, and reclassifying others which were felt to be more in the nature of means

228

rather than goals. Upon reflecting on these two goals, I find that they are perhaps actually parts of one overriding, comprehensive goal. They can, in effect, be combined into one, as follows.

Government should be primarily concerned with ensuring the full and unfettered development of the individual's capacities and capabilities. It should not act the role of guardian over private morality. It should, rather, protect and extend the personal freedoms of all. In order to insure this, there should be wider, more extensive, and direct participation on the part of as many individuals as possible in the decision-making process as well as assuring more direct accountability of decision-makers to the community.

I was more convinced of this as I reviewed the various alternatives suggested to accomplish these goals. They could not really be divided as means for goal number one and goal number two. Rather, they were all various alternatives for the goal as synthesized above. It is, then, in this sense that I have listed the alternative means.

1. Maximize use of educational television and the educational system in informing the electorate of citizen responsibilities. Consider making ETV directly responsible to the legislature. Use media, such as ETV, to communicate directly with the electorate on legislative and executive matters.

2. Eliminate artificiality between the legislative and the executive branches of government. Institute a parliamentary system of government with a high degree of accountability and sensitivity to the electorate. Establish a full-time legislative body aided by selected technical consultants on a full-time basis. Establish a school for legislators. Consider a unicameral legislature. Eliminate county governments in favor of a single all-comprehensive state government.

3. Reform elective process by such methods as com-

mon, presumably public, funding sources so as to equalize opportunities for political participation — or, set a limit on campaign expenditures by candidates.

4. Encourage and develop, through governmental resources, the capability, ability, and inclination for disadvantaged areas to participate in the political process so as to enable residents of the affected areas to seek such changes in the decision-making process as may be to their advantage.

5. Consider establishment of parallel community governance machinery alongside existing formal governmental institutions with decision-making authority to act as a spur to formal institutions.

6. Consider establishment of citizens' councils for community action whereby representatives from each neighborhood or community agency would assist in advising the respective city councils in their decisions.

7. Base present representational districts on criteria other than geographic, as for example, technological competence, knowledge and appreciation of human values, and occupational categories. Or, large districts could be reduced to a number of smaller community districts with full-time representatives. In this respect we might consider town halls or cluster communities as ideal representative districts.

8. Restructure or reorient political parties in such a way that they would be more concerned with issues that affect all people, and not be preoccupied with winning the 51 percent necessary to control the decision-making process.

I am not at all certain that professional futurists will agree that we have followed the model of social-systems designs accurately. But I am certain that there is a very strong sentiment for a serious and extended review of current processes of decision-making and the law in Hawaii, judging from both the preconference task force discussions and the workshop sessions of the conference itself. I write the foregoing, even though I am well aware of the fact that there are some apparent variances between the two bodies in terms of subjects of emphasis.

On the latter point, it should be reported that the composition of the two bodies differed. During the six-month deliberations of the parent task force, a nucleus of ten members attended sessions quite regularly. However, because of the timing of the conference itself, which fell during two weekdays, only two of the original ten task-force members attended. The conference partici-pants spent only about a day and a half in their workshops compared to the extended deliberations of the parent task force which began to meet fully six months before the actual conference date. The contributions of the two groups should thus be evaluated against the foregoing background.

In addition to the time element, there were noticeable differences in the two groups in terms of age. The precon-ference task force members were basically over thirty, while the conference workshop attendees were generally younger.

In short, we had two different groups working on the report of the task force on decision-making. This point should be made clear. Once clearly noted, one can perhaps more easily understand why I have chosen to report separately on the deliberations of the preconference task force as against the points raised by members of the conference workshop sessions.

Be that as it may, there are significant similarities of themes between the two groups, even while acknowledg-ing seemingly different emphases. For example, there is concern in both groups that increasing socioeconomic and technological complexities will make necessary a search for institutional reforms and restructuring, enabling more direct participation in the decision-making process. The preconference discussions zeroed in on needed reform of the existing legislative, executive, and judiciary departments and processes in order to make the point that the voice of the people must be given a more direct and effective opportunity to express itself. The workshop sessions, on the other hand, pointed to present systems of electoral districts that need to be overhauled to make for more direct and effective communication between citizens and their representatives in government.

But there was one recurrent theme running throughout both groups which seemed most significant. The feeling appeared to be that there must be a drastic change in orientation regarding society's approach to acts which are now classified as "crimes." The first group emphasized the need for a rehabilitative and correctional, rather than a punitive, attitude to certain classes of behavior now termed criminal, such as drunkenness and the possession of marijuana. The second group felt that the definition of crime should cover only those acts which clearly harmed the lives, freedom, or property of others. Where such harm to others did not occur, as in gambling and prostitution, the claim was that these acts should not in the future be classified as criminal behavior. I should also emphasize that while it took the foregoing stance with respect to "individual" acts, it strongly recommended the strengthening of economic and governmental controls to insure the protection of individual rights and freedoms.

It has occurred to me upon reflection that it doesn't matter whether or not we have followed the model of social-systems designs in our deliberations. For one thing, I believe it entirely possible for a professional futurist to diagram the discussions into "if . . . then" propositions in much the same manner that a grammarian can dissect the involutions of Spinoza.

What is important is that two basically different groups, totaling ten to seventy individuals at different times, came to view governmental problems and solutions in much the same manner. Considering notable divergencies in age, professions, ideologies, and the like, this agreement was especially significant.

Our group early decided that our report would not be the work of one man, the chairman. Rather, the group preferred that the final report incorporate the views of all the participants as much as possible. In retrospect, no wiser decision could have been made. Given the difficulties of making something coherent out of the random, rambling, and often discursive thoughts of so many individuals, we can say that this report is reflective of the entire group. In this sense, it is journalistic rather than academic, reportorial rather than theoretical. But I think we've done the job.

The Economy 2000
Thomas H. Hamilton

Thomas H. Hamilton is emeritus senior professor of political science, and former president, of the University of Hawaii. He was previously president of the State University of New York, and earlier held professorial and administrative posts at Lawrence University, University of Chicago, Chatham College and Michigan State University. At the time of the work of the task force he was president of the Hawaii Visitors Bureau. He is now special advisor to the trustees of the Kamehameha Schools/B.P. Bishop Estate. He has published works in the social sciences.

am terribly suspicious of the utility of predictions about the future. A simple exercise that is engaged in by too few individuals is to read the predictions about 1970 that were made in 1940. Very few of them make any sense in the light of what actually happened.

There are, of course, a number of reasons for this. When trying to predict what is going to happen to the whole of society or even to a major facet of it, there are such an infinite number of variables involved in terms of both their nature and their force, that even with a computer a man can hardly program for all the contingencies. But even more risky is the fact that new variables will enter the picture. Remember we are talking about the year 2000 which is no greater distant than the year 1940 was from 1970. Yet in 1940, almost no one except a few scientists even knew that it had become possible to split the atom, let alone knew what incredible force could be thus unleashed. And again, except for a few scientists,

the words "genetic code" made no sense whatsoever.
And the other terms we bandy about so freely these days,
ecology, pollution, environment, conservation and the
like, were hardly household words.

The problem is, and this haunts me, that at this very
moment someplace in a library or a laboratory, an
individual may be doing the preliminary work which will
change our lives as much as nuclear energy and the war
in southeast Asia.

The task force's consultant, Kenneth E. Boulding,[1]
depicted the problem nicely in a letter to me.

**I share your guarded skepticism regarding predictions
of the future, especially those which attempt to look more
than a relatively short time ahead. I have argued indeed
that the future of social systems is inherently unpredictable in detail because they contain knowledge as an essential element, and we cannot predict what we are going
to know without knowing it now. There has to be, therefore, in such systems what I call "fundamental surprise,"
and any planning for the future must take account of this
in the sense that all images of the future must be subject
to revisions and sensitive to new information. All plans,
likewise, must be subject to revision in the light of our
revised images of the world. There is hardly anything
which is more potentially destructive than a rigid plan.
On the other hand, we must make projections of the
future and we must make plans simply because all decisions are among alternative futures. A great many human
dilemmas indeed can be summed up in the aphorism that
all knowledge is about the past and all decisions are about**

1. Kenneth E. Boulding, professor of economics at the University of
Colorado, is author of *The Meaning of the Twentieth Century* (1964),
Beyond Economics (1968) and a score of other books. A native of Liver-
pool, England, and an honors graduate of Oxford, he has taught in
Britain as well as in the United States, Japan, Jamaica and other places.
He has been president of the American Economic Association and of
the international Peace Research Society, is a fellow of the World
Academy of Art and Science and a distinguished fellow of the American
Economic Association. He holds fourteen honorary degrees.

**the future. While it is extremely important to make projec-
tions about the future, therefore, it is equally important
not to believe them too much and to be prepared to revise
them continuously.**

*There even are some positive dangers in spending
too long speculating about 2000. It could be that we shall
become so busy and so preoccupied with that date thirty
years away that we shall have neither the time nor the
energy left over to solve tomorrow's problems. In short,
speculation about the year 2000 could indeed be criticized
as a new form of escapism.*

*There also is the danger that we may be too optimistic
about what can be accomplished in thirty years. Thus we
could unrealistically heighten social expectations which,
when they are not met, will but increase the frustration
level. To a degree we are now suffering from this. If one
promises the Great Society often enough, eventually he
is expected to produce it. And when it is not forthcoming,
the people become bitter.*

*Yet man always has thought about the future and will
probably continue to do so. It is important to remember
that many things we do this year will still be with us at
the very least in effect in 2000. Our present action should
be undertaken only with this in mind. I suppose the most
appropriate caveat for this paper is one written by a caustic
economist reviewing a book which he disliked very much.
"The possible harm of this book," he said, "is that it might
be read and believed by the very young." With this caveat
let us proceed with the exercise.*

*There are three major questions which have to be
faced before one can write meaningfully about the year
2000. Should the approach be descriptive or normative?
Can human nature be changed? And what is included in
the term "economy"?*

*If one is to take the descriptive approach, then all
that is involved, and heaven knows this is enough, is the
projection of present trends, assuming that the same forces*

which have shaped our economy thus far will continue for at least thirty years into the future. The normative approach, of course, calls for a consideration of only what should *be the case as far as the economy is concerned in 2000.* The approach taken in this paper is that both must be considered. If we take only the descriptive projections we simply admit that we cannot change basic forces. I would point out that there are a number of writers who sincerely believe this to be true. There are technological determinists who contend that we have set in motion a technology which has its own immutable laws that cannot be altered by man. I refuse to believe this, but such validity as there is in the case has to be taken into account. The approach as taken in this paper is that we must consider both the descriptive and the normative. In short, it holds that we cannot ignore the forces currently at work, but still holds that man has some control over his future.

The second major question, "can human nature be changed?" is enormously complicated. Robert Theobald in An Alternative Future for America[2] takes the position that from our present concept of human nature has come the system which uses for motivation "the carrot and the stick." And he further holds that when the world learns what it means to be "self-actualizing" we shall no longer need these motivating devices to move people. But when I reread my Herodotus, Thucydides, Machiavelli, et al., I find that not too much has changed in the intervening centuries. Thus I cannot hold that radical changes will be accomplished in the next thirty years. Yet I do feel that perhaps human nature can be redirected. In short, I am optimistic enough to feel that in thirty years we can get rid of the whip, but we shall still have to retain at least part of the carrot.

An equally puzzling problem is what we mean when we talk about the economy. One can assume that this simply means all that is involved in the production and

2. Chicago: Swallow Press, 1968.

distribution of goods and services. This of course makes the problem more manageable, but to many it is too confining an approach. At the other extreme one has those who would interpret the word economy to mean the totality of man's life. But if one takes this approach, the problem becomes intellectually unmanageable and, more often than not, one ends in tautological propositions which prove that all the world is all the world, a true but meaningless statement. Thus the approach here will be someplace between those two extremes. Recognizing the necessity to limit the scope of the inquiry on the one hand, but never failing to bear in mind the impact of economics on all other phases of life and, in turn, the extent to which economics are influenced by those other phases.

The problem of inclusion under the head of the economy has not only the functional aspect outlined above but also the geographical. Are we speaking only about the economy of Hawaii or do we include the nation and, for that matter, the world? Again a rather arbitrary decision has to be made. The position taken herein will be that we are primarily concerned with the economy of Hawaii but recognize that we are very much dependent on what happens to the mainland economy and, to a lesser degree, throughout the world. It is simply a fact of life that when the national economy sneezes, Hawaii at the very least has to say "Gesundheit."

A further element some may wish to include in the term concerns its structure. Is it capitalistic or socialistic? This raises questions of social organizations. These, too, we have excluded from our considerations, important though they are. Their inclusion would have complicated an already complex undertaking. They are more appropriately a part of a concern with life-style.

PROJECTIONS

At one time I held that the first thing to do was simply to project geometrically growth for the next thirty years at the same rate as growth has taken place for the last thirty years. But this rather quickly appeared to be a difficult, if not useless, exercise. For one thing, it is very difficult for a man who is not trained as an economist to find the data to make such extrapolations and indeed, in some instances, the data did not seem to be available. Fortunately, Robert C. Schmitt, the State statistician, has done some of these extrapolations, which are cited below to illustrate their limited utility.[3] Here are his extrapolations.

1. The civilian population would grow from 737,000 in 1969 to 1,379,000 in 1999.

2. The University of Hawaii enrollment would grow from 35,000 in the fall of 1969 to 416,000 in 1998.

3. Agricultural employment would drop from 14,450 in 1969 to 3,800 in 1998.

4. The average annual wage in manufacturing would grow from $6,310 in 1968 to $51,000 in 1997.

5. The consumer price index in the next thirty years would increase 171%.

6. The median monthly rent on Oahu would grow from $147 in 1969 to $1,070 in 1998.

7. The assessed value of real property would grow from $6.6 billion in 1969 to $127 billion in 1999.

8. Motor vehicles would increase from 374,000 in 1969 to 2,126,000 in 1999.

9. Vehicle miles would grow from 2.9 billion in 1968 to 13.3 billion in 1998.

I computed how many visitors we would have by the year 2000 if the growth over the next thirty years equaled that which occurred from 1940 to 1970. The result is an astounding 78,400,000.

MORE REASONABLE PROJECTIONS

It becomes apparent, at least to me, that simply projecting the future on the basis of the past is not very sensi-

3. Schmitt, Robert C. *Long-Range Forecast for Hawaii; the Statistics of Tomorrow*, mimeographed, Honolulu, 1970.

ble other than as it may give some indication of direction. One can see the difficulties by simply looking at some of the internal inconsistencies. During the past thirty years not all of our institutions and other factors have grown at the same rate. For example, taking the above would mean that approximately one-third of all of the inhabitants of the state of Hawaii would be students at the University of Hawaii in the year 2000. Thus Schmitt concludes, "No one seriously contends, of course, that more than 2 million motor vehicles will clog Hawaii's streets and highways in less than thirty years, or that the assessed value of real property will reach $127 billion. Either situation would be intolerable. Something would have to occur to forestall such developments. These projections should be viewed as simply illustrative — as indications of what will take place if present trends continue unabated, or if a preventive action is not forthcoming."

Fortunately there do exist some projections which are not straight extrapolations, but are modified by other insights. These have been made by the Office of Business Economics of the United States Department of Commerce and some also by the Department of Planning and Economic Development of the State of Hawaii. These figures are summarized in Table 1.

Schmitt summarizes these projections nicely and in the following words.

These projections are obviously subject to all of the limitations outlined earlier. Some will err on the high side. Others will fall short of actual developments. Even so, they provide a degree of insight into many of the changes likely to take place in Hawaii.

First, they point to rapidly increasing congestion. In addition to more than 1.5 million residents in 2000, there will be almost 200,000 visitors in the State at any given time. These totals imply a parallel growth in business and industry, housing supply, hotel accommodations, school enrollment, and beach usage. Airport and highway

Table 1

	1970	2000
Population	736,750	1,555,000
Employment	320,000	501,000
Personal Income*	$2.35 billion	$8.23 billion
Per Capital Income†	$3,034	$6,932
Per Worker	$6,054	$12,747
Farmers employed in Agriculture	12,900	8,600
Employed in Construction	25,500	39,400
Employed in Manufacturing	21,500	39,000
Employed in Services	75,400	170,900
Civilian Employees in Government	26,900	38,300
Visitors	1,400,000	11,000,000
Motor Vehicles	294,000	660,000

SOURCE: Robert C. Schmitt, *Long-Range Forecast for Hawaii.*
* 1968 dollars.
† Constant dollars.

facilities will be strained far beyond their present
capabilities, resulting in traffic jams of truly incredible
proportions, both on the streets and aloft.

Second, these projections suggest a far more affluent
future. Per-capita personal income and per-worker earnings seem likely to grow far faster than consumer prices.
Whether high wages will compensate adequately for congestion and loss of amenities is an important question.

Third, the "official" projections, high as they may
seem, are significantly lower than the 2000 levels implicit
in growth rates of the 1940–1970 period. In population,
for example, demographers generally anticipate a decline
in fertility and a leveling off in net in-migration. Some
of these trends may occur naturally, even though no
specific action is taken; increased housing costs may
reduce birth rates as successfully as family planning programs, and erosion of the Hawaiian image may discourage
both in-migrants and visitors. Such consequences, however, are far more inevitable. Many important trends are
susceptible to purposive intervention. If the residents of
Hawaii want to temper or redirect current growth rates,

or to avoid the levels of economic activity, congestion, and pollution implicit in the rates of 1940–1970, they should take effective remedial action. Otherwise, developments may — as they have in the past — overtake the statisticians, and create a Hawaii that no one wants.

WHAT DOES HAWAII WANT?

Thus we must inevitably come to the normative. What do we want the economy of the state of Hawaii to be like in the year 2000? There is a great temptation on the part of those who write to assume that what he wants everyone else wants or at least a majority of the citizens want. My guess is that if we really could get everyone's desires articulated we would be impressed with the range of desires for the future. Thus it would seem, if this be true, that we ought to provide within the limits of prudence as large a freedom of economic choice as is consistent with broad objectives. Choosing these objectives is sometimes difficult because the choice often involves giving up a measure of freedom in order to provide direction in the social interest.

There are two very nasty problems involved in talking about the future of the economy, neither of which is essentially economic in nature. One has to do with population, another with our value system.

An economy which is called upon to provide a decent standard of living for only 700,000 obviously cannot provide the same standard of living for a population twice that large. Thus those who would discourage economic growth have to face up to the problem of preventing population growth. But how is this to be accomplished? It seems likely that as far as births here in Hawaii are concerned this objective is attainable and probably with some planning and work constitutes no impossible problem. But in-migration is another matter. If we maintain a healthy economy and a pleasant environment, individuals are going to want to migrate here, and there is very little the state of Hawaii can do about it.

Being a state of the union we have no control over in-migration from the Mainland. In-migration from foreign countries is the province of the federal government. About the only possible solution, and I am not even sure it is possible, is to limit job opportunities in such a way that there will not be jobs for individuals not citizens of Hawaii. But this probably would ruin us as a culture for it would mean that new and exciting minds which from time to time in the past have been interjected into our society would no longer be forthcoming. In time the results might be quite deadly.

The limitation of population via the limitation of job opportunities seems doomed to failure for another reason. If, as will be discussed later, 2000 finds a minimum income base for all, this will have to be a responsibility of the federal government. And the individual will be able to live and spend it where he will.

Perhaps equally if not more difficult of solution, is the problem relating to our value system. At what level of economic well-being will most of the citizens of the state of Hawaii be willing to say, "This is enough — I want no more"? This is the carrot part of the carrot-stick problem and while, as I indicated earlier, I think we can get rid of the stick; I am not so sure about the carrot. It is not so much that evil people will dangle carrots as a way of motivating people to work, but rather that our nature, at least to this point, seems to be such that far too many of our citizens always want more. And, as a matter of fact, if they did not, the system would not work. And this desire for more is not confined to any one economic or social class.

In any event, let us try to develop some objectives. In 2000 Hawaii should have an economy which would be characterized by the following features.

1. The provision for a minimum decent standard of living for all citizens. *By 2000 it seems unlikely that any economic system which permits some citizens to be ill-fed, ill-housed, or ill-clothed by reasonable standards will be able to persist. The political, social, and moral climate will not permit it, and sound business reasoning will not advise it.*

It seems quite likely that this will be a matter resolved by the federal government rather than the State. Whether this is accomplished by a guaranteed annual wage or some other means is to a degree irrelevant. But by 2000 this minimum standard of living concept should be accepted. In 1970 dollars the amount for a family of four should be about $10,000.

2. The Hawaiian economy should be more diversified than is now the case. *Lack of diversity is the single greatest weakness in our economy now. This is compounded by the fragile nature of some of the "industries" on which we rely so heavily. Federal spending in Hawaii has its volume controlled by the legislative and executive branches of the federal government which, at times, can act capriciously. The need for Hawaii as a military base becomes, with the invention of new weapons, increasingly less.*

Our agricultural business is concentrated largely in sugar and pineapple. Sugar sales are influenced, in fact in part controlled, by political decisions which may have no relationship to the conditions of the marketplace. Pineapple now operates in a very competitive market, and there is every indication that this will continue and even increase. There are some who hold that in ten years Hawaii will not be a factor of much consequence in the pineapple market. This may be too pessimistic a prediction, but the problems of the pineapple industry are and will continue to be great.

A prosperous tourist business depends primarily on the presence in the national and world economy of leisure time and disposable income. It is an industry which is very sensitive to a decline in the economy. (There is a real question as to whether it is among the more sensitive. But the evidence to establish whether it is or is not was not available to me.)

Thus the need for diversification is evident when one considers that in 1967 fifty-five percent of Hawaii's gross state product came from these three industries.

3. Ways should be found to maximize the satisfaction which each individual finds in the work he chooses in the economy of 2000. Writings which depict all of those who work now as victims of mind-numbing repetitive tasks which depress the spirit are, of course, exaggerated. However, there is enough truth here to concern us. There is too much of "after I get through work I shall enjoy myself." Somehow we need to find ways in which there is pleasure in work as well as in leisure.

4. Virtue should be made profitable. This may sound like a startling or even shocking statement, but I think it has some merit. I, along with many others, have spent a great deal of time over the years trying to "do good." I do not criticize those efforts. Frequently they are most productive. I see nothing wrong with people's volunteering their effort to try to improve society. But I must say at times I have been depressed at how little progress is made, and cannot help but note how fast things can be accomplished if individuals stand to profit from such accomplishments.

Perhaps this is a base motive, but it does seem to work, and I cannot believe that it will be without motivating power even in the year 2000. In short, all that's being said here is that the man who contributes positively to society should be rewarded more than one who does nothing, and still more than one who injures the society of which he is a part.

5. Hawaii's population should be decentralized. A major part of our population problem even now is not numbers but geographical concentration. Our largest

island, Hawaii, now has only about seven percent of our population while our third largest, Oahu, has about eighty-four percent.

HOW DO YOU ACHIEVE THAT WHICH IS DESIRABLE?

The following steps would seem to be promising in terms of achieving the above desired goals.

The provision for a minimum decent standard of living for all citizens probably cannot come about through the action of the state of Hawaii alone. But there is good indication that steps in this direction will be taken by our federal government. Thus we as a state will participate.

It seems likely that by 2000 with cybernetics, automation, and computerization our gross national product can be increased to the point where this provision of a minimum standard can be achieved without too much difficulty in the United States.

But there is a larger problem which will be a long time in resolution. Ultimately this decent standard of living must be provided for all individuals throughout the world. This is true for both altruistic and selfish reasons. Altruism dictates that a man cannot desire for himself what he is not willing to accord to others on a universal basis. From a selfish point of view we shall not have a healthy world nor a stable one if it remains divided between the haves and the have-nots.

Diversification and stability of the Hawaiian economy is a subject amenable to specific and immediate actions. But one first must turn to the question as to what kind of diversity is feasible. Here we would do a disservice by not being extremely honest about our situation. As far as is known, Hawaii has no minerals with the exception of some low-quality bauxite, and the materials to make cement and titanium. It is always possible, although not likely, that some will be discovered. There is always the chance, as we learn more about the ocean, that this might provide some mineral resources. But at this point it does not appear prudent to count on either of these.

We probably shall never be able, even if it were desired, to engage in heavy industry. Even though shipping costs may in time become considerably reduced, it still appears unlikely that it would make sense for us to import materials and export heavy industrial goods.

In agriculture we should immediately increase our efforts to diversify. There has been some increase in this field, but it certainly has not been as dramatic as that of the balance of the economy. Since 1960 the sales of diversified agricultural products have increased only 2.1 percent per year. [4] Probably the principal ingredient needed to expand this kind of agriculture is increased research and better methods of getting the results of that research in understandable terms to the practitioner.

It is possible that there may be further development of the manufacture of jewelry. Black coral and olivine are found in Hawaii, and pink coral of gem quality is being extracted from Molokai's deep waters.

In 1967 Hawaii's annual catch of fish was valued at $3.1 million. With better methods, equipment, and more knowledge, this could be increased. The expansion of sports fishing also may hold promise. As a matter of fact, we must watch developments in the sea with care, for there may well be opportunities here as yet undiscovered. The present experience in shrimp cultivation is a case in point.

There would seem to be considerable merit in trying to attract to Hawaii what might be called "the foot-loose industries." What is in mind here are those industries which are not engaged in fabrication, but rather in some sort of a service which, with modern communication technology, does not necessarily have to have a headquar-

4. *The Economy of Hawaii in the Tenth Year of Statehood*, Department of Planning and Economic Development, State of Hawaii, 1969, p. 35.

ters immediately adjacent to large population centers. The headquarters of huge insurance companies would be an example, as would those companies that engage in financial services. The attractiveness of the state of Hawaii might for many of these firms be a real asset in terms of attracting high-quality personnel. These are clean industries and the compensation of employees, while varying, usually is reasonably good.

We should continue and intensify our efforts to attract to the state more companies concerned with research and development. Considerable progress has been made in this area in the last few years. In 1964 there were only 7,573 individuals employed in Hawaii by research and development organizations. By 1968 there was an increase by 75.2 percent to 13,273. [5] Again, this is a clean industry and its employees are highly paid. As more federal funds become available, as eventually they surely will for oceanographic studies, this may be a field of great growth between now and 2000.

Absolutely essential to this growth, however, is the presence of a truly great university. The University of Hawaii has made considerable progress toward this goal in recent years. The direction needs to be accentuated and accelerated.

It is possible that Hawaii might become a communication center for the Pacific which would both diversify our economy and achieve another goal of drawing together the Pacific community.

These efforts at diversification should receive wide support. However it is important that we not throw the baby out with the bath. It seems likely that by 2000 federal spending, sugar, pineapple, and tourism will still remain, regardless of how successful our efforts at diversification, quite central in the Hawaiian economy. However, there may be within these industries desirable changes that

5. *The Economy of Hawaii*, p. 39.

should take place, and indeed some may change in character. It is quite possible that an increasing number of our visitors, for example, could be attracted by our availability as a place for conferences, new learning experiences, and the like.

Achieving diversification, growth, and stability requires forethought. Contingency plans should be prepared to help adjust to changes that could be induced by reductions in military spending; for example, of the rapid growth in a particular industry. Perhaps a board or commission on futuristic thinking should be created to address itself to these and related matters.

The decentralization of population with due regard for appropriate distribution of talents and skills can be approached in several ways. Every effort should be made to see that future growth in visitor destination areas takes place off-Waikiki on Oahu, and on the neighbor islands. The latter in particular deserves emphasis. Thus any growth in the daily census of tourists and those employed by that industry would be better distributed throughout the state.

Essential to this redistribution of population is the provision of economical interisland transportation either by surface or air or both. It takes less time to get from Molokai to downtown Honolulu, even now, than it does to get from many New York suburbs into the city. Given economical transportation, there is no reason why those who work in Honolulu might not live on a neighbor island.

New businesses as they develop should be encouraged to locate on the neighbor islands. It would be a proper function of government to assist in solving those problems that make such location difficult. In this connection, there is a rationale for considering provision for a variety of economic life-styles.

It would appear that these objectives for 2000 are not unreasonable, provided we really wish to attain them and are willing to work.

EPILOG

One thing seems certain. The economy in 2000 is going to provide some people with more leisure than they ever had before. The important human question is what will they do with it? Just as the young are now asking the older, affluence for what?, their children may ask them, leisure for what?

It was noted above that we should make work more enjoyable. Perhaps the same, plus the additional dimension of social constructiveness, can be said of leisure.

Science and Technology 2000
Terence A. Rogers

Terence A. Rogers is dean of the School of Medicine at the University of Hawaii. A physiologist by training, he has done research in fluid and electrolyte metabolism, especially with respect to the effects of starvation and severe environments, such as the Arctic. He was born in London, England, and came to the United States in 1952 to undertake graduate work at the University of California. Prior to joining the University of Hawaii in 1963, he taught at the schools of medicine of the University of Rochester and of Stanford.

INTRODUCTION

The most fundamental motivation for technology was the provision of food, clothing, and shelter. Our technology today already has the capacity to provide these essentials for everyone on earth; the obstacles to doing so are political and economic, certainly not technological. As primitive man developed an agricultural technology, becoming a farmer rather than a hunter and gatherer, he assured himself of a more reliable food supply, but at the same time let himself in for a lifetime of grinding, monotonous work. Accordingly, another extremely important motivation for technological development has been to lessen the brute labor required of man. In general, any device which cuts down on the amount of necessary brute work can contribute to a better life for man. Perhaps this originally indisputable fact is the basis of the disastrous modern assumption that any technological device improves the quality of life! The original motivation leading to a

251

technological innovation may be the improvement of human life, but its continued production is motivated by the usual goals of "business."

Despite the dire predictions of Marx, the system has improved the quality of life. The basic life-style of the well-paid American industrial worker may lead to quiet or violent desperation, but it is undoubtedly and immeasurably superior in more than the material sensse to that of fifty or seventy-five years ago. The unsatisfactory aspects of life today sometimes cause us to romanticize our agrarian past, but at the turn of this century farm laborers lived little better than the animals they tended, even in the advanced countries of the world. As has been lucidly described by Galbraith,[1] the modern industrial corporation no longer operates on the simple principles of what the market will bear, and the lowest possible wages. Despite this new and more intricate relationship between the corporations, government, and the market, the basic motivation of the purveyors of technology is to convince their fellow men that their wares will improve the quality of their lives, by giving them less work, and higher status, by restoring their youthful vigor, by removing noxious insects from their proximity, or by providing a fantasy life of saccharine sweetness or bloody violence.

Problems related to technology today stem from a variety of causes, some of which can be briefly listed as follows.

1. Modern technology, chiefly through improvements in food production and advances in public health, has permitted an explosive increase in world population, unchecked by the "natural" controls of famine and disease.

2. The rate of technological innovation is not only very great, but the rate itself is increasing so rapidly that society is unable to assimilate the innovations. This tendency will accelerate.

1. John Kenneth Galbraith, *The New Industrial State.*

3. *Technological innovations are imposed upon society with a seeming mindlessness completely different from the ingenuity that goes into their development.*

4. *The pesticide problem is a new and serious one, but generally our pollution problems arise from the scale of our activities. Samuel Johnson's London was a polluted nightmare, but it was also just a speck on the edge of the fields and forests of Europe. Now we are faced with gigantic cities that spread from Boston to Washington, D.C., or potentially from Tokyo to Osaka, and the total pollution becomes worldwide rather than local.*

5. *It is now realized that none of us is a consumer. We are all processors who produce sewage and garbage of all kinds. Improvements in the methods of handling sewage are among the principal causes of our diminished early death rate and, therefore, of the population explosion. In general, however, the disposition of man's garbage has not received as much of his attention as has the prime production of goods.*

In our society the production and distribution of goods is in the private sector of the economy, whereas the collection and disposition of garbage is in the public sector. As has been pointed out by many authors, the public sector of our economy is underfunded.

6. *Perhaps in consequence of the fatalistic character of many of the world's religions, most of mankind believe that the future will just happen, and they cannot adapt to the idea that the future will be exactly what we make it.*

7. *In the Western countries, the Christian emphasis on the individual was enhanced by an acceptance of over-simplified Darwinism; with the comfortable idea that progress comes about through competition between individuals. The value of cooperative planning has been demonstrated time and time again, but our public ethic is still largely based on the sanctity of the individual and his rights as an entrepreneur.*

NATURE OF THE TASK

The distinctions between science and technology are not clear-cut, but generally we can think of science as concerned with the search for basic information about the laws of nature, and technology, with the application of the discovered laws to achieving material goals. For example, an investigation of the nature of radioactivity is "science," and the application of the results of that investigation (along with many other kinds of information) for the construction of a nuclear power station (or weapon) can be regarded as "technology."

Although the exact distinctions between science and technology are hard to define, the distinctions are not purely academic in at least one sense. Our society has clearly reached the point at which technological development and applications cannot be allowed to proceed without restraints from society, whereas it is difficult to imagine a system in which scientific curiosity could be shut off (other than by the relentless elimination of anyone showing scientific curiosity). Science can be regarded as "thinking," and technology as "doing," and this distinction serves to emphasize the difficulties of control.

The task-force members reached a limited consensus that their task fell into two broad categories.

1. Prediction of what would be technologically feasible by 2000, but without any value judgments about possible developments; and

2. Exploration of the means by which society could channel technological advance into directions beneficial to mankind and the world, without further contributing to the destruction of our environment.

An articulate minority suggested that we should also consider a third category: concerning mankind's problems which arise simply in consequence of our habitually separating technological and ethical considerations, just as is epitomized by the separation of the first two categories.

PREDICTIONS

"Straight-line" predictions from existing technologies are fairly simple, but if history is any guide, they will represent only a small proportion of the innovations by 2000. Furthermore, it was the impression of the task force that the kinds of scientific advances predicted in the popular magazines are more likely the technology of 1985 than that of 2000. That is not to say that they will all be implemented by the year 1985, but that they will be technologically feasible and their application will depend on economic and political factors.

The real difficulties in scientific and technological predictions lie in predicting the unpredictable. Several times in the next thirty years, discoveries will open up a whole field of technology unimaginable to us now. Other kinds of predictions would lie somewhere between the straight-line predictions from today and the unpredictable. There are major recalcitrant problems in engineering and medicine, for example, in which there seem to be generally promising approaches, but which await some flashes of genius to solve difficulties.

One possibly useful approach to prediction is to take the past as a paradigm for the future, but we cannot simply think of 1940 as thirty years earlier than 1970, just as 1970 is thirty years earlier than 2000. Arithmetically this is correct, of course, but the average rate of development in the next thirty years will be at least two or three times that of the preceding thirty years. Instead then, we should use the year 1910, or even the turn of the century, as a datum point for predicting 1970. The appalling difficulties immediately become apparent; our world today is so wildly different from that of seventy years ago. It is hard to see how anyone could have envisioned the world of universal radio and television, computers, air travel, antibiotics, and nuclear power, to name just a few technological commonplaces of today. In a tantalizing way, however, the threads were there in 1900 for an especially sensitive mind to see, because many of the basic principles of 1970 technology were visible at at the turn of the century. The roles of coal and steel were already firmly established. The basic work on radioactivity had been undertaken; electricity and magnetism were moderately well understood, with generators, electric motors, electric lights, and radio telegraphy in use. Development of the internal-combustion engine was imminently feasible, and viewing the future from 1900 with our 1970 knowledge we could easily project the important role of petroleum products in our part of the twentieth century. In other fields the threads were there, but less close to modern applications, and accordingly harder to predict from. For example, the work of the Curies and Roentgen had laid the groundwork in radioactivity, but the development of nuclear power could not be so clearly predicted as the mechanical engineering developments just discussed. Similarly, modern microminiature circuitry may be logically descended from the state of the art in 1900, but no one could have predicted the direction and distance we have traveled in electronics.

ELECTRONICS

The explosive development in this vast area of science and technology makes it extremely difficult to predict even ten years ahead, far less thirty years. Almost all that can be said is that the last third of the twentieth century will be regarded as the onset of the electronics age, much as the last half of the nineteenth century is considered the steam age.

One basis for projection is the microminiaturization of integrated circuitry; the importance of this can hardly be overestimated. Complex circuits need now occupy only one one-thousandth of the volume of transistorized circuits a decade ago. The power requirements and heat production are correspondingly diminished. This means, among other things, that the kind of computer that originally occupied a whole floor of an office building can become a desk-top or even a pocket-sized machine, and that large computers can have undreamed of potentials.

The new silicon chip circuits are much less susceptible to damage than vacuum tube or transistor circuits, and so we can expect electronic equipment of long life, high stability, and reliability.

Of special interest to our future in Hawaii is that for products of this kind, the weight and volume of raw materials and finished products are so small that one could conceive of an exporting electronics industry in Hawaii. The shipping costs would be an insignificant part of the total manufacturing costs, and so our distance from markets and suppliers would no longer be economically critical.

Small-scale circuitry will also be critical in the advance of orbiting satellite communications. In addition to the existing TV- and telephone-relay satellites, we can expect that the regulation of the world's air traffic will be mediated by satellites, not only for communication but for pinpointing the location of each aircraft. We can reasonably expect Hawaii to become the center for the regulation of all trans-Pacific traffic, whether or not we continue to be a way-station for actual landings.

Small size and small power requirements will also lead to extremely flexible personal communications, with pocket radiotelephones linked to the regular telephone system only a very few years away. We predict that improved equipment and simpler techniques for computer information storage and retrieval will lead to generations of personalized, potentially pocket-sized computers. Through these, the individual citizen will have instant access to vast stores of information. It is already clear that the source of power in the world of today and the future is largely through access to information, as it was once through control of land, and then of raw material supplies and manufacturing facilities. Accordingly we can expect the government (and other groups) to endeavor to limit access to some kinds of information, and we will see many *constitutional battles fought over principles we can only dimly perceive at this time. Related to this is the vast problem of secret electronic surveillance of our citizens — good or bad. Devices already commonplace in 1970 make it possible to bug anyone almost anywhere, and the scale and sophistication of surveillance described in Orwell's 1984 can already be regarded as underestimated for that date. It would seem that individual privacy can be best preserved by constant vigilance regarding the rules of evidence and by laws through which the private citizen could more readily get restitution from snoopers, rather than by attempting to control the technological developments which (incidentally) lead to better snooping devices.*

Because of the electrical nature of the functions of the human nervous system, most of our information about it is derived from electronics; thus, advances in neurophysiology will continue to be largely dependent on advances in electronics. Reciprocally, it is now clear that the behavior of an animal (including man) can be profoundly affected by electrical impulses administered through electrodes implanted in the brain. Savage rage or serenity can replace each other in seconds through such impulses. Sexuality, sleep, anxiety, the whole gamut of behavior seem to be accessible. The implications of these well-established observations of today are among the most profound that can be considered for 2000.

On the good side, we can see that surgical implantation of a brain stimulator could potentially help the violent schizophrenic, the autistic child, or the mentally defective. These are not solid predictions, of course, but simply examples of the kinds of applications that might be possible. The ethical problems arise through the fact that the stimulator would be controlled from somewhere, by someone. Who is to bear the godlike responsibility and power (through a switch, no less) to control the mind of another?

In the same context of behavior modification, elec-

trodes can be implanted in the brain of an animal and hooked up in such a way that impulses are delivered when the animal presses a bar in his cage. With proper placement of the electrodes this produces what we anthropocentrically consider to be intense "pleasure" in the animal, because he will go on pressing the bar several times a minute for long periods. The results are astonishing, because most pleasurable stimuli eventually cloy, and one will voluntarily desist. A possible explanation is that these self-stimuli simultaneously evoke appetite and satiety, whether the appetite is for food, sex, physical comfort, or we know not what. The horrifying prospect is that a man could be hooked up in the same way, and spend the rest of his life in tube-fed bliss, perpetually stimulated and satisfied in a private heaven of his own.

In addition to the developments in electronic instrumentation, we considered the electrical aspects of large-scale engineering and manufacturing processes. There are two large unknowns in our immediate future. One is the availability of nuclear fusion power, and the other is the possible development of superconducting alloys that retain this property at normal temperatures, and not just in a liquid helium environment ($-271\,°F$). The largest power costs today are the fuel costs and the losses in transmission. A superconducting distribution system coupled with nuclear fusion power stations would meet virtually all of mankind's conceivable energy requirements. We would need to rethink our entire approach to what is energetically feasible.

Furthermore, superconductors in electric-motor windings would mean that the motor would consume practically no current, so that the cost of industrial energy for machines would become insignificant. These developments, if they come about, will have almost incredible effects on the economy and, conceivably, even on international rivalries.

COMPUTERS

As with electronics, this vast area of technology is expanding so fast that even far-out predictions for 2000 are likely to be old hat by 1980.

Already some large-scale engineering projects exist which could not have been carried out without computers, not only because of the volume and complexity of the mathematical computations, but because of the brute volume of administrative detail in purchasing, inventory control, disbursements, and so forth. We can expect even more complex projects in the next thirty years that will be completely dependent upon computerization. The capacities of the computer to store and retrieve data, to correlate data, and to make predictions based on stored data are almost limitless. The great question and area of uncertainty concerns the possibility of their exercising judgment or imagination. It has been said that the first computer more intelligent than man will be the last invention man needs to make. If judgment comprises only the selection of the best option in any circumstance, then computers can make judgments now, provided they have all the facts and have been instructed about priorities. The difficulty now is to present the computer with all the data. Some existing computers which control machines actually learn from experience, and derive new information not programed in from "the outside." A computer that could itself acquire data from the random environment would be able, for example, to pretest the ecological impact of a technological innovation. Such a breakthrough cannot be predicted with certainty, but it would have profound effects.

As previously noted, access to information is a major source of power today. The centralization of data about our citizens by the Internal Revenue Service has already caused concern, especially among those who can appreciate the fantastic potential of electronic data pro-

cessing. As taxpayers, we can take comfort in the fact that the computer makes it harder for our fellow citizens to dodge paying taxes, but we are not entertained by the thought that some Big Brother of the future may have the same obliging computer provide him with regional lists of all those who claimed deductions for contributions to the American Civil Liberties Union (or the Boy Scouts of America).

Nearly all of the average citizen's routine interactions with government or business are computerized already; in the next thirty years this trend will continue, and will include his interactions with the health-care delivery service (not with his doctor, note), the courts, the schools, and others. All this can only increase the alienation and despair of men; so we predict that the limits of computer science will be set not by technological feasibility, but by human tolerance of the tireless intrusions upon privacy and autonomy. This limit of tolerance is already apparent in the "bent card syndrome," in which people deliberately mutilate punched cards to "frustrate" the computer. We can expect legislation aimed at preventing such activity, just as we have laws against disrupting a railroad.

Since credit-card sales offer a possibly closer control of inventory and other factors than cash sales, we predict an even greater promotion of the cashless society.

Technological developments will be necessary to insure the limited accessibility of computerized data. Devices may protect the privacy of medical records from the casual snooper, but they will not deter eager prosecuting attorneys or determined "personnel researchers." The myth of the privacy of bank accounts was exploded long ago, and computerization in this area just makes things easier for the authorities. The very volume of health transactions and bank transactions will make computerization essential, but the outlook for privacy is frankly grim. We conclude that privacy cannot be guaranteed by technologi-

cal devices, but only by the relentless administration of good laws limiting the utilization of information stolen from the various data banks.

On the more positive side, we see that advances in information retrieval and display will permit the physical dispersal of a great deal of professional and business work away from the great cities. We even predict that more people will work at home, and that advances in holography and television will permit socializing without the participants' actually gathering physically in one place. Such developments may be spurred by the murderous insanity of city travel, and optimistically we could view them as partial solutions to the transportation problem. Before 2000 we may logically regard information transmission as part of the same overall social need as transportation.

TRANSPORTATION

Cities in the next thirty years will experience a transportation revolution. So complex are our country's transportation needs that moving people and goods efficiently from one place to another will require a total and balanced transportation system, with a compatible interrelationship of highways, skyways, railways, and waterways, with each mode performing the task it does best. We predict the gradual separation of the principal public transit vehicles from all other types; there will be separation of cargo-carrying from passenger-carrying vehicles; and there will be separation of pedestrians from everything that does not walk.

It is conceivable that a generation hence cities will be webbed with grade-separated, multilevel arteries. Free of the automobile as we know it, streets may become "people places," served only by mini-buses. Overhead, travelers will use elevated, covered moving sidewalks, while still higher will be express tubes for "people capsules." Linking with the transportation systems below, escalators will deliver pedestrians to stations where automatically controlled capsules parade endlessly by.

We predict that electric vehicles will replace the internal-combustion-powered automobiles, and electronic highways will be constructed to move more cars per lane per hour, and to increase safety. Downtown areas of extreme congestion will be denied to privately owned-and-operated automobiles, but urban public-transit systems will have the flexibility and service of the private automobile. Such a system would employ small, municipally owned, low-powered vehicles which would be made available at a price to any occasional user. The user would pay for a device that would unlock any public car that he finds, which he would then use and leave parked at his destination.

Fast intraurban transit to move large numbers of passengers between central cities and suburban growth centers will be quieter, smaller, and less demanding in guideway requirements than current high-speed intercity systems. Linear motors for propulsion, air-cushion support and suspension for higher speed ranges, and automatic vehicle control, ticketing, and ridership counting equipment, will all contribute to safe, flexible, reliable service.

The dial-a-bus, a hybrid between an ordinary bus and a taxi, will serve low-density areas. It would pick up passengers at their doors or at nearby bus stops shortly after they have telephoned for service. The computer would know the location of the vehicles, how many passengers were on them, and where they were heading. It would select the right vehicle and dispatch it to the caller according to some optimal routing program which had been calculated for the system.

In the air the tendency will be toward specialization in certain types of traffic with hypersonic and supersonic transports for most long-haul personal travel. Improved flexible arrangements for rapid travel between airports and to and from city centers will be necessary. The vertical-take-off/short-take-off-and-landing aircraft and the compounded rigid-rotor helicopter are means of providing rapid connections independent of surface traffic.

Sky cranes capable of carrying ten-ton loads at over one hundred thirty miles per hour will find an expanding role in transporting heavy cargo to inaccessible places; airlifting cargo from ships at sea to docks on shore; and transporting people in sky lounges between major airports and numerous local points of boarding.

At sea we predict nuclear steam or gas-turbine engines for larger merchant ships and oil tankers on long routes, air-cushion vehicles and hydrofoils on short- and medium-length routes, and possibly submarine freighters on rough-weather routes or on routes under Arctic pack ice. Cargo ships will be highly automated and will remain at sea for years at a time, while cargo, supplies, and crews would be transferred by giant sky cranes as ships sail along the coast.

Finally, there will be standardization of containers, so that they can be transferred quickly among rail, road, water, and air vehicles. Thus, goods moving considerable distances will travel each segment by the most economical mode available, rather than being confined to one or two modes due to the difficulty and cost of intermodal transfers.

ENERGY SOURCES

Introduction

Coal has been used as a source of energy for over eight hundred years, and petroleum for just over a century. However, one-half of all the coal ever produced has been mined during the last thirty-one years, and over 50 percent of the world's cumulative production of petroleum has occurred since 1956. In brief, most of the world's consumption of energy from fossel fuels during its entire history has occurred during the last twenty-five years. Unless alternate sources of energy are developed, the growth in power requirements will seriously deplete known fossil-fuel reserves.

The United States, with only 6 percent of the world's population, accounts for nearly 40 percent of the energy expenditure. By 2000 the current generating capacity of 325,000 megawatts in this country will increase to over 1.5 million megawatts. The energy requirements for Hawaii will probably run ahead of the national norm, both from the standpoint of population increase and per-capita use of electricity. Existing power capability on the island of Oahu is 765 megawatts, with the peak load in 1970 running in excess of 600 megawatts. Consultants to the Hawaiian Electric Company predict a system load of about tenfold by 2000. The pattern for the state as a whole will probably match or exceed the growth rate projected for Oahu.

Fossil Fuels

Coal resources are reasonably well-defined, and will play a significant role in total power generation until alternatives are developed. Coal is not a potential source of unlimited power, particularly if it has to fill the void created by the depletion of petroleum resources. Crude oil, natural gas, and oil shales provide over two-thirds of the total energy used today. Every hour over 1.5 million barrels of petroleum are pumped into the energy-hungry devices of the world. These are nonrenewable stocks, and time projections for their depletion are from thirty to one hundred years.

Nuclear Energy

Fission. Uranium 235 is the only isotope spontaneously fissionable by the capture of slow-moving neutrons, and it is the initial fuel source for all subsequent power development based on the fission reaction. Unfortunately, it represents less than one percent of natural uranium, and the conventional light-water burner reactor can utilize only this fissionable isotope. The known uranium reserves that can be mined and processed economically are limited to about 500,000 tons which, at the present rate of growth of light-water reactors, could exhaust the total uranium supply within twenty to thirty years. This would be a tragic waste of an extremely valuable resource.

It is possible to convert most of the natural uranium into other fissionable fuels in the so-called breeder reactor. This permits the generation of nearly fifty times the energy from the same amount of nuclear fuel, and greatly extends the energy-generation capacity. Initial studies indicate that the minimum practical size of the breeder reactor is in the 1,000-megawatt range.

Fusion. The nuclear reaction produced by uniting heavy hydrogen nuclei to form helium is called fusion. This is the process by which energy is radiated from the sun and the stars. Enormous quantities of heat are released when deuterium or tritium is fused into helium, and the uncontrolled consequence of this process is the hydrogen or thermonuclear bomb. Intensive research is directed at the problems of confining and controlling the plasma in a steady-state fusion reactor. The Atomic Energy Commission predicts that prototype systems will be in operation by 1985; demonstration power plants by 1995; and full-scale fusion power plants should begin operation around the turn of the century. These plants will be extremely large, probably in the 4,000- to 20,000-megawatt range. Advantages of the fusion reactor include an inexhaustible fuel supply, minute quantities of radioactive waste, and minimal environmental degradation. Since only small quantities of the fuel are required for heat generation, the likelihood of an uncontrolled explosion is remote.

Water Power

Hydroelectric plants. There are five hydroelectric plants in existence in the United States with power capacities exceeding 1,000 megawatts each, and the total installed capacity in this country approaches 50,000 megawatts. The world's water-power potential is estimated at 2,850,000 megawatts, but nearly half of this capacity is in parts of Africa and South America where there is little demand for energy. There are many desirable aspects of hydroelectric power, particularly from the standpoint of the total absence of air pollution, but this is partially offset by the area of scenic or productive land inundated behind dams, as well as by the realization that these reservoirs may ultimately be clogged with sediments; the usefulness of any water-power site seldom exceeds a century.

With the steep drainage paths and rapid runoff rates in Hawaii, there are apparently a few sites adaptable to hydroelectric power. To date the one site that has been given serious consideration for this purpose is at Kokee on Kauai, where it is estimated that a 12-megawatt hydroelectric plant would be feasible. This represents less than one percent of the anticipated power requirement of Hawaii in 2000. Nevertheless, because of its unique advantages, there may be greater development of hydroelectric power in Hawaii, particularly in those areas of extremely high and frequent rainfall, where large reservoirs would not be necessary.

Tidal power. Tidal power is similar in many respects to hydroelectric power except that it is obtained from the flow of water in the filling and emptying of partially enclosed coastal basins during the rise and fall of the oceanic tides. The number of sites with a suitable basin configuration and a large tidal variation is limited, and there are none in Hawaii. The average potential power of all possible sites throughout the world totals only about 65,000 megawatts.

Ocean waves. There have been several ideas for harnessing the tremendous energy of ocean waves. It has been computed that a 7-foot wave in 30 feet of water possesses 20 horsepower per foot of wave front — or roughly 140 megawatts per mile. The advantages of ocean-wave power generation are obvious: (a) the motive power is free; (b) capacity can be increased indefinitely by adding more units along the coast; and (c) there is no negative effect on environmental quality. Equally obvious are the disadvantages, which include zero power generation during periods of calm and the difficulties of economically converting wave energy to electric power.

Geothermal Energy

Natural steam. In certain volcanic areas underground water is trapped in porous or fractured rock and becomes superheated. Tapping these sources permits the superheated water or steam to be used as an energy source for a conventional steam-electric power plant. There are a number of installations like this in Italy, New Zealand, and the United States, providing clean, inexpensive energy.

In 1961 five holes were drilled on the Big Island to a maximum depth of 700 feet, and temperatures of 237° Fahrenheit were encountered. There was, however, no pressure buildup, and the conclusion was that the volcanic rock is too porous to permit an adequate pressure buildup, even though both heat and water are available.

Gordon Macdonald, University of Hawaii volcanologist, reports that the possibility of finding natural steam in sufficiently large amounts and under the right conditions for commercial development "appears to be very limited and very uncertain." He comments on the general abundance and free circulation of ground water which test wells proved seldom exceeds a temperature of 95° Fahrenheit. Although not optimistic, he points out that geothermal power would be of such enormous benefit to Hawaii that "we cannot afford to overlook any possibilities." He lists Puna, West Maui, and West Molokai as the most likely sites.

Volcanic heat. A related source of geothermal energy is the direct use of volcanic heat. Macdonald reports that there is a large body of molten rock at a temperature close to 1200°C. (2200°F.) at a depth of only 10,000 feet or so below the floor of Kilauea Crater, and other sources of hot, partly liquid rock that extend into rift zones even closer to the surface.

Even though these hot rock formations exist at shallow depths, and it is entirely feasible to drill holes into them, the problem still remains of how to make adequate use of the heat. The obvious answer is to circulate water through some type of heat exchanger, but the capacity of this type of arrangement is severely limited by the very low thermal conductivity of rock. It would be extremely difficult to obtain sufficient heat flow through the rock on a continuous basis to establish a commercially feasible power plant. This type of problem, however, will probably receive much additional research and attention in the future, particularly in Hawaii.

Solar Energy

Theoretically solar energy is a prime candidate as a potential power source, particularly since it has the virtue of remaining nearly constant over time periods of billions of years. A practical commercial solar installation, however, in the range of 1,000 megawatts and with a conversion factor from solar to electrical power of 10 percent would require an energy absorbing area of 42 KM^2, or a square area roughly 4 miles per side. This is technologically feasible, but a gigantic undertaking. There are also certain special uses of solar energy, such as solar furnaces, home heating and air-conditioning systems, and satellite power sources, but we predict that the generation of solar power in commercial quantities is unlikely — even in sunny Hawaii.

Environmental Effects

A typical fossil-fuel power plant releases tremendous quantities of combustion by-products into the atmosphere. In contrast, the proponents of nuclear energy have presented it as the way to clean, safe, and smokeless power generation. Although nuclear power is still in its infancy and currently provides only about one percent of the nation's output, estimates are that by 2000 it will probably be the source of half of the nation's total energy. Already serious misgivings have been raised by conservationists and others regarding types of pollution from nuclear plants.

The most obvious danger — a nuclear explosion — is extremely remote; to date, nuclear plants have the best safety record of any major industry. The areas of primary concern are: (a) the possible release and unknown effect of even minute quantities of radioactive material; (b) the long-range problem of dealing with radioactive wastes; and (c) the amount of heat that must be dissipated. The present efficiency of nuclear power is appreciably below that of fossil-fuel plants, and thus thermal pollution of the environment — usually a river, a lake, or the ocean — is approximately twice as great as for the conventional plant. At some locations, and this could include Hawaii, there is potential benefit from this thermal by-product. It is speculated that discharging hot water deep within the ocean would cause an upwelling of nutrients that would enrich the near-surface zone and stimulate growth of marine life, including commercial fish. (Paradoxically, tropical waters support less life than the colder waters of the world. The nutrients lie in the colder layers at great depths.)

The wastes from a nuclear power plant contain isotopes with half-lives of around thirty years, and so they must be isolated at least 600 years in order to render them biologically harmless. Some of the current practices for storing and disposing of radioactive wastes are criticized as inadequate for the next six centuries, particularly in areas subject to earthquake activity, such as the Hanford Plant in the state of Washington. Some states have already established new and considerably higher standards for radioactive waste disposal than those advocated by the AEC, and until the legal implications of these regulations are resolved there will be much hesitancy in initiating additional nuclear power plants.

If, however, current standards of living are maintained for the increasing population base, greater quantities of power must be generated. This can be done either at a higher rate of depletion of the limited fossil-fuel reserves, and a corresponding increase of pollutants to the environment, or through rapid conversion to nuclear power — accompanied by adequate provision for eliminating radioactive contamination. The specialized "clean" sources of energy such as water, solar, and geothermal power are unfortunately limited, and will probably have little impact on meeting the world's escalating power demands.

Summary

The probable long-range pattern for meeting the increasing global power requirements involves a gradual transition from fossil fuels to breeder-reactor nuclear power over the next quarter century , with nuclear fusion emerging as a proven power source around 2000. By the middle of the twenty-first century, the majority of the world's energy requirements will probably be supplied by controlled nuclear fusion.

As far as the state of Hawaii is concerned, it is enticing to visualize a coordinated power system consisting of solar collectors on Haleakala and Mauna Kea; a series of ocean-wave generators strategically located off the Banzai Pipeline and at other storm-surf coastal zones throughout the state; a major geothermal installation drawing energy from the depths of Kilauea; and a massive nuclear fusion plant on Molokai — all tied in to an interisland electric grid connected through superconductivity transmission along the ocean floor, or by microwave and laser.

More realistically, however, because of the relatively small projected power demand and the inability to tie in to a coordinated grid with adjoining states, the conversion to nuclear power in Hawaii will lag appreciably behind that of the Mainland. By 2000, unless there have been major step increases in the power demand curve, there will probably be only limited conversion to nuclear power. However, public concern and support for the preservation *of the quality of the environment may accelerate the introduction of nuclear power to Hawaii well ahead of the rate that would be justified on economic considerations alone, and could also provide financial encouragement for development of some of the specialized energy sources such as geothermal power.*

At any rate, there should be no deterrent to the development of Hawaii in 2000 because of the lack of availability of an adequate energy supply.

MATERIALS

Supply

The various published predictions of future availability of materials are all based on some "straight-line" assumptions. We would assume that free-world trade will prevail, so that it is necessary only to consider world reserves, rather than national or regional reserves.

Metals. The supply of iron is adequate and so are reserves of the important alloying elements cobalt, chromium, nickel, molybdenum, and vanadium. Serious shortage of manganese (mostly used as a refining element in steel production) may develop shortly and will force utilization of sea-floor nodules and possibly mining of old slag heaps if no substitute is found. Another metal of concern is tungsten. Approximately 75 percent of world reserves are located in mainland China. Even if politics do not interfere with availability of these reserves, the metal probably will be exhausted before 2000. Two opposing trends make the prediction somewhat uncertain. One is the tendency to replace tungsten carbide cutting tools (presently responsible for 40 percent of consumption) with titanium carbide material, and tungsten-containing high-speed steels (17 percent of consumption) with molybdenum alloy steels. The other is the strongly growing demand for tungsten metal for service in extreme environments. It has the highest melting point of any metal and is used considerably for nuclear, space, and similar applications.

Some shortage could develop in copper, but low-grade ores are available. Substitution of copper conductors (for example, by aluminum or by cable with liquid sodium core) will influence the trend. There is sufficient aluminum and an abundance of magnesium (obtained from seawater) and of titanium. The supply of tin depends largely on the future of tinplate. The metal may be used up by 2000.

Gold for industrial applications may become scarce if no change takes place in current government use of the metal as basis for monetary systems. A serious shortage of lead will develop in the next few decades. Some relief (17 percent of usage) can be expected if lead additives disappear from gasoline. On the other hand, any increase in battery-driven transportation will accentuate the shortage. Zinc also will be scarce long before 2000. Some ease of the pressure on this metal can be expected as better "self painting" steels are developed and decrease the demand for galvanized steel. Silver will be scarce shortly, and its usage in coins will probably soon be discontinued. The platinum group of metals has reserves to 1980–1990, but the industrial use of these metals is rapidly growing. The most serious problem in the metals group is presented by mercury. This metal is difficult to substitute and present reserves will soon be depleted.

Nonmetals. In general, the supply of most nonmetals is adequate, although local shortages of sand, lime, and others already exist. There is an abundance of phosphate rock and potash, and the supply of asbestos and of fluorine should be adequate. The supply of mica should be adequate until a substitute is found (it is largely used in the electronics industry). Some shortage in sulfur could develop; however, new supplies may be obtained from the production of low-sulfur oils and, if necessary, from seawater. Large industrial diamonds will become scarce (the smaller ones can be produced artificially).

The main problem in Hawaii appears to be the resource of beach sand. Some of it is presently being depleted for concrete manufacture. It would appear that mined and crushed coral or limestone could well be used as a substitute.

Summary

For 2000 the supply picture can tentatively be summarized as follows.

Abundant: oil, coal, iron, magnesium, titanium, potash, phosphate rock, sand, lime

Adequate: cobalt, chromium, nickel, molybdenum, vanadium, copper, aluminum, asbestos, fluorine, mica

Possible shortage: manganese, tungsten, tin

Definite shortage: gold, platinum group

Severe shortage: silver, lead, zinc, mercury, large diamonds

It should be noted that by 2050 shortages will develop even in the groups labeled "adequate" and "abundant."

Possible New Sources.

New ore reserves may be found for some of the metals as exploration teams comb through the few remaining surface areas of promise. Improved exploration methods will make it possible to locate completely buried ore bodies of many metals and to survey the continental shelf areas of the oceans. Better technology for crushing and extraction of minerals from mineralized rock will make it feasible to utilize some of the lower-grade ores. Furthermore, advances in undersea mining technology and in ocean engineering will enable us to utilize the minerals of the continental shelves and possibly to mine the deep sea for manganese nodules. At the same time, we can expect an increased use of synthesis to produce items such as medium-sized diamonds, rubies, certain intermediate minerals, and others.

Seawater may be used as a source for some materials. It is now used as "ore" for magnesium, bromine, salt, and fresh water only. It is technically, though not necessarily economically, feasible also to get iodine, calcium sulfate, potassium, gold, silver, uranium, and deuterium from the water. With the expected increased use of nuclear plants for desalination it will be more profitable to "mine" the concentrate from these plants.

While the possible gains from all these sources are not fully predictable it is clear that we cannot expect any *El Dorado.* The attractive possibilities of solving all problems by obtaining unlimited amounts of metals from seawater or from base rocks have often been mentioned, but the energy required and the waste-disposal problems are so enormous for most metals that these speculations are highly unrealistic. The deep-ocean floor presents other problems. Even if it were possible to develop technology for mining under the ocean floor (and that would take a large effort) it is expected that the geologically recently formed rock there will show but little mineralization.

Thus, while new resources may change the supply picture somewhat, there is no doubt that shortages in important metals will begin to develop in a few decades and that many metals of importance to our type of industrial and postindustrial society will be in short supply a few generations from now. It is necessary, therefore, to change our wasteful ways and institute measures to conserve our limited minerals resources.

Role of Hawaii

Our local natural resources are meager. Those in danger of exhaustion (for example, beach sand) should be protected. A close inventory of resources and potential resources should be kept and small-scale efforts to utilize more local materials should be supported (such as ventures like the attempt to use pumice in production of light-weight concrete, the use of lava as abrasive or building material, use of local woods or of bagasse in constructional materials, and so on). If nuclear plants are constructed for power production and desalination we should consider using the necessary backup capacity to run a magnesium plant during periods of lesser power demand. We should, of course, contribute our share, or more, to the success of the other measures outlined above.

MATERIALS OF THE FUTURE

In the year 2000 the bulk consumption of metals will, as now, concentrate on aluminum and steel. The two account for about 95 percent of the total usage of metals and little change is anticipated, except that aluminum will continue to take over markets previously held by steel. There will be large increases in the use of titanium and magnesium.

There will be some trend toward using high-strength, low-alloy steels for all sorts of structures. This will be particularly useful for us in Hawaii if better self-painting steels are developed to the point where the oxide coat can withstand our atmosphere. These steels can then radically change the construction on our steep hillsides and certainly lead to more aesthetic design. Steel will remain the major material for body and frame of transportation units because of its great ability to absorb impact energy.

The field of construction has traditionally been extremely conservative, partly because of the building-code system. It would be amazing if we were to see this industry move much past the utilization of already existing technology within the next thirty years. There will be increased utilization of plastics, laminated woods, glasses, glass-ceramics, and composites. Concrete will still be the mainstay of high-rise construction, and will probably include corrosion inhibitors, permanent coloring, and surface-preparation agents. There will be increased use made of prestressed and of lightweight concrete. The trend toward factory-made modular units will force the industry to adopt stricter quality-control measures. For economic and efficient utilization of materials, the main need in this field is to change from the building-code system to one based on performance specifications, but we predict it will take at least thirty years to reach agreement on this point.

Better materials for high-temperature service will gradually develop and make it possible to use higher operating temperatures in power-generating equipment, resulting in improved conversion efficiency. The gas turbine for the passenger car may be economically feasible by 1980. The materials problems of seawater desalination will have been solved well before 2000.

In the presently backward area of biomedical materials, we can expect the development of corrosion- and fatigue-resistant implant materials that can be left in the body indefinitely, of fatigue-resistant plastic heart valves, or materials for prosthetic devices, and others.

There is some possibility that superconducting materials with transition temperatures above that of liquid nitrogen can be developed, although some special breakthrough is needed. This could revolutionize many areas of electrical technology and would certainly make it feasible to transport power over long, difficult distances (for example, from geothermal fields on Hawaii to Honolulu). The copper conductor will have largely disappeared in a few decades, having been replaced by other metals. New battery types (for example, the sodium-sulfur battery) may make the use of electric cars more feasible without cutting into our reserves of lead, although the development problems are tremendous.

The area of electronic materials that gave us "surprises," such as the transistor and the laser in the past two decades, also has the best odds for repeating the surprise performance. This is because the properties of these materials can be completely handled by solid-state physics theory. Apart from such surprises we can expect a tremendous growth in the production and utilization of these materials by their gradual development and improvement in performance, and in their adaptation to new fields.

There will be increased tendency toward micro-miniaturization, toward use of solid-state switching and control systems and toward use of electroluminescent materials instead of low-power light bulbs. There should be developments in laser technology that will enable us to use this tool in much higher energy-output applications, such as fabrication.

There will be increased use of glasses and ceramics (in particular, alumina) in structures, especially if the attempts to develop partially plastic glasses are successful. Inorganic plastics will be soon available with stability at higher temperatures. Better paints with longer life will reduce maintenance costs for ships, and the like. Injection-moldable thermosets will make the mass production of strong plastic items possible in a decade or so.

In general, there will be increased use of composite materials, some of them based on whiskers of directionally solidified materials, of cladding, and of materials of high strength and resistance to environmental attack. Most of the developments will be gradual. Materials closer to theoretical strength will be available and processing control will narrow the spread in property values. We should be able to develop better ways of characterizing materials and variables introduced by processing so that a total systems approach can be used to select materials for design.

Summary

Advances in many areas of technology now hinge critically on the development of materials to fit more stringent requirements. While we may see surprise revolutionary developments in the area of electronic materials, the development in most other groups of materials will be gradual. Of course, even by gradual changes one may cross "threshold" values which lead to development of whole new branches of technology. There will be some change in usage toward high-strength, high-stability materials in all groups and toward usage of ceramic and plastic materials instead of metals. However, steels, aluminum, and concrete will still constitute the bulk of materials used.

Of particular importance will be improvements in control of materials properties, in "microdesign" of tailor-made materials, and in development of quantitative or semiquantitative means of selecting materials.

MANUFACTURING

Conventional manufacturing processes will improve. High energy-rate processes will be common, and will eliminate many costly machining and heat-treating operations. We will see increased use of continuous steel casting, electrochemical machining, electroforming, electron beam and laser welding, vapor deposition, injection molding of thermosets, and other processes.

Because of the large capital requirements and decreasing transportation costs, the main production industries will be even more concentrated than today, with computers handling inventory and many aspects of process control. Better nondestructive testing methods must be developed and materials will be produced to much closer tolerances in properties, composition, and other characteristics.

The increasing automation and complexity of manufacturing will increase the output of "lemons" in all areas. For this reason, large numbers of service industries will thrive, and 2000 could well be the year of the repairmen.

Manufacturing in Hawaii will be restricted to very bulky products, such as building materials, or to very light, complex items such as integrated circuits.

MEDICINE

Introduction.

There is always a gap between scientific advance and its technological utilization, and there is an even longer gap between its first practical availability and its widespread availability to the population as a whole. This is very true of medicine, and will probably continue to be so. A sense of outrage at the inequality of medical care available to the different citizens of the world (or of our state) is quite understandable. This has led some activists inside and outside the medical profession to call for a moratorium on medical research spending until we have caught up on some of the gross inequalities in the delivery of presently feasible health care. The recent virtual elimination of poliomyelitis as a threat argues best against such a moratorium. If resources had been diverted from basic research to more adequate care of the crippled, we would be faced with endless care of a growing population of the afflicted, rather than the outright elimination of the disease.

Specific Predictions in Medical Science

It is possible to make a good many straight-line or surprise-free projections in the medical sciences. There will also be many brilliant surprises. Since we cannot predict the surprises, the following are all straight-line projections.

A. Status of fundamental understanding. *Improved understanding of the following basic areas can be expected.*

1. *The immunological response, including identification and synthesis of specific antibodies, confirmation of autoimmunity as the basis for many diseases and an understanding of the influence of environmental and physiologic factors on the autoimmune process.*

2. *Discovery of a host of "enzyme diseases," new enzymes, and the basis for enzyme specificity. Possible control of enzymatic activity by induction or depression of synthesis.*

3. *The basic biological control substances (DNA, RNA), permitting synthesis of nucleic acids (up to*

viable viruses) for potential use in transmission of genetic information.

4. Interrelations of environmental factors in disease and the relation of these to physiologic factors. In this category lie the following: recognition of carcinogens and cofactors for carcinogenesis; accelerators and decelerators of the aging processes; developmental biological processes and their relation to fetal and neonatal environment; regulation of social and biologic sexuality; the relationships of noise, radiation, climate, altitude, and the like, to health and disease, particularly mental disease; a clearer delineation of the organic and chemical bases for neuroses and psychoses.

5. The etiology of atherosclerosis, myocardial infarct susceptibility, cerebral vascular accidents, and the debilitating and progressive forms of hypertension.

6. The causes of obesity and mechanisms for control.

B. Diagnosis. Improvement here will depend upon three broad factors: computerized data processing, early recognition of disease processes, and improved analytic techniques. We predict massive screening from early in life (starting in utero) to identify genetic defects, to detect and predict disease processes, and to evaluate applicability of preventive measures. All information on an individual will be cumulatively stored for rapid retrieval and automatic search for correlatives and predictions.

C. Therapy.

1. Techniques and procedures. Surgical advances will include availability of adhesives to replace most suturing, development of a clinically useful series of mechanical hearts, kidneys, and other "organs" capable of implantation. (This will be accompanied by a parallel development of highly advanced techniques for in vitro maintenance of tissues and organs for use in

transplants.) Organ banks will be common-place, and major decisions will have to be made about the use of organs or the substitution of mechanical devices. Mechanical aids for the deaf and partially blind will include surgically implanted "receivers" and "amplifiers."

2. *Cure and control of disease. Virtually all infectious diseases will be controlled or have been eradicated prior to 2000. New, mutant forms will occur and there will be a continuing fight to handle both new vectors and agents (especially new viruses) and to maintain our immunological resistance to common organisms.*

A major concern for society will be the right of the individual to be ill and die as a result of his own action or inaction. This will not slow down the mass use of immunizations, drug additives, and supplements of many kinds which will be compulsory on a mass basis by 2000.

3. *Drugs in therapy. Drugs will remain a major means of altering disease processes. Chemical therapy will be of significant value, for example, in the cure or prevention or modification of: hypertension, edema, congestive heart failure, emphysema, autoimmune diseases, all manner of infections, anxiety-tension states, depression, aging in its several aspects, asthma, and cancer.*

D. Euphoric Drugs. *Euphoric drugs will become bigger and better. They are not recent phenomena, although alcohol has been around for so long that no one thinks of it as a euphoric drug any more.*

Man's interest in escaping the hard edges of his perception is probably as old as man. Sumerian carvings from 5,000 years ago show men drinking beer from heroically large pots, and all of recorded history has instances of the use of alcohol, opium, and possible references to peyote-like substances. It would be comforting to think that alcohol is associated chiefly with gentle conviviality or sacramental purposes, but the brutal fact is that it is (and was) used chiefly to make life more bearable. The wide range of socioeconomic circumstance, educational level, and religious fervor over which we find drug abuse (including alcohol) suggests that we cannot anticipate any widespread change in life-style in the next thirty years which will diminish the demand for euphoric drugs. The enforcement difficulties of Prohibition and now of marijuana laws make it unlikely that control of manufacture and distribution of drugs of this kind will change matters much in the future.

Our most optimistic prediction is that newer drugs will have fewer destructive side-effects, and yet will still be highly efficacious in doing whatever we need to have done to our view of reality. There is, however, good psychiatric evidence that the alcoholic gets some gain from the self-destructive implications of his addiction, as well as from the obvious surcease from reality. Accordingly, we would predict that safe substitutes for alcohol (or the narcotics) will not necessarily replace it.

In the electronics section we referred to the possibilities of lifelong euphoria through selective stimulation of parts of the brain. The same possibilities lie in drug developments, and society must consider the implications. Apart from the problems of voluntary cop-outs, we again have the specter of Big Brother administering happy drugs by stealth or compulsion to whole populations, leaving them happily unconcerned with public policy.

E. Genetics. Progress in genetics suggests that it will soon be possible to alter human genetic makeup, and perhaps even to change the course of human evolution. For our society this has very serious implications that will have to be faced before 2000.

At this time it is theoretically possible to produce genetically identical human beings by asexual means. This process, known as vegetative, or clonal, reproduction, has been accomplished in frogs. These same experiments are being attempted with mammals and there are no theoretical reasons why they should not be carried out with human cells. Possible misuses of this scientific potential would include the development of an army made of identical soldiers, derived from an individual selected as a soulless killing machine, or we could conceive of a work force of nearly mindless slaves.

Another means of asexual reproduction is by parthenogenesis, which is the development of an egg into a new individual without its being fertilized by a spermatozoon. This occurs naturally in several species of invertebrates, and artificial parthenogenesis has been accomplished in the eggs of amphibia and some mammals, such as rabbits. Even in humans, parthenogenetic births are possible, but modern claims along this line are usually met with derision. The era of genetic engineering is imminent. Techniques will be developed which could, if applied, produce individuals of highly desirable qualities or the correction of many genetic abnormalities. Older eugenic ideas are also becoming more feasible. Sperm from "superior individuals" can be stored indefinitely and used for artificial insemination, thereby increasing the frequency of desirable genes in the human gene pool. Methods have also been developed for the in vitro fertilization of a human egg and the implantation of the fertilized egg in a proxy mother, who effectively incubates the egg until she delivers the full-term newborn.

F. Transplantation. The enormous difficulty in transplanting organs is that the tissue introduced from the donor individual is vigorously rejected by the recipient. This is because it is made up of "foreign protein," that is, cells with a different array of genetic information. The rejection is through the body's immune response mechanism, which serves as its chief defense against invading microorganisms. Rejection of a transplanted organ can be minimized by use of certain drugs which inhibit the immune response, but this renders the transplant recipient correspondingly more susceptible to infection, and so the postoperative management of a transplant patient is extremely difficult.

The whole idea of the immune response is under the most intensive investigation, and we can certainly expect that ways of selectively inhibiting rejection will be developed within the next thirty years. In addition to problems in transplantation, several important diseases come about through disruption of the ordinary immune reaction following a fairly routine infection. In consequence of this disruption, the body rejects part of its own structure as if it were a foreign protein. Rheumatic fever is a prime example of this kind of disease, but this is no longer so serious a problem because the precipitating streptococcal infections can be controlled by antibiotics. Ironically enough, another disease of probably autoimmune etiology is glomerular nephritis, which is one of the diseases leading to kidney failure and to making a kidney transplant necessary.

FOOD

It is anticipated that the present world population of around three billion will double by 2000, but in the strictly technical sense we predict that the world will be able to feed that population. Food distribution is a political, economic, and social problem. The number of persons on earth is ultimately limited by the amount of space a person needs to work and live in reasonable comfort, and is not limited by the production of food.

If we calculate the area needed for a person in an affluent society, the estimate is 0.087 acre per person for urban use. Recreation would add an equal amount per person. These estimates might be low, but represent approximately 0.19 acre per person. If to this is added the amount of land necessary to support life per person, and we then divide the amount of land available by the total land needed for each individual, we arrive at a figure of 146 billion people. To feed this number we will need approximately 15 percent of the land surface of the world.

It is interesting that the number of persons who can live on the earth can be increased only a little by increasing the yields per unit surface, because most of the land is necessary for purposes other than growing food. Thus, a crop yield increase of 40 percent leads to an increase in the maximum number of people by only 3 percent.

A balanced diet requires an adequate supply of high-quality protein and vitamins, as well as fuel (calories) in the form of carbohydrate or fat. Vitamins will present no problem, in that all will be synthesizable by 2000. Because of a different distribution in plants of the amino acids that man's body cannot synthesize, plant protein is generally not as good as animal protein. This is another way of stating the uncomfortable fact that the best food for an animal is another animal. Because of the expense of producing animal protein, in terms of land and caloric efficiency, the next thirty years will see a great deal of ingenuity directed at ways of improving the nutritional quality of plant proteins.

Some combinations of plant proteins, such as the traditional soya bean and rice, have an amino acid distribution almost as good as that of animal protein, and other combinations will be developed. Another technique we predict is the supplementation of a plant protein with those amino acids it does not contain, or has only in short supply. The supplemental amino acids may be made by direct chemical synthesis, or by controlled microbiological synthesis, such as was used for penicillin production. Synthesis of materials by the selective growth of microorganisms has potentials completely unknown to the general public. Some microorganisms are grown even on crude oil: the products are refined gasoline and considerable tonnage of microbial protein of high biological value. We predict many more such innovations.

The oceans trap an enormous amount of the sun's incident energy in photosynthesis by the minute plants comprising the phytoplankton in the surface layers of water. We do not predict that this photosynthetic capacity will be exploited directly for human food, but it will continue to be the basis for the food-chain in the ocean, and so will continue to provide us indirectly with fish. Fish yields from the ocean will increase, both as a result of greater efficiency in catching deep-sea fish, and the development of inshore fish-farming. In any event, though, the fisheries will provide chiefly an added source of high-quality protein, and only a few percent of the world's bulk caloric requirement.

Our conclusion, therefore, is that our ability to feed any population present in 2000 will be easily within the grasp of mankind as far as science and technology are concerned. As stated, the number of persons supportable on earth is ultimately limited by the amount of space a person needs to work and live in reasonable comfort, and not by the production of food. At the present projection, overpopulation is our major problem — not starvation.

THE REGULATION OF TECHNOLOGY

This part of the task force's responsibility was much more difficult to carry out; there was more difficulty in agreeing on goals, priorities, and even definitions. The more important ideas that emerge with a limited consensus are outlined below.

1. A Scientific Advisory Committee

The administration and the legislature of this State should clearly have some formalized scientific input when decisions or legislation with any scientific content have to be made. We would recommend, therefore, that a scien-

tific advisory committee be established by law. The chairman of this committee should be a nonscientist (that is, with no professional ax to grind), and the other members would be representative senior scientists (including social scientists). They would operate largely by their appointment of highly specialized ad hoc committees drawn from the whole scientific community, from industry and the hospitals, as well as the university, to deal with each specific task.

2. Institutes For Technological Assessment

With reference to the long-range control of the introduction of new products or processes that might damage the environment or otherwise interfere with the quality of our lives, it was proposed that new products or processes should be referred to one of a series of institutes, set up for the specific purpose of objectively evaluating the impact of any such innovation. These, it was felt, should operate at the national level.

Computers offer one way of evaluating the possible impact of an innovation, but only to the extent that all the environmental variables can be foreseen, and suitable instructions given to the computer. We are unable to foresee any advance in computer technology that would permit it to take into consideration an environmental factor it has not been informed about, and so we can never expect perfection in this sense. Therefore, in addition to prejudging any potential innovation, the institutes must be equipped to initiate the recall of any innovation which shows itself to be damaging to the environment after a year or two.

3. Classification of Environmental Threats

A proposal in this context was that any new device or process should be graded from 1 to 10 (for example) as a hazard. Grade 1 would be something so insanely lethal that it should not be considered for a moment. Grade 2 would be something extremely dangerous, to be con-

ducted only under the closest controls and by the most highly qualified personnel. Then the grades would run the gamut of hazards requiring licensure, such as for firearms or automobiles, up through things like power lawnmowers, and so on up to Grade 10, which would be (provisionally) rated as completely benign to man and his environment.

Education 2000
Robert E. Potter

Robert E. Potter is professor of education at the University of Hawaii and was formerly associate dean for academic development. He is the author of *The Stream of American Education* (1967), a book on the history of American education.

THE FREE MAN AND HIS
LEISURE: 400 B.C. — A.D. 2000

ur modern word "school" is derived from the Greek word for leisure. Among the ancient Athenians the word scholē meant a learned discussion engaged in by men of leisure, the fortunate citizens who were free both politically and economically to devote much of their time to the arts of politics and philosophy. Their leisure was not spent in idleness, but rather in an intense and sustained search for truth and beauty. During these leisure discussions great teachers like Socrates were surrounded by younger men who were stimulated by their challenging questions and bold ideas. It was an education to make the free man free, to liberate him; hence it has become known as "liberal education."

By 2000, America, if not the whole world, will be approaching the point where most of the people may well be within the class of freemen. This free society will be based not upon the slavery of other men but upon the enslavement of the machine. Technology will free all but a small percentage of the population from work most of the time. Work days will be shorter, work weeks may be only a couple of days, long vacations will be more common, workers will start on their careers later in life and *retire earlier than at present, free to seek an avocation. Everyone, whether he works or not, will receive a guaranteed annual income.*

The American of 2000 will be much like the Athenian freeman of the time of Socrates — with some major differences: (1) there will be no favored class — all men will be free; (2) it will not be freedom for males alone — technology will make possible freeing women and children as well; (3) the range of intellectual, aesthetic, and other options open will be infinitely greater than Socrates dreamed of; and (4) the support facilities for leisure and learning will be one of the most expanded institutions of human society, with progress in the next thirty years being greater than it has been in the 5,000 years since the first teacher's only educational aids were his own voice and a stick to scratch drawings on the ground.

By 2000, education will again become synonymous with leisure. And since there will be plenty of time to learn, there will be no need for compulsion. The free Athenian did not have to be forced to attend school — he went because it was pleasurable, exciting, and worthwhile. The new freeman — whether he be five years old or eighty-five — will attend "school" for the same reasons. When he wants or feels a need to learn, he may join others in schools to learn what he wants or needs to know. But he may also choose to learn all by himself, and the technology of 2000 will make that possible. He will not need to transport himself somewhere to learn what he can teach himself — the teaching materials can be delivered to him.

When he doesn't feel like studying, no one will compel him to. No one will ask for a note from his parent or his physician excusing him for absence or tardiness. There will be no necessity for compulsory attendance laws or truant officers. New legislation may be necessary to protect the child from exploitation by parents — or perhaps protecting parents from exploitation by children — so that when a person wishes to learn, he will be free to do so. He will be equally free to take a vacation or a nap.

But most people need meaningful activity. One of the present causes for unrest among young people is that most of the activity they are forced to engage in has no significance. Schools are irrelevant because they have little apparent relationship to life as it really is. But instead of reforming education so as to make it so exciting and challenging that students will prefer learning to idleness, we cling stubbornly to the status quo and coerce students into attending. Some of the coercion comes from compulsory attendance laws, but much more comes from the social and economic coercion of grades, diplomas, degrees, parental dreams, teachers' assignments, and the whole range of subtle devices by which we make the nonattender and the inattentive feel guilty and threatened. By 2000, imaginative educators will find ways of bringing education in tune with the times — we will have our schools crowded with people, young and old, who want to learn. Then education will be a pursuit of the truly free man and then will be truly liberal.

AVOIDING THE TYRANNY OF WORDS

In talking about education in 2000, we must use words whose current meanings must change radically in the next thirty years, or else be replaced by new words and phrases. Among them are "school," "university," "teacher," "student," "educator," "class," "grading" — indeed many of the words which we now understand and use continually when talking about education. Those words are our framework for discussion — we have no other way of framing our thoughts but in words. Yet we must realize that the very way we use words is a form of tyranny of the present and of the past over our attempt to visualize a better future. Whenever we use these words, we must be aware that their future meanings will be vastly different from today's meanings.

PURPOSES AND CONTENT OF EDUCATION

In the schools of the future the purpose of learning will be identical with the purposes of living, for learning and living will be inseparable. John Dewey's criticism of formal schooling of the late nineteenth and early twentieth centuries is still significant today, and it must be of continuing concern in the future. There is a grave danger in any establishment of formal education, for schooling "easily becomes remote and dead — abstract and bookish."[1] It tends to become concerned with learning the symbols in which the accumulated knowledge of society is preserved while ignoring the real cultural experience for which the symbols stand.

Learning in the schools of 2000 must not be limited to the acquisition of literacy, however important a skill that may yet be thirty years from now. Much learning will still be through the verbal symbols of language, but only because we will have discovered ways to make the use of language "more vital and fruitful" in "its normal connection with shared activities" of life, the social processes of living, working, and learning together.[2]

To be productive, people must learn skills; in the schools of the future they may seek to train for new jobs or for advancement in their current ones. With the rapid changes in technology, many people will be completely retrained several times in the course of their short careers. The schools must provide that opportunity. More importantly, in all vocational training we must include concern for maintaining an environment that will make possible the survival of mankind.

To understand themselves, people must learn about themselves as humans and as individuals. This will be an important step in retarding — perhaps preventing — the increasing incidence of mental illness that so

1. John Dewey, *Democracy and Education* (New York: Macmillan, 1916), p. 9.
2. Dewey, *Democracy and Education*, p. 46.

debilitates both individuals and society. The schools of the future must give more attention to helping people learn to understand the self.

A significant correlative to learning about the self is learning about others. One aspect of the future which is not likely to change is man's dependence — socially as well as economically — upon others. We cannot tolerate a world where man preys upon man, individually or by ethnic groups, economic classes or nations. Schools must give attention to the critical problems of learning to live with others. This will probably be one of the most controversial aspects of education, for there is much about learning to live with others that we have refused to bring out in the open.

We have been too afraid or too ashamed to examine our religious beliefs honestly and to admit that religious irrationalities can be just as destructive of humanity as any other form of irrationality. We must be prepared to admit that churches have often promoted religious persecution and wars in the name of gods who supposedly offered all mankind love. Candor in examining man's religious relationships will demand that the evil be weighed with the good.

Another taboo which must be broken if we are to be fully educated about human relations is the reluctance to discuss sexual relationships. Many who wish they could talk openly about these relationships between men and women, indeed those between men and men and women and women, find themselves engaging in circumlocutions, avoiding the use of frank words which they hesitate to admit they know, furtively wiping their damp palms, and hoping no one smells the sweat under their armpits. But uncomfortable as it may be for many of us today, the schools of the future must be free to speak and read as openly about sexual relationships as about political and economic ones — perhaps an unfortunate comparison

294

since we rarely bring out the whole truth about those relationships either!

In order to learn their political responsibilities as citizens in a democracy, which we hope we will be able not only to preserve but make more truly democratic, people must be able to practice democratic citizenship in the school setting, where they might be helped to analyze the successes and failures of their practice and thus improve themselves in effective citizenship.

With increasing hours of leisure, schools must provide opportunity for people to learn many forms of creative expression — music, games, individual sports, painting, drama, dance, and conversation — as a performer as well as a passive appreciator. The distinction between curricular activities and what are now called extracurricular activities will disappear.

How will these purposes be reflected in courses? The arbitrary divisions between bodies of subject matter must be broken down. Problems in life do not come in neat textbook isolation. If schools are to be related to living, the problems that the learner encounters in his actual life must be the starting point for his education. Those problems cut across many of the subjects which schools now attempt to treat in sterile isolation — and the higher the school, the more sterile becomes the container in which the learning is encased until eventually, in a good doctoral program, the process is suddenly reversed and the student is encouraged to seek solutions to a problem which is important to him. Of course, few doctoral programs are really good, and many students are forced into one more sterile exercise that results in much work, little learning, and additional unread clutter on library shelves.

How can we be sure that the student will learn everything important if we don't require him to take certain courses? The answer is simple. With all the knowledge and skills to be learned today, no one can possibly learn all that somebody may assume to be important. Learning is most effective when the learner has an interest in what he seeks to learn — and that rarely occurs when he is forced to take a subject. Dewey pointed out that "learning takes place in connection with the intelligent carrying forward of purposeful activities," and that

when we speak of a man as interested in this or that the emphasis falls directly upon his personal attitude. To be interested is to be absorbed in, wrapped up in, carried away by, some object. . . . We say of an interested person both that he has lost himself in some affair and that he has found himself in it. Both terms express the engrossment of the self in an object. [3]

If a subject is important enough for someone to be interested in it, he will learn it. If he isn't interested, then let him learn what he is interested in. There's too much to be learned to waste time in struggling ineffectually with something that may never be of interest anyway. If the time ever comes when he needs it, he will learn it then.

Remember, in this connection, that we will not be concerned in 2000 with trying to get students out of school quickly. What will be the purpose of rushing them through school only to have them wait until some job demands their talents? Nor are we thinking of an education that begins with grade one and proceeds by annual increments to grade twelve or sixteen or even twenty. If a student wants to leave the educational institution at any time — whether it be to work or vacation or loaf or pursue a different interest — there will be no need to compel him to come to school. Learning will be a process of many starts and stops, but at the same time continuous and unbroken, for the intervals between involvement in school will provide much of the experience upon which further learning will take place. In that kind of setting it will be possible to capitalize on education as the "reconstruction or reorganization of experience which adds to the meaning

3. Dewey, *Democracy and Education*, pp. 149, 161.

of experience, and which increases ability to direct the course of subsequent experience." [4]

The purposes of education will be coextensive with the purposes of life itself, and the searching for answers to life's problems will define the structure of education.

SCHOOLS — THE LEARNING ENVIRONMENT

Schools will not be at all like the present complexes of classrooms and offices and playgrounds. Students will not be segregated by ages into elementary, middle, inter-mediate, secondary, or higher education. The school of the future will be an educational center where people of all ages gather to learn together or individually. The wide range of learners and teachers (including the learners themselves) will make possible learning opportunities that are virtually undreamed of in schools of today.

The buildings will not be crowded for six hours a day, five days a week, thirty-six weeks a year, and empty the rest of the time. They will be open virtually all the time. Some people will want to study at night, on weekends, during holidays or vacations. Others will want to be absent between nine in the morning and three in the afternoon Monday through Friday. That may be their time to work — or the surf may be up! Schools should be kept open for the convenience of those who want to learn, not restricted to an arbitrary set of hours when the brain cells are required to get into gear and do in six hours all the thinking that should be spread over twenty-four.

The buildings will be designed to provide greater flexi-bility of program and increased individualization of instruc-tion. In 1966, Louis Bright predicted that "within another ten years almost the entire academic portion of instruction will be on an individualized basis in most schools." [5] *There may be a delay in the realization of this prediction, in*

4. Dewey, *Democracy and Education*, pp. 89–90.
5. R. Louis Bright, "The Place of Technology in Educational Change," *Audio-visual Instruction*, April 1967, p. 341.

view of the slow progress since Bright delivered his paper four years ago; but by 2000, much learning will take place as a student works individually with prepared units of materials.

Suppose he wants to learn about a fundamental skill in mathematics. He will get from the learning center a package of programed materials, perhaps in book form, perhaps in a combination of books, slides, and tapes, perhaps as a film or TV tape. It may be used in conjunction with a computer station, or it may be complete in itself. As he finds difficulties which he cannot solve even with the programing or the computer, he will seek assistance from someone in a teaching role, although that may be another student working nearby. He records his progress so he will know where he should begin his next session — or the computer records it for him and keys his next lesson when he plugs in again.

Or he may want to learn about some scientific concept. A set of materials that will enable him to read about what he wants to know will be available; a single-concept film-loop may illustrate it or may give directions for setting up a laboratory experiment. He draws the necessary lab equipment from the learning center, enters a lab station, and runs his experiment. He may be the only student concerned about that concept and doing that experiment, and he may not perform any of the experiments being done by others around him. His interest calls for that material at that time.

Not all learning will be programed or taught on a one-to-one basis. There must be opportunity for free and spontaneous creativity but with the availability of help and criticism. There must also be provision for testing ideas through discussion with others.

Suppose the student wants to learn an artistic skill — he joins a studio group or works with an artist-teacher, who again may be another student — young or old — just a few stages ahead of him and who learns more effectively by teaching another what he is trying to master himself.

Suppose he needs to understand how other people think — he becomes a part of a group of learners and teachers dealing with social issues where the validity of his own thinking is on trial in the active interchange of ideas with others.

According to the learning problem he has, he may be in a classroom, a library, a soundproof listening booth, a laboratory, a concert hall, a gymnasium, a swimming pool, a conference room, a lecture hall, a private study carrel, his bedroom, or under a tree with a thoughtful companion or a good book. Indeed, he may be encouraged to try different, even apparently unsuitable environments in order to trigger novel reactions and bring innovative solutions. But the schools of the future will as little resemble present schools as the rambling mazes for learning we now build resemble the rural one-room schoolhouse of the nineteenth century.

TEACHERS — DIFFERENTIATED STAFFING

A modern hospital doesn't have just one kind of physician; it has many medical workers and aides. The hospital administrator and his staff keep the plant operating and carry on the business functions. The technicians do the laboratory work. The nurses have their many duties, divided up according to the training of the nurse or the aide. The physicians have their specialties. When a patient needs his back rubbed, he doesn't expect to have it done by a surgeon, but when he needs a broken back mended, he deserves the most expert orthopedic surgeon he can get.

Schools will be much like that in the future. The staff will include the business office to see that the school plant is taken care of and that all facilities operate effectively. Technicians will instruct students in the use of the learning machines and see that the machines are in constant operating order. They will also help other members of the staff, including the students, develop new units of learning materials. Each school will have a number of resident specialists in fields like mathematics, languages, history, sciences, composition, reading, geography, and physical education. Others will be available through telephone or closed-circuit TV from other schools or universities, called upon as consultants when their highly specialized knowledge is needed.

Central to the whole system will be specialists who know how to help students understand what problems they really want to learn about and to give them guidance in accomplishing their goals. They will be the counterparts to present-day teachers, but perhaps they should be known as learning clinicians. With the subject-specialists and technicians, they will take much of the leadership in developing new learning materials as students indicate a need for them.

Other members of the staff will be specialists in counseling, helping students understand themselves and select goals which reflect their interests and abilities, but not channeling them into any arbitrary direction. If the student makes a bad choice and "wastes" a couple of years before he discovers for himself that he has insisted on the wrong goals, he may have to retrace his steps, but what will he really have lost? He will have been learning, even if the only significant lesson is to know himself better.

There will be two other classes of people who help others learn. In a school where students are free to move about and talk with each other, where there is no competition to see who can outdo the others in earning grades, where the goal is to learn for self-satisfaction and there is no worry about cheating, where many learners will be more experienced in some field than those who are just starting, much of the teaching will be done by those whose major role is that of student. This cooperative arrangement will be of value to both the learner and the teacher. As anyone who has ever taught knows, you learn most effectively when you try to help someone else learn. And the learner profits by aid from one who can understand his question, the latter often having recently asked the same question himself. The danger of the student-teacher is that he may be tempted to simply give the answer and not help the learner find it for himself. One role of the learning clinicians will be to help the students learn to help others learn so that this valuable resource is used as effectively as possible. This may also be the first step in recruiting and training new faculty members. More on that later.

The other class of teachers will be part-time, volunteer members of the staff. They may earn their living at another job or they may be retired. It may be their choice to spend at least a part of their leisure in teaching others as well as learning. They may have an avocation which they want to share — playing golf, writing poetry, playing a musical instrument, digging for archeological artifacts, refinishing furniture, or collecting insects. They may be persons engaged in vocations related to learning activities of students — auto mechanics, museum curators, stenographers, computer operators, research scientists, musicians, nurses, airline stewardesses — and be willing to share some of their professional information and skills, or some of the knowledge picked up incidentally in their work. There would need to be some screening of these volunteer teachers — just as there must be of the other members of the staff — to make certain that the learners are not exploited or abused, but careful supervision by the regular staff can make this part-time staff an invaluable resource.

LICENSING, ASSIGNING, AND RETAINING FACULTY

To create differentiated staffing and to break the pattern of a "standard" teacher in every classroom, it will be necessary to change the recruiting, certifying, and assigning practices of the schools and colleges. These changes will not come easily, for they strike at the principles which vested interests have fought to establish and defend. The "Master Plan for Public Education in Hawaii," released in 1969, says boldly that "rigid certification requirements and rules and regulations must give way to the thought of using effectively the tremendous resources that are available either on a volunteer or paid basis."[6] Endorsing the relaxation of certification requirements by a state department of education is heresy; yet this is the kind of heresy which must be uttered if we are to develop the kind of school staffing needed in the future.

Similarly, universities must get over their myopic insistence that the primary license for college teaching is the Ph.D. Indeed, considering the responsibilities usually assigned to the new assistant professor, the Ph.D. is perhaps one of the biggest handicaps he must overcome. After several years of becoming a specialist in a very narrow field, he finds himself expected to introduce freshmen classes to the discipline in its broadest scope. Furthermore, he understands very little about the relationship of his discipline to any related body of knowledge — he wasn't permitted in his own graduate program to stray from the straitened path to explore the byways his students find profitable and interesting. We must have the courage to resist the statistical despotism of the accrediting associations which measure the quality of an institution by the percentage of faculty with doctoral degrees. We must make every effort to retain and reward those who have demonstrated their ability as teachers and their capacity to continue to grow intellectually, without regard to degrees earned. Socrates, Buddha, and Jesus of Nazareth never earned degrees, nor could they qualify for teaching certificates.

6. Department of Education, ". . . Toward a New Era for Education in Hawaii": Master Plan for Public Education in Hawaii (Honolulu: Department of Education, 1969), p. 71.

TEACHER RECRUITMENT AND EDUCATION

The cooperative atmosphere of the school of the future will create an ideal source of selection for prospective teachers. As students, young and old, help each other learn, the faculty will be able to identify those whose personality and interests suit them for the professional roles on the faculty. Some of these may be young people still looking for their first career; others may be mature adults ready to move into a new vocation. Counselors might suggest that they consider education as a vocational field.

Beginning with informal suggestions from the learning clinicians and proceeding to seminars of those interested in giving more time to helping others learn, students may begin their preparation as teachers, counselors, or technicians long before they have completed what we now view as secondary education. With the unified educational center and the free flow of students from one campus to another, it will be possible for the prospective faculty member to maintain a very close relationship between what he is studying — whether it be the subject matter he would like to teach or the theory and methodology by which he will operate — and actual practice with learners. In the case of the prospective technician, even as a beginning student he may help with the production of materials, developing artistic abilities at the same time that he is learning technical skills. In short, the professional preparation for faculty members will not be a period in which the prospective teacher, technician, or counselor is removed from contact with the learners he is preparing to help. Nor will it be the traditional student teaching situation in which a prospective teacher practices with someone else's course and materials. He will work with students and other faculty members in planning, developing, and implementing learning experiences. As he does so skilled learning clinicians should challenge him continually with questions of why and how. Why does he propose particular objectives and material? How are materials, activities, and methods related to purposes? Are the materials and methods consistent with the latest research? The need for studying the theory of pedagogy or subject matter should grow out of the practical problems of assisting learners, not from the arbitrary decisions of a faculty of professors.

Just as other vocations will need continual retraining, teachers will need to be involved in in-service education. Again, the close relationship among levels of education will make such education almost automatic. The visiting specialist will teach the teachers as he helps the students. The constant development of new teaching materials by teams of specialists, learning clinicians, and technicians will be a major force in preventing teachers from stagnating. Special seminars on pertinent subjects can easily be fitted into the flexible schedules of faculty members. The security of the guaranteed annual income and the incentive of satisfaction of a job well done will remove the need for accumulating credits that may be traded in on a higher salary.

The teacher who fails to keep up with the world, who just does the minimum necessary to fill the job, will be retired. The guaranteed annual income will remove the embarrassing job-security aspect of tenure, which will then be a bulwark of academic freedom. Those who are teaching only because it is a way of making a living, who have no commitment to the learning process itself, can be excused from participation.

EDUCATIONAL TECHNOLOGY AND METHODOLOGY

Perhaps the most glamorous aspect of the schools of the future will be the fantastic advances in technology, both the hardware and the software. The computers, projectors, recorders, language laboratories, multimedia auditoriums and carrels, science laboratories, and gymnasiums will be matched by an almost infinite number of combinations of learning materials. It will take a com-

puterized information retrieval system to be able to select the proper set of materials for a particular student at the particular stage of his development. No human memory can master the volume of information needed to prescribe properly. Librarians in the learning centers will be specialists in knowing how to tell the computers what is available and how to ask the computer to repeat it when they want to help a student or learning clinician make the proper selection. The descriptions of the technology for education in 2000 sound like science fiction, but those who describe it have seen enough in action to know that the dreams are indeed possible, even probable. Undoubtedly the biggest problem will be to produce the generation of teachers — learning clinicians — and other staff members who know how to utilize the full arsenal of weapons against ignorance. We are already a couple of decades behind in our teacher-education programs, and unfortunately we seem to be doing little to catch up.

But technology will not be the only change in how learning is conducted. Even when students work in groups with a learning clinician in something resembling the present teacher-class relationship, there will be exciting methodologies for involving students in learning. Teachers will have their classrooms augmented with multimedia presentations of sound and light, perhaps even of smell and taste sensations, as they work with students. Students will be encouraged to express themselves through creative drama, where they make up their own roles and act them out spontaneously. Educational games and simulations will give students the challenge of complex situations, but under controlled conditions so that they may learn effectively. Play will not be something permitted only at recess, but a standard opportunity for learning. Actual work experience, getting into the community or taking a job for a period of time, can be a very effective way of learning. Following up any of these methods, there must be a session which the modern educational methodologist calls the debriefing session. It is the time when the teacher and the learners examine the experience to see what actually happened, what they did, and what they learned. It is the period when they attempt to relate the experience to what they had learned previously, in other contexts, and to apply it generally to other situations. In short, the debriefing is the truly educative part of the experience; it is the epitome of Dewey's definition of education as the "reconstruction or reorganization of experience." [7]

ESCAPING THE INFLEXIBILITY OF BUILDINGS AND ADMINISTRATION

One barrier to significant change is that existing buildings are not flexible enough to be adapted to serve radically different educational programs. The buildings now in use will probably still be usable in 2000, but some remodeling of programs within buildings is just as possible as remodeling walls. John Holt has commented that an office building may contain many firms, each operating independently although sharing maintenance workers, janitors, elevators, and other facilities. Large school buildings can be used in the same joint manner. One building may house several separate schools. The several schools could thus provide in one locale a number of very different educational options.

In Hawaii, with its single school-system, there would have to be major structural administrative readjustments to make this possible. There could still be the concept of centrality of funding, with equality of opportunity for all children in the state, but an encouragement of decentralization of program development and experimentation. The kinds of school programs designed for Kauai might need to be very different from those proposed for Kalihi or Kaimuki or Kahala. The limitations placed on education by definition of program from a central office must be resisted vigorously.

7. Dewey, *Democracy and Education*, pp. 89–90.

Similarly, in higher education the long life of physical plant must not be permitted to constrict adaptability of program. Fortunately some of the current new programs planned for university campuses for fall 1970 demonstrate that innovation is possible even within existing structures — physical and administrative.

One more giant step needs to be taken to achieve the educational complex which might be appropriate in 2000. That will be to integrate the separate systems of lower schools and higher education into one program of educational opportunities from early childhood to mature adult. A first stage in producing the nonschool school of the future may be making the dividing line between high school and college a membrane permeable to student passage, back and forth, in order that learners may have access to the full range of educational experiences.

NEEDED: A REVOLUTION IN EDUCATION NOW

Some futurists warn that life is endangered on our planet. There is a finite amount of natural resources that we are depleting and destroying rapidly. If there is to be life for our grandchildren, we must develop a new education which will make life possible — and we must do it swiftly. As H. G. Wells warned, "Human history becomes more and more a race between education and catastrophe." [8]

To win that race, we need a revolutionary change in education. Programs in our schools and colleges are creeping timidly into the 1970s. We need the bold leap forward. Students are registering their dissatisfaction by dropping out of school, attending only under parental or legal pressure, turning to narcotics and marijuana as escapes, complaining of the generation gap and the irrelevancy of schools and universities, protesting against society in general, and yet we continue to put them through that

8. H. G. Wells, *The Outline of History* (New York: Macmillan, 1920), p. 594.

same routine which was already irrevelant for my generation. We dare not delay any longer. We must act now.

We must incorporate youth in our plans, and not just
the complacent, conforming, "safe" students who agree
with what the teachers and professors plan and what the
school board and regents will accept. That is Uncle Tomism
at worst, tokenism at best. The student as nigger is a concept we must reject. The learner must become a fully active
participant in curriculum planning.

Suggesting radical changes will rock some boats and
make some people very uncomfortable, particularly
teachers who have their lesson plans all worked out
from twenty years of experience — perhaps very slightly
changed over those twenty years. But others who will be
uncomfortable are those parents who can't understand
what their children are studying, who are bewildered by
new math, embarrassed by sex education, frightened by
an objective study of religion and politics, and resentful
over the substitution of intramural sports for interscholas-
tic varsity events. Students who have been dutifully working for good grades and election to the honor society
or Phi Beta Kappa will be frustrated if grades are not given,
if they have no report card to demonstrate their superiority
to their classmates. Students who hesitate to make decisions will complain about the lack of required courses.
Legislators and taxpayers will be increasingly uncomfortable at the continually rising financial demands of quality
education, which does not come cheaply. But unless
somebody does begin to rock the boat, to get it out in
the waves and start it moving, we aren't going to get anywhere!

Don't worry about rocking the boat so much that it'll
capsize. We've got a pretty big boat here, and so far all
the rocking in the field of education is about as much
as one tipsy sailor might rock an aircraft carrier by staggering down the flight deck. Even the wildest statements
in this paper are only minor changes compared to what

education in 2000 could be like if we really turned on our collective imagination and then worked to make our dreams come true.

One of the most moving experiences I ever had came in listening to Richard Kiley sing "The Impossible Dream" in The Man of La Mancha. When I hear this song, I often think of some of the educators who have dreamed impossible dreams. I think of Comenius, who in the sixteenth century dreamed of education accessible to all men; and while the education we have may not be what he would have wanted, and certainly isn't what we want, we in America — and particularly in Hawaii — have committed ourselves to post-high-school education for every person who wants it. I think of Pestalozzi who, in the eighteenth century, dreamed the impossible dream of a school in which the child and his interests would be central, and where discipline would result from love; and while some of us may blunder at times, at least officially we are committed to the centrality of the child in elementary education. I think of some of the educators in Hawaii in the early 1930s who feared that their dream of secondary schooling for everyone was an impossible dream. This was the time when the Territorial legislature, at the behest of local industrialists who were concerned that "boys were being educated away from the canefields," decreed that at least one-fifth of all ninth graders must be shunted out of school, to complete their education on streetcorners and in pool halls. The industrialists further insisted that those who did continue into the senior high school should pay tuition for the privilege. But now we have a system of community colleges from which no person is barred. I think of the frustrated liberals who even now wonder sadly if they may not be dreaming an impossible dream when they envision schools in Mississippi, Alabama, and Florida, in Chicago, Detroit, and New York, attended by children both black and white, and staffed by teachers and administrators chosen on the basis of *their competence and without reference to their pigmentation. But while their dream is far from realization, we have faith that it is not, in fact, an impossible dream.*

As a historian of education, I know that over the centuries educational progress has been made when, and only when, a small number of irrepressible prophets have dared to dream impossible dreams. That is what we are being asked to do in 1970, to dream an impossible dream and then, because we have dared to dream, to fight the impossible fight. And if we give our full devotion to fighting that impossible fight, we may yet reach that unreachable star. There might be a year 2000. [9]

9. The much longer version of this essay published in *Preliminary Task Force Reports (July 1970)* contains specific suggestions for changing education in Hawaii, including analysis of the *Master Plan for Public Education in Hawaii* and documents relating to the plans for the University of Hawaii.

The Arts 2000
Reuel Denney and J. Meredith Neil

Reuel Denney, professor of American studies, was born in Manhattan and educated at Dartmouth. His career has taken him from Wall Street to the Houdaille Shock Absorber Corporation, to high school English teaching, to an editorship of *Time* and *Fortune*, to a professorship of social sciences at the University of Chicago, and to his present post in the University of Hawaii. He is the author of *The Connecticut River* (poems, 1939), coauthor with Riesman and Glazer of *The Lonely Crowd* (sociology, 1950), *In Praise of Adam* (poems, 1957), and *Conrad Aiken* (literary biography, 1964).

J. Meredith Neil, associate professor of American studies, was born in Idaho and educated at Yale, the University of Wisconsin, and Washington State University. He has taught at Sam Houston State College in Texas. The author of *Paradise Improved: Environmental Design in Hawaii* (1972), he serves as historian of the Hawaii chapter of the American Institute of Architects.

> But here, upon this bank and shoal of time
> We'd jump the life to come. But in these cases
> We still have judgment here . . .   *Shakespeare*

Preceding ages show us that changes in art occur because societies and artists have new needs. New aspirations emanate from every epoch. The artist, being always of his own time, is influenced by it and, in turn, is an influence. It is the artist who crystallizes his age — who fixes his age in history. Contrary to general notion, the artist is never ahead of his own time, but is simply the only one who is not way behind.   *Edgar Varèse*

PRESENT AND PAST

Art is engaged in its familiar habit of being nonart and antiart. Contrary to a widely accepted view, this is not entirely new. And if some modern philosophies, including Zen, are any guide, it is not an unhappy state of affairs. Let the contradiction work itself out or not work itself out. In either case, even if we throw out the word art, the meaning of the world will not be entirely exhausted by science or religion — or the Dow-Jones averages.

Hawaii has shown some resourcefulness in dealing with social and cultural differences that turned out to be complements of each other rather than negatives of each other. This report suggests some of the ways in which this capability relates to the future of art (and artistic nonart and antiart) in the islands. This report is not a conclusion, but a kind of starting place. And road-signs are only a direction, not the journey.

One way in which this thought was reflected by participants in the 2000 conference — some in the arts task force and some in other task forces — was most interesting. They declared that it was antifuturistic by definition to deal with the arts in a separate task force and report.

The people of Hawaii, like other Americans, have a strong interest in the arts as long as they do not have to pay for them directly. The television arts, which we bill ourselves for indirectly through advertising and taxes, are an example. So is the symphony, a natural loser that stays the course only because of non-box office supports including gifts, rental discounts, and awards from tax-exempt foundations. Nevertheless, the arts grew in Hawaii from 1950 to 1960. And it is a sure bet — when the census comes in — that they grew from 1960 to 1970. Between 1950 and 1960, according to the U.S. census, the sharp rise in disposable income in Hawaii was accompanied by a:

200 percent increase in designers of various kinds
100 percent increase in dancers and dancing teachers

(a rate of increase roughly equal to disposable income increase)

60   *percent increase in radio and TV repairmen*
50   *percent increase in architects*
15   *percent increase in graphic artists and art teachers*
8   *percent increase in musicians and music teachers*

Toward the end of the 1950s the approximate median incomes of some of the professions were: architects, $7,500 (20 percent less than in San Francisco); artists and art teachers, $4,000 (20 percent less than in San Francisco); and authors and editors, $5,000 (25 percent less than in San Francisco).

Generally speaking, only designers, with their markets in architecture, decoration, and merchandising, added to their numbers at a rate exceeding the growth in disposable income. Many artists in Hawaii were no better off than the unemployed and, indeed, declared unemployment in the arts was present, including that among people forced to work at nonart jobs in order to maintain their stake in an art form.

This unemployment situation in the arts between 1950 and 1960 may have been due in part to the amiable willingness of the artist to gamble optimistically on his economic future and the psychic income of those who came to Hawaii from the outside in order to practice an artistic profession. That is, these entrants may have been willing to trade some of their income off against their gain of enjoyment in living in Hawaii. It may also have been occasioned by the need of immigrants to wait in other jobs before becoming locally qualified and accepted in their own professions.

If this is true, these factors are perhaps measured roughly by the tolerated unemployment of individuals in one field and another. Such 1950–1960 unemployment, in order of descending percentages:

1. *architects (highest unemployment)*
2. *authors and editors*

3. musicians and music teachers

4. actors, dancers, and entertainers

5. artists and art teachers

A selected group of university students was asked in early 1970 to second-guess the results of the 1970 census with respect to the arts and artists in Hawaii. Their opinions were that:

1. the arts and crafts related to hand production might show one of the greatest 1960–70 growth rates;

2. this would be related to participation in the arts, especially among the young;

3. the other arts and sectors of the arts would show continued growth, at least following, if not paralleling, the disposable income curve;

4. the fashion arts would show rapid growth, since they partly involve the increase noted in item one above and so also would mass-produced fashions; and

5. design and decoration would grow as before, along with construction contracts of the 1960s.

Yet if past performances and present projections are reliable, we could say that the arts in Hawaii in the 1970s are not necessarily going to increase greatly their share of public interest and may lose in proportion to disposable income in some areas.

The State of Hawaii General Plan Revision Program, Part II, "Goals for Planning,"[1] suggests some of the art-related concerns of the people of Hawaii. It is headed by Julian Huxley's statement: "Our next step in civilization: the positive attempt to make our environment a work of art." In this report the highest-ranking goal expressed by consulted people in all islands was "preservation of Hawaii's natural beauty." (Surely artistic sensitivity and productivity can be both a cause and an effect of the

1. Honolulu: Department of Planning and Economic Development, 1967.

art-related suggestions made by the task force on the natural environment.)

"Goals for Planning" also mentions the popular "assurance to all citizens that each individual will be provided with increasing opportunities to enrich his life and the lives of his children, according to his own basic desires." How this goal could be pursued without attention to the arts is difficult to see.

The same report speaks of the continued need "to enrich the cultural life of the state in a manner appropriate to its plurality, cosmopolitanism, and decreasing cultural distance from the mainland."

This comment is accompanied by the observation — which may not be completely true — that "Hawaii is fortunate in that no single ethnic or cultural group can dominate the life-style of any other."

The report goes on to suggest that more and better ways must be found to continue Hawaii's access to, and contribution to, the great traditions of Western and Eastern cultures, while at the same time preserving the so-called little traditions that are associated with them. The great traditions are embodied in great works of the various cultures; the little traditions are embodied in the popular attitudes and sensitivities expressed daily by these cultures. Our small, diverse population living in a limited space, with strong local ties, must pursue a difficult balancing act in order to share in the universals of the great traditions without downgrading its little traditions. This is clearly seen in the defensive, exploited, surviving elements of the Polynesian-Hawaiian culture.

"Goals for Planning" almost necessarily has a wishful generality, an absence of more assertively specific hopes for the arts in Hawaii. The legislature of the state of Hawaii, however, has in recent years taken a much more specific step toward the encouragement of the arts. It established and funded the State Foundation on Culture and the Arts. This organization actually began its work when the gover-

nor of the state appointed the first members of this commission in early 1966. Since then, with the help of federal
funding, it has become a significant contributor to the
life of the arts in Hawaii. The legislature has also provided
that one percent of the cost of certain public structures
be earmarked for the purchase of artistic objects to be
associated with or incorporated within the structures themselves. The State Foundation has the considerable responsibility of contracting for the actual millions of dollars
involved in these adventurous budgetings.

Yet it seems almost certain that even minimum artistic
goals expressed in "Goals for Planning" will not be
approached in the future if general social conditions are
unfavorable. But were they ever? Let us look at the past.

Man does not select the sites where he lives and places
his most precious symbols. He discovers them. The act
of discovery contains cosmic meanings. Man's pursuit of
these cosmic meanings in an act of discovery contains
among other things the activity we think of as art. Presumably the first artistic acts that brought about the discovery
of Hawaii by the Polynesians were the discovery of form
in the heavenly constellations and the craft by which these
forms, with geographical assistance, could be organized
in stick-charts for navigation.

The discovery of the Sandwich Islands by Captain
Cook occurred within a context of western European cosmic meanings. The future of art in Hawaii after Cook's
discovery was determined for a long time by European
cosmology. The European psyche in Hawaii has in many
ways been unable artistically to reconcile a split in its own
identity. As much as any other place, the Hawaiian Islands
are the islands of the blest which were sought in spirit
by medieval mystics and in fact by explorers like Ponce
de Leon.

Having arrived at the islands of the blest, Europeans
could not do otherwise but change the place from what
it had been, first in the hands of nature and later in the

gentle hands of machineless Polynesians. At some conscious level, this was regarded as progress. At some deeper level it may have been recognized as an act of desecration. After Hawaii, at any rate, there were no more earthly paradises available.

Nor was there even in Hawaii. Most Polynesian art forms, except the performing arts of dancing and surfing and singing, were soon destroyed by culture-contact.

Afterwards, in the period roughly 1820 to 1850, the principal new expressive forms brought in were western church music and the literary arts based on biblical and secular literature — both in their English-language versions.

After 1850 the rise of commercial and agribusiness interests developed audiences interested in western drama and secular music. Monarchic circles encouraged the graphic arts to some degree.

With the large increase in water supply following the discoveries of reserves in the 1880s, the agrarian landscape was increasingly engineered into profitable and handsome forms. The surplus water was employed to change the foreshore from arid to verdant. This encouraged the affluent to create beautiful gardens which generally imitated the English style of planting.

In the later nineteenth century, music in Hawaii took the popular form of a blend of native patterns with south German and Austrian folk-song, and American popular music. It was enriched by Latin-European instruments and local Hawaiian variations on the conventional use of plucked strings.

In the earlier twentieth century, music from Hawaii had greater international impact than we recognize. Henry Pleasants [2] (writing in consultative comment on earlier drafts of this paper) says:

2. Consultant Henry Pleasants, born in America but now resident in London, is a composer, music critic, and musicologist. He studied in conservatories in the United States and abroad. He is possibly the first

I wonder to what extent Hawaiians are aware of the enormous influence their native musicians had a few generations ago in shaping the character of what I call Afro-American music. Do they know, when they hear a Chuck Berry or a B. B. King laying down those anguished or exultant glissandos on an electric guitar, that the origins of this device are Hawaiian?

The historical fact, of course, is that touring vaudeville troupes and minstrel shows, in the early decades of the century, frequently included Hawaiian instrumental and dance groups and teams of Swiss yodelers. One may speculate that the propensity of the black (and white) blues singers for the use of falsetto may have been stimulated by the Swiss yodelers. But there seems to be no doubt that the use of knife blade, bottleneck, and brass or iron ring to bring to the guitar the sliding cadences of human speech is traceable to the effects achieved by the Hawaiian guitarists.

Many students of the blues and, indeed, of many other Afro-American styles including jazz and gospel song, believe that the characteristics of phrase, of attack, of cadence and of color which distinguish this from any previous western music may be attributed to the black singer's impatience with the restrictions imposed by the white man's addiction to precise pitches pretty rigidly ordered in a stereotyped scheme of scales and modes. The Hawaiian guitarists showed them a way around this restriction, going beyond the compromises they had already made in flattening certain intervals or certain pitches in their vocal inventions.

After the 1870s Hawaii experienced a decline of people skilled in the use of the English language. Immigration of non-English speakers also contributed to the develop-

musicologist to notice the contribution of the Hawaiian slack-key guitar to the development of American jazz and popular music after the 1930s. His writings include *Serious Music and All That Jazz* (New York: Simon and Schuster, 1969).

ment of substandard local English which was of very limited use in the literary arts. In these circumstances, the arts of writing did not flourish and the most well known writings about Hawaii were contributed by short-term visitors who found that the local color was interesting to English-speaking people all over the world.

The later, rising standard of general literacy in the English language has a most significant relation, for example, to drama in Hawaii. On the one hand the drama and related arts have made a great contribution to rising speech abilities as a consequence of their appearance in the schools and outside of them. This widened public has in turn created the audience and the skill base upon which Hawaiian-produced dramas have made notable advance steps in recent decades. New producing companies of high competence are the order of the day.

Hawaii arrived in the midtwentieth century and statehood with a large number of pleasing architectural and engineering structures, but with no visible local style. The nearest thing to it was perhaps the style represented in the C. Brewer & Company building, the Academy of Arts, and some other pieces of distinction.

By this time the English (or Southern California) garden effect was already being transformed by a degree of orientalism. The beauty and dynamism of some of Hawaii's gardens and parks (and wilderness areas) brought strong new interest. Their presence stimulated new ambitions in ecological balance and site designs. Their threatened position also dismayed the artistically sensitive and the ecomanics.

And in the post–World-War-II years, Hawaii found itself, like the rest of the country, saturated by TV and all the other new art and communication forms of the electronic, mass-media age. As was pointed out in the conference, these mass-production processes have had two effects on the older handcrafts in wood, clay, textiles, and other materials. On the one hand, they have removed them from the center of daily work and consumption; on the other, mass-production has stimulated a revolt against itself in a wide resurgence of the crafts in Hawaii. Space does not permit more than this mention here of the craft renaissance and its new higher levels of skill and creativity.

THE CONVENTIONAL WISDOM

So much for a brief glance at an eight-hundred-year past. Conventional wisdom tells us that human nature and art do not ever change much. It adds that it expects the institutions of the United States and Hawaii to be able to weather the storms facing them now and in future decades. According to this view, we shall probably see many changes in our way of life — but these changes will come by way of progressive adaptation. In this process Americans, including islanders, will conserve familiar values even while accomplishing this through novel practices. Assuming that there is not another world war, the political institutions of the nation and the state will maintain their flexibility as well as their legitimacy and authority. They will provide a social setting in which the arts and the artist can flourish at least as well as now — and, hopefully, better.

The arts, by this view, have always been important to island people as well as to other Americans. Constitutionally guaranteed freedom of expression and general prosperity will continue, even as they did before, to nourish the arts. Repressive censorship is improbable, especially in view of recent trends that seem likely to maintain themselves in the future. And the increase in consumer purchasing power and leisure that will come with great growth in the gross national product not only will widen all kinds of demands for the arts but create stimulating rewards for artists. Moreover, this prosperity will probably increase the number of people whose relation to the arts is enriched by their being part-time producers, as well as consumers, of the arts.

By this outlook, there may well be a continuance of the conflict between the younger and the older generations. Legislative, executive and judicial institutions will be severely tested by this. And many in the younger generation, rejecting the older relationships between art and society, will seek to establish, in the forum and marketplace of tastes and ideas, new patterns of this relationship. The younger generation will in fact shortly rise to artistic, economic, and administrative control of the mass media. In doing so, it may reverse many current practices. Thus, it is possible that its talented members could virtually nationalize the electronic media by 1980 and use these media to celebrate and confirm their conquest of the channels of expressive and communicative power. But in all this they would simply be carrying on the tradition of previous generations, and their Federal Communications Commission, *while different in attitudes from ours, would still be the legal and legitimate institution that it is today. Still subject, that is, to the rule of law.*

The reason for all this optimism is the faith that the existing institutions and structure of public opinion will accommodate the new forces. In certain parts of the society, to be sure, the changes might reverse the present in a massive way. Thus, a universal guaranteed income could build an economic floor under the aspirations of artists quite as well as under those of all other citizens. Again, the social context of many art works may increase their dissenting messages to the point where they oppose national habits in sexuality, economics, and styles of representative democracy. But these developments will find a not-disapproved place in the pluralism of American and island social and political structures.

Even the current belief system, with its trust in the rationality of science and its nearly blind faith in technology, will bend to accommodate its angry critics. American notions of religious freedom especially, defended by the courts and accepted by the people, may assist in these processes. The acceptance of widespread variation in matters of belief and conscience will permit the permissive coexistence of radically different life-styles. And if the ideas of such coexistence can be protected, along all sorts of lines, including the ethnic as well as the metaphysical, then conflict, including violent conflict, can be moderated. There will be no final two-sided struggle for total power between the old and the new.

In this situation, in Hawaii, the arts will conceivably widen their already plural role. They will symbolize and forward the attitude that values individual difference and personal autonomy. At the same time they will not drop one of their historic missions: the creation of symbols which, because all can share them in some degree, hold out some hope of social harmony. In Hawaii, moreover, where present fear of physical and psychological crowding is great, the arts may do even more. They may supply the cues for personal sensitization, thus increasing the capacity of island perceptions to master rather than fall victim to eco-psychological stress. For this, they will surely be honored by all who value peace as much as they value various dreams of wealth and power.

OR A WAR OF CULTURES?

The foregoing prospect, according to a not-so-conventional wisdom, is complacently self-deceptive. How could American and Hawaiian societies and their arts continue such a peaceful evolutionary partnership and development in the troubled future? In the United States, some 6 percent of the world's population find themselves using about 40 percent of the world's total resources. What makes us think that this can possibly continue? And if this cannot continue, what about the rest of our voiced, and unvoiced, expectations about the future? In the view of some observers, the United States and Hawaii will be

lucky if they reach 2000 without experiencing atomic war

and the decay of democratic institutions, or, more probably, both.

The rise in the United States and Hawaii of what is loosely called the counterculture appears to announce a movement that defines many present institutions as decadent in spirit and potentially bankrupt in political, social, and economic terms.

The result is that many people today predict increased attempts at repression of the various parts of this counterculture. This is based on the belief, which may be correct, that the recent and current political administrations of the U.S. recognize, and recognize correctly, that the counterculture is subversive of their own power, and the belief that such administrations will increasingly move toward crushing the countercultures.

Just how this might occur may lie outside the bounds of the American historical imagination, even though the nation has already experimented with concentration camps (called relocation centers) and has survived one episode in police-state tactics under McCarthyism. And it is possible to think that such a repression would never be attempted, partly because the political conditions for its success either never existed or, if they did, may already be past.

Assume, however, that we are entering such a war of cultures. What might be the results for the arts, not to speak of the results for the securities and liberties of the individual? Many young people, and older ones as well, regard the counterculture as a prime source of artistic and intellectual productivity in recent years. The same large number of people are likely to regard what they call the Establishment as half-dead in these respects. If this is a matter of taste, it is also a matter of taste carrying strong aesthetic and moral conviction. A repression of the counterculture would substitute the dead hand of the past for the living forces of the present.

This might be thought of as an escalation of what appeared as a generational conflict in the 1960s. But what is worse, it could not be simply a generational conflict. An increasing number of cultural leaders and opinion-makers in the United States today, including businessmen and lawyers, regardless of age, identify positively with this or that aspect of the counterculture. Therefore, conflict leading up to the point of attempted repression would result in a massive extension through all age-groups of what Alan Ginsberg lamented in the first page of Howl: *"I saw the best minds of my generation destroyed by madness, starving, hysterical, naked. . . ."* [3]

The probable results might include a flight into aesthetic blandness, along the lines of the late Walt Disney, or plastic sensuality à la Playboy, *as the only tolerated modes of cultural expression. A sort of technological totalitarianism would prevail, and it might be tempted to use coercion against all dissenting artists or thinkers. This, in turn, might undercut the long-term staying power of the Establishment itself. It might become increasingly static, defensive, and brittle in its attitudes. Educational institutions might be compelled to dedicate themselves to skill-training accompanied by brainwashing. We could have, in short, an Americanized version of the culturally repressive mechanisms of Stalin's Russia and Mao's China, with the difference that American productivity and wealth would permit much more in the way of bread and circuses.*

OR A GATELESS GATE?

The gloomy prospects associated with a culture conflict do not dishearten the various members of the counterculture. They have faith in their survival even against odds and they sometimes act and write as if many present institutions will fall a good deal more quickly than the Roman Empire. Such a belief may be especially prevalent in the youthful perspective to be found in several sections of

3. San Francisco: City Lights Books, 1959.

the counterculture attached to the idea that expressive love rather than continued conflict and violence will be the "gateless gate" to the future.

A representative but highly articulate and deeply artistic evocation of this hope is found in the work by Gary Snyder called Earth House Hold.[4] *A collection of essays with poetic supplements, it has evoked a strongly favorable response among young and old. It may become the "anti–Waste Land" of its generation, in the sense that it opposes religious and ecological hope to the disillusionment expressed in the poem written by Eliot about fifty years ago.*

Snyder's book amounts to a forthright return to a much earlier American literary tradition. It casts off the fashion of art for art's sake in order to employ literature as the vehicle of a religious, moral, and social message. The message, to be sure, is closer to Thoreau and Whitman (and Tolstoy and Gandhi) than to those poets — such as hell-fearing Wigglesworth — who were once read by the missionaries to Hawaii. In a uniquely personal way, it expresses the world-view of no little group of Americans, especially young Americans today.

Historically, according to Snyder, man has moved through roughly five previous stages of history into a present age cruelly dominated by applied science. In this age "the more we conquer nature the weaker we get." The intolerable war in Vietnam is the natural result of the tendencies of an age in which "nationalism, warfare, heavy industry and consumership are already outdated and useless."

The next necessary step is to bring to the surface the "great subculture" of the world. This has existed everywhere in all the dominant traditions. It was represented in China by Tao and in the West by heretical groups begin-

4. Subtitled "Technical Notes and Queries to Fellow Dharma Revolutionaries" (New York: New Directions Publishing Corporation, 1969).

ning with the Gnostics. A main characteristic of these groups is their belief in the divinity of man and nature — the indwellingness of God in man and nature. Modern followers among the so-called hippies, a word that Snyder understandably avoids, are the spiritual descendants of such groups in the Middle Ages as the Brotherhood of the Free Spirit. Such groups denied that God was "out there," preferring to believe that he was "in here" and often pursued their idea of human perfection in a state of undress.

Such groups will move us in the direction of casting off our allegedly male-centered system of kinship and replace it with a family in which descent is reckoned through the female. In sexuality, this will correspond with a movement away from romantic love, with its obsession for merged identities. It will move toward a more truly intimate bond forged by a love which aims not at the possession of the other, but at perfect self-possession. Such institutions may well be nurtured by communal styles of living. In this movement, the Westerner will need assistance from his own forgotten past and from the Orient. Says Snyder: "The mercy of the West has been social revolution; mercy of the East has been individual insight into the basic self-void. We need both." The ethos of this new order will be a discipline that is not defined as self-constraint but rather as the self-control required to do what one truly wants to do.

This is a perfectionist rather than a utopian prospect. The utopian sets up a goal he never expects to reach but would like to approach. The perfectionist sets up a goal of human realization that he resolves to live in. This view is familiar to us as the Christian heresy of Pelagianism and is related to William Blake's revolutionary notion that there were two sources of evil in the episode of the Garden of Eden: one was the Evil that was distinguished from the Good; the other evil was the making of that distinction itself.

Believers in such a view, including Snyder, do not assure us that we shall all enter this blessed state. But they rather assume that those who do not will be the out-of-date, unfortunate outsiders of the future. From such a viewpoint, the so-called economy and so-called state are designed to sacrifice the present to the future in a devilish search for nonhuman efficiency. What is required to check this, among other things, is a meditation (not necessarily assisted by "pot") against the machine. This may bring us to the insight that will teach us to moderate our search for material exploitation of the earth and man while there is still time.

In the herb leaves of these doctrines we can read a possible future for Hawaii and its arts. If Hawaii were to go through the gateless gate, it might make heroes of its flower-children and clowns of its developers. Efforts to improve the gross economic product of Hawaii might be much damped down. It would no longer be believed that the economy had to expand in order to generate new jobs. Major multipliers of both productivity and congestion, such as automobiles, might well be banned.

Immigration would be discouraged and the birthrate reduced. Large ranges of status items in the market, such as private swimming pools, might well be inaccessible because they would no longer be produced. Many firms that added to maximized efficiency might be taxed heavily as a penalty for doing this. Local and national use of prime natural resources might very well be forbidden, above low levels, by custom and even law.

This is a deliberate overinterpretation of Snyder but not, as we can see, an overinterpretation of some of the attitudes of the flower-children in Hawaii. Their parents to some extent diverted their attention from production to consumption. They themselves divert their attention from consumption to the enjoyment of time-present in process. In their future, almost all Hawaiians in 2000 would be artists, making an art work of the community life. If *we all could join such a mass aristocracy we might not miss our sports cars and our martinis.*

AMBIGUOUS SIGNALS

The perfectionist social background of art sketched in the preceding scenario of a possible future seems unlikely of total arrival even if there were no cynics left in the world. As a utopian hope and plan for action, however, it includes some of the this-worldly hopes that have always been deep in the western European consciousness. Such faith in the future may be one of the forces that will stand off the conceivable battle of the cultures. In any event, we would certainly wish to sidestep any battle of the cultures that would reduce us to a lower level of civilization and culture than we now precariously hold on to. Yet it also appears that such progressive development may come only if existing leadership in all fields demonstrates a superlative sanity and flexibility in its response to changing times. Since this is more and more regarded as a task of cultural rebirth on the scale of the Reformation and the Renaissance, it is almost an apocalyptic assignment to leaders who are merely human.

We think of art as working in the way nature does, and we realize that art also achieves some of its ends by working on nature. Can the prime mover of art's work be anything else but the spiritual unity of mankind? This does not mean dogmatic agreement among various branches of mankind. It means rather the import of recent discoveries and rediscoveries. The art historian Alan Gowans,[5] who shared ideas with us as a consultant, will

5. Consultant Alan Gowans, author and educator, was born in Toronto but moved to the United States when he was 25. He taught art history at Rutgers University and Middlebury, Vt., College before going to the Fleming Museum in Vermont as director and then to the University of Delaware, where he has been chairman of the Department of Art and Art History since 1956 and professor of art history since 1960. He also has been a visiting professor in Scotland and Sweden. His books range from *Church Architecture in New France* (1955) to *Images of American Living, Four Centuries of Architecture and Furniture* (1964) and *The Restless Art* (1966).

show in his new work that the cosmogonies of the world's peoples show startling correspondences. Moreover, says Gowans, these peoples passed through similar periods of artistic flowering with remarkable degrees of simultaneity. Some proof of this may be found in de Santillana's observation that the giant Samson, a great deity of Japan, and Hawaii's divine trickster Maui emerged as variations on the same vernal constellation in earlier stages of the zodiacal precession. (The zodiacal twelve require about 25,000 years to complete their cycle and start over again.) The neolithics, therefore, including the Hawaiians, may have been the world's first cosmopolitans — in the precise sense that they shared, the world over, some identical symbolic deductions from the pattern of the stars and planets and the precession of the zodiac. Hawaii, by inheritance, is not barred from a psychic share in this intersection of the earthly and the sacred.

Nevertheless Hawaii, like much of the rest of the world, is in the constant process of deciding what it is and may become. For art, the important point is that Hawaii is torn between localism and universalism. The universalism is represented in the not-unrealistic claims that it is a crossroads of the Pacific and a stepping-stone between East and West. The claim is true to the degree that it can be spiritually incorporated in our world-view and not sink into delusions of grandeur. And it is a necessary experiment in self-definition because it properly corrects our provincialism. To continue to think of ourselves as being on the fringe of things is to fail to rise to new concepts of our community and its life.

Since our mental environment is worldwide, we share in deep changes in man's view of his relationship to that environment. As Hawaii art professor Murray Turnbull sees it, in remarks he made at our task force's interim meeting, our perceptions themselves, which both affect and are affected by the arts, will change in their operation. One reason for this is the expansion of our scientifically originated controls (and decontrols) of consciousness. Still another is the recognition that our scientific world is not that of the rational materialists of the eighteenth or nineteenth centuries. It is rather a world perceived as containing irrationalities at the heart of nature, along with the presence of ambiguous signs and signals as well as unambiguous ones. The older mind-matter distinction has passed away, with profound implications for the future of the arts. It could be argued, in view of Turnbull's approach, that Hawaii is unconstrained in the time-arts of auditory communication (it can speak to everywhere and listen from everywhere, including the moon), but that it is conspicuously limited in space. Its arts might then try to probe the notion of infinity in time along with finiteness in space.

The task might be defined in this way: "How can Hawaii demonstrate by the least use of spatial means, its artistic control over aspects of both space and time?" By "least use" is meant this: to get the greatest possible artistic and human value out of the least commitment of space. The problem appears to be to allocate space artistically and to allocate its volumes and their appearances so that we get the most out of each square foot that is removed from some purely ideal natural condition. It can be argued that this is a fallacious and fictional concept in the sense that it identifies the human living space with the land, excluding the circumferential basis of the sea. True, but any and all uses of sea-space for almost anything but heavy transport (and, of course, tourist views) are fantastically expensive. And they need a land base.

The shortest way to the artistic conservation of space may be to substitute viewpoints and symbols for space itself. The suggestion is that Hawaii should lead in the miniaturization and transistorization of space uses — that is, learn how to get more amenity out of each unit of space than we do now. The challenge to our arts here *is to form an interface between limited space and less limited time, incipient crowding and expanded leisure.*

The difficulties we face in such ambitious hopes are suggested, in a down-to-earth way, in task-force member Evelyn Radford's thoughts on "Hawaiian Popular Music, a Dying Art Form?" She writes,

(1) What is the present position of Hawaiian popular music in its evolution? (2) toward what is it evolving? and (3) can its evolution be stopped or turned back; and if so, how?

There is within the Hawaiian community a nostalgia for Hawaiian music as it was. While most of the young sing the songs of mainstream America, they do include hapa-haole [6] music and verbalize a wish that Hawaiian music will never die. And although on the one hand they are chauvinistic about the superior expressiveness of Hawaiian music, they are embarrassed by its simplicity and denigrate it as a relic of the past.

One of the most obvious and often-expressed reasons for the decline of the music is the loss of the language itself. There are few Hawaiians under the age of fifty who can speak Hawaiian. Another factor is the professionalization of the Hawaiian musician. The spawning of luxury hotels for a "middle-mass" clientele at Waikiki following World War II has drastically changed the free and easy Hawaiian-tourist relationships of an earlier day. Though this has helped the Hawaiian entertainer by forcing him to the discipline of an Art and its perfection, it has eliminated the face-to-face sharing of a simple musical form. If tourism is the bulwark for the continued existence of Hawaiian music and if the perpetuation of Hawaiian music is essential to the health of tourism, then the hotels and clubs of Waikiki will have to assume more responsibility for its preservation.

Yet it is true that the late Kui Lee influenced the direc-

6. Mixed Hawaiian and Western.

tion of Hawaiian composition toward the ballad forms of Rod McKuen, and other poet-composers, retaining only textual reference to Hawaii. His music was so beautifully constructed and prosodically enchanting that he brought to pass the most pervasive change in Hawaiian composition since the introduction of hapa-haole music by Harry Owens in the 1930s.

As the current now flows, where do Hawaiians think this lovely art form is going? The most definitive statement I received was from a pianist at Reuben's piano bar. "By the year 2000 it will be like a Gregorian chant, the way it's going." By the year 2000 Hawaiiana, including the music, may be merely one of the ethnic-cultural studies in Hawaii by anthropologists, musicologists, etc.

Music is a mind expander and a space expander. What happens if a genial local popular tradition comes under pressure? The question might well be discussed in the light of the following suggested desirabilities for the future of the arts and the artist in Hawaii.

Desirabilities 2000

World peace.

Better balancing of technology and nature in the world and the U.S., including Hawaii.

Rebalancing of the overemphasis on the technological exploitation of nature and markets by supported development in the life-enhancing possibilities of the arts.

Imaginative new interconnections between the creative aspects of science and the human and humane aspects of the arts.

Improvement of the quality of all the arts and art audiences in Hawaii.

Reforms in U.S. and Hawaiian tax laws permitting artists to write off, retroactively, higher earning years against a longer period of early, low-earning years than now defined in revenue laws.

Measures of public support, comparable to advances

made to scientists for space and hardware, to assist studio artists in meeting high Hawaiian rents, use of public funds to award to artists the same privileges as to some Hawaiian medical students — such as subsidy for out-of-state study.

Improvement of mail and transportation facilities that now delay the arrival of timely cultural materials in Hawaii — and even then, at comparatively high cost.

Reexamination of governmental bidding regulations that increase the cost of artistic and other printed materials in Hawaii.

Scrutiny of the earnings of government-assisted mass media in Hawaii, such as TV channels, with respect to their support of the arts that are tributary to them. (The governmental assistance referred to here is the Federal Communications Commission's distribution of channels, an allocation of public rights of great value to private ownership).

More adequate representation of the arts in the curriculum and opportunities presented by the schools.

Continued efforts to preserve indigenous arts not so much by freezing them into tourist and museum exhibits (which have their merits) as by connecting them with the traditions of the contemporary.

Development of Hawaii-centered projects of high quality in the classic arts — for example, an edition of Asian classics issued from Hawaii in bilingual or English-translation form.

General vigilance with regard to constitutional safeguards of the freedom of expression.

Participants at the conference, having seen these recommendations, in some cases responded that they were not sufficiently specific or concrete. One of their own more concrete suggestions was that Hawaii should have more, and more widely distributed, art centers of the creative rather than the custodial type.

Hawaii and the Pacific Community 2000
George S. Kanahele

George S. Kanahele is currently vice-president of the international development division of The Hawaii Corporation. After
education at Brigham Young University and Cornell, he served
on the staff of the East-West Center, University of Hawaii, and
later became director of the Hawaii International Services
Agency, state of Hawaii.

INTRODUCTION

Recently a local public figure remarked that not a week
goes by without somebody's making a statement or the
newspapers' reminding us of our special role in the Pacific.
"We have talked about it so long and so loud," he said,
"that it's getting to sound like an old record." Hawaii,
the center of the Pacific — the crossroads of the Pacific
— the hub of Pacific trade — the Geneva of the Pacific.
. . . Any day he expected to hear somebody say,
"Hawaii, the center of the universe!"

The fact of the matter is that it is not an old record,
but rather variations on a traditional theme, a theme that
appears again and again in the rhetoric of modern Hawaii.
One can go back a hundred years and find it a dominant
idea in the statements of King Kalakaua (reigned
1874–1891). One can also go back fifty years when it
became the rationale for the founding of the first truly
pan-Pacific movement whose charter sounds as if it were
written yesterday: "We seek better understanding and real

cooperation for the advancement of the interests of all Pacific peoples.'' [1] *And ten years ago the East-West Center was established espousing the same basic philosophy and purpose.* [2]

So we are heirs to a long and proud tradition. It is also a tradition that makes good sense. Geographically, Hawaii is isolated in the middle of an ocean, with little in natural resources, few people, a small area and no place to move except outward into the Pacific. Unless we are content with our isolation — and we obviously are not — we can advance only outwardly, seeking contact with and sustenance from the world beyond us. This reaching out and being involved in the world community is and always will be our saving grace. The alternative would be deadly provincialism.

The Pacific is our world. It dominates and controls our entire lives — our environment, economics, culture, and politics. We need to become "Pacificans" with a new kind of awareness about the Pacific — not as an ocean, but as a community of nations and peoples.

Lest we suffer from what might be called Pacific egocentrism, we are also citizens of a larger world. We can no more restrict ourselves to Hawaii's shores than we can limit our horizons to the Pacific. Indeed, we live in a global village, but the Pacific is our backyard.

So, we look to this ocean that borders over a score of nations containing nearly half the world's population. Here lie some of the most advanced as well as least developed economies, and here lie opportunities and needs now and in the future. How can we help? How can we maximize our opportunities? What kind of role can Hawaii play in the Pacific? These are questions which

1. Charter of the Pan Pacific Union, 1920.
2. The East-West Center, founded by act of Congress in 1960, is a federally funded educational institution, administered by the University of Hawaii. Its formal designation is "The Center for Cultural and Technical Interchange Between East and West." — Editors.

will command our attention over the next thirty years just as they do today.

Our attempts to answer these questions are deliberately speculative. Wherein they are predictive, they are only as clear as our crystal ball would allow us to be. And insofar as they are prescriptive, they reflect our presently held values and biases.

Our assumptions, which reflect these values, are transparent throughout. People will still be around in 2000. Men can control their own destinies. Hawaii's population will increase. Economic growth is necessary. Government and business can work together. Our geographical location is an asset; it can also be a liability. Hawaii can retain its charm and appeal. Its people are more cosmopolitan than insular. Hawaii enjoys a favorable image in the Pacific. Tourism is here to stay. Education is our salvation. So is communication. There is a community of interests in the Pacific. Cooperation is both a desirable means and a tolerable end. Hawaii has many roles to play in the Pacific. Peace and not war is our most vital concern. Environmental control is imperative if Hawaii is to survive. And so on.

As with most assumptions, these are debatable. No one may survive a nuclear holocaust, or at least survive well enough to fulfill any of our predictions. It may be that we will reach zero population growth by 2000. The issue is not whether economic growth is necessary, but whether it is good or bad. Government could dominate business absolutely. Environmental damage could ruin Hawaii by 1984. For Asians to take us seriously we may need to change our image drastically. A single community of interests does not yet exist; in reality, there are many communities of interest. And so on.

Our predictions are tempered by these assumptions and their challenges. At best, our forecasting is an intelligent assessment of the future and at worst, it is an exercise in soothsaying. In either case, the last word has not yet been said.

COMMUNICATIONS

If Hawaii is assured of a future, it is a future in communications in the Pacific. Location makes the islands a natural communications center, a fact long recognized by both business and the military. The U.S. Pacific Area Command, for example, has set up massive and highly sophisticated communications installations which not only transmit but also process information. As for business, the Communications Satellite Corporation (Comsat) operates the world's largest satellite earth-station at Paumalu, Oahu. By building upon this base, Hawaii may become a communications hub for the Pacific world by 2000.

In the near future Hawaii will have its first island-wide computer net linking the University's campuses by radio — the so-called ALOHA system. For any campus needing computer services, ALOHA will provide direct connection with the computer center at the Manoa campus. This system will be only a stepping-stone to a larger network of educational computers in the Pacific via satellite communications. This in turn will lead to the development of the vast Pacific educational satellite network discussed later in this paper.

Such systems will contribute immensely to advancements in other fields apart from education. In medical diagnosis, for instance, people on remote islands that may not have a resident doctor may have a console hooked up to a medical diagnostic system based in Hawaii which would enable them to decide to give treatment or wait for medical assistance to arrive. This is a program that the regional medical program of Hawaii will develop first in American Samoa, Guam, and the Trust Territory, and eventually extend to other areas of the Pacific.

Recognizing the potential for communications in the Pacific, the University of Hawaii will greatly expand its program in this field — recruiting the finest talent, procuring the newest equipment, and enlarging its research capabilities. In conjunction with the East-West Center, the university will establish a Pacific school of communications which will draw students and scholars from all over the region. The school will also work interdependently with Hawaii's knowledge industry, each relying heavily on the other.

Perhaps one of the most important developments in communications over the next thirty years will be the establishment of what Robert Theobald calls the TERRAN communications center.[3] While the center will have both information-processing and -transmitting capabilities, its prime function will be problem-solving. That is, with its supercomputerized bank of information collected and programed from around the globe, it will simulate the exact conditions under which problems arise. This simulation capability will allow it not only to come up with solutions and alternatives, but also to anticipate problems, nipping them in the bud, so to speak.

The center will be staffed by some of the world's best minds, whose tasks will be primarily data analysis and consulting. They will attract other competent people from the entire Pacific region who will want to learn the techniques of problem simulation.

Imagine problem-solving requests pouring into Hawaii's TERRAN center from throughout the world — problems of every magnitude, on practically any subject, affecting any number of people or places. Hawaii's impact upon the world would be way out of proportion to its limited population and natural endowments.

EDUCATION

By 2000 Hawaii may become the central headquarters for the Pacific education community (PEC), a multinational body established to plan, coordinate, and carry out cooperative regional ventures in education. It will have begun to take shape as early as the late 1970s, with national and subregional educational and scientific organizations

3. Robert Theobald and J. M. Scott, *Teg's 1994*, pp. 101–108.

recognizing the need to pool their knowledge and resources in order to cope with common Pacific-wide problems. Organizations such as the Pacific Science Association or the Southeast Asia Ministers of Education Council already function in a regional capacity, but interaction is minimal. The PEC would serve to bring such groups together and thereby further joint educational undertakings.

But a good deal of the initiative and action leading to the founding of the PEC will come from Hawaii. These efforts would naturally flow from the University of Hawaii's traditional emphasis on and continuing expansion of its Pacific-oriented programs and the pioneering work of the East-West Center in intercultural and problem-centered learning.

Two important developments in this regard will be: (1) the extension of the state's community-college system to American Samoa, Guam, and the Trust Territory, and (2) the construction, internationally financed, of a trans-Pacific satellite educational network based on the original island-wide ALOHA system. In time, through the cooperation of the South Pacific Commission, the community-college system would be adapted to other island communities in Polynesia, Micronesia, and Melanesia. The cumulative experiences gained in the system would then be applied on a larger scale by the PEC.

The trans-Pacific satellite educational network will provide multichannel audio-visual communication to all major educational centers throughout the Pacific Basin. The network will play a major part in the strengthening of the Pacific university consortium (see below) as well as in the formation of the PEC.

It will open up educational vistas for many more Pacific peoples, especially communities in remote areas. Through the PEC, for example, telerama sets equipped with self-contained satellite receivers and computer printout units, accompanied by a technician, would be sent to or even airdropped into isolated communities. In addition to transmitting live broadcasts, such sets would be programed to play tapes in the local language, adapted to the needs and interests of the population. The portable teleramacomputer unit and technician may replace the hardpressed and fast-disappearing missionary.

By the 1980s, with the new University of Hawaii acting as a catalyst, leading universities in the Pacific will form the Pacific university consortium. The consortium will be looked upon as a means to relieve overburdened institutions, to meet the needs of a more rational allocation of academic resources, and to upgrade the instructional and learning levels of poorer universities. Also an important impetus for its formation will be the internationalization of higher education.

Functionally, the consortium will allow for: (1) mutual transfer of credits, (2) multiple exchange of faculty and staff, (3) the right of attending lectures, laboratory sessions, seminars, and other activities at member institutions without having to change one's registration, (4) the unlimited use of research and library materials, and (5) access to electronic tapes of lectures by a distinguished faculty.

One of the pet projects of both the PEC and the consortium will be that of getting the approval of governments for the elimination of visa requirements, and for free travel and communication, particularly for students and faculty. Success in either case will lead to mass movements of pupils and faculty throughout the Pacific academic world. What this will mean to the cross-fertilization of intellects is exciting to contemplate.

Capitalizing on the strengths of local educational institutions, the consortium will work jointly with the PEC in setting up regional centers. These centers will be designed to improve learning and research and to satisfy subregional and regional requirements for technical and scientific manpower. In Hawaii there will be two such centers, the creative leisure center in Honolulu, and the transcultural training complex in Hilo.

A closely allied program will be the establishment of eleven "biospheric" research stations located at Anchorage, Vancouver (B.C.), La Jolla, Santiago, Tokyo, Vladivostok, Shanghai, Singapore, Ambon (Indonesia), Sydney, and Honolulu. The station here will probably concentrate on environmental and weather control and on resource-conservation problems.

To insure its innovative leadership in the knowledge industry, Hawaii will set up its first all-computerized MIDOCRE (or microfilm documentation and information retrieval center) which will likely render traditional libraries obsolete. It will be the prototype for similar facilities to be built in other countries. The MIDOCRE will be linked with the Pacific satellite network, thus giving users from all over the region access to its stored information.

What began in the early 1970s as a debriefing program for returning Asia/Pacific students, to help them relate their learning and experience in a foreign context to their local situations, will become an integral part of the transcultural training program on the Big Island. The new program will attract many new students enrolled in the Pacific university consortium system who will spend time for "decompression" at the transcultural training complex. In addition to students, it will also draw others such as business executives, government officials, and professors.

In science and education, there will be spectacular growth and expansion of our capabilities in relation to the Pacific. State, federal, and private scientific institutions will expand their research and services in such fields as agriculture, biomedicine, genetics, oceanography, meteorology, astronomy, cybernetics, and ecology. Funds will come not only from the State and federal governments but also from other governments and multilateral financing institutions. Thus, along with a solid infrastructure of communications, informational storage and retrieval, and international linkages, our present population of scientists will grow into a first-rate international scientific community.

CREATIVE LEISURE

Tourism, as we know it today, will be transformed over the next thirty years into what can be termed creative leisure. It will be a new kind of travel experience because the future traveler, particularly the American, will, by and large, differ from today's tourist. First, he will have increased leisure, for by 2000, Americans for example, will work thirty-hour weeks, or work six months and rest six months. Some will prefer to concentrate their work during ten or fifteen years so that they can retire at age forty and spend the rest of their lives in leisure. Thus, the average American will be able to travel longer and better. Second, he will have a different attitude toward traveling, in that while he seeks relaxation and pleasure, he will be more interested in the educational content of his travel experience. His dominant needs will be psychological — developing his talents, improving himself as a person, achieving a new quality of life. If travel is recreation, he will prefer to view it as educational recreation rather than vice versa.

Given this new type of consumer-traveler, Hawaii's tourism industry will need to change and adjust — and it will have done so by the turn of the century. Instead of a visitor industry, Hawaii will pioneer the development of a creative-leisure industry. Hotels will no longer be mere hostelries or pleasure domes. Rather, they will be creative-leisure complexes staffed not by desk clerks or bellhops and the like (since their functions will have been automated), but by highly trained specialists in such fields as art, music, physical therapy, and psychology, or activity generalists in PR (pleasure and recreation).

The new complexes will be closely linked with educational centers. In fact, some will become integral parts

342

of the new University of Hawaii. The linkup is logical since many travelers will be people who will spend several weeks or months in refresher courses, special seminars and other learning or relearning activities. There will be joint appointments whereby faculty and staff may serve at both the university and creative-leisure complexes. Out of this working arrangement will eventually develop a single institution integrating in one physical facility the university and the creative-leisure complex.

In general terms, then, people will visit Hawaii not so much for fun and sun, but for reeducation, rejuvenation, and rebuilding of minds and bodies. They will come for long periods rather than a few days. In addition to sightseeing, shopping excursions, and nightclubs, the packaged tour will consist of educational seminars and course work, programed exercises in improving, say, extrasensory acuity or other talents, and reorientation or readjustment programs for people who may have undergone radical changes in their personal or occupational lives.

While the system will cater to leisured travelers in the main, there will also be a place for tourists who have neither the means nor the time to afford the creative-leisure complexes. While they will not be either a large or a profitable market, they will be important because they should represent the growing number of visitors from the developing areas of the Pacific. In short, Hawaii's creative-leisure industry will not preclude budget-class travelers from visiting the islands.

Indeed, the industry will be a magnet for students, professionals, and government officials from all over the Pacific who will want to study it to build up their own industries back home. The integration of the university and creative-leisure complexes thus will serve as an ideal training ground.

Following the pattern set in Hawaii, other creative-leisure complexes will be built throughout the Pacific. They *will be formed into a Pacific or worldwide integrated leisure (rather than travel) system with Hawaii as its operational headquarters.*

PEACE AND SECURITY

Commensurate with our claims to being the center of the ocean of peace, nothing would be more fitting than for Hawaii to become a center for peace. In the minds of many people, Hawaii is already a symbol of peace as represented in the racial harmony we have achieved. Over the past few years there have been a number of proposals for peace projects that go beyond the symbolic. These include the setting up of a peace institute and even a separate state agency for peace. The University of Hawaii has supported research in the problems of peace and the state legislature has already granted the university an appropriation for conducting special peace research. One of Hawaii's representatives to the Congress has authored and advocated legislation calling for a new federal department of peace. All of this evidences not only our humanitarian concern but our public commitment to resolving the issues and problems of peace.

Thus, Hawaii will become a major center for peace activities not only for the Pacific but the entire world. Out of current efforts in peace research centered at the university may emerge a peace institute dedicated to the study and promotion of peace. Such an institution may become an integral part of a Pacific-wide system of multinational consultation embodied in a Pacific community.

But while Hawaii may become a center for peace, it will also continue to be a key to American defense strategy. Geopolitical realities and the security of the state are factors that cannot be ignored even in the pursuit of peace. Hawaii is the headquarters of the Pacific Area Command; it will continue to be so even after the termination of hostilities in Vietnam or the reversion of Okinawa to Japan.

344

Eventually, the U.S. defense perimeter will be pulled

back from Asia, perhaps to Guam and the Trust Territory. It is quite likely that Hawaii may become even more vital as a defense base. Accordingly, Hawaii will continue to be the beneficiary of substantial defense appropriations which will provide a good number of jobs and a significant proportion of our gross annual product.

However, while Hawaii may remain strategically important for the foreseeable future, rapid improvements in sophisticated weaponry may alter this situation by 2000. Indeed, push-button war technology may make liabilities of Hawaii's present military assets. It may also make Hawaii an indefensible target.

CULTURE

Hawaii's rich and diverse cultural heritage combined with the large number of visitors who come here would make it a logical site for cultural performances representative of the Pacific. All the basic elements exist now, but they have yet to be brought together and organized into what could be a center for the performing arts. The cultural as well as the economic benefits that would accrue if such were to materialize are so great that it is a wonder nothing has been done about it up to now.

With sufficient leadership and backing, a center for the performing arts of the Pacific (CPAP) will become a reality for Hawaii. It would be to the Pacific what Lincoln Center is to New York City, but on a different scale. The center will bring together in one artistic community performers, instructors, and students representing the important art forms of all the major ethnic and cultural groupings in the Pacific basin. While its primary purpose will be to perpetuate the various indigenous art forms through regular performances, the center will also encourage the dynamic synthesis of the old and the modern as well as the culturally diverse.

Since few societies will be able to preserve entirely their indigenous art forms, because of the changes brought about by modernization, the center will seek to find and resurrect dead art forms or revive those now disappearing. Thus, it would encourage research and study. It would send out search teams to cultural pockets to discover, study, and record unique or little-known art forms that could be performed. In time, the center would become the outstanding repository for such material.

The CPAP, however, will be dedicated mainly to performance. The performance season will be yearlong, for the center will never close. It will feature not only professionals but the best amateurs. Its policy will be "every man is worthy of a good performance." So the center will be open to all at minimal cost.

To afford as many people as possible the opportunity to view performances, the center will make extensive use of the trans-Pacific satellite network by relaying televised performances. Or, the center would provide videotapes to small and isolated communities. In 2000 it may well be that the only way, say, the Papuans in the eastern highlands of New Guinea will be able to see their ancient dances performed at their authentic best would be through such means as the CPAP. Of course, there will be performances on location and these will attract live audiences from all over the world. Hawaii will thus become a cultural mecca.

For all of this to happen, however, an appropriate building will be necessary. An international committee with a local nucleus will be formed and funds will be secured from both public and private sources, locally and internationally. The center will not exist alone, for it will work intimately with the new University of Hawaii and other local cultural organizations and with many other similar institutions and groups around the Pacific. It will belong not only to Hawaii but to the whole world.

BUSINESS

Hawaii's transition from a goods to a service economy will be virtually complete in 2000. It will have capped a trend that is already underway. Right now most of our labor force is engaged in, and the greater percentage of our gross domestic product is derived from, service-related activities. Hawaii's transition may be even faster than the nation as a whole which, according to present projections, will have 65 percent of its workers deployed in services in 1975.

Many of Hawaii's export products in 2000 will therefore be prepackaged services. As the phonograph and tape recorder successively expanded the marketplace of the musician, so will computers and audio-visual technology expand the marketplace of the teacher and consultant expert. The canned services industry of the future (computer programs and self-instructional courses) will be quite similar to the present canned entertainment industry (books, films, and records). The advantages of such industries to Hawaii can be well imagined — high salaries, creative work, pollution-free production, and stimulation of the region's social, political, cultural, and economic activity.

A major factor in this evolution to a service economy undoubtedly will be a decision by the major agribusiness firms to make domestic agricultural production, especially sugar and pineapple, ancillary to their international operations. This will leave only a few enterprises producing goods, such as secondary manufacturing industries which likely will be geared to the luxury market. Even our primary industries, limited to marine exploitation and diversified agriculture by 2000, would still be heavily committed to service in the form of research and development.

For Hawaii's service economy to prosper, it will need to expand its markets — and expansion will take place mainly in the Pacific basin because the people are there. Almost half of the world's population between now and 2000 — and thereafter — will reside around the rim of the Pacific. The majority are in the developing countries, whose needs will increase as development continues into and beyond the twenty-first century. By 2000, areas such as Mexico, Taiwan, Hong Kong, Korea, Malaysia, and Singapore will already have reached the level of the advanced countries, while others may not be far behind. Hence, the market potential for a whole range of services will continue to grow over the next thirty years.

Hawaii's future commerce, therefore, will be almost exclusively in exporting skills and know-how to Pacific and world markets. We already have a good start as more than one hundred fifty firms are now active in this trade. However, we will face immense competition from other states, not to mention countries such as Canada and Japan; indeed, by 2000 Japan may be largely an exporter of sophisticated technical products and technological know-how, leaving to other Asian countries the export trade in manufactured goods which she now produces and sells.

In any case, Hawaii also will service this vast international activity in the selling and buying of skills and brainpower. The handling and organizing of this trade will be the central function of the state's new international trade center. Accordingly, it will differ from existing world trade centers which deal with the export or import of commodities. It will specialize in the worldwide exchange of services by acting as a gigantic clearinghouse for information regarding the availability, cost, quality, and delivery of engineering, management, consulting, construction, research, and other services. The most important part of the international trade center will be its information and retrieval system — a bank of computers which would provide all the pertinent facts for anyone requesting skills or data.

To cite one instance of how the system would work: Suppose that a private company in Indonesia wished to hire a team of experts in the cultivation of hybrid corn in tropical soil conditions. The firm might desire experts with special qualifications, such as previous experience in the area, availability by a certain date for a certain length of time, at a specific salary range, with good health, and good character. Failing to find anyone in Hawaii, the computer would supply names of experts around the world. In addition, the center would assist in the paper processing, contract negotiations, travel arrangements, and so on. Of course, fees would be collected so that, with other revenues, the center would be almost self-supporting. Such services would be available to governmental and international agencies as well. In short, it would be a worldwide employment agency.

Convenient and immediate access to such information and services will attract multinational companies which will dominate the world economy by the turn of the century. Some will establish regional or even international headquarters here. This will bring new kinds of businesses into Hawaii, such as legal firms specializing in multinational company law, public relations, insurance firms and other support services. Also, labor organizations may have to relocate offices here, and so may special international bodies created to administer or regulate multinational corporations.

Another attraction for multinational companies and ancillary service organizations to move to Hawaii will be the TERRAN communications center, which will ensure them not only of constant contact with points throughout the world but also of a supportive data base of enormous utility. Even more attractive to some may be the problem simulation and long-range forecasting capabilities of the TERRAN center.

Still another reason will be the movement of a substantial number of people through or to Hawaii for education, creative leisure, or "decompression." These people represent a large labor pool, albeit a shifting population as well, from which suitable employees might be found. More important, however, partly through programs of the transcultural training complex and the new University of Hawaii, the state will become a permanent community for transcultural employees — people who are multilingual and who by character and training are specially adapted to working in different cultural environments.

But a most important reason for multinational companies to base here will be special legislation providing incentives and other forms of assistance. These will include tax holidays, State-developed business parks, and Delaware-type corporate laws.

While the entire Pacific basin is our potential market area, Hawaii's businessmen will continue to focus on Oceania: Guam, the Trust Territory, American and Western Samoa, and the other island communities in Polynesia, Micronesia, and Melanesia. Proximity and familiarity work in our favor already, but the development of the Pacific satellite network and additional air flights connecting with Hawaii to form one vast grid will make our position even more strategic. While Oceania's population will remain small (now less than six million), it is a rapidly developing market for both service and commodity exports. Most importantly, the area will become one of the world's great playlands, attracting visitors from all over the world. Drawing lessons from its best experience, Hawaii will take on a major part in developing the tourism potential of the area.

The broad base for Hawaii's service economy will be the knowledge industry. A good deal of that industry will involve economic data on trade, investment, governmental policies, prices and wages, and economic conditions, mostly regarding the Pacific basin. With what might well amount to a monopoly of such information, Hawaii will develop into an international financial service center. We may emerge as a Geneva of the Pacific, playing an intermediary role between the financial markets of Tokyo, Hong Kong, Sydney, and Singapore, on the one hand, and New York, San Francisco, Montreal, and Mexico City on the other. In other words, Hawaii would serve as a clearing-house and servicing station for capital movements largely unrelated to commodity-trade flows. If not existing banks, then new firms will arise to offer portfolio management and mutual funds concentrating — to begin with — on Japanese, Australian, and Hong Kong securities. In time this will lead to the establishment of a Pacific basin stock exchange. Eventually, this will result in investment-banking functions in venture equity deals, mortgage banking, and land-development financing.

For Hawaii to emerge as an international financing center, the state legislature will have to amend present statutes or enact new ones affecting taxes, corporations, and banking. It will also seek federal legislation which will, in effect, make Hawaii a free-trade zone for capital, offering tax and other incentives to foreign depositors.

In general, it will be necessary for the State to review all its statutes in order to amend, repeal, or initiate laws to ensure the most favorable climate for the development of a service economy. It is a question of economic survival, and it will bring about closer cooperation between government and business.

The future development of Hawaii's economy in relation to the Pacific must be seen against the background of proposals and efforts to further multinational economic cooperation. The most notable examples are establishment of the Asian Development Bank and the Private Investment Company for Asia, the Pacific Basin Economic Cooperation Committee, and the series of Pacific trade and development conferences organized by Professor Kiyoshi Kojima. We will likely see over the next thirty years greater integration of Asian economies in subregions such as southeast Asia. The tremendous increases in intraregional and transregional trade will spur efforts to set up a Pacific common market or a free-trade area.

The State will not only monitor all such developments but will deliberately seek to exert its influence in national or international and regional councils so as to safeguard its own economic interests. To do this effectively, a new *department of Pacific affairs will be created, with a mandate to promote and strengthen our economic activities in the Pacific Basin. The department will also administer and staff a number of field offices around the Pacific rim to collect data, promote trade and, importantly, attract investment capital into the state.*

Significantly, the growth of the state's economy, especially the knowledge industry, will be due largely to the virtual integration of certain sectors of higher education and the private sector. As the private sector would move away from the production of goods to services and knowledge, it would naturally gravitate to the university and colleges. This increasing dependence will result in a constant two-way flow of professors into corporate consultancies or executive positions, on the one hand, and of managers and technicians going back into the classrooms, on the other. This marriage of industry and education will greatly determine the extent of Hawaii's involvement in Pacific developments.

THE PACIFIC COMMUNITY

Scientists say that because of the drifting land masses, the Americas will be nearly thirty inches closer to Asia by 2000. But there are many more powerful forces and pressures pushing the nations of the Pacific closer to each other. Trade, mutual defense, cultural exchange, communications and transportation, and politics have drawn them together — or kept them apart.

In the past twenty years, Pacific nations have themselves sought means of cooperation and interaction, as evidenced in the various regional organizations such as the Association of Southeast Asian Nations (ASEAN) or the Asian and Pacific Council (ASPAC). There are also a large number of examples of bilateral cooperation, such as those between the United States and her allies or Great Britain and her former colonies. Yet there is an even greater need for multinational cooperation on a grander scale involving all the countries bordering the Pacific.

The need is for a Pacific community distinguished by nations with shared viewpoints and mutual interests, seeking solutions to common problems. Establishment of a Pacific community would serve not only as a dynamic symbol, but as an equally dynamic vehicle for peaceful progress and cooperation throughout the hemisphere.

A community of interests in the Pacific already exists; what remains for the future is the building of a community. And this is what Hawaii will have to commit itself to because our prosperity over the next thirty years will depend on such peaceful regional cooperation.

This idea of a Pacific community is not new to Hawaii. It has a history that goes back nearly fifty years, when the first Pan Pacific Union was formed in Honolulu. Thus, it is consistent with our traditions and our own self-interests and aspirations. We will, therefore, continue to make every effort to foster any genuine cause leading toward the building of a Pacific community.

The process of institutionalizing an idea may take several forms. We may begin a systematic exploration, in concert with other interested parties, of identifying common interests or conflicting interests and seeking ways to strengthen the one and eliminate the other. Convening a conference with meaningful agenda and the right set of people — with adequate follow-up — is one way to start.

We may also take the initiative in establishing a Pacific council and a Pacific community institute. The council would serve as a kind of board of directors to the institute, which in turn would function as a clearinghouse for information and knowledge on background problems, current issues, and future prospects for multinational cooperation on a Pacific-wide basis. It would provide the means for continuing study and analysis on both short- and long-range problems. It would also provide a forum for free and full discussions among people on the differences that may divide them and the common aspirations that may unite them. In short, what the East-West Center does in the areas of educational and cultural interchange can be extended by the Pacific community institute to the field of public and international affairs.

Meantime, the State would urge our national leaders and other opinion-molders to support the movement, not only with rhetoric but action and money. In so doing we would be fulfilling one of our avowed responsibilities of influencing and shaping American attitudes and policy in the Pacific.

There will need to be a step-by-step buildup of machinery to handle consultations, negotiations, and discussions between governmental bodies or other organizations. In time, there will emerge a body of knowledge from which could be developed the rules, customs, and precedents essential to the orderly conduct of pan-Pacific affairs.

While this wide-ranging system of consultation is being developed there will be cooperative projects undertaken by participating countries and groups. Some of the more important ones probably will be the exploration and exploitation of marine resources, conservation, the promotion of free trade, and weather prediction and control, to name a few.

If luck is with us, there may well emerge even before the turn of the century a Pacific community. In that eventuality, Hawaii would be the logical site for its headquarters. As such, the U.S. Congress may grant Hawaii special status as an international state allowing us extraconstitutional privileges in order to conduct our affairs with the Pacific community. Hawaii may indeed render its greatest service to the nation and the world in this capacity.

SUMMARY

One flight into the future does not make a well-seasoned traveler. While this exercise has made us a bit more knowledgeable and confident, it has not freed us entirely of our fears and reservations. We can still ask our-selves the hard questions: Where will all the money come from? Who will assume the leadership and accept the risks? Is there sufficient public commitment? And will there ever be? Does our cup run over with ambitions? Have our visions outstripped even our greatest capabilities? Will we as a society reach our level of incompetence sooner than we think? Will time run out on us — and mankind?

We have given a great deal of margin and play to our optimism and idealism, nonetheless, for it will take all of that and more to accomplish some of the alternative futures we have described. Some may insist that Hawaii's location is no assurance that anything big will happen here. True, but the point is, will it happen somewhere else? We are betting on ourselves' making things happen here first. The race is to the swiftest and the "firstest."

But one thing we cannot allow is for events in the Pacific to bypass us. We must be where the action is. For in both the short- and long-run our future will depend not only on what happens in the Pacific, but most impor-tantly on what we cause to happen there.

5 NEIGHBOR ISLAND FUTURES

Overview
Editors

The creation of task forces to explore the futures of the neighbor islands of Hawaii, Kauai, and Maui was in keeping with the spirit of decentralized participation that marked the Hawaii 2000 project — but it was initially unplanned. It was not that the neighbor islands had been forgotten — efforts had been made to include their representatives on the advisory committee, on the statewide task forces, and in plans for conference participation — but we had failed to provide for their autonomous participation as distinct identities.

Some neighbor-island folks who attended the February mini-conference for task-force members were first to see the possibility for county versions of the statewide effort and the advisory committee was quick to agree. Supplemental appropriations were obtained to support the work of the neighbor-island groups and the leaders of the local community colleges were asked to serve as chairmen. Resource persons from the committee, including James Dator, were sent to the neighbor islands to help get things started.

The island of Hawaii was especially active. Futures activities were led by Kaoru Noda, provost of the Hilo campus of the University of Hawaii, by Mrs. John Zelko, a leader of the League of Women Voters, and by David Treacy, an assistant professor of English. These leaders formed a group of about ninety persons, including the *island's respected, dynamic, and imaginative mayor Shunichi Kimura. Like the eighty-seven-member Kauai and sixty-three-member Maui groups, they modified the ten statewide topics to fit their own needs. Two Big Island innovations, for example, were to create task forces on youth with Coreen Sekimura and Tim Bryan as cochairmen and a group on the spiritual environment led by professor Hideo Aoki.*

The momentum and enthusiasm of this island group was so great that they held a Hawaii county conference on the year 2000 on August 22, 1970, just two weeks after the governor's conference. At this conference of about two hundred persons, Mayor Kimura summarized both the future aspirations of the group and the need for engaging wider participation. "We say now," he declared, "that this island, its land, its sea, its air and most important, its people, are a national and human treasure — a treasure not to be modified unless said modifications enhance its quality." He further stated that "a unique scientific and cultural reserve also requires a unique political process. We should devise a process by which participatory democracy will work and provide representation, accountability, and effectiveness."[1]

The neighbor-island task-force reports that follow will be found to convey a sense of concreteness and a local flavor sometimes missing in the often more analytical statewide reports. They grew, of course, out of the more intimate atmosphere of small communities. The effort to integrate the work of separate groups into an overall concept of community identity seems particularly successful in the case of the Big Island, whose present combination of agricultural and scientific research institutions conditions its views of the future. The concerns of Kauai with brain drain and the exodus of youth seem distinctive. Salient on Maui, then site of controversy over whether

1. *Honolulu Advertiser*, August 23, 1970, p. F–3.

deviant life-styles should be permitted in an area called the "Banana Patch," [2] *was concern with civil rights.*

In retrospect, as at the height of their activity, these island community efforts suggest exciting possibilities for further decentralization of anticipatory democracy to neighborhoods, organizations, institutions, ethnic groups, occupational groups, and families, as well as to individuals.

2. See explanation on p. 157.

Hawaii (the Big Island) 2000
Charles M. Fullerton and Kaoru Noda

Charles M. Fullerton is director of the University of Hawaii's Cloud Physics Observatory on the island of Hawaii. He has participated actively in programs of the Hawaii Island chapter of the Hawaiian Academy of Sciences, serving as president and director of the 1968 island-wide science fair. He originated the proposal that the entire island of Hawaii be designated as a national scientific preserve, a provocative idea that caused considerable discussion, both pro and con, at the Hawaii 2000 conference.

Kaoru Noda, zoologist, assistant chancellor of the University of Hawaii at Hilo, was born in that community in 1924 and was educated at Grinnell College and the University of Iowa, with postdoctoral studies at the University of California at Los Angeles. In World War II he fought in Italy and France with the 442nd Infantry Regiment. He joined the University of Hawaii in 1957 as a parasitologist in the experiment station and two years later moved to the Hilo campus as assistant and associate professor of science. He was named director of the Hilo campus in 1962, provost in 1967, and assistant chancellor in 1970. Dr. Noda has served on the Big Island's charter commission, on its commission on children and youth, and in other civic organizations.

I f the state of Hawaii is to have a meaningful future in the next thirty years it must begin today to look to the relatively unspoiled islands which lie beyond crowded Oahu; in particular, to the island of Hawaii, which contains 63 percent of the total land area in the state and has a current population density of less than sixteen persons for each square mile. These 4,030 square miles form a majestic natural environment with clean air and clean water, high mountains and deep oceans. Here, 63,468 persons are creating Hawaii's future.

If the island of Hawaii is to remain the Hawaii of the visitors' dreams and the land of aloha we all want to preserve, it is up to us to learn how to plan and how to achieve the future we want — not simply how to adapt to the future which suddenly arrives. We bemoan the urban sprawl and overgrowth of Waikiki while working diligently to bring Mainland to Hawaii direct air flights into Hilo. While the flights bring tourists (hence, dollars) and while occasionally a Big Island resident going to the Mainland can avoid the interisland hop to Honolulu — is the resulting air, noise, and people pollution really worth it? We do not suggest either a yes or a no answer. We do emphasize the need to examine closely all proposals for "progress," to be sure that our island and its people do not exchange short-term economic gain for long-term disaster.

Much of the charm and peaceful environment of the Big Island stems from the emphasis on natural pursuits such as agriculture and ranching. The principal uses of island land are for grazing (31 percent of the area), forestry (25½ percent) and sugarcane production (4½ percent). Hawaii Volcanoes National Park covers some 8 percent of the island with lands reserved mostly for recreation. Almost all of the remaining land — 750,000 acres, or more than 29 percent of the total — is classified as barren (lava) land. This area has tremendous potential for a variety of useful purposes. The state economy is dependent mainly on military spending ($585 million annually), tourism ($375 million), manufacturing, sugar, and pineapple (agriculture contributes $635 million to Hawaii's economy each year). The economy of the Big Island is based largely on the twin pillars of sugar ($74 million) and tourism ($43 million). Because of excellent natural conditions for scientific research in a number of fields, research and development is of growing economic importance on the island and currently contributes perhaps $5 million annually.

A large part of the island's population is involved in the production of sugar. Present political and economic considerations suggest the strong possibility that it will not be profitable to grow sugarcane in Hawaii by 2000. For the island, this poses an enormous problem, which might be analyzed in the following way. As technology or economics reduces the number of people needed to produce sugar (or even totally eliminates the sugar industry), we will have a large portion of the population who can no longer depend on the land as a source of livelihood. One need only look at the turmoil in Latin America, India, Southeast Asia, much of the Middle East, and large parts of Africa, to see that this poses a serious problem — alienation from the land for a basically agricultural people. The people might well take steps to alter the pattern of traditional land ownership by the violent transfer of land holdings from present ownership to their own hands. In short, one of the possible life-styles of 2000 on this island could be one which is already illustrated in Viet Nam and elsewhere in Southeast Asia — a life-style of political and guerilla warfare over land ownership.

The only major alternative to sugarcane production that has been seriously discussed is tourism and land development. Economists point out, however, that tourism is a particularly unstable economic base for any area. In addition, tourism tends to develop exceedingly unwholesome social attitudes and to attract social types that are generally not conducive to increasing the quality of life. Thus, a total emphasis on tourism and a completely open pattern of allowing Hawaii's planning and development can bring two possibilities.

1. A garishly opportunistic society, in which all natural beauty sites have been usurped, and local people are devoted primarily to serving and exploiting the tourists in hotels and restaurants as gaming operators, tour-bus

drivers, prostitutes or procurers, operators of souvenir shops, and so forth.

2. A severe economic depression, population loss, and intensified struggle for small livelihood opportunities, and a real possibility of a desperate and frightened people's attempt to regain control of their island by force.

We know that such futures, while possible, can and must be avoided. To determine more desirable alternative futures we must first look at our basic natural resources.

The island of Hawaii possesses fertile soil, benign climate, more than adequate rainfall, and a variety of promising environmental settings. In addition, the island boasts 320 miles of shoreline. It is this boundary zone between the land and the sea (the littoral) which generates more varied life forms, both plant and animal, and produces more potential food than perhaps any other environmental setting. As a place for collecting food, through gathering and fishing, the littoral has been used by man throughout his entire history.

It is possible to envision the production of highly nutritious, high-priced foods along the coastline of Hawaii by 2000. It is biologically and technically possible to conduct all of the following aqua-technological operations on the Big Island: production of shrimp, crab, lobster, opihi, abalone, turtles, clams, oysters, and edible seaweeds. Such production requires the involvement of well-trained, highly skilled, and well-paid workers or owner-operators. Most importantly, such persons would be engaged in direct extensions of the day-to-day practices of thousands of island people who actively pursue subsistence, sport, and semicommercial fishing.

In addition to the immediate seashore, there are areas on the island which could easily lend themselves to the large-scale production of edible froglegs as well as fresh fish, shrimp, and crayfish. No one, to our knowledge, has explored the possibility of utilizing lava tubes as nurseries for mushrooms.

In addition to such environmentally based industries, which would produce high-protein, high-quality, and high-priced market foods, a plan for the future must provide for proper utilization of those lands now used for sugarcane production. Much of this land could be divided on a profit-sharing basis into individual truck farms producing high-quality vegetables for the domestic markets and for export to expanding markets such as Japan and the United States mainland. Beyond that, much of the land now devoted to sugar could be converted into pasturage of a quality unequalled anywhere else in the world. Through the use of grass silage and fresh grasses, one could envision the development of a first-rate dairy and veal industry, freeing Hawaii from the need to import and producing a large surplus for export — in particular, to Japan. Milk, cheese, butter, ice cream, and other dairy products are in great demand in Japan; Hawaii has a transportation and economic advantage over any possible competitors for this market.

Independent farm businessmen, working in cooperation with large agricultural corporations and the State and federal governments, can develop an integrated food production center in the mid-Pacific which will not only produce large amounts of food for export to both the East and the West but will also increase Hawaii's standard of living.

Cooperative endeavor among State, County, and federal governments, individuals, and interested concerns, could explore the possibility of reseeding the now-vanished sandalwood groves, which once brought millions of dollars to Hawaii. Experimentation with the growing of high-priced and high-quality hardwoods for veneers and quality furniture, and the like, may once again provide a land-based source of income. These considerations suggest a future for the island of Hawaii based on its natural resources, a future which would see the disappearance

363

of the large plantation and its replacement by a profit-sharing tenant population.

Much of the aqua-technological picture of the future as just described depends upon intensive research and experimentation, as well as upon economic transitions. It is expected, therefore, that there will be a growth of research groups and institutions devoted to scientific studies. Here, then, is a completely compatible future for the island of Hawaii, based on its ideal nature as a locale for many kinds of scientific investigation.

This island is a unique scientific resource. Almost all the scientific facilities located here are concerned with natural observations, with studies dependent on the relatively undisturbed environment of the island. This condition results primarily from the island's isolation, limited population and development, and an almost total lack of heavy industry. All these factors appear, however, to be changing — some slowly, some rapidly.

Consider the scientific studies particularly appropriate to Hawaii Island: seismic and volcanic research at the volcano observatory; astronomy at the Mauna Kea observatory and at the solar coronagraph station of the National Center for Atmospheric Research on Mauna Loa; numerous experiments in tropical agriculture carried on by a variety of federal, State and private organizations; atmospheric studies by the Mauna Loa observatory, by the cloud physics observatory of the University of Hawaii and by visiting scientists; oceanographic, tsunami, and marine biology programs; and evolutionary and ecological studies, such as the Hawaii terrestrial biology subprogram of the international biological program.

The island of Hawaii is the only place in the United States where active volcanic processes may be studied. The highest lake (Waiau) in the United States, the largest single mountain mass and the highest mountain (measured from its ocean-floor base) on earth are found here. It has been said that the island may be the finest place in the world for evolutionary and ecological studies. Because the island of Hawaii represents a truly unique natural scientific laboratory, the conditions which make it so must be preserved. To this end, it is suggested that it be designated a cultural and scientific model community by appropriate governmental and citizen action.

What would such a model community designation mean? Would it prevent visitors or reduce their number? Would it cause the end of the sugarcane or cattle-ranching industries? Would resort development be prohibited? The answer to each of these questions is no. What would be required is an appreciation of the ecological importance of the island and the legal authority to prevent any man-made degradation of the natural environment.

One of the major developments essential to the State's planned growth and the preservation of the Big Island as a cultural and scientific resource is a high-speed, reliable, safe, clean (nonpolluting), and economical system of inter- and intra-island transportation. These considerations, particularly the need to eliminate wherever possible all forms of pollution, suggest a ground-based transportation network. This involves the technological problem of linking the principal islands together by bridges (elevated airways), not for normal automotive or even pedestrian use, but for a rapid mass-transit system, and for carrying power and communication cables. As an engineering feat the construction of such bridges would be sufficiently difficult to be interesting, but by no means impossible.

The monorail, pneumatic tube, antigravity spin tube, or whatever system adopted, would transport people from a single central overseas airport to the most distant point on the major inhabited islands in no more than one hour. The interisland transportation system would be linked with similar networks on each island, providing a statewide rapid transit facility.

All air traffic into and out of the state would be handled at a central overseas terminal, a floating airport, located approximately twenty miles south to southeast of Honolulu. A surface transportation system, as previously described, would transport passengers between the airport and Honolulu in about ten minutes. Interisland travelers not leaving the state would have no need to visit the central airport. There would be no scheduled aircraft landings on or flights over any of the islands. Discussion of a major statewide system of transportation involves the consideration of power — the energy necessary to operate this system and to fulfill the growing requirements of a more technological society.

While atomic energy may well become the major source of energy in Hawaii in the next few years, certain critical problems of thermal pollution and disposal of radioactive wastes remain unsolved. We should, therefore, not neglect other possible energy sources, some quite esoteric. For example, the earth's crust and upper mantle is subject to stress; this stress gradually builds until it is suddenly relieved by internal rock fracture; the result is, of course, an earthquake. Small earthquakes are valuable in that they release crustal stress without damage before the stress can accumulate to produce a major earthquake.

If we could tap the energy of earthquakes, we could simultaneously prevent the death and destruction caused by major earthquakes and gain a relatively clean source of power. Studies currently underway in California may indicate a mechanism for the controlled release of earth stress.

On the Big Island we expect volcanic heat to be used as a source of clean energy. Subsurface heat-transfer chambers will be constructed in the vicinity of volcanic vents and located carefully so that natural volcanic processes are not disturbed. A high-efficiency heat-transfer agent, perhaps liquid sodium, will be circulated through the chamber and the extracted heat used to operate a seawater steam generator which, in turn, will run a turbine to generate electricity. The spent steam will not be recirculated, but condensed and pumped into an irrigation water system. Precipitated salts will be automatically removed and segregated. Such a system could yield an inexpensive source of power, water, and fertilizer, with essentially zero pollution.

Within the context of the Big Island as a model community will develop a major university, concentrating on education and research in those fields particularly suited to this unique environment. Certainly those sciences already mentioned will be a major part of the curriculum, but no less important will be cultural and artistic studies, and historical, religious, philosophical, and anthropological programs. We anticipate substantial work in the field of tropical agriculture.

The island would accommodate a large variety of compatible uses. Much of the land will be preserved in its present natural state with walkways, bikeways and hiking trails providing limited access. Historical displays will recall life in earlier times in Hawaii. Resort and other development would be encouraged as long as no deleterious effects on the environment or on historical artifacts occurred. Special attention would be given to preserving the shoreline and offshore waters for aquaculture, scientific studies, and public usage; no major industrial development would be permitted.

Could we afford to limit the development of heavy industry on the Big Island? Considered as a part of the total United States, the island of Hawaii contains about 0.11 percent of the nation's area. It is probable that no other 0.11 percent of the United States contains the variety of cultural conditions and environmental factors found here. From the viewpoint of national self-interest can we afford not to set aside this unique cultural-scientific-environmental resource for future studies?

The year 2000 should see the development, or more properly the redevelopment, of a village pattern of living, to the degree that people working in a specific area would

367

live in concentrated residential clusters. A population increase should be anticipated in Kawaihae and in the Puna and Ka'u regions as they become commercial centers. There will be complete rebuilding of living structures presently occupied by most island residents. Housing will be made available by maintaining strict control of land prices and building costs through surveillance, and by developing inexpensive forms of construction utilizing native materials and island-adapted designs, featuring open space, screening, and so forth. In some villages, communal bathing facilities may reappear so that the cost of the most expensive part of a modern house may be shared by all. Development of small marinas and boat harbors along the coasts will provide jobs for harbor masters and boatmen and more opportunity for recreational activity based on the environment.

By 2000 there will be a sharp rise in ethnic consciousness and pride so that celebrations and festivals honoring the various ethnic groups will be common. Government will be much more dispersed. Each village will have a representative of the government (a position for the retired and experienced) whose job it will be to know the conditions and needs of his community on the one hand, and the services and facilities of the government on the other. He will be the link between the people and the government, acting as a facilitator, explainer, and protector. The day-to-day business of government will continue to take place in metropolitan centers, but the government representatives will see to it that when governmental services are needed, the people will not be required to come to the government, but rather, the government will come to the people.

In 2000, people will come to Hawaii from throughout the rest of the world to study what is happening for the people rather than to them. The central focus of future planning for Hawaii and the Pacific should be the quality of life in Hawaii, and the effects this may have on the relationship of this island community to other communities of the Pacific and the world. The concept of quality of life includes an individual's personal satisfaction with his own life-style and tolerance and appreciation of diversity. Hawaii's leadership in the Pacific will stress interpersonal and cultural relationships. The state will be known for openness and acceptance, and Hawaii, with its cultural and religious pluralism, will become a natural laboratory for experimentation in cultural understanding and dialog. Hawaii should strive to be a model through solving her contemporary problems of transportation, population, pollution, economics, and tourism. Through developing solutions, or at least finding possible courses of action, Hawaii will be a model to the Pacific communities that will be meeting these problems in the future. These problems will be solved with respect for and protection of the environment given first priority. Pollution and the destruction of natural resources must be controlled and halted; therefore any potential development must first be examined for the possible effects it may have on the quality of island life.

Any solution proposed will require both legislation and changes in present educational goals. Programs must be focused on individual growth, with value placed on diversity and self-generated satisfactions, to provide for the inevitable abundance of leisure that will exist in thirty years. The educational system should teach students to value people for their degree of happiness and peace of mind rather than for their material possessions and "success." Skills for self-development and for finding peace of mind and value in doing what one enjoys will be imparted. Sensitivity training and individual evaluation will be part of this new system.

Simultaneously, the educational process will encourage interpersonal contact and new concepts of associative living and community design. Cultural diversity and various ethnic identities will be preserved and perpetuated;

thus, some sources of conflict will be minimized, and specific means of problem-solving will be emphasized. In short, we propose a system of education that will prepare people to develop their own satisfactions, and that will give them techniques to analyze long-range development, to fully understand their environment, and, most importantly, to appreciate and accept change.

The product of the new educational system and of technological development tempered by environmental considerations will be a new type of person with a value system that will allow him to adapt to the ever-changing world in a peaceful manner. Any methods and solutions developed will be shared with other communities that desire them. And this, rather than economic, military, or cultural dominance will be the basis of Hawaii's relationship to the Pacific community.

The first effort of education will be to teach survival. Robert Theobald told Hawaii 2000 task-force members that any rational visiting Martian would report back that there is less than a one percent chance of this planet's making it to 2000. Overpopulation and other ecological disasters show that the world is in serious danger; these signs should be taken seriously. Following survival training, students should be taught to enjoy some of the quality and richness of the human experience available with increased leisure.

With the perfection of computer education, much of learning will take place through computers; likewise, television instruction at home will be improved and the need for compulsory school attendance will therefore diminish. Teachers will be trained to become serious users of television, not just knob-turners. The development of vast resource centers will take place during the next decade, and the audio-visual department might become the most powerful one on campus. Teachers whose function is to produce and create TV and computer programs will appear in greater numbers.

Research on drugs and the relationship between them

and learning will receive more attention in the coming decades. Research already indicates that certain drugs cause increased retentiveness; other experiments suggest that learning can be transferred chemically.

One of the task forces which the Hawaii Island commission on 2000 added was that on youth. Members were high-school and university students — all under twenty. It is instructive to see how these students view the education of today and of the future; they reported that youth feels disgust and dismay toward school. One member described the existing educational system "as being marked by some unprofessional teachers, by methods that are outmoded and restrictive, by courses that do not provide incentives to learn, and by grades which are in reality artificial goals to please teachers." Such a system will not meet youth's expectations in its search for wider horizons.

Students foresee that education in 2000 will be left up to the individual, and independent study will be foremost. Teachers will serve strictly as resource people, grades will be eliminated, and students will evaluate their own success or failure. "Youths will be learning not to please their parents or teachers, but to live up to their own personal expectations."

Another task force (adult) suggested a possible way both to promote diversity and to deal effectively with the public school crisis through a plan whereby government would allot each child "educational credit" which could be used to purchase education in private, parochial, or public schools. This plan would enable the child and his parents to select the kind of education most desired, and at the same time would promote diversity in our educational institutions.

It is reasonably easy to visualize many of the technological advances which will have a major bearing on our way of life. Control of the environment will permit a greater distribution of population by substantially increasing the areas of the earth's surface considered desir-

371

able for habitation. Advancement in the communications industry should certainly permit us to reach the point where concentration of population is no longer necessary because of economic factors or cultural advantages. Not only should our present monetary and banking system be outmoded, but so also should credit cards. A central computer bank recording debits and credits for individuals, ownership of assets (if that be still permitted), economic areas requiring expansion, and the like, should be well along toward becoming reality.

Under the conditions conjured up by such prospects, it is easy to understand the frustration of those who would plan to the point of imposing their standards of human behavior on the populace as a whole. The argument that by 2000 man will no longer need to be gainfully employed and therefore must participate in a cultural revolution may be valid, and the stage should certainly be set to permit him to do so. Unfortunately, the visionary, while espousing the cause of individual freedom, will often favor a controlled economy, directed by those who "know best what the people want." The logical extension of this is direct control of all activities, including research and manufacturing, by the government. The study of the economy thus becomes futile, since the economy is no longer free in such a society. Production schedules and efficiency, together with judgments as to what is good for the people, then become the game.

Consider another example of dilemma in a society in which choice is controlled. With the advent of machines to sustain life, for example kidney machines, and their high cost of operation, there arises the question of who should be selected to be kept alive through the use of machines? The affluent? The intelligent? The poor — as a matter of equal protection? Who should decide who gets to use a kidney machine? Doctors? A bureaucrat? The question of allocating life-preserving machines is one for lawmakers to ponder.

In the economic sphere, society may continue to permit the consumer to express his desires through the marketplace. The current attention to ecology has been interpreted by some as a desire by consumers for even greater government control of the economy than at present, and as a disenchantment with the capitalistic system. It is more likely, however, that the opposite is true. The consumer is only now becoming really aware of the amount of power he has. He is shocked by the fact that, in meeting his demands, industry has polluted the environment and that he himself is therefore a despoiler.

He is becoming aware that he must temper his demands and curb his own appetites if he is to look to the future with confidence. Since he is selfishly motivated, it is the threat to his own well-being which is arousing him. The consumer, in recognizing that it is his tremendous spending power which controls the economy, also recognizes that he has not received the attention he should have had over the years from industry, labor, or government. This awakening of the consumer need not result in a desire for greater government control but rather in greater discrimination in his buying practices. If this assumption is correct, then a free economy which permits the individual to be compensated according to his contribution to society and to exercise his control over it in the marketplace would still be a part of our picture in 2000. Since such an economy is a servant of the consumer rather than his master, its planning must necessarily be geared to an appraisal of the consumer's future needs and aspirations.

With regard to the economy of the State and of the island of Hawaii, it would appear that protection of the environment and provision of a political atmosphere that will maintain the state as a suitable place to live and work, are our most important economic factors. We should keep in mind that, as other areas become more attractive environmentally and climatically, we will become comparatively less attractive unless we can provide a quality of life unmatchable elsewhere. It is conceivable that because of instantaneous communications our community may become a place to live and work and play. We will then no longer be a separate community; it would be well to plan now to become a quality suburb in the national and world picture.

It is important to realize that the type of economy we will have in 2000 will depend not upon what we want for mankind but rather upon the political aspects of how we attempt to achieve our wants. Politics will be the major determining factor. If we are to plan and control the economy, we need political supervisors, not economists; and there appears to be little choice between the present outlook for complete annihilation through ecological strangulation or for complete subjugation of individual choice in a puppet world.

If, on the other hand, we are to use our planning to provide the consumer with the additional knowledge to enable him to control the economy through freedom of choice, then we must apply ourselves diligently to providing an economy which will react to the demands of an enlightened marketplace. Admittedly, the second choice is much more difficult to plan for; possibly for this reason it would appear to be the most worthwhile.

In the new society, where increasing numbers of persons are rejecting traditional institutions and life-styles, it will be necessary and salutary to permit and recognize new institutions and statuses. For example, homosexual "marriages" would be recognized. Laws which would permit divergent subcultures with their own "tribal" laws may best serve the interests of the larger society. Thus, drugs, sex, private versus communal property rights, and other areas could be dealt with by the group or community.

There appears to be a need to create a new kind of property. Property — gold, land, and other tangible forms of wealth which have thus far constituted property — is increasingly being replaced by forms of status and by governmental largess. Examples of this are professional licenses and vocational and occupational certification. Welfare benefits, social security, pensions, government contracts and other forms of direct governmental largess are replacing the more traditional forms of property. The result is the creation of a much greater dependency upon government, forming a kind of feudalism where the "serfs" are centered around the "lord," which is the government. There is, therefore, a need to re-create independence for the serfs, perhaps through an experimental homestead act for the twenty-first century. For example, equities such as securities could be purchased through government loans, held in escrow, and paid off in a number of years by their dividends and capital gains. These equities then would be granted to persons otherwise propertyless.

Another concern is the need for controlling the increasing assaults on privacy and for preserving constitutional rights. The government should not be permitted to condition benefits upon complete acquiescence to its demands.

The foregoing only sketches the kind of life we could be living on this island in 2000. There will be problems; this is not a utopia we are talking about but rather a possible society with solutions to present problems, solutions which retain the patterns prized today. New and effective means of maintaining standards of living, and active interests in life, for the retired elderly must be developed. An increase of ethnic pride must be prevented from increasing xenophobia and racial competition. Newcomers will continue to arrive and programs of assimilation must be formally undertaken. Because the environment will always be threatened by man, a constant watch on environmental quality will have to be developed. Government's increased role as servant must not be allowed to justify increased control of life activity.

Nonetheless, the picture painted is entirely possible.

It is simply the development of a social organism designed to make life as good as possible for as many people as possible without destroying our environment. At the same time, it would ensure that the island of Hawaii, perhaps alone in the civilized world, could maintain a well-fed and healthy population, should world disasters occur and the island find itself left to its own devices.

Hawaii, as a cultural and scientific model community, may provide values and a way of life for others to emulate; all of us who are privileged to live and work there can contribute to the building of this model society.

A foundation for Hawaii's future has been established to carry on the work of the 2000 committee. Other action-oriented groups are joining together to assure that Hawaii becomes and remains a model society for the future.

Kauai 2000
Philip K. Ige and Ralph S. Hirota

Philip K. Ige, assistant superintendent of instructional services, Hawaii State Department of Education, was provost of Kauai Community College at the time of the Hawaii 2000 conference. He was born on Oahu and educated at McKinley and Kaimuki high schools, the University of Hawaii, and Teachers College, Columbia, where he received a doctorate in English and education. His career has included teaching and administration at the intermediate, high-school and community-college levels.

Ralph S. Hirota, chairman of the Kauai County Council, has also been a farmer and businessman. Born on the Big Island, he moved to Kauai in 1948, and in 1961 became executive assistant to the then county chairman and later became director of the Kauai office of economic development. In 1966 he was elected to the board of supervisors which, through a charter change, became the county council. He has been a leader in efforts toward adequate staffing of the planning department, upgrading of county personnel, and redirection of the county's goals to seek a more balanced growth.

KAUAI'S PEOPLE AND LIFE-STYLE

Overview

auai, the Garden Island, 550-square-mile home of 30,000 people, has always been slightly off the beaten track, geographically more isolated, historically more independent, and economically more conservative than its neighbors to the east. Such isolation has contributed to a distinctive way of life, easygoing and friendly, persistent in its cultural pluralism, and relatively free from the pressures of modern urbanization.

Yet for all its natural beauty and the good life it offers,

Kauai is faced with a cultural crisis of major proportions: for twenty years, young people have been leaving Kauai, causing a serious brain drain. With the exodus of its most highly educated and most upwardly mobile segment, much of this society's creative potential is being short-circuited. This in turn generates a leadership vacuum, with negative implications for all phases of Kauai life.

Why have the young been leaving? First, lack of meaningful job opportunities. Second, lack of educational diversity. Third, lack of adequate housing. Fourth, lack of cosmopolitan entertainment. Subtle psychological factors also contribute to the flight of Kauai's youth. Despite the changes of recent years, the attitude persists among many residents that Kauai is unchanging and unchangeable. A recent article in the Garden Island (newspaper) referred to "Kauai-nitis," a disease characterized by "indifference, apathy, and relentless monotony." Young people who are eager to participate in the twentieth century and who are no longer in the shadow of plantation life find such attitudes discouraging and incompatible with their personal goals.

Despite the exodus of its youth, Kauai's many assets still outweigh its liabilities. Only a week in Honolulu is sufficient to restore a proper perspective. Urbanization, overbuilding, air pollution, and plastic aloha are not yet part of Kauai's life-style. But without energy and imagination to chart a different course, what is to keep Kauai from plunging headlong into environmental and cultural disaster long before 2000?

The Probable Future

Unless Kauai's brain drain is reversed, it is likely that by 2000 the island will be overwhelmed by economic pressures to "develop" to its "highest and best use," thus squandering its natural resources and failing to cultivate its human resources.

In the short term, society will continue to fragment, and the leadership vacuum will grow worse. Young people will continue to leave because there will be nothing to attract them; their elders will continue to rule because there will be no one to replace them. Planning will be nonexistent because "who needs it?" In the absence of long-range objectives, the fast buck will prevail. And Kauai will develop, and overdevelop, and overdevelop . . .

By 2000, traditional Kauai will long since have disappeared. A population whose children refuse to stay cannot long perpetuate itself. On the other hand, immigration will accelerate, bringing newcomers whose cultural referents will be the suburbs of Los Angeles, Chicago, and Kansas City. The population could well reach 250,000 by the end of the century. One day, the newcomers will have their fill of old-style Kauai politics and will vote in their own leaders. By then, it will be too late to save the traditional life-style of Kauai's people.

Alternative Futures

If the brain drain can be arrested, cultural catastrophe might be avoided. The leadership vacuum will have to be eased, however, and new immigration to Kauai must be regulated with considerable skill. By 2000 it is possible that Kauai will have retained its easy informality, close parent-child relations, freedom of movement throughout the island, and cultural pluralism. But it will have to be the kind of society in which youth can satisfy personal as well as professional aspirations; in which growth is orderly, the natural environment is respected, and development is ecologically sound; where economic integration with the rest of the state can create more challenging job opportunities without sacrificing the quality of life; where housing is available in greater diversity, imagination, and price range, so that people can raise their families as they choose but can also be near relatives and friends, forging a sense of community and local pride; where continuing education and individual growth are possible for people of all ages and interests; where citizens can participate in political process without fear of intimidation, and where political initiative and innovation are applauded rather than condemned.

Suggestions for Action

1. Develop new educational programs for all levels of instruction, focusing on cultural traditions, values, and variations among all ethnic groups that have contributed to Kauai's population.

2. Sponsor, with adequate funding, an annual folk festival featuring cultural traditions found on Kauai.

3. Survey, through the community college, all college students in the county to document their interests, aspirations, and suggestions for Kauai's future development.

4. Build neighborhood facilities, similar to Kapaa's, around the island, where young people can meet, talk, and simply fool around. Consideration might also be given to private development of youth barges that would moor offshore on Friday and Saturday nights.

5. Construct vest-pocket parks in all urban areas, starting with park benches in front of the County building in Lihue.

6. Initiate physical-education programs, including swimming, surfing, and horseback riding, at the community college, to encourage greater use of Kauai's natural assets.

7. Develop new planning tools to weigh the ecological impact of any given development, in human as well as physical terms.

8. Develop new economic planning tools to measure population growth as carefully as inflation, and develop policies to encourage or discourage new growth according to long-range objectives.

9. Institute public education programs to promote greater understanding of long-range economic and land-use planning.

10. Encourage oceanographic and ecological research as new industries offering meaningful opportunity to Kauai's youth.

11. Offer more amenities of urban life, particularly culture and the arts, commercial diversity, and nighttime entertainment, with appeal to young people.

12. Lower the voting age to 16 by 1980.

THE NATURAL ENVIRONMENT

Overview

Kauai's land offers some of the most breathtaking views in the world, but certain developers see only immediate profit in the form of maximum density. This State has some of the most progressive land controls in the country, but Regulation 4 of the County land-use law permits development in conservation-zoned areas without approval from the County planning commission. State taxing procedures encourage development rather than coordinated planning; under the concept of highest and best use, cow pastures stand no chance against resort hotels. Littering is against the law, but tons of rubbish mar Kauai's highways and beaches.

Kauai's air is relatively clean, but air pollution anywhere is cause for concern. On Kauai, primary abuses involve the airlines, sugar mills, and automobiles. Promises have been made, but must be followed by action. The sea around Kauai is also in need of protection. And most importantly, whatever Kauai's optimum population might be, rampant population growth always has an irreversible impact on the natural environment.

The Probable Future

Severe strains may be expected to increase on all segments of the natural environment. A number of Kauai's rare and endangered species, such as the āe'o, 'ō'ō, and nuku-pu'u birds, as well as dozens of rare plant species in the Alakai Swamp, will become extinct. We will also see continuing erosion of open spaces and beach areas, the end of marine life in the Wailua and Hanalei rivers, and smog over Lihue-Kapaa. By 2000, prime agricultural land will have been converted into suburban tract developments, and the H-5 Freeway will encircle the island with its six-lane thoroughfares. An international jetport at Kilauea will dump thousands of visitors per day onto Kauai. Urban high-rises will dominate government renewal programs aimed at clearing up unplanned, unimaginative, and overpriced subdivisions. Fishing and hukilaus will come to an end, and there will be $20 greens fees and $10 tennis fees on overcrowded facilities. Ni'ihau will be the site of Disneyland West.

Alternative Futures

With intelligent planning, the future for Kauai's environment could be exceptionally bright. By 2000, rights to clean air and water will be constitutionally guaranteed, and man's stewardship of public lands will be enforced by law. Much more will be known about the limits of environmental insult, and, through applied ecology, miles of Kauai's interior will be accessible to permanent residents and visitors alike. By 2000, we can envision well-planned cities and towns, surrounded by open space, bridle trails through much of the interior, and an island-wide mass-transit system. Old-style twentieth-century roads will become public gardens, the automobile having been banned in 1980.

Suggestions for Action

1. Begin education programs immediately to acquaint the public with the dangers of pollution, the principles of ecology, and civil responsibility concerning Kauai's unique environment and ecology.

2. Develop an ecology research center on Kauai, while the island is still relatively rural and underdeveloped.

3. Undertake a "SIMMAP" program [1] to adorn Kauai's highways with flowering trees and shrubs that will bloom throughout the year.

1. A computer-run mapping process used to pick out and illustrate various phenomena and frequency of types of land use while leaving out the rest of the map. — Editors

4. Expand State watershed management, reforestation and erosion control programs.

5. Amend Regulation 4 of the land-use law to extend the County's authority over the development of conservation-zoned property.

6. Extend jurisdiction of the County planning commission over all new highway and mass-transit development on Kauai.

7. Double the staff of the County planning office immediately, as a first step in a major expansion.

8. Insist that adequate public notice be given for hearings on all matters affecting the natural environment.

9. Amend "highest and best use" to read "highest and best public interest," and create new tax incentives for more imaginative land use by private owners.

10. Establish an architectural design tradition which integrates Kauai's man-made environment with its natural environment and appoint a design-review board to scrutinize all plans for government buildings and hotel complexes.

11. Research the impact of a hotel surcharge or a landing fee, to be called an environmental quality tax and to be used to protect Kauai's natural environment.

12. Declare a moratorium on all new buildings, except single-family residences, until the County adopts a comprehensive zoning ordinance or general plan. Further delay simply invites disaster.

THE ECONOMY

Overview

The economy of Kauai is presently based on two major industries: sugar and tourism. The pineapple industry, once important, has all but vanished. Diversified agriculture, once stable, faces an uncertain future.

Sugar has retained its stability on Kauai, with the introduction of innovative technological improvements, and high-yield crop varieties. The tourist industry, inasmuch as its growth came when pineapple was floundering, has had a profoundly beneficial impact on the economy. But tourism's growth has been a mixed blessing; Kauai was largely unprepared for the onslaught of hotels and visitors, and is currently adjusting to the many problems triggered by its growth.

Scientific research and development have gained a foothold on the island in the form of the U.S. Navy's Pacific Missile Range. Combined with the NASA space-flight tracking station at Kokee, research and development account for a number of widely diversified jobs for local residents. Technical specialists must be brought in from the Mainland, however, and the installations are dependent upon federal funding.

The Probable Future

According to projections by the County's planning consultants, the local population will grow from 29,761 in 1970 to 90,000 in 1990. This projection is based on the assumption that tourism, as the prime economic growth factor, will be allowed to grow at the accelerated rate of the recent past. It also assumes that practically all other economic development between now and 1990 will be related to tourism. By 2000, it is probable that Kauai's economy will be almost entirely tourist-oriented, leading to pollution of the worst sort. By then, Kauai will be nearly devoid of its appeal to residents and visitors alike. The island's inventory of tourist facilities will have been over-built as tourist interest declines, thus raising the specter of widespread unemployment and business failure by 2000. Kauai will have been turned into a bizarre, honky-tonk, second-rate Miami Beach, with no trace of its traditional charm.

Alternative Futures

More desirable futures are possible, but will be difficult to achieve. Efforts to diversify Kauai's business and industrial base will hold the key. If successful, the sugar industry will prevail as a significant component. Tourism will remain a major industry, but its growth will be guided. Diversified agriculture (especially taro, anthuriums, guava, and winter-seed) will have regained its status, and will be joined by synthetic food production as a new industry. Kauai will become a leading international research center in a dozen fields. New markets will have been opened around the world, and Kauai's economy itself will have become integrated to that of the Pacific. Economic isolation will be a thing of the past.

Through the establishment of imaginative measures, discouraging rampant land speculation and wanton development, Kauai's growth will be orderly, with a population in the neighborhood of 60,000 by 2000.

Suggestions for Action

1. Continue and expand current efforts to diversify Kauai's economy, particularly in the fields of small business and labor-intensive agriculture.

2. Develop an educational program through the high schools stressing the importance of economic planning and the range of potential job opportunities on Kauai.

3. Create economic development work-study internships for top Kauai students, through the university system.

4. Develop new economic planning tools to monitor Kauai's population growth, and conduct research on the relationships among industrial growth, population expansion, and environmental pollution.

5. Sponsor legislation creating a new federal assistance formula which would take into account effective population rather than permanent population.

6. Develop new programs to stimulate private as well as public research facilities on Kauai, in the following fields: oceanography, ecology, human biology, medicine and public health, gerontology, cultural change, and economic development. Augment existing research in diversified agriculture, and establish "research destination areas" in order to attract grants under the new national oceanographic and atmosphere agency.

7. Undertake studies of the economic impact of various transportation systems on Kauai, particularly interisland ferries, international jet service, and island-wide mass transit.

8. Continue tri-county economic development conferences to explore all areas of possible economic integration among Kauai, Maui, and the Big Island.

9. Explore the possibility of eventual development of a free-port trade center, perhaps at Port Allen, to take advantage of the growing commerce between Hawaii and Pacific basin countries.

10. Develop a long-range promotional program to encourage visitors to Kauai who will stay longer and return more often.

11. Establish a tourist-ombudsman office at the County level to encourage visitor satisfaction and to stress Kauai's concern for the quality of its tourism.

12. Develop new sources of revenue for the County, to enable it to fund necessary economic planning services.

HOUSING AND TRANSPORTATION

Overview

Housing on Kauai developed where there was work — near sugar mills and major ports, resulting in dozens of plantation-owned communities scattered around the island. The plantations now find it uneconomical to maintain old camp housing and are generally phasing out their landlord functions. Some are building new subdivisions for employees — but many people, especially the elderly, resist moves requiring higher monthly payments and a disruption of old habits.

For Kauai, transportation is its lifeline to the world outside. Jet travel opened the gates for thousands of visitors but travel for Kauai's people is harshly expensive: it costs almost as much to make a round-trip flight to Hilo as it does to fly to the Mainland and back. Kauai has one airport facility and two deep-sea ports, all expanding. Ground transportation has centered around the car. Cane railroads were replaced by trucks a generation ago. Extensive changes are around the corner.

The Probable Future

Constructing new homes in the 1970s at the same rate new hotels were put up in the 1960s may prove costly in the long run; first, because housing takes up a much larger proportion of urban acreage, and second, because it initiates a vicious cycle: sugar land is taken out of circulation for housing development, causing more dependency on tourism, which takes out more sugar land. Once started, further urbanization is almost unstoppable. By 2000, the Garden Island may well be the glutted island.

The probable future for Kauai's transportation holds considerable promise, at least for the short term. A merger between the local airlines should greatly improve service and perhaps lead to reasonable fares. Also, the announced interisland ferry system should have a most welcome impact on Kauai's economy. The longer-range future is less appealing: mass transit, expanded highways, and a trans-Pacific airport all have costs which will rival their benefits. The costs will be ecological, visual, audible, and spiritual. SSTs over Hanalei Bay is not a happy thought. One prediction is safe: before 2000, Lihue will have its first traffic light.

Alternative Futures

No one wants Kauai to become like Waikiki. But inefficient and unnecessary development of prime agricultural lands and an international jetport could easily lead to this. On the other hand, diversified agriculture and a major research industry by 2000 could provide an alternative to mass tourism and a buffer against rampant urbanization. To attract needed specialists and to retain Kauai's young people, small-scale urban amenities may be necessary; to develop needed markets, international export facilities may be essential. Two concepts hold particular promise: creation of a central city embracing the Lihue-Kapaa complex; and development of international cargo facilities at existing air- and sea-ports.

It is vital to Kauai's long-term interests that the island diversify economically. To do this it must develop local leadership to its fullest capacity and must stem its brain drain. These ideas would combat urbanization with limited urbanization. Above all, Kauai's present leaders must recognize that public attitudes in the future are most likely to change in the area of housing (urban versus rural) and (single-family versus multifamily) and transportation (private versus public conveyance). It would be extremely shortsighted to make irreversible moves affecting the natural environment on the basis of popular attitudes which may soon be outmoded.

Suggestions for Action

1. Approve a comprehensive zoning ordinance for Kauai now.

2. Amend the building code to permit experimentation with new materials and new design concepts.

3. Provide tax benefits for development of urban-zoned land, to encourage urbanization there rather than in agricultural land.

4. Allow flexibility in the height of multifamily and office structures but not in tourist facilities, and permit controlled increases in urban density requirements.

5. Auction off unimproved State and County land in urban districts not intended for public parks.

6. Create a special land-use category for a central city and inaugurate a coordinated research and development program to reconstruct a new urban center for Lihue-Kapaa.

7. Sponsor a feasibility study of international cargo facilities at existing air- and sea-ports on Kauai.

8. Withhold approval of the proposed trans-Pacific airport at least until the impact of the interisland ferry can be assessed.

9. Develop integrated multimode transportation net-

works for recreation, including bridlepaths, bikeways, and footpaths.

10. Ban the internal-combustion-powered automobile from Kauai by 1980.

11. Do not complete the belt highway.

12. Develop a tourist railroad along old cane railroad rights-of-way, which presently lie dormant.

EDUCATION AND THE ARTS
Overview

Society's values are transmitted through education; individual values are expressed through creative arts. Institutional frameworks exist to facilitate the process. On Kauai the institutional aspects of education have traditionally been weak, and the means for individual creativity have been left up to the individual himself. As one of the task-force members said, "Kauai's educational facilities can only go up."

Kauai schools, however, are beginning to make some interesting noises, and reflect a new willingness to consider a more flexible approach to their traditional functions. The great burden for reversing Kauai's brain drain rests on the shoulders of its three high schools and the community college, as much as on the body politic; the need is to educate not only Kauai's youth but Kauai's people on the island's great potential. But preoccupation with matters concerning discipline, drugs, and extracurricular behavior could negate much of the new educational promise. In the arts, the cultural desert may be showing new sprouts. The museum is expanding, the library is busy, and special events are increasing. Most importantly, there is a new interest in understanding and preserving the rich but hidden folk art of Kauai's people. The band of people dedicated to supporting the arts is small, but growing.

The Probable Future

If we continue the present stress on control and rules in Kauai's educational system, by 2000 the elementary and high schools will be overcrowded "police states" run by faculties and administrators whose average age is over 40. Promising young students will leave the island for study, depriving Kauai's communities of any young input. Students who remain on Kauai will leave the educational system ill prepared for the rapidly changing world, thereby aggravating the problems of our society. The present controversy over the community-college site will still be raging.

In the area of arts, due to the facilitation of interisland travel and the increase in population and leisure, there will be a greater variety and frequency of cultural events. Some of the unique multicultural nature of the arts, however, will be lost as Kauai's culture changes and becomes increasingly homogeneous on the mainland mold.

Alternative Futures

The possibilities of massive changes in educational institutions and values are as great as in any other segment of our society. If these possibilities materialize, by 2000 schools in the traditional sense will cease to exist. Classrooms will be anywhere. Students will be anyone. Teachers will be anyone. Learning will be voluntary, and accepted as an enjoyable, lifelong pursuit; educational curricula will explode far beyond the confinements of the present system. Education will be geared to the individual's needs and desires. Kauai has every opportunity to be a center of educational innovation and experimentation. School buildings will function around the clock, and around the year, not in the present regimented style, but as community learning centers open to all. Through worldwide satellite computer networks, Kauaians will have at their fingertips every piece of information ever known by man.

Kauai will be known as a cultural center where East can meet West, where individuals can renew themselves intellectually; an island to whose shores music, drama, and folk festivals will draw persons of outstanding creative ability.

Suggestions for Action

1. Encourage a wide variety of experimentation and evaluation of school and classroom structures, materials, and curricula.

2. Transfer the policy-making powers in education to those who are being educated.

3. Keep up with current educational trends.

4. Provide adequate funding.

5. Eliminate the tenure system.

6. Initiate teacher evaluations by students.

7. Support better and broader teacher education that would prepare the teacher for the more human aspects of education, such as counseling.

8. Utilize nonschool personnel, materials, and settings to enrich the students as well as to involve a greater portion of the community in the educational process.

9. Provide public funds for culture and the arts in sufficient quantity to be meaningful.

10. Assess and promote public awareness of Kauai's multicultural heritage.

11. Strive to preserve an environment that will be physically and socially conducive to artists and educators.

12. Encourage and promote education as a continuing process important and enjoyable to all age groups.

POLITICAL DECISION-MAKING

Overview

Because political activity is one of the truly important arenas in any society, the best minds and best people should engage in it. Yet the words politics and politicians are so often linked with other words like dirty, corrupt, and dishonest that they trigger reactions of cynicism and hopelessness. To become a politician some say is to deliberately choose the crooked path. Public hearings are regarded as shows or shibais [2] put on by politicians to make points for themselves for the next election, but not to learn how the public feels or thinks about given issues. Some seem more interested in serving their private interests — through whatever means are available.

Kauai is no exception to this condition. Elsewhere in this report, the island is described as being beautiful, off-the-beaten track, feudalistic, behind the other islands in most things progressive, and still hung up with a plantation mentality. Many Kauaians admit to the ills of their political conditions. Yet election after election, they return the same faces into office.

The Probable Future

With all due respect to women's liberation, if Kauai were a woman, she might truly be called beautiful but dumb. But some Kauaians see a small ray of hope in changes which are beginning to take place. Some of the young people are beginning to return. New blood is flowing into Kauai. And some of the ordinary citizens of the island are beginning to learn to protest political actions they feel are not in the best interests of the public. It is possible that by 2000 these small changes will grow to dominance. Native brain power may return in significant ways to provide a new kind of leadership, and the level of political sophistication of the people may rise accordingly.

But perhaps it is more probable that old habits and attitudes will prevail, at least for the short term. The mass of voters will continue to be politically naive and uninformed on important public issues, easily fooled by back-slapping politicians. Voters will continue to be manipulated. Racial campaigning, economic reprisals, and other kinds of intimidation will continue to be significant.

2. From Japanese, meaning a play or drama. In Hawaii this has come to mean a deceptive performance in social or political life, concealing reality. — Editors

And charges of corruption will continue to be made. Until one day — people will get fed up and we will see Kauai's last hurrah.[3]

Alternative Futures

But too much is at stake to permit the old-style politics to continue much longer. The Garden Island's future as a beautiful, unique place is seriously threatened. If decisions are not made, and made soon, with all of the wisdom we can muster, Kauai as we know and love it will not be around by 2000.

One can dream of a future in which, through enlightened political, community, and educational leadership, Kauai voters can be lifted to new levels of political maturity. They will be issue oriented, interested in the quality of their candidates, rather than in their racial background or personality type. Politicians will be responsible, and responsive to the public will, able to make hard, tough decisions, and to establish priorities. All citizens will be politicians, in the finest sense of the word.

Suggestions for Action

1. Let the schools and the community college make concerted efforts to teach political science and citizen responsibility.

2. Encourage community, business, and professional organizations to be more informed about the power structure of the community, about the dynamics of political decision-making, and to be more active politically.

3. Encourage students to participate in political discussion groups and campaigning.

4. Lower the voting age to at least 16 by 1980.

5. Identify and gather fair-minded citizens to conduct political workshops to evaluate grass-roots political strategy for Kauai.

3. Compare the end of a past era of political rule in Boston portrayed by Edwin O'Connor in *The Last Hurrah* (Boston: Little Brown, 1956). — Editors

6. *Limit the amount of money candidates may spend on local campaigns, and let the government pay for half the campaign costs.*

7. *Establish a city-manager type of government for the County in place of the current structure.*

8. *Establish a unicameral legislature at the State level, so that people on the neighbor islands can more easily follow what's going on in Honolulu.*

9. *Publish the economic affiliations of all candidates and politicians, and insist on establishing a sound ethics code at the County level.*

10. *Provide public campaign funds so that young people and others can afford to run for public office.*

11. *Increase County powers in all areas of taxation.*

12. *Create a youth advisory board to the County Council.*

Maui 2000
John P. Hoshor

John P. Hoshor is director of the Counseling and Testing Center, University of Hawaii. At the time of the conference he was provost of Maui Community College. He has served as professor of speech and psychology at the universities of Washington and Hawaii as well as associate dean of Arts and Sciences, University of Hawaii.

ur Maui is now an island community of 46,000 people living on 728 square miles. The task forces working on Maui 2000 have in general approached their goal by trying to see 2000 as it might be by simple projection of existing conditions and trends; next by describing 2000 as they would like to see it; and then by suggesting ways and means of getting to the more desired future. Certain general ideas have emerged from most of the groups. One of these is that a fairly clear distinction should be kept in mind between prediction and prophesy. A prediction of 2000 would be based on known factors, interrelationships, interdependencies, psychological or social "laws" (established theories) — and would be subject to rational explanation and logical analysis. Prophesy on the other hand is the result of a vision, inspiration, hunch, or insight; it is not generally susceptible to analysis. In discussing the future, both of these can play a part, but in general our task forces are working toward prediction rather than prophesy.

The point was also made that a prediction is not in itself a plan — though it may, and presumably should, be a guide to one.

EDUCATION

This group has met only a few times, but has carried on considerable discussion of the subject among the individual members. In general, it recognizes that the college of the future will be addressing itself to a different set of needs than has the college of the past. The preservation and passing along of culture, long recognized as a basic goal of our higher education, will be greatly deemphasized. The expanding of new frontiers of knowledge will remain as a goal but will also be deemphasized, and probably greatly changed in character. Three new goals will be added as needs to which higher education should be addressing itself: the preparation of society, providing a lifetime learning center for all segments of society, and providing sociotechnologic systems research.

One need to which the college of the future will definitely be paying much attention is that of preparing youth (and for that matter, people of all ages) for planning. The future society will recognize more clearly than we now do that planning should not be an individual matter only. People should be concerned not only with planning their own careers, their own marriages, their own pleasures, but also with planning the total or overall objectives of the world in which they live. In this way, forecasts or predictions can become self-fulfilling (man's landing on the moon is probably the best early example of such a prediction).

A second way in which the college of the future will be involved in preparing society is in the improvement of communication. It is an interesting observation that printed books were the last major change in communication to be fully accepted and exploited by universities. In the future we will be very concerned with helping society utilize fully such developing technological improvements to communication as computers, electronic information storage and retrieval systems, and instant global audio-visual communication.

A third way in which the college of the future will be involved in preparing society is in the acceptance of rapid change. One has only to stand back and take a sweeping view through time of virtually any aspect of man's behavior or environment to recognize that the extent and the rate of change is increasing on a geometrical rather than on a simple arithmetical basis. When one looks at the multitude of areas in which breakdown has occurred in recent years, it is easy to recognize that part of the problem is almost always the inability of people to accept change as rapidly as it is being forcibly thrust upon them.

The college of the future will more and more become a lifetime learning center for all members of society. This prediction is based on a clear recognition of many factors, some of which are: that education is maturational, that is, many things can be learned only over a period of time, and in conjunction with various kinds of experiences; that more and more retraining will be necessary in practically all jobs — because the rate of change referred to above is such that in most future jobs, skills, knowledge and attitudes will become obsolete within a few years without routine retraining; also, that the day of the single lifetime career is rapidly coming to an end. Most able people in the future will change careers at least once, sometimes oftener, during the course of their lives; the colleges must recognize this and be prepared to facilitate the process.

The complexity of man, his machines, and his technology has become such that only extensive control, experimentation, and testing of hypotheses offer hope for the future. Purely theoretical analysis will more and more be hopeless; the "logical" answer will more and more often be the wrong one.[1]

1. A good example of this might be the problem of slums and ghettos. The logical answer is rehabilitation — that is, model cities. Recent computer-based projections by a systems-research team at MIT suggest that this is exactly the wrong answer. A better answer is to tear down all the slum houses and build factories in their places. The people then successfully take care of their own housing problems.

On Maui this committee sees the need by 1980 for a separate public institution that would enable us to offer the complete range of services referred to above. Specifically, we see the need now for a separate campus offering the junior and senior years (bachelors degrees), and by 2000, graduate studies as well. We offer this suggestion: the area on the Wailuku side of the present Maui Community College campus should be acquired by the State and utilized for the purpose just referred to, making Maui Community College and the adjoining senior institution a complete learning center to service all of Maui County by 2000.

VALUES AND LIFE-STYLES

Our discussions were generally quite frustrating and inconclusive. It was difficult to concentrate on the question of future values and the life-styles that might result from them without considering such matters as education, political structure, law, economic systems, and various other constituents of the fabric of human society.

In a general way, however, our discussions did center around the question of what it is that makes for a quality life. There was a good deal of agreement on the following points.

Our present conception of the "good life" is not well thought out. As a consequence, some of the most revered of our modern life ideals have led to negative and often disastrous consequences; for example, societal crises and civil disorder. Many felt that contemporary values were largely shaped by minority private-interest groups whose motives were grounded in the desire for profit. Most of the group agreed that man's equation of the good life with things (that is, with the acquisition of material wealth) would have to change.

We agreed that we would plan for a world in which a variety of life-styles might coexist. It was recognized that the population would probably have to be stabilized for this to be possible. There was a strong feeling among the group that the future should not be straitjacketed. Though all agreed on the need for thought and planning, most were reluctant to specify a particular future they would like to see realized. In accordance with this feeling, most of the plans for the future were quite general. In sum, the group generally agreed that contemporary man had not yet begun to take seriously the question of what it is that makes a quality human existence. They felt that many of our present values are vacuous, others are blatantly detrimental to man's happiness, and some threaten man's very existence.

Considerable interest and excitement were generated by the realization that Maui as an island community has a much better opportunity than most areas of the world to exert some measure of control over the emergent lifestyle of 2000.

ART

Maui, remote island in the Pacific, both suffers and benefits from lagging fifty to one hundred years behind the mainland U.S.A. in technological developments and in social change. Foresight in planning can help resolve many problems before they develop.

Speculations on housing in 2000 ranged from total disaster to cloud nine floating tetrahedronal cities. On the moon, in the clouds, on the earth, underground and underwater, man-made structures now exist and will undergo transformations of new materials and forms, with increasing use of curved surfaces as contrasted with the current rectilinear structures. Transportable units of interlocking modules will increasingly be used for offices and apartments; population mobility will increase; and personally selected items in interior decoration will decrease. More and more packaged and check-out units with increased individualized instruction-education kits will coincide with and be made more feasible because of decreased individuality in those strata of society preserving and extending established systems of production.

MUSIC

All agreed that there will be more free time in the future, but some fear that too much leisure will lead to drink and drug use, crime and boredom. This emphasizes the need for education for leisure that will promote participation rather than passive listening or watching. Creativity must begin early in life. One desirable model might be "Mozartian man," a creator whose art does not live on conflict and who creates for and out of joy.

If present trends continue, we will find music on Maui created largely in bars and hotel dining rooms for tourists, played in dance halls by local rock groups who imitate as well as innovate, and imported from Honolulu on occasion for those with classical tastes. Elementary students participate in classroom bands, but at the high-school level, a college-prep course often eliminates time for band for the very student who has the most talent to offer. Church and school choruses will continue. String quartets are rare and ensembles nonexistent. Creative talent exists but is rare.

For the future, a concerted effort must be made to bring string instruments to Maui and to develop a youth symphony orchestra on each island. Making art and music a more important part of the school curriculum is essential for the leisure world of the future. More music will be imported from Oahu, and if there is no orchestra on Maui for youngsters to join, there should be small string ensembles, chamber orchestras befitting an island world still apart from Honolulu in 2000. The Honolulu symphony should be subsidized to the extent that almost a full season will be possible on Maui; an opera season should be available too. The other alternative is travel so swift and inexpensive that Mauians can easily attend the season in Honolulu. This will not satisfy the needs of the school population, however, and will necessitate some tours by the symphony and opera companies.

Focus on the Pacific basin by schools and colleges

will make musical festivals of various ethnic groupings popular and more elaborate than ever. Colleges will be the focal point for these studies in national music. Children will grow up familiar with songs, dances, and instruments of various Pacific countries, as part of their heritage that should never be lost. There has been so much music written that it would take a lifetime to acquaint oneself with all the musical treasures extant. To make this acquaintance easier, homes in 2000 will be plugged into libraries of recorded music. A punched card inserted, or a series of numbers dialed, will bring into the room not only the music you select, but also three-dimensional holograms. Mild drugs might heighten the sense of hearing, making it possible for the not-too-musical to derive utmost pleasure from music. But people change, and, besides passive listening, there will probably be an increasing desire to re-create sounds on an instrument or with the voice, for pleasure and for the feeling of accomplishment that such creative activity brings.

While nothing really innovative or startling is contained herein, it behooves us to make the arts exciting, interesting, and important to the young people of Maui so that leisure will not be a vacuum of boredom, but full of accomplishment and pleasure. This can result from active participation in music or from listening to the varied kinds of music that will be readily available in 2000.

THEATER

For fifty years prior to the coming of television, the Maui community theater was active in presenting first-class plays in their own theaters or in the Baldwin High School Auditorium. The introduction of television kept the audiences at home, as distances are great and working hours early. Also, many changes in the industrial scene meant that a majority of the most talented members left the island. The theater is now quiescent, with only an occasional play at Baldwin — which is at present expensive and difficult to use. The newcomers seem unable to give time to take part actively either as audience or performers.

At present, theater here depends upon the plays from Honolulu brought by the youth theater, the lyceum course, and arts council projects. A readers' theater is being organized by the Lahaina art club and next season will probably see one in central Maui. Excellent productions are given by the high-school drama clubs of Baldwin and St. Anthony's, with occasional ones by other groups.

The future will depend upon the completion of the fine theater to be built for the Maui Community College when funds become available. It could mean a revival of the Maui community theater and of its excellent seasons of praiseworthy performances. The number of theater-minded individuals living here is limited, however. Maui is also overorganized, and community-minded and talented people are overly involved, so that the problems are very different from those on Oahu.

TRANSPORTATION AND HOUSING

This task force concluded that certain assumptions as to possible conditions and problems for 2000 are justified. Among these are that Maui County population will increase from the present 46,156, to approximately 250,000. A minority of the group felt that 150,000 would be more realistic. There was agreement that there would be an influx of people from outside the state; that housing needs, already critically short, would become more and more pressing; that there would be a strong — possibly irresistible — tendency toward urban residential sprawl; that crowded roads and pollution of air, water, and living conditions in general would become a fact of life; that the means of livelihood for the majority of our people would change from agriculture to tourism, services for retired people, and construction.

There was also fairly general agreement on what the

group wanted to see happen, and on what it considered possible. Generally, it hopes to see greater use of data and theories from the social sciences to aid design of communities. This would include the designing of housing to meet social and psychological needs, to help certain special groups such as the "deprived," or those who want to experience communal living, and those who see the home as a bedroom and social center only (no kitchen). Some more specific suggestions were that separate cities be self-sustaining with intervening green belts. Some towns might be of high-rise construction, with condominiums or townhouses; some, of fee-simple ownership with single-family dwellings; one was proposed for about four hundred families, with a skyscraper that would occupy only one-fourth the land of a single-family dwelling. Flexibility in land use was also favored; as owners die, for example, government could appropriate land for parks or other public use.

Particular attention was given to the need for mass transportation, such as buses and monorails, and the need to change the thinking of people so that they will use public transportation rather than rely entirely on family cars. Other developments foreseen by 2000 were interisland ferries and electric cars that would be rechargeable on house current.

THE ECONOMY

This committee made several general suggestions for the development of Maui. The foremost was the need to develop a more balanced and diversified economy. Preferences were expressed concerning the nature of new industries to be recruited. The feeling was that the present major basic industries of the county — sugar, tourism, and pineapple — would not prove a secure basis for long-term growth. Nonpolluting light manufacturing, diversified agriculture, and flower growing were considered probable.

A second major consideration was the absolute necessity for the County to begin planning the construction of recreational facilities for both local and tourist populations. In particular, it would be advisable for the County to provide a larger number of developed parks and undeveloped wilderness areas. The committee also felt that it would be advantageous for the County at this time to develop a long-range recreational plan, including the location of needed beach rights-of-way, future park locations, and hiking areas.

A third suggestion was for the County to consider the future development of its coastal areas, with "blue-belt" bays in which there would be set aside ocean areas suitable for the recreational needs of residents and tourists. Hanauma Bay on Oahu is an example of such a park. A further use of our coastal areas might be the development of fish hatcheries, the construction of enclosed ocean areas that might be stocked for sport fishing, and the construction of boating facilities.

The committee's final suggestion concerned education and manpower training. It thought that in the long run it would be necessary to retrain many of the present agricultural workers for both the tourist industry and the new industries which the County should be recruiting.

THE NATURAL ENVIRONMENT: LAND, SEA, AND AIR

In general, this committee recognized the vital necessity of constant and efficient research to develop the data needed for wise decisions on preserving and enhancing the natural environment. It was felt that some of this research must be done locally by Maui-based scientists and researchers.

The principal problem discussed was pollution. In general, it was thought that there is some danger of an overbalancing growth of tourism that would inevitably lead to pollution of the land, air, and water unless controls are effectively applied.

POLITICAL DECISION-MAKING AND THE LAW

A general statement agreed upon by this committee was that the guiding principle behind the laws and their enforcement should be that a man's liberty be curtailed only in types of conduct that would transgress the rights of others. Vigorous enforcement of existing U.S. constitutional guarantees of basic rights would promote this objective.

Some specific recommendations were:

1. *Amend the State constitution to provide that criminal penalties may not be visited upon a person for the purpose of protecting him from himself, and that in all cases the legal presumption will be that individual conduct is not harmful to the public, with the burden of proving a legitimate public interest placed on the State.*

2. *Revise State and County criminal codes to clearly define what conduct is criminal and what is not, with no "catchall" statutes — which the United States Supreme Court has found to be suffering from the vices of vagueness and overbreadth.*

3. *Adopt the model penal code submitted by the State supreme court to the 1970 State legislature.*

4. *Establish regulations that would require private detective agencies to be licensed by the State, and that would assure the individual the right to see and challenge all data in file on him in private or governmental organizations.*

5. *Require extensive training in constitutional law for State and County police officers.*

6. *Increase the number of State-financed public defenders and expand other legal services for the nonwealthy public.*

7. *Develop a truly nonpartisan, professional method of selecting qualified candidates for district and circuit judges.*

8. Provide county governments with the authority to mitigate penalties and repeal laws in the areas of social legislation (that is, gambling and drug laws).

Special attention was given by this committee to the need to decrease the alienation and frustration felt by young people and to engage their creative talents in the general effort to meet the challenge of the future.

The committee also felt it imperative that Hawaii's political systems be efficient, future-oriented, and, most importantly, responsive to the needs and desires of all the people. In this connection, it was recommended that regulations be established to effectively control and publicize the political activities of well-financed special-interest groups, and to provide State financial assistance for political activity by groups representing the impoverished minorities.

A final recommendation was to establish permanent Hawaii 2000 committees to advise State and county governments as to long-range future problems and objectives.

MAUI AND THE PACIFIC COMMUNITY

As an outgrowth of many discussions held by this task force, a consensus was reached on recommendations to the conference. Most meetings revolved around discussions of Hawaii's future role in the Pacific community, serving as a center for Pacific expertise in agriculture, industry, science, and in intracultural studies concerned with preserving ethnic modes for future appreciation and use in improving the quality of life. It was felt that Hawaii is uniquely suited for leadership in the Pacific community — already she serves in a leadership capacity for educational programs through the University of Hawaii, the community college services, and the East-West Center.

The task force expressed its hope that the citizenry and government of Hawaii would strive to achieve a new direction for the state, to serve as a center of Pacific activity in science, education, and cultural appreciation, rather than to continue its present preoccupation with agriculture, tourism, and the military. Hawaii is unique, in part because of its environmental circumstances, but, more importantly, because of its unique cultural disposition and cosmopolitan atmosphere. These aspects form the attraction it has for people who see in Hawaii an opportunity to create a cultural oasis, a place from which to reestablish directions for what at present appears to be a tumultuous future.

6 CONFERENCE OBSERVER RESPONSES

Overview
Editors

To assist the advisory committee in carrying out the second and third responsibilities of our triple legislative mandate — to hold a conference, to evaluate it, and to make recommendations for consequent activities — we decided to engage four outstanding futures thinkers as conference observer-consultants. We asked them to read the preliminary task force reports, to participate in the August conference as observers, and then to submit a critical assessment of what had happened, together with recommendations for further action.

Two consultants brought us the benefits of global futures thinking as nurtured in Japan and Korea, where pioneering futures societies, unique in Asia and then among the few outside Europe, had been established in 1968. The first was sociologist Hidetoshi Kato, who had just completed the task of administering the Second International Futures Research Conference held in Kyoto, Japan, in April 1970. The second was Hahn-Been Lee, scholar-administrator, a founder and then president of the Korean Society for Futures Studies.

From Scotland via the Mainland came world-citizen John McHale, exemplar of the truth that the art, poetry, and science of futures studies spring from the same creative imagination. From Pennsylvania State University came Raymond G. Studer, director of the division of man-environment relations in its new College of Human

Development, who brought us the viewpoint of a behavioral scientist.

Each of these observers could have been a striking star of the conference as a featured speaker. Instead we asked them to devote themselves to watching, listening, reading, and thinking about what we had done, what we were doing, and what we ought to do next. Their responses are shared here.

A Wholly Unique Venture
John McHale

John McHale is director, Center for Integrative Studies, School of Advanced Technology, State University of New York, Binghamton. Author, artist, and sociologist, he has published extensively in the United States and Europe on the impact of technology on culture, mass communications, and the future. His latest books are *The Future of the Future* (1969) and *The Ecological Context* (1967). He is a fellow of the World Academy of Art and Science and holds French and other honors.

To render some useful measure of critical assessment, this report will express many caveats regarding various aspects of the conference. It should be emphasized at the outset, however, that the conference in itself was a wholly unique venture in that it was the first initiative of its kind designed to involve a whole state; the participants were drawn from as widely separated areas as possible, so as to involve people from all sectors of Hawaii — geographically, socially, and politically [1] — and the preplanning and general organization of the meetings matched up to the ideals expressed within the conference. Given the inevitable limitations contingent upon any large conference format, it allowed for the widest range of expression and flexibility of involvement by all participants.

In general then, one can say that it was an extremely

1. It may be compared favorably, in this regard, with the Commission on the Year 2000 conducted by the American Academy of Arts and Sciences — which was almost wholly confined to academics and other professionals.

important and significant event — not only within the local Hawaiian, but in the world, context. A new approach was taken to the consideration of the future, on a sufficiently large scale, involving a whole community and a leading role assumed which will have an extensive impact far beyond the event of the conference itself.

As will be stressed later in this report, the initiative taken should be sustained and encouraged so as to build upon what was accomplished in the preparatory work and in the workshops during the meetings. Finally, no matter what criticism may be offered in assessment of this project, all of those who contributed their time, knowledge, and experience are to be congratulated on the success of this unique venture.

PRELIMINARY TASK-FORCE REPORTS

Detailed substantive comment on the content of these reports seems to be out of place here. Much of this kind of detailed evaluation was carried forward in the various workshops. Two points might be made about the task-force reports overall. One is that some reports tend to consider Hawaii in rather autonomous fashion with insufficient attention to its place in the world context. Two, more attention might have been given to critical problems in the present and how their solution or further exacerbation would influence various aspects of Hawaii's long-range future development.

In terms of content, the complete report is an excellent and most useful collection of materials. Attention, therefore, will be focused here on the procedural aspects of the task-force organization, the report format, and its use as a working document, all of which may be helpful in any forward developments that may be planned.

Given the relatively short period during which this preparatory work was done and the wide range of topics explored, it is obvious that the individual group reports would vary greatly in quality. Some topic areas were easier *to deal with than others; some might have required a different organizational and methodological approach than was available in the discussion-group technique used.*

This variation in quality, however, is compounded somewhat by the lack of coherent relationship among the various reports. There seems to be no common data base in use throughout. Again, an obvious comment, due, no doubt, to lack of time and the difficulty of organizing such a common framework of data, expectations, and assumptions with so many groups. Insufficient use was made of visual material such as diagrams, charts, and tables, where these might have been applicable to communicate the main points in specific topic areas. Given the overriding theme "Hawaii 2000," one might have expected that more attention would have been given to the presentation of alternative holistic scenarios — within each task force and encompassing, in some measure, the overall task-force conclusions. The latter approach would also have linked the reports together in a more meaningful interrelated way.

The document itself was rather unwieldy to use as a conference text. Again, this is a question of time and energy available. It might have been useful to have provided as a separate item all of the summaries of the task forces together — and, as will be noted later on the organizational format, to have devoted some space to examining the expectations, goals, consequences, and implications of the various directions explored.

One might diagram the above comments as in Figure 2 with the suggestion that some such schema might be followed by those who may carry on the work of the conference.

In a simplified form one might schedule this interrelation and feedback procedure in the following way. Group the summary reports together. Select out and correlate their common objectives, examine the consequences and implications of one projected direction upon another.

412

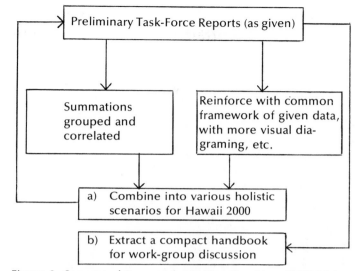

Figure 2. Suggested Process for Integrating Hawaii 2000 Ideas

For example, where Hawaii's resource limitations indicate certain aspects of economic and technological interdependence with mainland U.S.A., and with other Pacific regions, what are the socioeconomic and political consequences, and their implications for Hawaii's future? Conversely, if certain preferred life-style directions and goals are indicated, how do these affect or suggest changes and alterations in the economic and political sectors? Where a consensus of choices might be required to indicate an overall profile of alternatives, the various key sections in the interrelated summaries could be fed back to the task-force groups — to be ranked in order of priorities, preference, and desirability, by individual members. This process could be repeated several times so as to compile an interrelated series of projected futures in such a manner that the consequences and implications of various changes could be communicated in a more systematic way — and be used to compile various alternative scenarios. Table 2 shows a rather simplified version of this procedure as used by Nigel Calder to summarize the series of papers on our world in 1984.

413

Table 2

Major Technological Changes

Character of Change	Technical Aspects	Possibilities Arising	Effects on the Individual	Social Aspects	Global Aspects
1 Revolution in information: vast increases in computing and telecommunications capacity and wide use of electronic storage and retrieval of information.	Computers a good deal faster and easier to "converse" with. Computers linked in nation-wide and world networks. Messages by computer network (in digital code). Big increase in communications using millimeter radio, laser beams or communications satellites.	Television-telephones. "Dialling for news, books, etc." World-wide weather and disaster warning services using satellites.	Ready access to information (a data store in the home?). Close surveillance by government computers? Use of television links instead of business travel.	"Abolition" of libraries, paper-work and typists. Wide use of computers in every field of activity. Increase in local broadcasting. No more newspapers as we know them?	World-wide instantaneous reporting. Language translation. Big investment in communications (but increasing nationalism in these services?).
2 Revolutionary consequences of biology.	Understanding of living systems, including the human brain. Manipulation of genetic structure. Development of "bio-engineering." Understanding of ageing process.	"Biochemical machines" for food production, energy, transformation, chemical manufacture and information storage. Alteration of cell heredity. Engineering controls modelled on biological systems. Transplantation of organs and wise use of artificial limbs and organs. Modification of the developing brain. Conquest of viruses, heart disease and cancer?	Longer life. Better treatment of mental disease. Inhibition of ageing or "medicated survival"? Loss of individuality by surgical implantation?	Better understanding of human behaviour. Need for moral criteria in biological manipulations. Danger of a racket in transplantable organs. Danger of "mind control."	Understanding of complexity of living systems. Opportunities for enlarging food production.

From "...," The Series Summarised," New Scientist, August 20, 1964. Published by Penguin © New Scientist, IPC.

This also tends to suggest that it would have been advantageous to have three additional working groups whose sole functions would have been to coordinate, that is, combine summaries into scenario/alternatives, and feed them back to the task forces; to provide the common data base, through such means as charts and diagrams; and to be responsible for designing and compiling a working handbook for conference use which would give a synoptic and holistic view of the overall task-force reports.

Some of this interrelation of topics might have been more directly aided by using one of the modified Delphi techniques — an approach which could also have been extended into the conference itself, giving a further participatory dimension to the proceedings.

CONFERENCE PROCEEDINGS

Overall, the conference itself was extremely well organized. The opening sessions — particularly the main speaker on film, the audio-visual futures presentation, and the youth panel — were excellent. Points of general criticism would be that there was no real opportunity for discussion with the major speakers. Of course, this is always difficult to do in plenary form — but this lack tended to isolate their contributions somewhat from the ongoing work in the task-force groups. There was also a feeling expressed by various participants that generally more discussion could have occurred in plenary sessions. Of course, it is extremely difficult to keep such a large conference format flexible and responsive enough to allow for internal changes in schedule, organization, and so forth.

A second point would again be directed toward the lack of visual presentation material. Perhaps this could have been aided by an exhibit by the student participants, providing data and perspectives on present problems and their consequences and implications for the future. The present-problems issue tended to hold up much of the discussion of the future of Hawaii. Perhaps this gap could have been bridged by more deliberate attention and time allocation to this, or to special sessions or presentations on the ways in which solutions to immediate and present concerns would influence and direct overall future considerations. Many participants, particularly the students, felt that this seeming avoidance of present problems vitiated the longer range focus on the future.[2]

This issue, if properly handled, could be one of the most important areas for consideration and would have broader educational implications not only for students but for all participants. By avoiding, in a few cases, some of the more emotionally laden economic and political issues which constrain present decision-making, and powerfully influence futures alternatives, much discussion of the future is rendered somewhat pointless. One way of handling this within the conference itself would have been through a wider representation of economic, political, and even military sectors in the conference discussions. It was encouraging to see the number of legislators who did attend the conference but the other sectors — for example, corporate industry — seemed underrepresented.

CONFERENCE WORKSHOPS

All the workshops were visited, but I spent most time in those devoted to Hawaii's people and life-style and the natural environment. The workshop on Hawaii's people and life-style appeared to be the most coherent and productive group. This may have been due to my longer acquaintance with its discussions as they developed; I also consider the preliminary report of this group to be one of the most holistically oriented and useful in the report volume. The chairman, Douglas S. Yamamura, is to be complimented both on the report and on his

2. This schism between the consideration of present crises and future choices is noticeable when one compares the reports of the Hawaii Youth Congress, *An Aquarian Perspective Toward the Year 2000*, with the task-force reports on Hawaii 2000.

responsive guidance of the discussions. It seemed that the chairman's role was a critical one in wide-ranging discussions of this nature — and, in some cases, it might have been better to have formally established a different chairman for each day, with a permanent cochairman for continuity.

The life-styles discussion itself suffered a little from lack of feedback from other task forces, as mentioned earlier. It seemed difficult to ground the discussion, to reduce its level of abstraction, toward identification of those factors — economic, political, and legal — which encourage certain life-style directions and militate against others. Again, the input of economic and other data, and the conceptual elaboration of such factors, would have been aided by more preliminary work by the coordinating and synthesizing group suggested earlier. The closest approximation to this area of discussion was grouped around questions regarding the necessary conditions for diversity of life-styles in a modern cultural context such as Hawaii; how much uniformity was required for the society to remain cohesive; and what necessary common sets of understanding and expectations would require to be encouraged.

With its emphasis on the Hawaiian identity, which involved so many diverse participants, this particular topic seemed to be a potent one for further development as a postconference activity. Also, as it inevitably brought into focus many considerations and questions bearing upon it from other task-force areas, it would make for a continuing and lively basis for their integration into more holistic and multivariate scenarios of Hawaii's future.

The group on the natural environment was not observed as much as that above, but the major impression was one of a somewhat overcontrolled workshop in which the platform panel tended to direct and constrain discussion rather than to encourage more imaginative exploration. Discussion also seemed to be hampered by lack of *a common framework of understanding about the key issues involved. Here, one might say that the preliminary task-force report covered its topic area extremely well and brought forward many excellent and imaginative pro-posals — for example, that of "time zoning" in land-use reform, and so forth — but this good work tended to get lost in the discussion. This particular topic area would have benefited greatly by more visual communication of some of the basic data parameters of the problem and prospects being examined.*

The same basic schism that affected the conference as a whole, that is, present issues versus futures concerns, was particularly noticeable in this group. There was a strong preoccupation with questions of immediate environmental pollution that were most difficult to contain within longer-range considerations of the overall environmental context.

This schism might have been headed off by more attention by the preparatory task-force group to Hawaii's position in the global environmental context. They chose mainly to deal with Hawaii almost as an autonomous environment rather than as part of a large whole in which various international forces — economic, political, and military — powerfully affect local actions which have identifiable long-range consequences and implications. Also, where attention was focused locally, many issues affecting present and future environmental concerns were some-what glossed over where they might be too controversial for detailed consideration; for example, commercial land use and development, questions of land rights and owner-ship, military uses of land, corporate responsibility for environmental deterioration, the political aspects of environmental health, and so forth. These background issues were often those around which the present versus the future division became exaggerated — but their lack of emphasis did seem to detract from the overall direction and usefulness of the discussions. Again, as with life-

styles, this area of concern with the quality of the natural environment, in the long range, seemed a most fruitful and productive basis for postconference work, embracing as it does so many issues that touch all participants in every aspect of their lives.

POSTCONFERENCE SUGGESTIONS

Many participants expressed their genuine disquiet regarding the possibility that, once the conference was over, there would be no organizations or channels through which they might continue and widen their discussions. I met with several small groups of varied representation to discuss this question — and would certainly like to emphasize that, as the conference in itself was so success-ful, every attempt should be made to create and support the necessary organizations, institutions, and communica-tion channels to keep its spirit alive. The conference gener-ated so much enthusiasm and energy in every age range and social sector represented that it would be a great waste of enormous potential value to the Hawaiian community as a whole if this unique initiative is not sustained in some way.

Obviously, one direction would be to set up a more permanent council on Hawaii's future drawn from and broadly representative of those participants who con-tributed to the conference. This body could continue the work of the conference and initiate various postconference evaluation and study groups — as well as compiling and disseminating further information on futures concerns. Such a council should have attached to it various other more practically oriented working groups who might deal specifically with communications — for example, how can the issues raised in the conference be disseminated more widely and conveyed more vividly to the largest part of the Hawaiian community — and also have attached to it a group which might conduct a large-scale series of Delphi explorations involving a cross-section of that community.

An important direction of this council should be to gain access to newspaper and journal space, and to radio and television time, to reach out further into the community to involve a much larger proportion of the local society in futures considerations. The modes which might be employed to communicate this awareness of the future would also encourage new forms of individual and group participation in community affairs. New images of change, of future alternatives, of ways of circumventing present dilemmas could evoke a fresh sense of social directions. Providing more direct participation would widen awareness of our potential abilities to control change and engage with the wider decision-making processes in society.

This aspect of the council on the future's work may be one of the most crucial. In general, it should seek to go beyond the more traditional use of mass-media channels as presentational and expository means — to devise ways in which the larger community might feed back its reactions, ideas, and proposals on the issues presented to them — for example, through game formats, citizen panels, and experimental formats of all kinds. By larger audience one means here not only the expert professional, but all sectors of the society — from the child to the elder, from the plumber to the politician. It is only through some such mode of interactive feedback that we can expand our range of possible futures options and alternatives.

A world futures study center should be set up to work with the above council. (A number of ideas like this were proposed in the closing sessions of the conference by diversely representative participants.) This would be a kind of lookout, monitoring, and study center whose function would be to collect, analyze, and disseminate futures materials — and to place Hawaii's future problems and prospects within the global context. The nucleus of professionals and students for such a center already exists within the more active members of the task-force groups. To make this a more effective instrument however, the attempt should be made to secure different funding from as many varied sources as possible to make such a unit relatively autonomous and independent of any specific sector in the society. For example, it might be located within the University of Hawaii, but its support base should enable it to act as flexibly and experimentally as possible.

The initial structure of such a center should be an "open" one, designed to allow for change within itself. One might envisage a relatively small core staff to maintain continuity, with the bulk of the work of the center being carried out by work teams composed of students (high-school, undergraduate and graduate) and nonstudents from various sectors of the community. These work teams would have as their consultants various leading futurists from around the world who might be invited for varying periods — a week to a month, or more. Each visiting scholar might be asked to outline in advance a specific area of futures research which he would like to conduct during his stay and he would then carry out this study, or studies, in collaboration with one of the center's work teams — which would have the effect of broadening the base of the center's function as an educational focus for futures studies, and would more directly involve students and nonstudents in practical work.

The output of the center would greatly augment and enrich the activities of the council on Hawaii's future and would enable the kinds of data, and presentational and experimental programs to be devised for the council which have been tentatively outlined.

DECENTRALIZATION

A key aspect of any of the above postconference directions would be to ensure that such activities are not confined to and controlled by the center of Hawaii, but that they be diffused throughout the islands. The organizational model should be that of a series of networks rather than of one centrally located entity. Specific foci for *various kinds of experimental futures studies might be more suited to one or other of the islands and be located there, rather than grouped together on Oahu. Likewise, the decision-making structure of any organizations set up should reflect this decentralization and participatory aspect in its decision-making arrangements. In general, though quite specifically organized activities have been suggested here, every effort should be made to encourage all kinds of individual and group initiative and experimental projects.*

CONCLUDING REMARKS

As earlier emphasized, these notes, though critical in some details, should be taken as a strong recommendation for the continuance in as many ways as possible of the work of the Governor's Conference on the Year 2000. The success of this conference should give the necessary impetus and encouragement for such continuance and should encourage the community support necessary for its work. The message which emerges from the conference is very clear — the range and scale of our present problems indicate the urgency and gravity with which all societies need to confront their futures. Hawaii has given the leadership which one may now expect many other states, and whole societies, to follow. It is only through such attempts to confront our collective futures that we may indeed assure all mankind that there are ways out of our present crises. "Hawaii 2000" was, and is, an extraordinarily important challenge.

Toward Liberation of the Future
Hidetoshi Kato

Hidetoshi Kato, sociologist, served as executive secretary of the Second International Future Research Conference (Kyoto, 1970). Among his research projects has been a study of the future of TV and radio for the Japan Broadcasters Association. He has taught at Kyoto University, Stanford, Grinnell, and in England, and has served on numerous Japanese government advisory groups.

GENERAL IMPRESSIONS

an is the only creature that has acquired the ability to think about the future. Animal psychologists have demonstrated that certain animals have some sense of future in terms of delayed response, but that such a response is a preconditioned one in which alternative "futures" are not expected nor imagined by the animals and, above all, the time scale is usually very short from a human viewpoint. Can a dog or a mouse learn to wait three days for a reward?

In contrast, a man is capable of thinking and working for futures three years, fifteen years, and even thousands of years ahead. Moreover, it seems that curiosity about the future is almost an innate part of human nature. We cannot help but think about, expect, and imagine times to come. Man is essentially a future-oriented animal.

However, it is embarrassing to discuss the future or futures, because nobody can tell what will happen nor what can be done about it — or them. Though we know that the future will be different, we do not know just how. The images are rather vague and always uncertain.

More embarrassing and perplexing is the experience of being addressed as a futurist, even if the term is used as a compliment. And I often suspect that many people today are looking for certain magical powers in futurists, considered as the contemporary version of crystal-ball gazers. Like traditional villagers who rush to magicians to know whether a sick man will live or die, people in contemporary societies ask the futurists what will happen in the coming ten, twenty, or thirty years. This action is really inexcusable, because, in my opinion, there is no professional, expert "futurist." Futurists are those men and women, young and old, who are keenly interested in the future of man and his environment from the view-point of their own disciplines and professions. What we do have, in other words, is a huge group of future-oriented people: scientists, taxi drivers, medical doctors, farmers, educators, business executives, factory workers, house-wives, and longshoremen, and the term "futurist" — or, sometimes with a little mystic connotation, "futurolo-gist" — is shorthand to mean such a person.

It is quite misleading, therefore, to assume that there is a small number of professional futurists who can forecast and solve every problem man will encounter in the future. As a matter of fact, even a cynic who is skeptical about the future and futures research, is essentially a futurist if he buys insurance or finances his house or automobile, because, in either case, he is making a contract with future conditions. There is other evidence that man is the animal living for and working with the future: look at your appoint-ment book. It will show your future engagements. Reflect on your Friday shopping: your supermarket basket pre-pares for the week to come. Hence, we are futuristic ani-mals, are we not?

Another important aspect, as we know from experi-ence, is that we choose one future out of an unlimited number of different futures. For instance, you have many alternatives for the next weekend. You may invite friends in for a drink, you may go out for a picnic, you may paint your house, or fix your bathroom. The possibilities are numerous. And the fact that you do something over the weekend means that you chose one kind of behavior out of many alternatives; you chose one future out of many. In other words, we are, without exception, committed to the future. We cannot escape from it, and it is the most dangerous fallacy to think that the future is solely in the hands of "experts."

In this connection, the Governor's Conference on the Year 2000 in Hawaii took the most sensitive and reasonable approach toward the future, because it encouraged the participation of great numbers of amateurs. When I say this, I am thinking of several meetings and conferences of a similar nature in the past few years. The organizers of these conferences were well aware of the importance of amateur participation and tried to ensure it, but because of technical difficulties, so far have not been successful. But the Hawaii organizers were different. The most significant contribution of the conference to the history of and to the future of futures research was that, for the first time, we were able to have the lively participation of ordinary citizens.

I was most impressed by the presentations of the younger generation. In my opinion, to have young people take part in an occasion like this is extremely important since, obviously, the younger the person the more he or she is concerned with the future.[1]

It is my feeling that the young must be given more opportunity to express their images of and wishes about the future, even if such images seem to be fantastic. In-

---

1. Overall we have a somewhat different impression. We found many young persons impatient with discussions of the future, while many older persons, who would not live to see 2000, were keenly interested in it. Probably age is not a sufficient explanation. — Editors.

deed, reflecting my own experience, I confess that futurology has been mostly carried out by men in their forties or fifties; and we have tended to lack fertile imagination. It is the young who potentially have such ideas and imagination. Hawaii 2000, in this sense, was a breakthrough in futures research.

Amateur participation, I repeat, is a good thing, and the conference demonstrated that it is possible. I would not say that all the papers presented and all the discussions that followed were excellent. Sometimes, they seemed rather naïve; but this naïveté should be cherished, because this approach may be the only basis for the development of a realistic and better future.

Aside from these general impressions and evaluation I would recommend the following actions by the people concerned.

A FUTURES SCENARIO CONTEST

There were two types of papers and discussions during the conference. On the one hand, there was a group of people whose approach to the future is steady and analytical, but not so inventive. They tend to project the present into the future. We may label this group the realists. On the other hand, we have dreamers, or idealists, who construct various future images not necessarily connected with present conditions. This polarization of realists versus idealists is not new in human intellectual history; it sometimes seems impossible to reconcile the two. Futures research is no exception; the extrapolative future and the visionary future are two examples of such a dichotomy.

To bridge the gap, I feel that it would be interesting and fruitful to have a scenario contest. In this contest, each contestant (an individual or a group) would be asked to present a desirable and imaginative future as well as realistic steps to attain that ideal. The topic or the subject matter must be specific, such as housing, transportation, hospitalization, an educational system, and the like. By this procedure, a combination of utopian thinking and realistic policy interest could be achieved. The policy proposals submitted by the contestants would be, without doubt, worthwhile for administrators to examine and to consider putting into practice.

As stated earlier, the participation of the young was one of the most impressive aspects of the conference; however, these young people did not have enough time to present their ideas completely. They were able to deliver only fragments of their thoughts. Part of the purpose in having a scenario contest is to encourage these people to design futures in a more logical fashion. I am sure that this second chance would also be a good opportunity for them to further reflect.

Preferably, each scenario should be accompanied by a visual presentation, and each contestant given the opportunity to present his ideas orally, so that the ideas and images can be fully developed.

The judges, for technical reasons, may be appointed, but they should represent a cross-section of the population of Hawaii, and where possible, again, mass participation is desirable. In the course of such a contest, groups may make a joint effort to furnish new images and ideas; such developments are most welcome.

If this kind of informal and participatory process could mold a consensus of the people concerned, the scenario may be not only reflected but also adopted by administrators as a matter of urgent policy orientation. Citizens have the right to ask the government to heed a consensus, and it is the duty of administrators to respond to such an appeal. This response, indeed, is the only means of liberation of futures.

In fact, as far as I know, planning for the future has usually been in the hands of the few in many parts of the world. The future has been given to the majority by a small group of people. As I stressed earlier, this is not good; design of the future, or futures, must be liberated and put into the hands of the people. I would very much like to see Hawaii as one of the first places in the world where this liberation is achieved.

I therefore think that this scenario contest must be announced as soon as possible, so that many people of Hawaii can start to work on it before the excitement of the conference dies down.

A FUTURES RESEARCH INSTITUTE

At the conference, the participants discussed the future of Hawaii; over and over again it was pointed out that the State cannot be an isolated unit, and that its future is heavily dependent upon the futures of related areas, that is, the mainland U.S.A., and the countries of Asia and the Pacific in general.

And often during the conference I felt that Hawaii is one of the very few places in the world where local problems inevitably have to be converted or interpreted into the problems of the larger area. For instance, many participants emphasized that Hawaii cannot survive if the import of oil and foods is stopped for any reason. This feeling of crisis, of being on a tightrope, cannot be shared by continentals who enjoy self-sufficient, if not abundant, natural resources. Even as a visitor, when I stand on one of the scenic points of Oahu, I feel a kind of uneasiness. All I can see in front of me is the vast Pacific Ocean, and at my back, I see a tiny island with a population of several hundred thousand. This island is really a contemporary technical miracle in the sense that the people here live in the belief that ships and aircraft will come — an affluent version of the Cargo Cult!

We must see the interrelatedness of Hawaii with the outer world, and see that this feeling of interdependency is the very starting point for contemplation of and research into the future of the world and mankind. Unlike most continental societies, Hawaii is destined to be an open, not a closed, system. It is therefore my opinion that Hawaii

428

can claim to be a most suitable site for establishing a new research organization for the study of world futures.

This, I think, is a realistic and urgent proposal, because we now have a great number of problems that cannot be solved locally. For instance, the Pacific Ocean is increasingly polluted. Who is responsible for the misuse of this huge area of the planet? Are we going to convert the ocean into an international garbage disposal? An organization devoted to the study of that kind of new problem is needed. I would very much like to suggest that a futures research institute, which would work not just for local interests but for the betterment of the whole earth and its inhabitants, could be founded in Hawaii.

AN URBAN TRAFFIC EXPERIMENT

As observed, Hawaii is, and should be, an open social system. But geographically the islands are a closed system; this physical isolation means that many experiments are possible. I would be most interested to see one performed here with urban traffic.

Whenever I come to Honolulu, I usually rent an automobile. It's nice to drive around, but, in the past few years, I have often wondered if I am doing the right thing, because automobiles are quite incompatible with the life of an island like Oahu. For one thing, automobiles, especially from the United States, are designed from a continental cultural background. They are built so that you can drive 500 miles a day on an interstate highway. At this stage of civilization, they are a useful and necessary means of transportation in a vast space like the U.S. Midwest. Also, in most parts of the mainland U.S., in northwestern Europe, and in Japan, an automobile must protect itself and its passengers against low winter temperatures. To meet these requirements, automobiles have become bigger, more comfortable, and more powerful.

429   If you keep these characteristics in mind, you will

feel uncomfortable driving a standard automobile in the islands. Is there much chance that you will drive more than one hundred or even fifty miles a day? Long-distance driving is alien to Hawaii, unless you have an air-cushion vehicle to drive on the surface of the ocean. Further, is it necessary to have a car with a heavy, sturdy body for commuting and supermarket shopping? My thought is that it is impractical and nonsensical to use standard automobiles on a tropical island, where space is limited and the climate is always charming.

It is for these reasons that I would like very much to see a fundamentally new means of transportation invented: a very small, handy, and safe vehicle. My image is of a kind of battery-operated wheelchair, with a maximum speed of about thirty miles per hour. This idea has been presented by many thoughtful traffic engineers and city planners, but has never been realized because the total replacement of vehicles old and new would be a fantastically expensive business. However, I feel that Hawaii could try this experiment successfully, because its size is compatible with such a change. This is the advantage of the compact nature of the state — an advantage that must be developed. Hawaii has also been famous for its conspicuous cars. Several years ago, the pink Jeep with a fancy top was fashionable, and today the sandbuggy and other strange-shaped vehicles are tourist attractions; so that, in my opinion, battery-operated wheelchairs would be accepted by tourists, whose minds are full of easy curiosity.

I emphasize this experiment because automobile traffic is today's universal problem, about which administrators all over the world are making desperate efforts. If Hawaii could be the first region where the automobile age came to an end, it would encourage other peoples of the world who search for an imaginative transportation future.

I may be optimistic, but I feel that this experiment

could be carried out in cooperation with the present automobile industry, because thoughtful manufacturers today know that the automobile age is only one transitory period in the history of human movement, and that a new surface vehicle for private transportation must be invented. These people may well be interested in helping the experiment. I sincerely hope that somebody or some group of people of Hawaii will undertake the challenge of this seemingly fantastic project, because, someday, the automobile-dominated traffic problem must be solved by somebody. It could be done now, by you.

Need for Complex Human Systems Design
Raymond G. Studer

Raymond G. Studer is professor and director of the Division
of Man-Environment Relations in the new College of Human
Development, Pennsylvania State University. He formerly
headed the Planning Analysis Project at Brown University and
taught architecture at Columbia, Arizona State, and the Rhode
Island School of Design. His research includes design of information and control systems for environmental planning and management, and physical systems for experimental human settings.

This conference was well organized and apparently so were
the events which led up to it. The inevitable formalities
did not detract from, and often enhanced, meaningful
communication among participants. Various community
interests appeared to be well represented, and within the
constraints of context, time, and requirement for orderly
discourse, all were afforded an opportunity to contribute
to the planning of Hawaii's future. The information generated thus forms an excellent base from which to move
to the more operational aspects of realizing a viable human
environment in 2000. If the momentum of this effort can
be consummated into an operational program for the kind
of future envisioned by the participants, this will indeed
be a significant historic event. Because of its geographic
and social setting, Hawaii undoubtedly has an opportunity
to give exemplary leadership to the United States in moving from imminent social and environmental chaos toward
a more optimistic future.

A CONTEXT FOR EVALUATION

To comment on and make recommendations in response to so complex an array of information, one must establish a context. The sources of information available to me included observation of a portion of the February 1970 mini-conference, the preliminary task-force reports, random observations of the formal and informal proceedings, and sundry reports informally issued by various interest groups. Extensive as these sources of information are, they obviously constitute but a fraction of the information actually generated during the development of the documents and events preceding and included in the conference. My comments must, therefore, be somewhat impressionistic, and any misinterpretation of the actual intentions of involved persons may reflect a lack of information beyond that noted above.

As an ordinary citizen I join most conference participants in a commitment to fundamental change in the institutions and environment which have produced the present state of affairs, both here and in the more critically affected Mainland. I feel, however, that dramatic, orderly, and permanent change in complex human settings must involve the innovative, compassionate and thoughtful application of scientific thinking. I do not share, then, the current antiscience, anti-intellectual subjectivism which is embraced by many social change enthusiasts.

My professional and research interests are primarily focused on a search for more effective planning and design methods through the integrated application of several scientific disciplines. As a planning methodologist I feel that there are several aspects of the reports which require attention as further development is contemplated. Comments regarding the substance, the quality, and accuracy of the information per se in the reports and proceedings will be minimized in favor of comments regarding the class and structure of this material. Emphasis will be upon some

433

of the procedural problems and possibilities involved in these task-force efforts.

Contemporary human systems at almost any scale exhibit unprecedented complexity; they also exhibit critical and pervasive dysfunction. It is this combination of complexity and dysfunction which challenges us toward collective efforts to change the course of human events. No longer can we assume that "natural" processes will produce a viable human environment. If we are to realize an alternative environment, it must be designed. We either become a planning culture or face certain disaster. A planning culture is one in which collective planning is an integral aspect of the various members' thought and behavioral repertory — an enculturated view of existence.

In the proceedings and task-force documents there has been great emphasis upon the various technological (physical) futures we can expect. Another area which might be investigated is the methodological future. The viability of future human settings depends not only upon ambitious goals and the availability of various physical and human resources, but also upon our ability to organize these into a coherent, appropriate structure. As Yehezkel Dror pointed out in his presentation, without effective planning methods we cannot hope to get to the kind of future we seek.

Planning and designing complex human systems (for example, economic, political, and physical) is an extremely technical undertaking, and future deliberations of this conference require the implementation of a technical analog to support ordinary discourse on the various issues. Unless there is a mechanism for transforming and evaluating concepts in terms of their functional implications, evaluations of these will become increasingly arbitrary and discussions will become increasingly circular. The methodological objective is to operationalize general notions of desired states, to facilitate essential decisions, and transform general goals into explicit programs. A systems analytic perspective is, needless to say, fundamental to the entire enterprise.

Human systems design involves both normative and empirical dimensions. The need to satisfy both of these often confuses a planning process committed to empirically based decisions. The proposition is quite simple: one cannot deduce an ought from an is. Planning and design functions involve: (1) normative ends; (2) an empirical understanding of natural constraints; and (3) an understanding of the available resources to realize states which satisfy (1) and (2). Coherent goal structures thus become intrinsic to the design of futures. Blurring ends with means — problem with solution — will confuse any planning and design effort from the outset, and the task-force reports were not entirely free of difficulties in this regard.

The most inevitable aspect of the future is uncertainty. Human goals and the impinging environment change in unpredictable ways. Any decision-making structure of value must be dynamic. We are neither technically nor ethically justified in designing one future. As has been mentioned many times, we must conceptualize many futures. But we must also adopt a dynamic methodological structure to get to any future. We cannot and/or ought not to deduce the future from the present; the design of futures involves not merely extrapolation, but invention. Futures thinking of the sort this conference was intended to nurture is a necessary heuristic device, for invention requires that we imagine the unimaginable, that we break down conditioned preconceptions regarding the possibilities. It is fairly obvious that extant environmental structures are not producing appropriate human outcomes. We are, therefore, justified in considering entirely new taxonomies of human settings, those which exhibit alternative patterns and interrelationships. For example, could not elements of support systems for the administration of justice (and corrections), education, recreation, commerce, transportation, and housing be interrelated in *ways which facilitate greater effectiveness in meeting objectives? Obviously, they could. Should not the physical environment reflect a less disjunctive organization of human processes? These processes are intrinsically interdependent and in need of entirely new kinds of support systems. Extant structures, while perhaps functional in less complex times, are simplistic and grossly suboptimal in reinforcing viable human interaction patterns and goals. These structures need to be questioned and reconceptualized.*

Existing dysfunction is a product of existing environmental structure; this is the empirical reality. Well-intentioned moves to overcome these, for example the "hitchhiking" gambit, are excellent symbolic gestures. Persuasion and social pressure are necessary to change people's attitudes — hopefully even their behavior. However, unless alternative environmental structures are institutionalized, permanent behavioral change is not likely to occur; that is, the system will probably return to something approaching its original (dysfunctional) state. This is no time to make small and harmless plans for the future.

In retrospect, several critical observations can be made regarding the nature and structure of information generated in the various task-force areas. These general criticisms are not intended in any way to question the activities to date. When putting into motion processes involving groups of people democratically addressing so complex a task, it is difficult to anticipate the outcome and to order the flow of information. The most important task is generating a collection of concepts and information elements — this, the task forces have done quite admirably. The amount of information necessary to proceed is no doubt available in these reports, and there is nothing to suggest a false start in the comments which follow. Rather these are suggestions for ordering, building upon, and utilizing the information contained therein.

The division of labor for the ten statewide task forces — that is, the taxonomy of planning domains for the future — was undoubtedly a product of great deliberation. But, logical as it may seem at first glance, something seems amiss in this structure. These describe different classes of phenomena which impinge on the planning task in quite different ways. Science and technology, for example, constitute a class of available resources to realize certain environmental states required by another class: "quality of personal life." The general categories identified certainly require inclusion, but a reading of the reports and observation of the ensuing discussions indicate a degree of confusion regarding the interdependence of these various domains. Not only are these domains interdependent, but, as noted above, this interdependence is in most instances hierarchical. How can one conceptualize and evaluate a housing and transportation system, an educational system, an economic and certainly a political system until a social and behavioral structure (that is, a life-style and quality of life) has been conceptualized. These latter classes are, after all, the independent variables for designing the systems required to realize them. In not recognizing the interdependences, emphasis tended toward excessive generalization, a descriptive mode of discourse and/or a superficial consideration of the behavioral and social goals in order to get on with the assigned task of describing economic, political, and educational futures.

In terms of the appropriateness of the information generated, one inclination was to describe, perhaps to excess, things as they are rather than things as they could or ought to be. This kind of exercise is new to most of us (in nonplanning cultures), and we often shift to a forecasting mode, a related but different kind of exercise. In developing these forecasts for the future in various domains, an element of economic, technological determinism crept in. In designing the future, as opposed to forecasting it, the question is not how an economic system will affect our life-style, but what kind of economic system is required to support a defined life-style. The former question confuses ends with means, and this kind of thinking (for example, economic man) is where we just came from. In the future we will have to do better.

The ambivalence in setting about to conceptualize significantly different futures in each of the areas in question was, I contend, a direct consequence of the apparent nonrecognition of their hierarchical interdependence. The result was one of persistent redundancy of certain elements and issues in the reports. Greater coordination among task domains may have effected a more integrated product and have avoided certain inconsistencies, for example, the levels, the classes, and the structure of the information produced. The intergroup inconsistencies among domains will make for enormous difficulties in integrating this vast array of information into a coherent plan for dealing with various explicit futures toward which Hawaii may desire to move.

The actual procedures involved in developing the task-force reports were not available to this evaluator. In observing the conference proceedings, I noted that the mode of discourse took the form of a series of minimally structured "rap" sessions. (The various chairmen were extremely careful to allow everyone to participate in the sessions I observed.) Rapping allows ideas to begin to flow and is an appropriate mode at preliminary stages. As participants become involved, however, a structure should be developed so that the group will not be required to constantly review the same points. One problem of open discussion as the primary mechanism is that ideas are not allowed to be developed fully before they are evaluated. Small utterances by individuals in large group meetings represent but minute elements in a larger system of concepts. Fuller contextual development of these ideas may reveal greater, or lesser, merit than is apparent. In several sessions some ideas were neutralized or even dismissed as a result of immediate aversive responses by other participants holding alternative points of view. (This problem became most apparent in the unofficial meeting of the "young people.") As activities move to the next stages, more highly structured means of discourse must be developed.

Control of the population to be served by the Hawaiian community was a recurring theme in virtually all of the task-force domains. Beyond the fact that population control is a general survival issue for all humans, there is good reason for concern. The quantitative and qualitative dimensions of the population to be accommodated constitute the basic defining characteristic of the systems (economic, political, and physical) under analysis. Population characteristics for 2000 (quantitative, and to some extent qualitative) must therefore be settled within reasonable limits, otherwise planning and design of the various support systems will probably be spurious. This constitutes a difficult ethical and technical issue, but it must be settled (for example, as a series of "if, then" states) before you proceed much further.

The underlying dichotomy which quite naturally gripped this conference at both interpersonal and intrapersonal levels was action versus planning. The irony of confrontation between these two means of dealing with problems was apparent to many participants. The motivation for this unprecedented conference is obviously the pervasiveness and intensity of current dysfunction. Clearly both planning (that is, where do we want to go?) and action (that is, how do we get there?) are critically needed. Action without program often makes matters much worse; the behavior of complex economic, political, and physical systems cannot be understood intuitively. Program without significant action can also lead to increased dissonance, that is, to outbursts of frustration resulting from unconsummated expectations, and waste of time and resources.

Commitment to fundamental change seems essential to our biological and extrabiological survival. Reasoned action is a part of this commitment. The challenge is to operate in both action and planning modes simultaneously, for these are clearly complementary aspects of the same problem. However, talk of action issues when in a planning mode is noise; talk of planning when in an action mode is likewise noise.[1] This was intended as a planning conference; but the muddling of these two issues was apparent.

The need for large- and small-scale social and environmental experimentation emerged toward the end of several sessions. This was a most gratifying and possibly the most significant development in the conference proceedings, since experimentation is the bridge between planning and action. Many reasonable people appear conservative not because they are protecting the status quo (many actually are, of course), but because they are uncertain of the implications of a proposition in terms of the common good. For example, one of the many exciting recommendations of the Hawaii youth congress was an item concerning the evaluation of teachers. All competent educators feel that objective evaluation of teachers by students should somehow be implemented. What they fear is not a contexturally defined test of their knowledge and skill but subjective, self-gratifying evaluations by persons less knowledgeable and experienced than themselves. Under extant systems both competent and incompetent teachers are protected from irrational actions. What is required is a series of fairly large-scale experiments wherein both teachers, students, and other related interests are insulated from intimidation by one another. In time a new system of evaluation that embodies the appropriate set of contingencies would emerge.

More generally, our knowledge of both the behavior of systems under analysis by the task forces and their inter-

1. Compare McHale discussion on p. 419. — Editors.

system characteristics is limited. We cannot accurately predict the behavior of alternative system structures under the control of new goals. The tendency is, therefore, to hypothesize future systems rather conservatively for fear that untested hypotheses may actually be implemented. Fair enough, but if we conceptualize alternative futures in an experimental context and otherwise facilitate social and environmental experimentation, we are more likely to realize vastly different possibilities with minimum risk and unnecessary dogma. What I am proposing is that all citizens become "scientists" as well as "artists" in designing and organizing their lives. We need methodological structures to allow this. The importance of techniques of simulation to future design efforts should be noted in this regard. Development of high-fidelity simulation tools will allow the pretesting of complex systems and also facilitate the involvement of the affected population in this pretesting function.

In the opinion of this evaluator, the most relevant information contained in each of the task-force reports is the following.

1. Historic backgrounds. Implicit in the evaluation of existing systems are the cultural baselines that must be taken into account in bringing about change. Also certain historic states embody artifacts of functioning human systems which may have value for future designs (beyond any notion of cultural determinism).

2. Evidence of the causal structure, or intrasystem functional relations. Since we generally have incomplete scientific knowledge of economic, political, and other systems, knowledge (even conventional wisdom) regarding how they function in the Hawaiian setting is important in the design of future systems.

3. The interdependencies between the system under analysis and other related systems, that is, precisely

what functional relations have been observed between the political and economic domains and between these and the educational?

4. Existing dysfunctions generate the need for alternative systems. A careful delineation of these dysfunctions, their nature and intensity, is a precondition for designing aspects of alternative future possibilities, (that is, we know what doesn't work).

5. Inventories of constraints, restraints, and possible resources in the various domains that condition the design of relevant systems (an excellent example of this class of data is contained in the report on science and technology).

6. An array of possible future systems invented in each domain.

RECOMMENDATIONS FOR FUTURE ACTIVITIES

As mentioned earlier, previous conference activities have produced, on the whole, the quantity and quality of information required to proceed to other stages of planning. The recommendations I would make are implicit in the criticisms noted above.

A methodological structure is needed to sort out, organize, and interrelate the information generated in the various domains. The conference participants must, if this planning process is not to become stymied, develop a consensus methodology which becomes public and formal and which is capable of operating at various levels, that is, from metaphor to technical, and even to quantitative levels. This is necessary to reduce the complex task of analysis and information handling to manageable proportions. What is needed is a planning mechanism which can receive, classify, analyze and act upon information coming from many sources. This mechanism must also be capable of dealing with the complexity of interrelations *among the various domains. The format suggested is obviously a systems analytic one in which the processes of: (1) analysis (what is . . .), (2) modeling (what ought to be . . .), (3) simulation (what would happen if . . .), (4) implementation, and (5) testing (what happens when . . .), are seen as interrelated but discrete functions. It should be noted that this methodological format should be neutral with respect to substance and allow inputs from all legitimate sources, that is, permitting free flow from general idea to technical implications.*

A technical team *should be selected to assist in subsequent activities of this conference. It should be clearly recognized that further development involves highly technical dimensions if the intentions of the various participants are to be organized into a form which will lead to appropriate, programed action.*

New organizational structures *around which subsequent planning activities can be more effectively developed should be investigated. The existing categories (task-force domains) should be reexamined with a view toward realizing alternative ones based upon functional domains that recognize the hierarchy of interdependencies of the various classes of phenomena. It is now quite clear that conceptualization of goals, normative, social, and behavioral structures, are prerequisite to the design of economic, political, and physical support systems and cannot proceed disjunctively. Several means of structuring activities are suggested including the possibility that new teams be formed as follows: several members from each task force could be regrouped into new teams, each of which would set about to design more comprehensive futures. They would (a) identify through intense participation a set of goals, (b) conceptualize a desirable social / behavioral structure, and (c) conceptualize interrelated future systems in the various domains, for example, economic, political, and physical. "Specialists" from the* original task-force areas working together toward coherent, fairly detailed plans for Hawaii 2000 would seem a reasonable next step.

Purging of preconceptions *(a continuation of previous exercises) regarding the possibilities for future settings is essential if alternative futures are to be fully explored.*

New modes of discourse *should be investigated as alternatives to rap sessions. One reason for adopting a formal methodological structure is to receive, analyze, and act upon the suggestions and needs of the population affected. Involvement of these populations in all phases of the planning process would be enhanced by effective information storage and retrieval tools. Such modes of discourse as participation in simulation and in problem-solving games should be implemented so that the implications of propositions can be more fully explored within the constraints operating and the resources available. When possible, a general task area should be so structured as to afford the assignment of subtasks to individuals and small groups without producing redundant or highly overlapping information on future design elements.*

A dynamic decision structure *is necessary if the many changing interests, goals, and events of the present and the future are to be accommodated.*[2] *Complex systems, including human biological and extrabiological ones, invariably change. Beyond this, the need for experimentation, the possibility to hypothesize and systematically test alternative systems is essential to realizing the most effective possibilities. What is suggested here is a dynamic methodological framework that will permit systematic response to changing goals, constraints, and human outcomes. Such a system should also facilitate simulation, experimentation, and monitoring as well. If a sophisticated, dynamic planning and design mechanism can be realized, it would not only* assist *designs for the future, it* would be *the design of the future.*

2. Compare McHale's suggestions in Figure 2 on p. 413. — Editors.

Toward a Pacific Conference on the Twenty-first Century

Hahn-Been Lee

Hahn-Been Lee, founding president of the Korean Society for Future Studies (1968) and former dean of the Graduate School of Public Administration, Seoul National University, is one of Asia's pioneers in action-oriented futures thinking. Innovative administrator, diplomat and scholar, he is a former director of Korea's Bureau of the Budget, ambassador to Switzerland, and author of *Korea: Time, Change and Administration* (1968).

T he Governor's Conference on the Year 2000 was a pioneering enterprise of public futurism undertaken by the state of Hawaii. Its outstanding characteristic was that it was a publicly based futures conference. The conference was a cross-section of all kinds of Hawaii citizens — legislators, government executives, businessmen, professors, educational administrators, journalists, social workers, and youth. The collection of thirteen task-force reports, prepared before the conference began, was a very useful document. The buildup of participation through the interim program was impressive. Here was community involvement with participants who did their homework. This made the conference a purposeful one. The breadth of participation and the depth of preparation were the distinctive features which made this conference different from other futures conferences held before elsewhere. For example, the First International Futures Research Conference held in Oslo in the fall of 1967 was a very small *gathering of professional futurists who came mainly from Europe. The more recent Second International Futures Research Conference held in Kyoto in the spring of 1970, again, was attended mainly by professional futurists, this time with an addition of a handful of representatives from Asia and Latin America.*

The early involvement of community leaders and the legislators in the very idea of holding a conference like this was a most effective way of planning, and this seems to have been the key to its success.

Conference speakers were well chosen and the sequence of their speeches was generally good. The profile of the technological possibilities of the future depicted by Arthur C. Clarke was judiciously offset by the humanistic suggestion of Robert Jungk that man, not technology, is the real frontier of the future. Yehezkel Dror's practical admonition that futures thinking must be translated into a set of priorities expressed in terms of plans and policies provided a much-needed realism to the conference. The national perspective given by Charles Williams was a useful one, although it could have been spelled out in a more suggestive manner. Saburo Okita's closing speech was a valuable contribution, [1] giving an Asian perspective to the future with the focus on the prospect of U.S.–Japan relations, although it would have been more effective if the order had been exchanged with that of Dror's speech. The conference deserved a concluding speech which could at once open an exciting vista of the future for Hawaii and realism toward implementation of some of the ideas generated in the conference.

Several programs both at the beginning and the end of the conference seem to have been designed to bring the focus to Hawaii. The multimedia presentation at the opening hour was an effective way of giving a sense of urgency for thinking ahead about the future. The panel

1. Because of space limitations, addresses by participants Charles Williams and Saburo Okita are omitted from this volume.

of all task-force chairmen toward the end was a fine show of force and common thinking. One could observe a swelling sense of shared gratification among the participants.

I sat in on the workshop on Hawaii and the Pacific community which dealt with the task-force report on the subject prepared by George Kanahele and his group. Earlier I had had an opportunity to read this report — which in my view is a most imaginative and conscientious document — and to write a critique on it. In this light, it is a pity that the workshop did not have time to discuss the ideas of the report in full measure, due to a few fundamental reservations persistently expressed by some dissident members. In spite of the inadequate treatment of the Kanahele report in the workshop sessions, the final session in which George Kanahele presented the recommendations of the report, together with the proceedings of the workshop, was a productive one, in the sense that basic rethinking of the role of Hawaii in the Pacific community was aroused. The spontaneous floor remarks by an elderly Hawaiian lady, who expounded on the meaning of A-L-O-H-A, were a most appropriate note of conclusion.

Recurring counterpoint notes were provided in the conference by dissident youth. The fact that the youth leaders were given ample opportunities to express their views, first in a regular session on the first day and then in informal sessions on Friday and Saturday, in addition to their full participation in various task-force deliberations, contributed materially to the conference in terms of diversity and relevance. In spite of some apparent diversionary effect, the added push provided the conference and the community a genuine sense of participatory futurism.

Another extraordinary feature of the conference was the exceptional coverage of its proceedings and sidelines in the local mass media. The two Honolulu dailies, the Advertiser and the Star-Bulletin, did a very conscientious job of covering the conference for the benefit of the community. *Compared even to the patently futurology-minded Japanese newspapers, whose treatment of the recent Kyoto futures research conference left much to be desired, the Honolulu papers really zeroed in on the themes, debates, and evaluations of the conference. To cite a few good examples: the* Honolulu Advertiser's *coverage of the children who shall inherit the earth (August 6), of women in the future (August 7), of neighbor isles delegates (August 8), and the editorial of the* Star-Bulletin *at the end of the conference (August 10). This editorial, "Sights on 2000," observed:*

The several hundreds of people who got together last week to talk about the future — specifically the future 30 years from now in the year 2000 — ranged from pessimistic to sanguine, frightened to hopeful, young to old, pragmatic to visionary, involved to uninvolved.

There was a noticeable "anti" (or was it masochistic?) tendency to applaud all criticisms, including those aimed most squarely at the conferees.

There were typical concerns about the burden of work falling on a few, about non-participation, about papers unread and homework undone.

There were concerns about spotlights on the wrong faces (from those in the shade).

There were up-tight didactic tirades from young people who wanted action here and now to settle things for the year 2000 — and up-tight responses from over-30s who have already trod half their path to the year 2000.

There was a general recognition that the rate of change is accelerating — and some feeling that the sum total of changes in the next 30 years may more closely equal those of the last 3000 than the last 30.

There were dreams of a new and better politics with more participation . . . or "interest communities" growing up around the State where people with similar concerns might live together . . . of comfortable and pleasant transit systems instead of crowded highways . . . of wealth more evenly distributed . . . of leisure used profitably and lovingly.

The villains included notably the auto, the hordes of people who aren't in Hawaii now but may want to come, the single family home that contributes to urban sprawl, comfortable traditionalists who can't abide others "doing their thing," and, of course, the establishment now in charge and thereby accountable for all things evil.

Youths proposed that government might well subsidize and study more experiments in new life styles like Banana Patch, that government officials be held personally and financially responsible for development errors, that wealth be limited, and that population be controlled.

On the balance it was an extremely worthwhile exchange.

Professional futurists were ecstatic, if only because it gave their budding profession a boost that it has seldom had before. (Proposals to continue and to institutionalize the effort were frequent.)

New ideas were advanced. Opinions were exchanged. Understanding was perhaps enhanced.

Amid all the exchanges one observer offered a realistic (was it also pessimistic?) insight: The people who will direct human destiny from now to the year 2000 are already alive. Those who will guide Hawaii, America and the world through at least the first part of the way are already adult, many of them are already our leaders. We will have to make our trip into the fast-changing future with the same kinds of fallible humans and fallible leaders that we already know quite well.[2]

The conference will have several important effects on the public life of the citizens of the State, if adequate follow-up efforts are made. It will raise the level of public consciousness regarding the citizens' future in relation to Hawaii's future. A chain reaction of such a heightened

2. *Honolulu Star-Bulletin*, August 10, 1970, p. A–20. Reprinted by permission of the *Honolulu Star-Bulletin*.

public consciousness might be, hopefully, a higher style of public discourse on such occasions as political campaigns, legislative deliberations, and so forth. The highly future-sensitizing editorial style of the two leading Honolulu dailies may be a good indicator of the trend.

Viewed from a larger perspective, this conference was an imaginative project of citizen education — educating not only about the possibilities and catastrophes of the future, but, above all, against the catastrophe of nonaction and lethargy. This is the kind of education all people everywhere need very badly now and in the years to come. In pioneering a new style of citizen education, the state of Hawaii has set a good example not only for other states, but also for other countries in the Pacific basin. The Hawaii conference was local in design but international in effect.

The real impact of any kind of education takes place in the minds of individuals. In this regard, the simple words of a conference delegate who "never got past the seventh grade" are worth quoting, "In my open heart, I wanted to come. It's something new to me. It gives me an idea how to advise my kids what to expect in the future." [3] *If indeed, through this conference and follow-ups, Hawaiian fathers can talk with their children over the supper table about their future, the conference will have done a great wonder. It may be worth many times the $65,000 investment. As was observed by the* Star-Bulletin, *the conference was on the whole "an extremely worthwhile exchange." Now, the key is follow-up.*

CONTINUING COMMUNITY INVOLVEMENT

The first step of follow-up should be to encourage the various islands and communities to hold mini futures conferences, adapting the format of the governor's conference. Already the Big Island follow-up conference at the end of August 1970, was a good start in this direction, and will help keep alive the futures fervor ignited by the

3. For context, refer to p. 134. — Editors.

statewide conference. The network which was mobilized for the interim program should be maximized in subsequent activities. A parallel statewide forum of continuing futures outlook should be anchored in the various high schools, to capitalize on the already aroused enthusiasm of the teenagers, who will be in their prime by 2000. This action would cultivate a broad group whose vested interests lie in the future, and would gradually inject long-range views into public thinking. While there is great advantage in exposing the young early to the prospects and problems of the future, there is one danger inherent in this: that of arousing parochial reactions and possibly reinforcing defensive tendencies. This could be remedied by continuous injection of wider viewpoints — best done at the university level.

UNIVERSITY COURSES AND INSTITUTE

It will be highly advisable to institute futures courses as part of the general education of freshmen or sophomores in all the community colleges and universities throughout the state. The ecology-centered human survival course, to be offered by a group of University of Hawaii faculty beginning in fall 1970, is on the farthest frontier in the futures field. As an underpinning for all general public education, it will be necessary and desirable to establish an institute of futures studies at the University of Hawaii, building upon existing talents and resources. The institute could provide in-depth research on futures problems and methodologies on the one hand, and facilitate regional and international connections on the other.

FUTURES COUNCIL

Futures thinking has to be rooted in the people, and capable of being translated into the current decision-making of the community. In other words, it has to be related above all to the administrative and legislative processes of government. And the mainsprings of ideas that are brought to bear on these processes should be non-bureaucratic-nongovernmental institutions with a public orientation are needed. One way to fill this need might be by the creation of a futures council of Hawaii, with dual functions. One function would be that of crystalizing and synthesizing futures thoughts and proposals originating from various organizations and forums in the state. The council should keep a running inventory of various concrete alternatives for Hawaii, and conduct a continuing series of discussions on these futures toward formulation of a broad consensus. Another function would be that of watching and monitoring the extent of implementation by the legislature, executives, and corporations, of the futures ideas generated and accepted by the community. The futures council will thus become a major nonofficial forum of futures-oriented public opinion.

The membership of this council should not be too large — approximately thirty, with various subcommittees. The membership of the present thirteen task forces would be a good base for this council. The kind of high-quality communal thinking that went into the present task-force reports, as well as the extent of trust in the work of the task forces shown by the participants, set a favorable stage for the evolution and effective functioning of a futures council in Hawaii. The members of the futures council could be appointed by the governor to relatively short terms, say two years, and should be, of course, nonpartisan. Individuals from the press, the university, and the business community would presumably constitute the main part. The council secretariat could be housed at the university.

INVOLVEMENT OF LEGISLATORS AND PUBLIC OFFICIALS AND THE PACIFIC SCHOOL OF LEADERSHIP

It cannot be too emphasized that futures thinking must be tied to planning and decision-making if it is going to have real impact. It must be translated into concrete legislation and even organizational structure; thus, the recent creation of a State office of environmental quality control is a concrete step forward. But environmental control is only one important area of futures concern — other problems such as education, communication, and trade will also be vital to the future of Hawaii. There is a constant need to secure the alternative that suits Hawaii best — growing out of the continuing debate through such mechanisms as a futures council — for the benefit of those who make plans and decisions affecting the entire state. Hence, there is a continuing need to involve and reorient legislators and other public officials who have heavy responsibilities. In this regard, the idea of a Pacific school of leadership, proposed by Harlan Cleveland, president of the University of Hawaii, merits keen attention. Tied to the burgeoning concern for the future in the state of Hawaii, this school could serve as the major orienting and reorienting ground for those who wield great influence on the public life of Hawaii — notably including legislators, state and county executives, mayors, educational administrators, editors, pastors, labor chiefs, and women- and other community-leaders.

A PACIFIC CONFERENCE ON
THE TWENTY-FIRST CENTURY

One danger in the thinking of some citizens of Hawaii, which became clear in the course of the conference, is the persistence of parochial thinking. This was expressed in such ways as, "We don't want to be the center of the Pacific." Hawaii's obvious role, stemming from its singular geographical location as well as from its relational uniqueness to the mainland United States, gets obscured in this kind of thinking. There is yet a great need to widen our horizons and set the role of Hawaii in the Pacific context. On the other hand, the futures outlook which the people of Hawaii are beginning to have must also be shared by other peoples of the Pacific. One way of sharing a futures

453

outlook with other Pacific countries would be to plan and hold a conference for the region in the near future. The East-West Center conference on the problems of modernization in Asia and the Pacific, held immediately after the governor's conference, was a good beginning.

Specifically, a Pacific conference on the twenty-first century, sometime between 1972 and 1976, working toward the bicentennial of the United States in the latter year, would be a significant project for the state of Hawaii to think creatively about from now on. By 1976, there should be many countries around the Pacific having futures studies societies. (At present, only South Korea and Japan have such societies — both organized in 1968.) The prospect of rapid change and development, accompanied by a growing intellectual and public concern about the future in Pacific and Asian countries, will make any continuing initiative by Hawaii in this field, especially in its brand of public futurism, of enduring significance to Hawaii and its Pacific neighbors.

I would like to conclude this evaluation by again quoting the wise words of an ordinary Hawaii citizen, Alfred Pasatiempo, Sr.: "The conference makes a lotta sense in a lotta ways. Because there is so many ideas come out of it. If they don't follow through and do something about it, though, it's waste." [4]

4. For context, consult p. 135. — Editors.

7 TOWARD THE FUTURES

Alternative Hawaiis
Editors

Hawaii 2000 is both a continuing process and a successive set of outcomes that serve as points of new departure. This book, describing as it does the origins, process, products, and evaluations of the Governor's Conference on the Year 2000, is one kind of outcome. But Hawaii 2000 is still being created. Thus in this final chapter we intend to summarize the lessons we think we have learned so far, to describe some of the projects underway as of early 1972, and to attempt to visualize some alternative futures for Hawaii in 2000 and beyond. We hope that this will interest not only those of us in Hawaii but also persons throughout the world who, like ourselves, are concerned about their futures.

We think that the Hawaii 2000 experiment has expressed the following principles: emergence of the idea in the private sector, but attempts to realize it within the framework of overall public responsibility; the support of top-level political leaders, including the governor, legislative leaders, and other members of the legislature — but not political domination; encouragement of multipartisan participation by all parties and groups; primary emphasis upon local intellectual as well as organizational leadership and initiative instead of dependence upon outside authorities; balancing efforts to contribute global, national, and intersocietal viewpoints through consultants, speakers, and observers, as a defense against parochialism; encouragement of diversified citizen partici-

*pation rather than exclusive reliance upon experts; open-
ness to expanding participation rather than organizational constraint; responsiveness to demands for decentralization; preparation for program flexibility versus
rigidity; provision for external evaluation as well as self-
assessment of significance; encouragement of youthful
participation versus adult exclusiveness; and finally, something that we do so habitually in Hawaii that we sometimes
fail to perceive it as one of our most important public
principles, the pursuit of multiethnic participation versus
ethnic exclusion. The initial composition of the advisory
committee, for example, created without special futurist
considerations, is illustrative. In our group were those of
Hawaiian, Japanese, Chinese, Filipino, and Caucasian
extraction.*

*Overall we believe that the net result of the Hawaii
2000 experiment thus far has been worthwhile. It has
demonstrated the need of and desire for continuing wide
lay participation in efforts to design alternative futures for
the islands. But, in retrospect, the shortcomings, even
the failures, of the conference and related activities must
be recognized if subsequent efforts are to benefit from
what was wrong as well as what was right.*

*Focusing attention upon the year 2000, then thirty
years ahead, may have had a constrictive effect. For some
of us it was too far, for others too near. We may continue
for a while to use the phrase "Hawaii 2000" but it should
be understood as a general symbol for futures thinking
rather than as a rigid time constraint. Eventually perhaps
we should replace it with a term like "Hawaii's futures."
Flexibility in temporal perspective should be an imperative
for anticipatory democracy. Those of our citizens who find
it more congenial to think in terms of short- middle- or
long-range futures should be able to gather together to
do so. Then communication and organizational devices
should be sought to bring about a creative interaction*

among these temporal perspectives.

We failed to obtain an integrated overview of alternative Hawaiis in the years ahead. The ten task-force approach produced a fragmented picture of Hawaii's future. Beginning with traditional specialized concepts we were, in essence, both prisoners of the past and producers of partial pieces of a futurist puzzle that can be assembled, if at all, only with the greatest of effort. The combined panel of task-force chairmen that we planned near the end of the conference was favored by neither the time, the creative atmosphere, nor the proper guidance to produce one or more alternative Hawaiis. In retrospect, we now see how more-integrated images of Hawaii 2000 might have been created. We might have established at least one and possibly several competitive task forces on this theme. We might also have asked a variety of existing community groups to offer their own versions which could then be presented by the advisory committee in parallel, semi-integrated, or fully integrated fashion. Or we might have experimented with alternative modes of combining overview scenarios with more specialized study-group efforts. For example, separate overview and specialized study groups might be formed and members might alternate their participation between them.

There were signs, unheeded by us, right from the start of our initial February mini-conference that numerous task-force members felt uneasy about their given subject. They tended either to view it as covering everything about Hawaii (for example, "life-style," or "economy"), or to feel that whatever they suggested about their particular subject really should depend upon assumptions to be made about the future state of Hawaii as a whole. In future efforts, certainly we can do better in meeting these felt needs for general relevance and specific competence.

Another shortcoming lay in the fact that we did not generate enough ideas and practical programs about how we might make the transition from Hawaii today to Hawaiis of the future. This was a product of several things. Most

*importantly, we did not stress it as a task-force or confer-
ence goal, although we clearly so thought of it. At first,
we believed, it was more important to evoke creative community imagination. Almost all of several billion humans
spend most of their time being "practical," we argued,
therefore it could do no great social harm and perhaps
ultimately some good, if a few hundred of us or potentially
a few thousand of us here in Hawaii, began to cultivate
creative societal imagination.*

*Another reason for the relative scarcity of precisely
planned forward-action programs and legislative proposals
was that task-force chairmen simply did not have the time
to develop them. Although they were deeply interested
and enthusiastically invested their talents, there was just
not enough time in three to five months for them to assess
adequately the state of their present fields, to create and
evaluate alternative futures, and then to develop policies
and actions needed to move us from where we are to
where we might want to be.*

*Also, although all men are "futurists," in the sense
that they envisage and plan for things neither past nor
present, few of us were really well trained for the tasks
of first writing imaginative alternative future scenarios and
of then developing action programs to realize them. We
began to explore this kind of education only slightly in
our mini-conference and in a workshop James Dator held
with task-force chairmen. But if we could do it again, we
would favor widespread preliminary exercises to train as
many persons as possible in alternative methods of projecting futures and paths to reach them, especially in the
writing of future-action scenarios, or purposive "future
history." But this should not be at the expense of shackling
creative and sometimes "naïve" imagination. Because we
are creatures of our conditioning and our well-grooved
habits and attitudes, we need mind-stretching and an
impulse for free-flowing dreams if we are to break out*

of the constraints of contemporary experience.

Another related but somewhat different problem was our consistent failure to bridge the gap, or to establish a meaningful dialog, between the creative futurists and what might be termed the "critical presentists." Some might argue that this gap can never be closed, that there is an irreconcilable gulf between "radical" — sometimes even "revolutionary" — critics of present institutions and those who would seek to remove the defects of present society partly from a constructive futures point of view. Nevertheless, we would like to invite consideration of a form of organization and communications procedure that might possibly bring the two points of view into a more useful dialog. That is, any given study group or a conference as a whole might be subdivided into three sections: those most comfortable with creative imagination about the future and willing to engage in serious study of it; those most creative in ways to eliminate the bad and to preserve the good features of the present; and a third group of "action programers," mainly concerned with drawing innovative programs for concrete action out of the creative tensions between the "futurists" and "presentists." A fourth "conference committee" (analogous to a joint committee established to reconcile differences between two legislative bodies) should be composed of representatives of the preceding three groups. It should be guided by an expert in creative communication processes in groups composed of persons with widely different backgrounds. Perhaps proceeding in this way, providing scope for futures imagination, present outrage, and constructive policy articulation, under creative catalytic leadership, we might be able to take a step further beyond polemics, beyond the usurpation of the future by the present — and vice versa.

Another suggestion we have along this line is to subject the consequences of varying emphases upon past, present, and future in group deliberations to comparative social science experimentation and evaluation. For example, we might have established four groups matched in talent, procedures, and in instructions to create alternative images of and pathways toward Hawaii's future. The groups would differ only in the sources of knowledge that they would be expected to employ. The first group would be instructed to emphasize the present, the second to stress the past and present, the third to combine the future and present, while the fourth would be told to draw upon past, present, and future in its deliberations. By studying the outcomes of these four group processes, differing only in the weight attached to temporal sources of knowledge, we might be able to evaluate critically the number, quality, and eventual validity of the future goals and implementational action programs recommended by them.

Our experience shows that most of us need training in the creation of alternative futures. Most of us are the creatures of an either/or, right/wrong, yes/no culture. This shows up in our images of the future where we often find what we want opposed to what we do not want — a single "heaven" opposed to a single "hell." As analyzed by Gerald A. Sumida, of our total of thirteen task-force reports, only one (Kauai 2000) envisioned six alternative futures, two produced three, one imagined two, and nine contained only one alternative future each. Perhaps dichotomous thinking was functional for a past of scarcity, ignorance, and authority — and perhaps it will make a powerful contribution to the future as illustrated by the binary heart of the contemporary computer — but the potentials for pluralism in future societies probably make it necessary to prepare for more alternative outcomes than ever before.

Although we tried, we failed to engage all the possible talent available to us. For example, having developed a list of more than fifteen hundred outstanding community leaders — and being aware of the possibility of extending it — we might have benefited immediately from the con-

tributions of at least twice as many citizens as we did. That is, we might have had twenty-six study groups and fifteen hundred participants in one or more conferences. Furthermore, we failed to engage the participation of all segments of Hawaii's people. We wanted to, and made efforts to do so but we are as much dissatisfied as encouraged by the results. A more satisfactory outcome would have meant that Hawaii 2000 thinking would have benefited more from the ideas of men and women who feel less comfortable in standard English than in pidgin, Hawaiian, Japanese, Cantonese, Mandarin, Korean, Pilipino (Tagalog), Ilocano, Visayan, Pampango, Samoan, Portugese, and other languages of Hawaii's peoples. This would have required translators, interpreters and a deliberate effort to promote intercultural communication about Hawaii's futures. But to gain the active contributions of all Hawaii's people regardless of background, age, or occupation would require more than just linguistic skills; it would require more widespread knowledge of the project, more energetic efforts in recruitment, and a belief among our people that participation would be beneficial. Thus Hawaii 2000 must be dedicated to extending its social outreach as an essential feature of anticipatory democracy.

We have already commented earlier about possible shortcomings associated with use of conventional concepts as foci for task-force activities, and failure to make full use of consultant potential.

Nothing we have said here should be taken to minimize the splendid work of the task forces — whose chairmen and members deserve an entire state's gratitude — but only to propose to others who may emulate the Hawaii experience that our effort can be improved upon.

This was symptomatic of a range of questions and issues which immediately faced the Hawaii State Commission on the Year 2000, mandated by the legislature before

the August 1970 conference, but established afterward as

a natural outgrowth. *Eight of nine members of a temporary commission were named by Governor Burns on March 23, 1971.*[1] *The commission's responsibilities were to study the impact of technology and social change on Hawaii and to promote a general awareness of it; to assess the future of Hawaii and identify desired economic, political, cultural, social, and environmental state goals; to recommend legislative and administrative actions to achieve these goals; to assist and coordinate activities of those groups concerned with the future of Hawaii; and to submit an annual report to the governor and the legislature.*

All through its first summer the commission wrestled with role and goals — questions of how it could best function to meet its responsibilities, what were the desirable and yet manageable boundaries of its work, what kinds of projects it should undertake, and so forth. The commission was made permanent on November 11, 1971.[2]

After a series of meetings, the commission agreed upon three basic assumptions in terms of what, why, *and* who. What *the commission is aiming for: to bring about such real, visible, and significant change as seems desirable in Hawaii's society and institutions.* Why *the commission has this aim: because it believes that the choice facing Hawaii's people is either to act now to seek to fashion the hurrying future or to be overwhelmed by it, and because it firmly believes in the ability of Hawaii's people to help shape or alter their destiny.* Who *the commission*

1. George Chaplin, chairman; Gerald Sumida, elected vice-chairman; Mrs. Robert W. Guild, elected secretary; Walter Dods, Jr.; Harry Flagg, Keiji Kawakami, Linda Luke, and Claudio Suyat. Kunio Nagoshi, head of the Center for Governmental Development at the University of Hawaii's College of Continuing Education and Community Services, became staff director. An informal group of advisors was also established, including Richard J. Barber, James A. Dator, Thomas H. Hamilton, George S. Kanahele, Guy R. Kirkendall, Hahn-Been Lee, Ralph M. Miwa, Glenn Paige, and Richard Takasaki.

2. Members included the incumbent chairman, six original members (Linda Luke had resigned to attend a mainland university), and two new members Stanley W. Hong of Honolulu and Thomas S. Kaneshiro of Keaau, island of Hawaii.

is concerned about: all the people of Hawaii, not particular elites or interest groups or socioeconomic strata or organizations.

On these assumptions, the commission settled on the following goals for itself in keeping with the responsibilities mandated to it by the legislature: (a) to create, sustain and intensify an awareness among Hawaii's people that our future may be and is being shaped in several different ways, and how this may occur and is now occurring; (b) to promote and maintain the active participation and involvement of Hawaii's people in a statewide effort to depict, assess and establish political, economic, social and cultural, and environmental goals for Hawaii; (c) to devise and recommend legislative, administrative, and citizen action to accomplish these goals; (d) to assess, evaluate, and review periodically these goals and the action being undertaken to accomplish them; and (e) to promote, assist and coordinate programs, activities, and plans of individuals and organizations, whether public or private, concerned with the future of Hawaii.

In pursuance of these goals, the commission in the final days of 1971 worked out a phased action program designed to create public awareness, bring about widespread participation and involvement, and provide coordination and promotional services. Elements of the program ranged from establishment of a speakers' bureau and film library, utilization of mass media and cosponsorship of various futures-oriented conferences, to futures clubs and possible scenario contests in schools, and preliminary work toward a large-scale "Hawaii 2000" project that would stimulate broad discussion of island futures down to the neighborhood level. Consideration was also given to stimulating in the private sector an alternative economic futures project for Hawaii. This came into being with support of business and labor, under the cochairmanship of the president of the Dillingham Corporation and the Hawaii 2000 commission chairman. It was anticipated that scenar-

ios would be produced by 1975 for several overall economic futures for the islands, with recommendations for action by public and private decision-makers and the citizenry.

As the program of the commission itself moved from planning to action, it cosponsored conferences on communication in the future and on the role of the judiciary in a changing Hawaii, and presented a public lecture by futurist John McHale. An experimental project was begun in three Oahu high schools — Kailua, McKinley, and Roosevelt — to engage students in community planning efforts and to provide them an opportunity to formulate and advance their own ideas of preferred possible futures.

Meanwhile there was a widening impact of Hawaii's futures activities. A continuing flow of inquiries — mostly from the United States mainland, but some from abroad — came from institutions and individuals, including newspaper editors, several members of Congress, planning agencies of a number of states, corporation executives, and college and university officials. In May 1971, a delegation from Hawaii attended the World Future Society's first general assembly in Washington, D.C. In September the Hawaii commission chairman and the president of the University of Hawaii were among some forty delegates from sixteen countries participating in a United Nations–sponsored conference in Rensselaerville, N. Y. This meeting, organized by Undersecretary General Simeon O. Adebo, led to a decision to create a Commission on New Perspectives in International Cooperation devoted to global concerns for the future. An invitation from Hawaii's governor was conveyed for the U.N. commission to hold its inaugural meeting in the islands. As of early 1972, this commission was still in the process of being formed; Hawaii's invitation is still outstanding. It is hoped that eventually the futures aloha of the islands can be extended in this way to the United Nations family.

It may be, as some mainland friends have said, that

Hawaii is leading the way in the study and utilization of futuristics in the United States. Certainly, the legislature and the governor of Hawaii have tangibly demonstrated faith in the proposition that the people should try to determine their fate. This has been reflected not only in support for the conference and the commission, but in considering a Hawaii research center for futures study at the University of Hawaii.

All this is heartening, but just a beginning. For the future is already upon us, calling for the best that can be mustered in intelligence, imagination, and flexibility. Can there be developed in these islands a productive model of what people can really do about their social, political, cultural, economic, and physical environment? Hawaii should have no illusions that it will work miracles, but neither should it desist from trying to continue its experimental efforts in anticipatory democracy.

We cannot foretell all the alternative future Hawaiis that creative community efforts may envision and seek to realize, but we can think of some of them. We share some here briefly as a stimulus to further thought. We argue neither their reasonableness nor plausibility but only their provocativeness. All arise out of the principal creative resources of our islands. These include tensions between multiethnicity and ethnic convergence; between ethnic balance and ethnic domination; immigration and emigration; population growth and population stabilization; nature-destroying and nature-enhancing technology; private economic interest and public economic good; wealth and poverty; land, air, and sea for living or dying; narrow or broad participation in community decision-making; centralization and decentralization; parochial and more encompassing identifications (local, national, regional, and global); beauty and ugliness; individual freedom and social responsibility; and varying emphases upon past, present, and future concerns.

One vision is that of Hawaii as a futurist version of

an ideal American state, an island community where all of the traditional dreams come true: freedom, equality, justice, abundance, and virtually unlimited opportunity. This is a Hawaii without racism, poverty, unemployment, crime, slums, pollution, mental illness, moral degradation, and family disintegration. Future versions of rugged farmers and skillful fishermen draw sustenance from land and sea, while equally rugged entrepreneurs and faithful workers vigorously operate the productive facilities of postindustrial society — all enjoying happy leisure in unmatched natural beauty. Business, labor, government, and the military balance and bargain with minimum friction, and statesmen rule with the informed support of a wise citizenry. There is a stock market and although some are richer than others, no one really suffers. Other people's problems are far away and there is little incentive for involvement except to trade, to travel, and to keep up with scientific inventions and artistic creations via the world communications satellite systems. The world's woes, although available to everyone's television receiver, challenge cerebral, not substantive involvement. Happy visitors from near and far throughout the globe share Hawaii's charm and acclaim it as the pride of the American nation.

Another vision is of Hawaii as a battlefield for protracted struggle. The poor, the racially oppressed, the psychologically scarred, the pure-minded youth, and the cast-aside aged, conduct constant warfare against formidably entrenched businessmen, landlords, politicians, bureaucrats, media controllers, police, militarists, teachers, and other assorted authority figures. The revolutionaries of the world are seen as models and allies in the grand effort to defeat capitalism, racism, militarism, and imperialism. The battle will not be easy; the enemy will be cunning and powerful, but doomed to eventual destruction, and on his ruins Hawaii will be able to build a truly new civilization. Land and tools will be held in common; public ownership of most industries, including communications and tourism, will prevail. The stock market will disappear. Abundance will reign and a powerful collective leadership will decide what is best policy for all. People will be taught that the social good overrides individual interests. Hawaii will become a revolutionary state, emerging either as part of an accompanying twentieth-century American revolution, or liberating itself violently against federal forces as a multi-people's republic supported by the nuclear umbrella of a reconciled China and Russia, with the encouragement of revolutionary Japan.

Another vision is of a futurist Hawaiian restoration, the establishment of a true kingdom of aloha. One path to such a community would be through a combination of granting preferential treatment to persons of Hawaiian or part-Hawaiian ancestry in all areas of social life (an expanded version of what has been attempted in veterans preference) and an "aloha-ness test" (more humanely comprehensive than the customary citizenship or loyalty test). The latter would guarantee the avoidance of a racist society — so far from the Hawaiian tradition — and ethnic Hawaiians would have to "pass" various versions of it along the life cycle or be encouraged to seek a more congenial society elsewhere. The aloha kingdom would attempt to achieve greater harmony among men and between man and nature. It need not revert only to fishing and subsistence agriculture but might progress to the highest levels of future scientific, technological, biological, informational, and humanistic arts. It might produce concepts of ownership far beyond polemical nineteenth and twentieth century rhetoric. The possession of human qualities within the capacity of individuals and groups might come to be regarded as the highest form of "ownership." The establishment of such a future "participatory monarchy" — genetically, psychologically, and culturally based — where the concept of aloha came to reign in place of a *physical king, would require separation from the Union or an achieved permissiveness in the U.S. Constitution to free states for radical social innovation.*

An alternative to the aloha kingdom would be the establishment of a Pacific "coconut republic," the playground of the world. Here, in a balmy climate, no one need wear clothes, except when it is chilly; partially computerized gambling in games drawn from the seven seas or monitored throughout the world would be at its finest; all the chemical euphorias of the world would be readily at hand; the finest medicines would restore health, obliterate venereal disease, and control births. There would be a golf course so long and intricate that it would take a lifetime to master it, and when players became too senile to hit the ball, they might continue to play through computerized remote-control armchair facilities until the moment of death. Tax-free shopping would be at its best for the affluent of the world — and for the poor, there would be produced little "dream Hawaii" packets either to spur achievement motivation to join the fun or to dull the pains of existence through creative fantasy.

Another Hawaii would be what might be called an "ecological commonwealth." This would require a truly radical departure from conventional concerns (capitalist, socialist, or communist) with power and property to focus upon man's relationship with the natural environment as the highest form of good. In effect this would mean profound community acceptance of the necessity for restraint in human power. Having recognized his capacity for poisoning land, sea, and air to the extent of annihilating human life — his capacity to influence nature to the point where it goes random in life-destroying chain reactions beyond control — men in Hawaii could decide to make their islands the world center for experimental man-environment symbiosis. Having failed to solve satisfactorily problems in subordination to gods in the age of religion, or to other men in the age of humanism, men and women in this vision of future Hawaii would turn to focus upon their creative relation to nature as a mode of approaching the most fundamental religious and human questions. The enrichment of the environment would replace the enrichment of man as the object of human life. Gardeners, landscapers, plant and animal disease scientists, waste-disposal experts, marine conservationists, wildlife protectors, and pollution inspectors — if specialized in a period of transition from the present — would be more highly rewarded than corporation executives, entertainers, and sports heroes. It would be fitting that Hawaii with its breathtaking inheritance of natural beauty and its resonance with the nature-enhancing traditions of Japan should seek to become a world pioneer in the ecological reorientation of human thinking. The signal for the creative vitalization of this kind of approach would be a world congress of nature lovers — not only militant anti-industrial crusaders — to share worldwide creative imagination and esthetic sensitivities about man-nature relationships of the future.

An ecological commonwealth might come in two versions: a back-to-nature version and a postindustrial technology–nature symbiosis. The first, much less likely, would require a radical reduction of population to levels supportable by fishing and agriculture. It would mean "technological disarmament" (probably achievable itself only through more advanced technology; that is, through dismantling or chemically dissolving high-rise buildings, roads, parking lots, and machine technology, including automobiles). Without technological aids, a massive labor force to restore nature would be required, undoubtedly beyond that supportable by subsistence farming. Therefore in a transition period, technology-reducing techniques would be preserved and the last technologies to be dismantled would be those that can be used to restore or enhance nature.

469　　　*An effort to construct a postindustrial technology–na-*

ture symbiosis would radically differ from the back-to-nature model in that it would stress the enrichment rather than the dismantling of technology as a part of nature itself. This would mean that Hawaii might support not one- but ten- or twenty-million people. Synthetic food, vitamins, and biological products rather than subsistence agriculture would sustain them. They would live in densely packed high-rise apartments, crammed at the bases of our mountains, or in floating cities on the sea. Mountain slopes, floors of valleys, and shoreline areas would be freed of all but minimal man-made structures: bikeways, cartways for the ill and aged, rest pavilions, and bases for the highly prestigious all-volunteer "Hawaii nature-service society." Waste recycling would be a major industry — as would all other occupations that could be pursued by a globe-encircling computer-satellite informational system.

There are at least three ways Hawaii might begin to move toward an ecological commonwealth. All of them involve State and county initiative. First is to shift patterns of land use and new building in the desired direction, while gradually seeking to remove older structures from places of beauty. The second is for the State to petition for federal assistance in becoming a "national park." A substantial start is already available in federally controlled military and other public lands, including the Hawaii Volcanoes National Park. Only long-term residents and specially skilled conservationists would be permitted as permanent residents in the park domains, then to be regarded as national treasures. Third, the whole state might be deeded by action of its own citizens, with national concurrence, to the United Nations as the first major "world park." The argument for this would be that Hawaii is too beautiful and too significant in potential human relations to be anything less than a subject of world concern and enjoyment.

470   This naturally suggests the idea of a future Hawaii as

the world headquarters of the United Nations [3] — combining the functions of a world park and the informational processing requirements of future world political, social, economic, and cultural institutions. In this kind of future, reaching beyond the regional concept of Hawaii's Asia-Pacific role, selective immigration on a global basis would be sought so that the people of Hawaii eventually would become a microcosm of the people of the world. Culturally, the beauty of aloha and of Hawaii would offer a priceless gift to all humanity in perpetuity. A cultural, educational, and health-restoring visitors' program on a public basis would be established, reaching more than just the world's affluent.

A further future alternative might be called "experimental Hawaiis." In such a society, continuous, pluralistic, relatively small-scale experiments would be encouraged by legislative action and supporting public opinion on a wide range of political, economic, social, cultural, environmental, and intersocietal matters. Overall creative monitoring would be by a futures-enhancing public leadership, held more accountable than today for facilitating anticipatory democratic innovations. Aspects of alternative Hawaiis, some briefly sketched above, might be allowed: for example, an effort might be made to create and to be worthy of a visitors' program that would demonstrate future-seeking Hawaii as a model American state (Hawaii does not now have a futures-oriented visitor-education center of this type); "revolutionary" pilot communities might be permitted; an experimental futurist restoration of the Hawaiian kingdom might be made on former crown lands; nonsexist toplessness — and eventually complete nudity — might be permitted from the sea to the nearest public highway; a world ecological congress might be held and land dedicated for the experimental exploration of an ecological commonwealth; an experi-

3. This was suggested by John McHale, *Honolulu Advertiser*, January 6, 1972, p. A–4.

mental valley and an experimental floating community might be comparatively explored as alternative man-nature postindustrial styles of life; military lands might be converted to national park use; parts of the state might be dedicated for a world park; a United Nations conference center might be established in Hawaii, and so forth. Ideas such as these and others that have been expressed in the Hawaii 2000 venture can be elaborated, transformed into experimental form, and scientifically and humanistically evaluated for results that can contribute to enriching life in "experimental Hawaiis."

By now, we hope that the reader is in a state of creative tension. So Hawaii has plunged into an experiment in anticipatory democracy! So there has been a conference, task-force reports, critical observer evaluations, and some imaginings about Hawaiis of the future! But better than anything that has been suggested for Hawaii 2000 thus far would be . . .

APPENDIX

A. TASK-FORCE MEMBERS

HAWAII'S PEOPLE AND LIFE-STYLES 2000

Simeon Acoba / *attorney*
Harry V. Ball / *professor of sociology*
James K. Clark / *state senator*
Fuifatu Fau'olo / *chief, community leader*
Wallace Fukunaga / *minister*
Ernest N. Heen, Jr. / *state representative*
Marianne Holu / *student*
Kenneth Ito / *high school student*
Larry Kamakawiwoole / *student*
Keiji Kawakami / *businessman*
Mrs. H. Baird Kidwell / *community leader*
Stephen Kohashi / *student*
Stephen W. Lane / *community worker*

Linda Luke / *student leader*
Melvin Masuda / *attorney*
A. Q. McElrath / *social worker*
Barbara Okamoto / *student*
Priscilla Sabella / *community worker*
John Sharp / *community worker*
A. A. Smyser / *editor, Honolulu star-bulletin*
Joe Tanega / *high school student*
Myron Thompson / *state administrator*
Michael Town / *attorney*
Herman J. Wedemeyer / *county councilman*
Douglas S. Yamamura / *professor of sociology (chairman)*

QUALITY OF PERSONAL LIFE 2000

Kay Asuncion / *community worker*
Carol Brown / *student*
Brian Casey / *city councilman*
Donald Char / *director, university student health services*
Walter Char / *professor of psychiatry*
Alfred Dela Rosa / *labor leader*
René Dubos / *professor, explorer of the biomedical, psychological, and social effects of the technological environment (consultant)*

Byron Eliashof / *president, state psychiatric association*
Robert Ellis / *businessman*
Shigeaki Fujitani / *university counseling and testing center*
Hale Hitchcock / *attorney*
Francis Hsu / *professor of anthropology*
Frank Judd / *state representative*
Marion Kelly / *anthropologist*
Anne King / *teacher*

Monta Kinney / housewife
David Kinzie / senior resident
in psychiatry
Robert Krauss / reporter
John D. Lanham / state senator
George Lee / state committee on
planning and economic development
K. Y. Lum / psychiatrist
Nengin Mahony / high school student
Thomas Maretzki / professor of
anthropology
Michael Martin / student
Floyd Matson / professor of American
studies (vice chairman)
John F. McDermott, Jr. / professor
of psychiatry (chairman)
A. Q. McElrath / social worker
Roderick McPhee / school
administrator
Robert Midkiff / businessman
Guy T. Nunn / director, labor
management education program,
university of Hawaii

Edward O'Rourke / dean, school of
public health
Richard Paglinawan / Hawaiian home
lands commission
David Pali / community leader
Alfred Pasatiempo, Sr. / laborer
Walter Quisenberry / director of
health, state of Hawaii
Lena K. Reverio / housewife
Patricia Saiki / state representative
Pat Schnack / community leader
Steve Shupe / student
Margaret Smalley / executive director,
child and family service
Charles Stewart / psychiatrist
James L. Swenson / protestant
clergyman
Lois Taylor / reporter
Robert Toyofuku / attorney
Fred Weaver / psychiatrist
John Witeck / youth leader
Leo S. Wou / architect
Vincent H. Yano / state senator

THE NATURAL ENVIRONMENT 2000

Gerald Allison / architect
Russell A. Apple / historian
James R. Bell / planner
Richard E. Bell / operations
research analyst
E. W. Broadbent / engineering
administrator
Nathan C. Burbank, Jr. / professor
of public health
Robert T. Chuck / manager, state
division of water and land
development
Walter K. Collins / businessman
(chairman)
Thomas H. Creighton / planner
Ramon Duran / state land use
commission
James C. Faries / businessman
Wayne Gagne / entomologist
C. Michael Hare / student

Howard Harrenstien / associate dean,
college of engineering
Thomas K. Hitch / economic research
administrator
Paul C. Joy / businessman
Ben F. Kaito / county councilman
George S. Kanahele / businessman,
political scientist
John S. Kay / businessman
Alison Kay / professor of
general sciences
Sunao Kido / chairman, state board
of land and natural resources
Clemente Lagundimao / designer
John Lanham / state senator
Ken Masuda / management counselor
Steven Montgomery / student
Garth I. Murphy / professor of
oceanography
Robert S. Nekemoto / engineer

W. Jan Newhouse / *associate professor of general sciences*
Richard Poirier / *consultant, state department of planning and economic development*
Peter Preis / *designer, draftsman*
Jane Preuss / *state department of planning and economic development*
Kenneth Norris / *marine biologist*
Saul Price / *regional climatologist*
Richard Schulze / *attorney*
Linda Anne Smart / *housewife*
Russell Smith / *businessman*

Philip E. Spalding, Jr. / *businessman*
Raymond Suefuji / *director, county planning commission*
Jack Suwa / *state representative*
Fred E. Trotter / *estate trustee*
C. Peairs Wilson / *dean, college of tropical agriculture*
John G. Wisnosky / *artist*
George S. Walters / *landscape architect*
Toni Withington / *planning writer*
Wendy Yin / *high school student*

HOUSING AND TRANSPORTATION 2000

William J. Atkinson, Jr. / *engineer (housing subcommittee chairman)*
Edison M. D. Chong / *student*
Gene Dashiell / *professor of anthropology*
William A. Grant / *architect, planner*
Karen Hiura / *student*
Harold Hostetler / *urban affairs writer (transportation subcommittee chairman)*
John J. Hulten / *state senator*
Lewis Ingleson / *architect*
Russell Johnson / *student*
Kekoa David Kaapu / *city urban renewal coordinator*
Robert J. Kasher / *student*
Shigeomi Kubota / *county councilman*
Aaron Levine / *planner (chairman)*
Roland Lagareta / *student*
Carl T. Mahoney / *architect*
Fujio Matsuda / *director, state department of transportation*

Bernice Midkiff / *community leader*
Mrs. Howard Moore / *community leader*
James F. Morgan, Jr. / *businessman*
John J. Morrett / *protestant clergyman*
Jane Ohara / *research assistant*
George Oshiro / *student*
Chester Rapkin / *professor of urban planning (consultant)*
Fred W. Rohlfing / *state senator*
Arthur Rutledge / *labor leader*
Roy Shimabukuro / *engineer*
Eddie Tangen / *labor leader*
George C. Villegas / *director, city traffic department*
Ned Wiederholt / *lecturer in public health*
Donald Wolbrink / *planner*
Yoshio Yanagawa / *director, state housing authority*

POLITICAL DECISION-MAKING AND THE LAW 2000

Byron Baker / *television and radio reporter*
David Benz / *publisher*
H. Edwin Bonsey / *protestant clergyman*

Mrs. Frank Butterworth / *civic worker*
Tom Dinell / *director of Pacific urban studies and planning program*
Mrs. Toy Len Chang / *housewife*
Elmer Cravalho / *mayor, Maui county*

James A. Dator / *associate professor of political science (consultant)*

Walter Dods / *businessman*

Claude du Teil / *protestant clergyman*

Mary George / *city councilwoman*

Tom Higa / *businessman*

Stuart Ho / *state senator*

James Kawachika / *university center for governmental development*

Dewey Kim / *associate dean, division of continuing education and community service*

Shunichi Kimura / *mayor, Hawaii county*

Morton King / *department of the attorney general*

Sharon Komata / *researcher, house of representatives*

Tyrone Kusao / *director, university center for governmental development*

Peter C. Lewis / *businessman*

Linda Luke / *student leader*

Robert R. Midkiff / *businessman*

Ralph M. Miwa / *dean, college of continuing education and community service (chairman)*

Eichi Oki / *attorney*

Patricia Park / *department of the attorney general*

Mary Ellen Swanton / *health specialist*

Pattie Thomas / *student*

Daniel W. Tuttle, Jr. / *political scientist, educational administrator*

Charles T. Ushijima / *state representative*

Antone Vidinha / *mayor, Kauai county*

Gordon Wood / *high school student*

THE ECONOMY 2000

Lawrence S. Berger / *president, KHVH television*

Kenneth E. Boulding / *professor of economics (consultant)*

William R. Fox / *student*

Wytze Gorter / *dean, university graduate division*

Thomas H. Hamilton / *president, Hawaii visitors bureau (chairman)*

Richard Henderson / *state senator*

Ralph S. Hirota / *county councilman*

Danny Kaleikini / *professional entertainer*

Richard A. Kawakami / *state representative*

Harry S. Kennedy / *episcopal bishop*

Shelley Mark / *director, state department of planning and economic development*

Richard Mayer / *community college instructor*

Adrian H. Perry / *housewife*

Mrs. John G. Simpson / *housewife and community relations specialist*

Patricia Won / *high school student*

SCIENCE AND TECHNOLOGY 2000

Nadhipuram Bhagavan / *assistant professor of biochemistry and medical technology*

Louis Casarett / *associate professor of pharmacology*

Ruth Denney / *public administrator, regional medical program*

Ruth Harada / *student*

Teruo Kawata / *protestant clergyman*

Melvyn K. Kono / *high school student*

Jorgen Larsen-Badse / *professor of mechanical engineering*

Herbert D. Long / *theologian, academic administrator*

Jung Lowe / *attorney*

Louis G. Nickell / *plant scientist*

Lawrence Piette / *professor of biophysics*

Terence A. Rogers / *dean, school of medicine (chairman)*

George Sarant / *student*

John W. Shupe / *professor of civil engineering*

George P. Woollard / *professor of geophysics*

Alvey Wright / *state department of transportation*

EDUCATION 2000

Tim Boyne / *college instructor*

John A. Brownell / *professor of education*

Charles M. Campbell / *city councilman*

Robert Clopton / *senior professor emeritus*

Robert Cushing / *director, Hawaiian sugar planters' association experimental station*

Daniel Dever / *superintendent, catholic schools*

Norman Geschwind / *college instructor*

Stanley I. Hara / *state senator*

Ralph Hirota / *county councilman*

Derrick Ho / *high school student*

Marianne Holu / *student*

Jean Kanahele / *student*

Monta Kinney / *housewife, community leader*

Ralph H. Kiyosaki / *superintendent of education*

Pilialoha LeeLoy / *student*

Lynn Nakkim / *teacher*

Robert E. Potter / *professor of education (chairman)*

Charlene Robello / *student*

Theodore Rodgers / *dean, school of medicine*

Mrs. John Sanders / *housewife*

Ralph K. Stueber / *associate professor of education*

Claudio Suyat / *high school principal*

Robert S. Taira / *state representative*

David Treacy / *assistant professor of english*

Daniel W. Tuttle, Jr. / *executive secretary, Hawaii education association*

Mrs. Jack Woltman / *housewife*

Sara Woods / *housewife*

Louis Yamauchi / *education specialist*

THE ARTS

Max Botticelli / *physician*

Kenneth Bushnell / *assistant professor of art*

Mrs. J. Russell Cades / *member, state foundation on culture and the arts*

Sherry Charles / *student*

William C. H. Chung / *businessman*

Mrs. Kathy Crockett / *community leader in the arts, Maui*

Reuel Denney / *professor of American studies (chairman)*

Howard Droste / *associate professor of art*

Wallace Fukunaga / *clergyman*

Lee Gomes / *high school student*

Jaci Gordon / *student*

Alan Gowans / *art historian (consultant)*

Bruce Hopper / *designer*

Richard Hoyt / *reporter*

Alvina Kaulili / *member, state foundation on culture and the arts*

Rebekah Luke / *student*
Barney B. Menor / *state representative*
Timothy Mitchell / *historic Lahaina foundation*
J. Meredith Neil / *assistant professor of American studies*
Prithwish Neogy / *professor of art*
Shirlee Novack / *art teacher*
Jayne Ohara / *housing researcher*
Henry Pleasants / *composer and musicologist (consultant)*
Alfred Preis / *director, state foundation on culture and the arts*

Evelyn Radford / *teacher*
Theodore Rogers / *assistant professor of psycholinguistics*
William Samways / *communications consultant*
Lee Stetson / *director, Hawaii performing arts company*
Wadsworth Yee / *state senator*
Pundy Yokouchi / *chairman, state foundation on culture and the arts*
John Wisnosky / *assistant professor of art*

HAWAII AND THE PACIFIC COMMUNITY 2000

Sophie Ann Aoki / *student*
Clinton Ashford / *attorney*
Robert Behnke / *businessman*
Harlan Cleveland / *university president*
Lloyd Evans / *student*
William Fernandez / *state senator*
Roland Force / *museum director*
John Griffin / *newspaper editor*
Alice Guild / *advertising*
Rhoda Hackler / *housewife*
Gail Harada / *high school student*
Walter Heen / *city councilman*
Robert B. Hewett / *director, east-west center public affairs*
James Hirai / *student*

Paul Hooper / *student*
Susan Ichinose / *state employee*
George S. Kanahele / *director, Hawaii international services agency (chairman)*
Hahn-Been Lee / *administrator, scholar, diplomat (consultant)*
Werner Levi / *professor of political science*
Henry T. Takitani / *state representative*
Tobias C. Tolzmann / *attorney*
Charles R. Williams / *businessman*
Don Wilson / *student*
Alexander Wylly / *businessman*

HAWAII (THE BIG ISLAND) 2000

Ronald Agrigado / *high school student*
Hideo Aoki / *professor of religion and philosophy*
Elena Bacgalupi / *spanish teacher*
Sam Boone / *automobile salesman*
Mrs. Sam Boone / *housewife*
Ann Bowen / *student newspaper editor*

Bill Brenneman / *cross-cultural specialist*
Mrs. Bill Brenneman / *housewife*
Carol Brice / *county librarian*
Ken Brown / *radio engineer*
Paul Brown / *student*
Penelope Brown / *student*
Leanne Bryan / *high school student*
Tim Bryan / *student*

Richard Cann / *policeman, motor patrolman*
Mrs. Richard Cann / *secretary*
Dante Carpenter / *county councilman*
Steve Christensen / *public defender*
Harry Chuck / *superintendent, department of education*
Hugh Clark / *reporter*
Dale Crowley / *language unit chairman, peace corps*
Ellen Curry / *student*
Karen Cushnie / *housewife*
Jeff Dann / *businessman*
Sylvia Dann / *businesswoman*
Frances De Silva / *school principal*
James Downs / *professor of anthropology*
Howard Droste / *associate professor of art*
John Farias, Jr. / *director, Hawaii county planning and development*
Juan Fernandez / *community college student*
Alan Ferreira / *high school student*
Jane Ford / *assistant professor of education*
Charles Fullerton / *acting director, cloud physics observatory*
Mrs. Charles Fullerton / *housewife*
Lew Genge / *businessman*
Hal Glatzer / *news media*
Herbert T. Hamai / *assistant professor of health and physical education*
Will Hancock / *teacher*
Sylvia Hara / *teacher*
Arthur Hoke, Jr. / *police lieutenant*
Charlene Iboshi / *student*
Robert Kim / *student*
Robert Knox / *instructor in art*
Ardis Kuniyoshi / *high school student*
Mrs. Hideo Kuniyoshi / *teacher*
Bobby Jean Leithead / *student*
John Y. F. Lin / *catholic clergyman*
Mrs. Walter Loo / *anthropologist*
Herbert Marutani / *university administrator*

Richard Matsunaga / *high school principal*
Peter McKnight / *protestant clergyman*
Kiyoto Mizuba / *deputy superintendent, department of education*
Jeanne Moulton / *unit assistant, peace corps*
Dwight Nakamura / *buddhist clergyman*
Kaoru Noda / *vice chancellor, university of Hawaii at Hilo (chairman)*
Norene Ogomori / *high school student*
Philip Olsen / *interim director, peace corps*
John B. Orr / *inventor*
Gerard Pilecki / *professor of english*
David Reed / *student*
Stanley Roehrig / *state representative*
Susan Rogers / *high school student*
Jim St. Leger / *attorney, law enforcement agency*
Harold Sanders / *engineer*
Coreen Sekimura / *student*
Robert Spencer / *psychiatrist*
Dennis Suenobu / *elementary school teacher*
Joseph Swaffer / *instructor in economics*
Joseph Sweeney / *reporter*
Ruth Tabrah / *member, board of education*
Harold Tanouye, Jr. / *businessman*
Eugene Tao / *reporter*
Alysen W. Taylor / *school administrator*
Charles Taylor, Jr. / *sociologist*
Donald Tong / *county planner*
David Treacy / *assistant professor of english*
Mrs. David Treacy / *housewife*
Steve Tsunemoto / *high school student*
Alan Tyler / *conservationist*

Ted Ura / *high school counselor*
Hiromi Urasaki / *high school student*
Mrs. Louis Warsh / *director,*
Hawaii county mental association

Steve Warsh / *student*
Priscilla Watson / *community*
college student
Dave Yamauchi / *high school student*

KAUAI 2000

Takumi Akama / *labor union official*
Dewey Allen / *police chief*
Dale Anderson / *plantation official*
Martin Arthur II / *student, radio*
broadcaster
Robert Asakura / *high school student*
Ardis Asaoka / *high school student*
Ivy Awakuni / *high school student*
Paul Bartram / *county researcher,*
writer
Dan Betsui / *student*
Bud Carter / *radio station manager*
William Carvalho / *businessman*
Francis Ching / *businessman*
Mrs. Connie Cuaresma / *school*
teacher
Debbie Cullen / *student*
Tad Eto / *sales representative*
Mrs. Peg Faye / *chairman,*
committee on aging
Mrs. Barbara Franklin /
instructor in speech
Gary Freitas / *high school student*
Clyde French / *bank official*
Doreen Fujita / *high school student*
Patrice Gokan / *high school student*
Gordon Haas / *student*
Darleen Hamamura / *high school*
student
Willard Haraguchi / *student*
Kenneth Harding / *businessman,*
anthropology instructor
Art Harrington / *director,*
Kokee job corps
Ann Haruki / *high school student*
Debbie Hashimura / *high school*
student
Kei Hirano / *county attorney*
Colleen Hironaka / *high school*
student

Ralph Hirota / *county councilman*
(cochairman)
Jean Holmes / *newspaper editor*
Leon Houghlum / *U.S. navy officer*
Jahne Hupy / *public health nurse*
Rodney Hustead / *high school*
principal
Bud Hutton / *farmer*
Mrs. Jane Ibara / *public health nurse*
Philip Ige / *provost, Kauai*
community college (cochairman)
Calvin Inouye / *high school student*
Warren Iwamoto / *high school student*
Mrs. Jalna Keala / *housewife*
Grace Kato / *high school student*
Ryosho Kondo / *buddhist clergyman*
Karen Koide / *high school student*
Kaymi Koide / *high school student*
Toru Kawakami / *businessman*
Robyn Lai / *high school student*
Fred Lawrence / *airport manager*
Phyllis Liu / *high school student*
Odell Lloyd / *teacher*
Anne Loquercio / *art instructor,*
community worker
Ronald Martin / *school principal*
Cynthia Masukawa / *high school student*
Lorna Matsuda / *high school student*
Allan Miike / *high school counselor*
Mrs. Bernice Midkiff /
businesswoman
Keith Mikasa / *high school student*
Michael Mikasa / *high school student*
Gary Miyashiro / *high school student*
Isamu Miyoshi / *school principal*
Tad Miura / *administrative assistant*
to mayor of Kauai
Dean Mizura / *high school student*
Lori Mori / *high school student*
Edward Morita / *curriculum specialist*

Ralph Mossman / land developer
Ann Murakami / high school student
Dyna Nakamoto / labor union official
Peter Nakamura / high school student
Edward Nakano / engineer, state
    department of transportation
Craig Nakatsuka / high school student
Leland Nishek / labor union official
Marian Olson / hospital director of
    nurses
Tetsu Omoto / shipping company
    manager
Ronald Oshima / high school student
Don Plucknett / director, agricultural
    experiment station
Linda Rabina / high school student
Gary Rodrigues / labor union official
Myles Shirai / high school student
Taka Sokei / county official,
    businessman

Janice Takaki / office worker
Clarence Takashima / labor union
    official
Avis Tamura / high school student
Chad Taniguchi / student
Fred Taniguchi / labor union official
Virgil True / director NASA tracking
    station
Burt Tsuchiya / director, economic
    planning and development
Cathy Van Ausdeln / high school
    student
Joe Vegas / student
Eberhard Widenmeyer / clergyman
Isao Yoneji / businessman
Penny Yoshimura / high school
    student
Mrs. Jennie Yukimura / social worker
Joann Yukimura / student

MAUI 2000

Robert Aitken / lay minister
    and youth leader
Duane Alexenko / professor of
    nursing and medical technology
Angus Ashdown / retired
    plantation manager
Peter Baldwin / dairy owner
Arkemio Baxa / plantation manager
Webb Beggs / executive secretary,
    chamber of commerce
Margaret Cameron / housewife and
    civic leader
Picho Cheida / student
Mrs. William Crockett /
    housewife and community leader
Jack Davis / businessman
Walter Frederickson / instructor
    in anthropology and oceanography
William Griffis / instructor in
    philosophy
William Haines / businessman
Hideo Hayashi / highways district
    engineer

Tim Head / instructor in history
Duff Hendrickson / student
Barbara Hoefler / librarian
John P. Hoshor / provost, Maui
    community college (chairman)
Adrian Hussey / labor union business
    agent
Wayne Ikeoka / student
Mabel Ito / home economist
Garner Ivey / businessman
Robert Johnson / reporter
Tom Kaser / reporter
Michael Kelly / instructor in history
Dominic La Russo / student
Martin Luna / attorney
Max Maude / contractor
Carolyn Medeiros / registered nurse
Joseph Medeiros / businessman
Barbara Miller / instructor in art
Jim Mitchell / executive secretary,
    Lahaina restoration society
Nobuo Miyahira / accountant
Guy Moen / attorney

Shigeto Murayama / *engineer*
Joseph Nuuanu / *catholic clergyman*
Bing Oen / *professor of history*
Robert Ohata / *engineer*
Robert Ohigashi / *businessman*
William Paine / *newspaper editor*
Bruce Palmer / *instructor in biology*
Phil Parvin / *botanist*
Harry Rice / *writer*
Jose Romero / *physician*
Peter Sanborn / *businessman*
George Sano / *school administrator*
John Siener / *businessman*
Joseph Souki / *director, fair employment opportunity*
Alan Sparks / *instructor in political science*

Cummins Speakman / *president, private college*
Jay Speakman / *student*
Charles Street / *plantation manager*
Neil Swanson / *protestant clergyman*
Lynn Thompson / *head ranger, Haleakala national park*
Bonnie Tuell / *home economist*
Mrs. Meyer Ueoka / *housewife and school counselor*
Katherine Vincent / *writer*
Michael Ward / *instructor in english*
John Wilmington / *farmer*
Cable Wirtz / *attorney, retired judge*
Ricky Yasui / *engineer*
Robert Yokoyama / *Maui county executive on aging*

B. CONFERENCE PARTICIPANTS

Norman Abramson
Josephine Achimore
Amefil Agbayani
Robert Aitken
Harriet Ajimine
Albert Akana, Jr.
Hazel Akim
Fay Alailima
Ruben R. Alcantara
Trinidad Alconsel
Dewey M. Allen
James Allen
Gerald Allison
Richard Alm
Martha Almon
Mrs. David C. Anderson
Edith Anderson
Don Angell
Toshio Ansai
Doris Aoki
Hideo Aoki
Sophie Ann Aoki
Tom Arakaki
Rosita Aranita
Bud Aronson
Robert Asakura
Kaye Asuncion
William J. Atkinson
Harry V. Ball
Anthony Baptiste, Jr.
Edward Barnet
Paul Bartram
Artemio C. Baxa
Mrs. S. James Beardmore
Richard E. Bell
Mrs. John A. Bell

Mrs. Harlan Frederic
  Benner
Edith Bennett
David Benz
Phillip Benz
Lawrence Berger
Julie A. Beyer
N. V. Bhagavan
Cobey Black
Duane Black
Thelma Bolling
Sam Boone
Susanne Boone
Charles R. Borns
Anne Bowen
Mrs. William M. Bowman
Hubert Boyd
Tim W. Boyne
Gordon Bradley
Dick Brady
William E. Brenneman
Edward Broadbent
Mary Brogan
Carol Brown
Kenneth F. Brown
Edward Bryan
Timothy O. Bryan
John A. Burns
Mrs. John A. Burns
Jerry Burns
Frank Butterworth
Mrs. Frank Butterworth
Margaret Cameron
Alberta Cameron
Charles Campbell
Mrs. Kenneth Campbell

Eugene Carney
Dante K. Carpenter
Norma Carr
Louis J. Casarett
C. J. Cavanagh
E. R. Champion
Susan Chandler
Carolene Chang
Rose Chang
John G. Chantiny
Esta Chaplin
George Chaplin
Donald Char
Walter Char
Mrs. Emmet Cheeley
Debra Mock Chew
Hung Wai Ching
Linda F. L. Ching
Noland Chock
Anson Chong
Edison M. C. Chong
Betsy Christian
Harry C. Chuck
Robert T. Chuck
Marian Chun
Stanley Chun
Mrs. Barry Chung
James Clark
Arthur C. Clarke
Robert Clopton
Ford G. Coffman
Joan Collins
Walter K. Collins
Jeanne Anne Collis
Jeanne Comer
Eugene B. Connell

Herbert R. Conrad
Bill Cook
Nancy Cook
Frank Cooper
Herbert C. Cornuelle
Howard Corry
Doak C. Cox
Samuel E. Cox
Thomas H. Creighton
Lucy Creps
Kathy Crockett
Kenneth Cundiff
Ellen N. Curry
Mrs. Richard B. Cushnie
Windsor C. Cutting
James A. Dator
Jack Davis
Richard H. Davis
Sue-Mar Dawson
Paul T. de Ham
A. V. Dela Rosa
Frank DeLuz III
Reuel Denney
Ruth Denney
Eliot Deutsch
Mrs. Eliot Deutsch
Daniel J. Dever
Joyce De Waele
Tom W. De Waele
Walter Dods, Jr.
Robert E. Doe
Herman S. Doi
Paul Domke
Yehezkel Dror
Howard Droste
Yone Droste
Robert Duncan
Claude Du Teil
Ramon Duran
Harold C. Eichelberger
Robert Ellis
Linda Engelberg
Jane Ervin
Timothy Ewald
Lung Piao Fa
Joni Fabrao
Gabriel Fackre

John Farias, Jr.
James C. Faries
John Farmer
Fuifatu Fau'olo
Alan P. Ferreira
Harry Flagg
Eureka B. Forbes
Lee Ann Forbes
Mary Forbes
Roland Force
Jane Ford
Morris Fox
Julie Franco
Robert Freitag
Duncan Frissell
Tatsuo Fujimoto
Doreen Fujita
Yoshiaki Fujitani
Sidney Fuke
Nobuko Fukuda
Robert T. Fukuda
Tadashi Fukumoto
Charles M. Fullerton
Mrs. Charles M. Fullerton
James Furstenberg
Wayne Gagne
Sandra Galazin
Nick Garcia
Mary George
Mrs. Peter George
Thomas P. Gill
Jack Gilliam
Harris Gitlin
Jill Glanstein
Mateo L. P. Go
Patrice Gokan
Eugene Gomes
Lee Gomes
Robert Goodman
Kathleen F. Goold
Jaci Gordon
Wytze Gorter
Mary A. Grandjean
William A. Grant
Ed Greaney
Peg Gressitt
John T. Griffin

Bill Griffis
Mrs. Sherman Grossman
Porfirio Guerra
Alice Guild
Douglas Guild
Mark Gurney
Francis Haar
Gordon W. Haas
Rhoda Hackler
Frank Hajeck
William S. Haines
Herbert Hamai
Scott D. Hamilton, Jr.
Leonore Hammond
Carl L. Hanson
Stanley Hara
Sylvia A. Hara
Edward K. Harada
Gail Harada
Kenneth R. Harding
Dorothy Hargreaves
James Harpstrite
Howard Harrenstien
Richard Harrington
Jim Harris
Eugene Harrison
Ann Haruki
Masato M. Hasegawa
Eloise D. Hayes
Joan Hayes
Florence M. Hayslip
Timothy E. Head
Clyde H. Hedlund
Walter Heen
Will J. Henderson
Duff Hendrickson
William Henry
Joan D. Hester
Robert B. Hewett
Tom Higa
Robert Higashino
Colleen Hironaka
Robert Hite
Derrick Ho
Alan Hoe
Barbara Hoefler
Jan Holt

Ralph C. Honda
Bruce Hopper
Pegge Hopper
Cheryl Horiuchi
George R. Horne
John P. Hoshor
Tosh Hosoda
Harold Hostetler
James Hunt
Jahne Hupy
Charlene Iboshi
Susan Ichinose
Philip Ige
Beryl Ikeda
Patty Illing
Lewis Ingleson
Kate K. Inokuchi
Kelvin Inouye
Kazuo Ishihara
Mrs. Leo Israel
Mabel Ito
Maurice Jackson
Virgil Jhoo
Edward H. Joesting
Mrs. Edward H. Joesting
Judith Johnson
Russell Johnson
Gardiner B. Jones
Larry Jones
Josephine Leigh
Paul C. Joy
Frank C. Judd
Robert Jungk
Kekoa D. Kaapu
Deborah Kahakui
Alice Kailewa
John Kamakea
Wayne Kanagawa
George Kanahele
Mrs. George Kanahele
Bert Kanbara
Keith Kaneshiro
Roberta Kaneshiro
Vilma Kaoihana
Richard D. Kartchner
Thomas Kaser

Hidetoshi Kato

Shoji Kato
Carol Kawasako
Fred Kau
Keiji Kawakami
Richard A. Kawakami
Juanita Keawemauhili
Chong Kyu Kim
Robert Kim
Toshiaki Kimura
Anne King
John M. King, Jr.
Morton King
Samuel P. King
Nancy Kinghorn
Monta Kinney
Phil Kinnicutt
Edith Kleinjans
Mrs. Yoshi T. Koga
Jane Komeiji
Ralph Kondo
Melvyn K. Kono
David H. Kornhauser
Liane Kosaki
Mrs. Richard Kosaki
Lawrence Koseki
Robert Krauss
Diane Kroll
Ardis Kuniyoshi
Clarissa Kuniyoshi
Edmund Kuroda
Ronald Kurtz
Tyrone T. Kusao
Nelson Y. C. Kwon
Roland Lagareta
Clemente Lagundimao, Jr.
Robyn Lai
Chapman Lam
Mrs. John M. Lambert
Stephen W. Lane
Jorgen Larsen-Badse
Kim LaRusso
Avis Lee
Frederick Lee
Hahn-Been Lee
John Leifhelm
Werner Levi
Aaron Levine

Leilani Lewis
Peter Lewis
Stuart Lillico
Prudence Limos
Alfred Littman
Clarence Liu
Phyllis Liu
Herbert Long
Ann Longknife
George Loo
Paul C. T. Loo
Anne Loguercio
Jung Lowe
Mrs. Dwight Lowrey
Clorinda Lucas
Stephanie Lui
Rebekah Luke
Doman Lum
Kwong Yen Lum
Mrs. K. Y. Lum
Harriet Lum
Sandy MacLaughlin
Wanda Maddigan
Carl Mahoney
Nengin Mahoney
Jacqueline Maly
Wesley Manaday
Frank Manaut
Andrew Maretzki
Thomas Maretzki
Shelley M. Mark
Geraldine Martin
Michael R. Martin
Larry Mastny
Ken Masuda
Melvin Masuda
Cynthia Masukawa
Floyd W. Matson
Fujio Matsuda
Colbert Matsumoto
Eleanor Matsumoto
David Mattison
Harilyn Mau
David C. McClung
John McDermott
Sally McDermott
A. Q. McElrath

Charlotte McFadden
John McHale
Maurine McIntyre
Graham McKay
John McKenzie
Phyllis McOmber
Roderick McPhee
H. Brett Melendy
Marian Melendy
T. Clifford Melim, Jr.
Doris Melleney
Rosella Melzer
Dolores Metivier
Charles J. Metelka
Robert Midkiff
Raymond Milici
Barbara D. Miller
Ellen Miller
William H. Miller
Mrs. George Mills
Hiroshi Minami
Luciano Minerbi
Timothy Mitchell
Tetsuichi Mitsuda
Ralph Miwa
Annette Miyagi
George Miyasaka
Kiyoto Mizuba
Guy T. Moen
Anita K. Moepono
Steven Montgomery
Mollie Moore
Willis Moore
Carol Morgan
James F. Morgan, Jr.
Lila Morgan
Ethel Mori
Lorre Mori
George S. Moriguchi
Dwight Morita
Edward S. Morita
Russell Morita
John Morrett
Aldyth Morris
Marian Morrison
Stanley F. Mukai
Roy Moser

Ernestine Munei
Leonard Murayama
Mrs. Leonard Murayama
Hugh J. Murphy
Kunio Nagoshi
Kazutoshi Najita
Haruo Nakamoto
Hisao Nakamura
James H. Nakamura
Joyce Nakano
Craig Nakatsuka
Lynn B. Nakkim
H. Kelley Naylor
J. Meredith Neil
Robert S. Nekomoto
Morton Nemiroff
Tuck Newport
Louis G. Nickell
Thomas Nickerson
Lelan Nishek
Grace T. U. Noda
Kaoru Noda
Shirlee Novack
Charles Novak
Guy T. Nunn
Joseph Nuuanu
Dennis E. W. O'Connor
Bing T. Oen
Jayne Ohara
Seido Ogawa
Robert Ogata
Mrs. Robert Ogata
Noreen Ogomori
Saburo Okita
Gary S. Oliva
Douglas Olson
Debbie Omine
Edward O'Rourke
Vladimir Ossipoff
Dixie Padello
David J. Pahk
Betty Paige
Glenn Paige
Jan Paige
Sharon S. Paik
Nicholas Palumbo
Alvina Park

Arlene L. Park
Phil E. Parvin
Alfredo Pasatiempo, Sr.
Mrs. William W. Paty, Jr.
Musette Payton
Michael K. Pearce
Betty Perry
Marya K. Pettit
Ronald Petty
Erika Pfeufer
Lawrence Piette
Donald L. Plucknett
Richard Poirier
Arlie E. Porter
Hebden Porteus
Larry Post
Prudence Potter
Robert E. Potter
Duane Preble
Alfred Preis
Rolf Preuss
Saul Price
Taylor Pryor
Lee K. Radner
Rogene K. Radner
Manjit Reddick
David K. Reed
Vera Reid
Jack C. Reynolds
Skip Riddle
Fred Riggs
Robert N. Rinker
Joyce Roberts
John Robinson
Robert Robinson
Theodore Rodgers
Fred Rodriguez
Terence A. Rogers
Frederick Rohlfing
Theodore F. Ruhig
Elena B. Russell
Shiro Saito
Henry Sakaue
William G. Samway
Bette Sanders
Harold A. Sanders
Ken Sanders

Wallace Sanford
George K. Sano
F. A. Schaefer III
Henry Schainck
George F. Schnack
Mrs. George F. Schnack
Richard P. Schulze, Jr.
Paul J. Schwind
Steven A. Scott
Mrs. Steven A. Scott
Miriam Shea
Glenn Shepherd
James Y. Shigeta
Betty Shimabukuro
Ann Shinsato
Harry C. Shirkey
Mrs. David Shupe
John W. Shupe
Mrs. John W. Shupe
Steve Shupe
Calvin C. J. Sia
Ann Simpson
Frank Skrivanek
Mrs. Fred B. Smales
Margaret W. Smally
Mrs. John L. Smart
Dale Smith
Doris S. Smith
Nellene Smith
A. A. Smyser
Wilfred Soares
Joseph M. Souki
Philip E. Spalding, Jr.
Allan R. Sparks
Donna A. Spaulding
Heinz Spielmann
Pat Stanley
Edward Stasack
Janet I. Stevenson
Barbara Stewart
Charles Stewart
Niels Stoermer
Robert Strand
Carol Strode
Walter S. Strode
Nancy Strode
487 Roger A. Stroede

W. H. Stryker
Charles Stubblefield
Raymond G. Studer
William Stuiver
Raymond Suefuji
Debra Sugitaya
Raymond T. Sugia
Paul D. Sullivan
Gerald Sumida
Jack K. Suwa
Claudio Suyat
Mary Ellen Swanton
James L. Swenson
Mrs. James L. Swenson
Robert S. Taira
Sakae Takahashi
Richard S. Takasaki
Roy Takayama
Henry T. Takitani
Norma R. Taliaferro
Eddie Tangen
Eugene Tao
Lois Taylor
Al Temple
Earle Thacker
Pattie Thomas
David Thompson
Lynn H. Thompson
Myron Thompson
Donald Timmerman
Betty Tobiasson
David Treacy
Mrs. David Treacy
Lucinda Treat
Fred E. Trotter
Steve Tsunemoto
Leonard D. Tuthill
Daniel W. Tuttle, Jr.
Thurston Twigg-Smith
Alan Tyler
Mitsuo Uechi
Yukie H. Ueoka
Hirobumi Uno
Lawrence Uno
Hiromi Urasuki
Charles T. Ushijima
John T. Ushijima

Esther Uyehara
Terrence Uyehara
Cathy Van Ausdeln
Wilma Van Dusseldorp
Joyce Van Zwalenburg
Amalie Vasold
Antone Vidinha
Mrs. Valdo Viglielmo
George C. Villegas
Katherine O. Vincent
DeWaine Wall
George S. Walters
Jess H. Walters
William E. Wanket
Michael D. Ward
Fay Warshauer
William Waters
Robert R. Way
Larry Weber
Shirley Weeks
Sandy Weintraub
Ken Weiss
Doris E. Wetters
Walter E. Whitcomb
John G. White
Jeanne Wiig
Nancy Wilke
Carl H. Williams
Charles R. Williams
Mrs. Charles R.
    Williams
Edith Williams
Don Wilson
Susan Wilson
John Witeck
Toni Withington
Donald Wolbrink
Bruce F. Wolgemuth
Mrs. Jack Woltmon
Patricia Won
Raymond Won
Robertina Wong-Leong
Gordon Wood
Mrs. Allen Woodell
Mrs. A. Jack Woods
Pamela A.
    Worthington

Alvey Wright
Alexander Wylly
George Yamamoto
Merle Yamamoto
Douglas S. Yamamura
Dave M. Yamauchi
Yoshio Yanagawa
Vincent H. Yano

Andrew Yanoviak
Mary Lou Yap
Wendy Yin
Dick Yoda
Samuel K. Yoshida
Nadao Yoshinaga
Akira Yoshioka
Pat Young

Le Roy Yuen
Jennie T. Yukimura
JoAnn Yukimura
John Yukimura
Vivian Zane
Mrs. John Zelko
Helene Zeug
Christ Zivalich

BIBLIOGRAPHY

A. HAWAII'S FUTURES

Note: Mimeographed materials have been placed in the archives of the state of Hawaii in the collection titled "Governor's Conference on the Year 2000 (1970)."

Chaplin, George. "The Future is Being Shaped Today." *Bulletin of the American Society of Newspaper Editors*, no. 541, May 19, 1970, p. 5.

Dator, James A., "A Framework for Futuristics in Hawaii." *In* Japan Society of Futurology, *Challenges from the Future: Proceedings of the International Future Research Conference*, pp. 229–240. Tokyo: Kodansha, 1970.

———. "An Approach to Popular Participation in Forecasting and Designing the Future of Hawaii." *In* Magoroh Maruyama and James A. Dator, eds., *Human Futuristics*, pp. 131–146. Honolulu: Social Science Research Institute, University of Hawaii, 1971.

Evinger, Jane. "Education in Hawaii 2000." *In* Robert Theobald, *Futures Conditional*, pp. 204–209. Indianapolis: Bobbs-Merrill, 1972.

Helton, William. "Science and Technology in Hawaii 2000." *In* Robert Theobald, *Futures Conditional*, pp. 125–130. Indianapolis: Bobbs-Merrill, 1972.

Hawaii Youth Congress. *Peace: A Common Goal, Report on the Hawaii Youth Congress 1970: An Aquarian Perspective on the Year 2000.* Honolulu: Vanguard Press, n.p., n.d. [1970, 27 pp.].

Kleinjans, Everett, ed. "Proceedings of the Second International Conference on Problems of Modernization in Asia and the Pacific." Honolulu: East-West Center, University of Hawaii, forthcoming.

Krieger, David. "Senatorial Perceptions of Hawaii's Past, Present, and Future." Mimeographed. Honolulu: Department of Political Science, University of Hawaii, 1970.

Paige, Glenn D. "Hawaii's 1970 State Legislators View 'Hawaii 2000': Report to the Legislature on Responses to a Questionnaire." Mimeographed. Honolulu: Department of Political Science and Social Science Research Institute, University of Hawaii, January 26, 1970.

Schmitt, Robert. "Long-Range Forecast for Hawaii: The Statistics of Tomorrow." Mimeographed. Honolulu: Department of Planning and Economic Development, State of Hawaii, 1970.

State of Hawaii, Governor's Conference on the Year 2000, August 5–8, 1970, *Preliminary Task Force Reports (July 1970)*. Mimeographed. Honolulu: Advisory Committee, Governor's Conference on the Year 2000, Room 102, 2500 Dole Street, 1970.

Wolbrink, Donald. "Land Use Availability Through the Year 2000." *In* State of Hawaii, Governor's Conference on the Year 2000, August 5–8, 1970, *Preliminary Task Force Reports (July 1970)*, pp. iv, 21–35. Honolulu: Advisory Committee, Governor's Conference on the Year 2000, Room 102, 2500 Dole Street, 1970.

B. GENERAL FUTURISTICS

Annotations by James A. Dator

Boulding, Kenneth. *The Meaning of the 20th Century*. New York: Harper and Row, 1964.
An excellent background book.

Clarke, Arthur C. *Profiles of the Future*. New York: Harper and Row, 1963.
Simple and interesting, by a long-time futurist. Good chart of expected developments at the end of the book.

Dator, James A., Sheo Panday, and Nirmal Jain. *A Bibliography of Futuristic Materials*. Honolulu: Social Science Research Institute, University of Hawaii, manuscript.

de Jouvenel, Bertrand. *The Art of Conjecture*. New York: Basic Books, 1967.
A must for those especially concerned about problems of prediction.

Ehrlich, Paul. *The Population Bomb*. New York: Ballantine, 1968.
It will scare you into action by its predictions of what will happen if you don't act.

Feinberg, Gerald. *The Prometheus Project: Mankind's Search for Long-Range Goals*. Garden City, New York: Doubleday, 1969.
How to develop values for the future. An exciting book.

Halacy, Daniel S., Jr. *Century Twenty-One*. Philadelphia: Macrae, 1968.
An overall introduction.

———. *Cyborg*. New York: Harper and Row, 1965.
On developing machine-augmented organisms, or organic machines!

Helmer, Olaf. *Social Technology*. New York: Basic Books, 1966.
A good background and explanation of the Delphi method of forecasting.

Japan Society of Futurology, comp. *Challenges From the Future*, Vols. I and II. Tokyo: Kodansha, 1971.
Papers of the Second International Future Research Conference.

Jungk, Robert and Johan Galtung, eds. *Mankind 2000*. Oslo: Universitetsforlaget; London: Allen and Unwin, 1969.
Papers of the First International Future Research Conference.

Maruyama, Magoroh, and James A. Dator, eds. *Human Futuristics*.
Honolulu: Social Science Resarch Institute, University of Hawaii, 1971.

Papers given at the American Anthropological Association's annual meeting in San Diego, fall 1970.

Michael, Donald N. *The Unprepared Society*. New York: Basic Books, 1968. Another background book, especially concerned about the role of education in preparing for the future.

Taylor, Gordon Rattray. *The Biological Time Bomb*. New York: World, 1968. Another must book, this on new developments in biology, and the social implications of genetic engineering.

Theobald, Robert. *An Alternative Future for America*. Chicago: Swallow Press, 1970.
A good summary of Theobald's exciting and provocative ideas.

Theobald Robert, and J. M. Scott. *Teg's 1994: An Anticipation of the Near Future*. Chicago: Swallow Press, 1970.
Historical interpretation of the world from a 1994 viewpoint.

Toffler, Alvin. *Future Shock*. New York: Random House, 1970. Introductory bestseller on problems of the future.